# NEW EXPLOR

# Critical Notes

ON PRESCRIBED POETRY FOR THE 2005 EXAMINATION
(HIGHER AND ORDINARY LEVELS)

EDITED BY
## John G. Fahy

CONTRIBUTORS
Carole Scully
John G. Fahy
Séan Scully
John McCarthy
Bernard Connolly
David Keogh

GILL & MACMILLAN

Gill & Macmillan Ltd
Hume Avenue
Park West
Dublin 12
with associated companies throughout the world
www.gillmacmillan.ie

Print origination and design in Ireland by O'K Graphic Design, Dublin

*The paper used in this book is made from the wood pulp of managed forests. For every
tree felled, at least one tree is planted, thereby renewing natural resources.*

# Acknowledgments

For permission to reproduce copyright material in this book the publishers are grateful
to the following:

Carcanet Press for complete poems and extracts from other poems by Eavan Boland
from her *Collected Poems*, and also for extracts from her autobiography *Object
Lessons: The Life of the Woman and the Poet in our Time* (1995);

Faber and Faber Ltd for extracts of poems by Séamus Heaney and for extracts from
*Preoccupations: Selected Prose 1968–1978* by Séamus Heaney.

# CONTENTS

P   = POEM ALSO PRESCRIBED FOR ORDINARY LEVEL 2005 EXAM

P = POEM ALSO PRESCRIBED FOR ORDINARY LEVEL 2005 EXAM

P  = POEM ALSO PRESCRIBED FOR ORDINARY LEVEL 2005 EXAM

P = POEM ALSO PRESCRIBED FOR ORDINARY LEVEL 2005 EXAM

# 1 *William* WORDSWORTH

Carole Scully

## *Seeking the significant moment*

### EARLY LIFE

William Wordsworth was born on 7 April 1770 in Cockermouth, Cumberland in the north-west of England, an area noted for its beautiful scenery. He was the second son born to John Wordsworth and his wife Anne. Wordsworth's family was comfortable both financially and socially. His father was an attorney-at-law and a land steward, while his mother came from a respectable merchant background. Less than two years later, his sister Dorothy was born and the two children developed a close relationship that was to continue into adult life. Sadly, this stable childhood world was rocked by the death of his mother, when Wordsworth was eight years old, and his father's death five years later. Some critics have suggested that the loss of his parents at such a young age had a lasting effect on Wordsworth, in that much of his poetry is underpinned by a sense of searching for an absent quality that will somehow fill a gap in his life. In one of his earliest poems, composed when he was about sixteen years old, Wordsworth writes:

> Now, in this blank of things, a harmony
> Home-felt, and home-created comes to heal
> That grief for which the senses still supply
> Fresh food; for only then, when memory
> Is hushed, am I at rest.

Two of their uncles became guardians to the five Wordsworth children and ensured that they were brought up in a manner suitable to their social station. Wordsworth attended Hawkshead Grammar School and, at the age of seventeen, entered St. John's College, Cambridge.

Wordsworth's career at Cambridge was undistinguished, but the long holidays gave him the opportunity to indulge in a favourite pastime, walking in the countryside. The appreciation of nature and the first-hand experiencing of the natural world became increasingly popular towards the end of the eighteenth century. In the summer of 1790, Wordsworth and a college friend went on a walking holiday through France and Switzerland, 'staff in hand, without knapsacks, each his neediments tied up in a pocket-handkerchief'. Wordsworth was impressed by the majesty of the Alps and wrote a series of 'Descriptive Sketches' detailing the scenery:

> The rocks rise naked as a wall, or stretch
> Far o'er the water, hung with groves of beech;

In later life, Wordsworth came to view these pieces as representing a time when he was enveloped by the visual aspect of nature, when he revelled in seeing, with little or no understanding of the spiritual quality of the natural world. At this stage, his writing was very much in tune with the poetry of the time, where natural beauty was described in detailed word pictures without intellectual consideration.

After receiving his B.A., Wordsworth returned to France with the intention of learning French. However, he was diverted by a growing interest in the revolutionary movement that was sweeping through France, and by his love affair with Annette Vallon. Annette bore him a daughter. However Wordsworth, under pressure from his friends and relations who were anxious about the political instability in France, returned to England and was not to see his daughter until she was nine years old.

## SAMUEL TAYLOR COLERIDGE

On his return from France, Wordsworth rather reluctantly published some of his work. The books were not particularly well received and sold slowly. However, another young writer, Samuel Taylor Coleridge, did read them and was immensely impressed, commenting: 'Seldom, if ever, was the emergence of an original poetic genius above the literary horizon more evidently announced.' The pair met in 1795 and became great friends, travelling and writing together. At Coleridge's suggestion they began to write a series of poems that was to become 'The Lyrical Ballads', generally recognized as marking the beginning of the Romantic Movement in English poetry. This collaboration resulted in Wordsworth  producing some of his most uniquely individual poetry, such as parts of 'The Prelude', the 'Lucy' poems and 'Lines Written above Tintern Abbey'. Coleridge regularly visited Wordsworth and his sister Dorothy at Grasmere, in the Lake District. Although she was a talented writer herself, Dorothy devoted most of her energies to caring for her brother until her death in 1855. Even when Wordsworth married Mary Hutchinson in 1802, Dorothy continued to live with the couple and was very much a part of the literary group that developed around Wordsworth. In 1810 the friendship between Coleridge and Wordsworth ended. During one of his visits to the Wordsworths,

Coleridge's addiction to opium led him to behave in an extremely difficult manner and Wordsworth grew tired of trying to cope with it all. When Coleridge discovered that Wordsworth had spoken dismissively of him to a friend, he was deeply hurt and the two men were estranged for quite a while. Finally they did patch up their relationship, but it was never the same. Coleridge wrote, 'A reconciliation has taken place – but the feeling can never return.'

## WORDSWORTH'S POETIC THEORY

It was a sad end to what had been a wonderfully creative friendship. Long discussions with Coleridge had led Wordsworth to formulate his theories on poetry, which he expressed in his famous 'Prefaces'. He saw poetry as originating 'from emotion recollected in tranquillity': that is, sensory memory is used to recreate a moment arising in 'everyday life', made significant by 'powerful feelings'. By revisiting the emotionally significant moment through sensory memory, a further quality is added to the original experience. The moment is uniquely personal to the poet, but because of the way in which he expresses it the moment takes on a more general relevance to all men. For Wordsworth, the poet has 'a greater readiness and power in expressing what he thinks and feels'. But he is, above all, 'a man speaking to men'. For this reason, the poet should use 'a selection of language really used by men' in such a way that 'ordinary things are presented to the mind in an unusual aspect'. In this way, the poet creates a new moment that has significance not only for himself, but for his reader as well. It encapsulates 'truth, not individual and local, but general, and operative; not standing upon external testimony, but carried into the heart by passion'. For Wordsworth, Nature played a vital role in this truth, since the poet 'considers man and nature as essentially adapted to each other, and the mind of man as naturally the mirror of the fairest and most interesting properties of nature.' Thus, 'Poetry is the image of man and nature.' Wordsworth believed that Nature was symbolic of the essential Truths that could give coherence to an apparently disordered world and, because of this, it triggered significant moments of emotion in the poet. Poetry, that expressed these moments of significance, enabled the reader to understand something of the Great Truths underlying both his own existence and the society and world in which he lived. For Wordsworth, this act of poetic creation helped both the poet and the reader to restore something that could be lost, all too easily, in everyday life: the power to escape from the physical limitations of time and place, to grow positively and strongly in the face of an apparently confused universe, to improve the social context of human existence, to experience joyfully the emotionally significant moment.

Wordsworth, by the Poetic Theory that he had formulated, came to view the poet, and therefore himself, as an individual set apart. His focus was on his own emotional reactions. In 'The Prelude', composed between 1799 and 1805, he traced the 'Growth of a Poet's Mind', that is, his own mind, with a series of vivid and immediate descriptions. Although Wordsworth himself considered this an acceptable poetic stance, and many of his devoted readers felt that it was an approach justified by his incisive observations, an equal number of his contemporaries viewed it as indulgently self-centred and egotistical. Indeed, this divergence of opinion regarding Wordsworth still exists today. Nevertheless, despite the mixed reactions, he continued to write in this personalised manner, stating 'Every author, as far as he is great and at the same time original, has had the task of creating the taste by which he is to be enjoyed.'

Yet, in truth, Wordsworth began to lose his creative way after 1808. For ten years he had written with an uncompromising vitality and an unshakable self-belief. When he completed 'The White Doe of Rylstone', he seemed to lose touch with the impetus that had driven his creativity. Perhaps he had simply used up all the self-focused moments of emotional significance from his memory. For whatever reason, after this time Wordsworth's work is never more than competent. He had peaked by the time he was thirty-eight and for the next forty years he tried, but failed, to climb again to that heady summit of creativity. Nowhere is this more evident than in his two versions of 'The Prelude'. The first version of 1805 is separated from the second of 1850 by some forty-five years, but by an eternity of emotion. The older Wordsworth seems to feel embarrassed, or at the very least uneasy, in the face of the intensities of his youth. However, by this stage of his life he had seen his great works achieve widespread recognition and approbation. As Thomas DeQuincy, a contemporary of Wordsworth put it, 'Up to 1820 the name of Wordsworth was trampled underfoot; from 1820 to 1830 it was militant; from 1830 to 1835 it has been triumphant.'

In 1843 Wordsworth was appointed Poet Laureate and received a state pension. He died at his home, 'Rydal Mount', at the age of eighty in 1850. He was buried in Grasmere churchyard, in the same beautiful north-west region of England where he had been born and had lived most of his life.

## WORDSWORTH – THE ROMANTIC POET

The terms 'Romantic' and 'Romanticism' are deceptively easy to use in a literary context, probably because they have a distant branch in everyday language. We tend to use 'romantic', with a lower case 'r', to denote a particular aspect of being in love. It also represents a kind of idealised quality connected with fictional characters. In the case of females, the 'romantic' heroine carries the connotation of intensity of repressed emotion, an apparent vulnerability concealing strength of passion; while with males, the 'romantic' hero usually exhibits an irresistibly attractive disregard for the rules of social behaviour, a sense of freedom from convention. In the 1980s 'New Romantics' appeared in the world of popular music, representing a backlash against the overt brutality and harshness of 'Punk' music with a less aggressive, gentler, more feminine ethos encapsulated by their white, frilly shirts and use of make-up.

There is a general sense of what 'romantic' means, but it is a great deal harder to actually define 'Romantic', with a capital 'R', in a literary context. Perhaps the most important factor to understand about 'Romanticism' is that it is a term that was applied after the fact to a particular style of writing and a group of writers. It was not until the nineteenth century that the 'Lake School', consisting of Wordsworth, Coleridge and Southey, and the later poets Byron, Leigh Hunt, Shelley and Keats, were grouped together under the title of the 'Romantic School', in a deliberate attempt to connect this disparate group with the 'Romantics' of Germany and France. At this time, the term carried a historical connotation, as Thomas Arnold explained in 1862: 'By romantic poems we mean, poems in which heroic subjects are epically treated, after the manner of the old romances of chivalry.' In the context of this definition, Coleridge, Byron and the novelist Sir Walter Scott were viewed as the great 'Romantic' writers. Indeed, Wordsworth was, to a large extent, placed on the margins of the Romantic group.

However, by the 1930s Wordsworth had been allocated a central role in 'Romantic' writing. Such writers as T.S. Eliot and F.R. Leavis reawakened an interest in his work. Although Wordsworth did not write about the historical subjects that Arnold, in the nineteenth century, considered prerequisite to 'Romanticism', he did express many of the features that were regarded as characteristic of it in the twentieth century. Firstly, Wordsworth represented the self-conscious individualisation of the poet when he advocated that the poet 'ought to travel before men occasionally as well as at their sides'. Allied to this was his idealisation of the poet's role to prophet-like status: 'The Poet, singing a song in which all human beings join with him, rejoices in the presence of truth as our visible friend and hourly companion.' In some twentieth-century definitions of 'Romanticism', this idealised individualisation was seen as enabling the poet to arrive at an understanding that would benefit human society in general. F.R. Leavis commented that Wordsworth showed the reader 'the significance of this poetry for actual living'. He believed that Wordsworth's poetry was 'the expression of an order and the product of an emotional and moral training'. Secondly, it was generally agreed that the impetus for the 'Romantic' writer sprang from his relationship with Nature. Once aqain, Wordsworth epitomised this relationship with his view that poetry 'is an acknowledgement of the beauty of the universe'. His combination of personal memory, imagination and observation was seen as representing the 'Romantic' approach to Nature. M.H. Abrams described 'Tintern Abbey' as 'the joint product of external data and of the mind'. Finally, Wordsworth's poetry expressed the intensity that is fundamental to the twentieth-century interpretation of 'Romanticism' both in an emotional sense, where he tried to write of 'the spontaneous overflow of powerful feelings', and on a sensory level, when he stated that poetry should 'treat of things not as they are but as they appear; not as they exist in themselves, but as they seem to exist to the senses'.

Thus for readers in the twentieth century, Wordsworth is a perfect example of a 'Romantic' poet, if there can be such a thing as a perfect example of a rather vague definition. M.H. Abrams summed up the problematic nature of the word 'Romantic' when he commented that it is 'one of those terms historians can neither do with nor make do without'. Perhaps the best way to ensure that we treat the term with caution is to remind ourselves that could we return to the eighteenth century and visit Wordsworth in his house, set in the beautiful mountains, he would undoubtedly react with bemused and disconcerted puzzlement if we were to greet him with 'You must be Wordsworth, the great Romantic poet'!

## *She dwelt among the untrodden ways*

Text of poem: New Explorations Anthology page 24
[Note: *This poem is also prescribed for the Ordinary Level 2005 exam*]

BACKGROUND NOTE

Wordsworth appears to have written the group of 'Lucy' poems when he was in Germany in the winter of 1799. They were first printed in the 'Lyrical Ballads' collection in 1800. This poem appeared second in a group of three, with 'A slumber did my spirit seal' the third of the group. The poems have an elegiac quality in that they lament the death of someone. However, the traditional elegy usually laments the passing of a notable person, such as a great poet or military hero. Wordsworth seems to deliberately emphasise how unknown Lucy was in order to highlight the fact that her importance came from her effect on him. Similarly, there is a sense of mystery in each of these poems not usually found in the traditional elegiac form. Wordsworth avoids the standard approach of detailing facts about the deceased in order to heighten the sense of loss. Instead, he simply suggests certain qualities while placing most of the emphasis on how he was affected by the death.

A READING OF THE POEM

In the first stanza Wordsworth introduces three important ideas in connection with the deceased 'Lucy': (i) she lived closely with Nature; (ii) she had a delicate, gentle quality; (iii) she lived away from the company of people. Lucy lived 'among the untrodden ways', suggesting an isolated and unspoiled countryside. This sense of unspoiled Nature is reinforced by the 'springs of Dove'. Modern advertising still uses the idea of 'natural spring water' to represent purity and untouched Nature. The connecting of Lucy with a spring called 'Dove' signifies a gentleness about her; this is certainly not a raging waterfall. There is the feeling that Nature in its extreme form would have been too overwhelming for Lucy. She found her home in a quiet and protective natural environment. Wordsworth emphasises the lack of human relationships in Lucy's world by using the words 'none' and 'few'. Lucy did not experience the positive side of human interaction, where 'love' and 'praise' support the individual. However, there is no real sense that she missed this – rather it appears that she accepted her condition; perhaps there is even the feeling that she neither knew nor cared about such things.

In the second stanza Wordsworth reinforces these ideas with the images that he uses in connection with 'Lucy'. By using the metaphor of the violet that is 'half hidden', Wordsworth implies a shy delicacy. There is the suggestion that the violet is content to remain hidden by the stone, just as 'Lucy' was content to remain 'among the untrodden ways'. The fact that the stone is 'mossy' conveys a more comfortable image than if it had been simply cold rock. It also indicates a sheltered environment, one where the delicate 'violet', and by implication Lucy, would be protected. The simile of the star is used in a similar way. Lucy is as 'Fair as a star' in that she is undoubtedly beautiful. The star image also conveys a sense that Lucy is somehow not of this world. She is set apart not simply by her physical isolation, but also because she is from a different physical environment. Man can observe the star from Earth, but he cannot come into contact with it because it is physically impossible for him to travel the vast distance that lies between him and the star, nor can he survive in the star's environment of space. So Wordsworth implies that although he was one of the few to have seen Lucy, there was, even for him, something unattainable about her. The idea that the star is the 'only one' shining also reinforces the sense of Lucy's isolation from normal human life.

In the third stanza, Wordsworth repeats the idea that Lucy was unknown in the general world of men. His use of the phrase 'few could know' suggests that to know of Lucy was a privileged or special experience – that he was lucky to have witnessed her existence. When it comes to communicating Lucy's death, Wordsworth does so in an undramatic way; Lucy simply 'ceased to be'. The very sound of the word 'ceased' reinforces the gentle, almost natural quality of her passing. There is no feeling of a violent separation caused by death. Wordsworth has carefully structured the poem so that this moment appears with a quiet inevitability. Lucy's existence is written about in the past tense. She is portrayed as having a delicacy and gentleness that almost melts away. Her close connection with the quiet things of nature implies that the manner of her death was simply an extension of the manner of her living. There is an acceptance of the fact of Lucy's passing in the phrase 'she is in her grave'. Wordsworth does not shy away from the reality of the situation, but the 'grave' image is not a very frightening one. After all, Lucy spent her life 'half hidden' by the natural world – it was not a great change for her to become completely hidden. Wordsworth ends the poem with a clear statement that Lucy's death had a significant emotional impact on him. However, he does not express exactly what he felt. This serves to highlight his avoidance of any specific details about his relationship with Lucy. There is a haunting air of mystery about his connection with her and, indeed, about Lucy herself.

## STYLE

The mysterious death of an often young and beautiful person was a popular theme among the Romantic poets, not only in England but in Germany and France as well. There was the sense that death was simply Nature reasserting its power over the person in a magical and inescapable way. Wordsworth takes this theme and uses it in an original way to communicate the emotional and psychological effects caused in him by the death.

In a similar way, the simple rhyme scheme of the poem and the use of such words as 'dwelt', 'untrodden' and 'maid' give the poem a historical, fairy-tale atmosphere, customary in this type of poem. However, Wordsworth was not content to simply relate the incident. For him, an incident gained impact by his meditating on it: 'emotion recollected in tranquillity', so that he was able not only to recreate the original incident but to weave into it the emotional and psychological depths that he had developed in his meditations. It is not really important for us to know exactly what effect Lucy's death had on Wordsworth; what is important is that we understand that it did affect him in a profound and lasting way.

## Alternatively

Dante Gabriel Rossetti, the nineteenth-century artist and poet, commented that Wordsworth was 'good, you know, but unbearable'. Perhaps Wordsworth is 'unbearable' in the way that he portrays Lucy as being perfectly happy with her rather limited life. She is the ideal fantasy girl dreamed up by Wordsworth. Their relationship is obviously unreal and not very well expressed. He could be regarded as even more 'unbearable' in the way that he is more worried about his own reaction, rather than about Lucy's death. He simply uses the idea of Lucy as an excuse to write about his 'unbearable' concern with his own 'unbearable' feelings!

# It is a beauteous evening, calm and free

Text of poem: New Explorations Anthology page 26
[Note: This poem is also prescribed for the 2005 Ordinary Level exam]

## BACKGROUND NOTE

This poem was first published in a group of various sonnets in 1807. It was actually composed in 1802.

## STRUCTURE

This poem is a sonnet, in that it consists of fourteen lines and is divided by the rhyme scheme into an octet (eight lines) and a sestet (six lines). This type of sonnet is called a Petrarchan sonnet, because it was first used by an Italian writer called Petrarca in the fourteenth century. Usually the rhyme scheme is *abba abba cdecde*. However, Wordsworth changes the sestet to *cdeced*, so it is not strictly Petrarchan.

Generally the octet is descriptive, telling the reader about a particular situation. The sestet then meditates on, or presents a reaction to, the octet. This difference in content between the two parts of the sonnet is often reflected in a change of mood or tone.

## A READING OF THE POEM

Wordsworth opens the poem with an accomplished description of a sunset over the sea. The octet is carefully structured so that there is a sense of immediacy for the reader; he wants us to feel that we are standing alongside him and witnessing the scene with him. Although we know that Wordsworth felt that poetry was created by using the memory of a significant moment, he deliberately uses the present tense throughout this poem, as if he is actually writing as the incident occurs. Similarly, his description uses not only the sense of sight but also the sense of hearing. This gives a greater depth to the picture and reinforces the immediacy of the scene.

Although the scene in the octet is not obviously dramatic, as a huge storm might be, Wordsworth describes it in such a way that it has great impact. He stresses the peacefulness of the sunset with such words as 'calm', 'quiet', 'tranquillity', 'gentleness'. For Wordsworth, this quietness comes from a sense of natural order. The sun sets according to an established pattern. The sea rises and falls in a rhythmical and regular way. Each natural object behaves in a constant and appropriate way, just as a nun follows her religious rituals with a dignified and quiet reverence. Wordsworth holds us in a moment of stillness. For it is only a moment. Although the sea moves 'everlastingly', there is the strong feeling that Wordsworth is only too aware that this scene is anything but everlasting, and that gives it an added impact.

However, although Wordsworth has put a great deal of effort into making us feel and experience the 'beauteous evening', it is only with the sestet that we realise why he considers this a significant moment. It is not the scene in itself that is significant; it is the contrast between his own reaction and his companion's reaction to it that moved Wordsworth to recreate this moment from memory. His companion does not react to the sunset in an intellectual way – she is 'untouched by solemn thought'; whereas Wordsworth, as we have seen by the type of language he uses in the octet, has been filled with solemn thoughts. But Wordsworth realises that his companion's reaction, although different, is a valid one; she is in no way 'less divine'. Indeed, he suggests that he is rather envious of the spontaneous way in which she does react. Just as the sunset is impressive because it is driven by a natural order, so his companion's reaction is enviable because it too is natural. For Wordsworth Nature symbolised, or represented,  Great Truths of existence. His companion, by reacting naturally, is more able to come to an understanding of these Truths; she can go into 'the Temple's inner shrine'. The implication is that Wordsworth, because his reaction is more self-consciously intellectual, is not admitted into the 'inner shrine'. Indeed, the final line of the sonnet summarises just this. He understands that his companion is always close to the Truth of existence, is always near to 'God', because she reacts to God's creations in an instinctively natural way. She does not continually think about it: she just enjoys it. She is happy not to 'know' intellectually, and as a result she knows in a much deeper sense. Once again, there is the strong suggestion that Wordsworth regrets that he cannot react in the way that his companion does. The 'dear girl' is accompanied by God, while Wordsworth is accompanied by the need to know.

### Alternatively

This sonnet simply shows the confusion underlying Wordsworth's whole Poetic Theory. After all, he stated in his 'Preface' that 'poems to which any value can be attached' are produced 'by a man who, being possessed of more than usual organic sensibility, had also thought long and deeply'. So, he emphasises the importance of thinking. Yet in this sonnet he suggests that thinking, or intellectualising, is not a good idea; rather it is better to react in an instinctive way!

In 'She dwelt among the untrodden ways' and 'It is a beauteous evening, calm and free', Wordsworth presents the female figures as idealised and unrealistic. He may have been able to describe Nature realistically from his observations, but he clearly had never observed females!

# Skating *(extract from* The Prelude*)*

Text of poem: New Explorations Anthology page 28
[*Note: This poem is also prescribed for the Ordinary Level 2005 exam*]

## BACKGROUND NOTE

This extract comes from a long poem that Wordsworth began to write in 1799. He expanded it in 1805 and revised it at intervals until 1839. It was not published until after his death in 1850. The title 'The Prelude' was chosen by his widow and means something that serves as an introduction. Wordsworth himself claimed that this poem was to serve as a 'preparatory poem' to another work called 'Recluse'. He intended to explain how he had arrived at a point where he could write 'Recluse'. Therefore 'The Prelude', in Wordsworth's own words, 'is biographical, and conducts the history of the author's mind to the point when he was emboldened to hope that his faculties were sufficiently matured for entering upon the arduous labour'.

## A READING OF THE POEM

Wordsworth opens the piece with a vivid and expert description of the setting for the skating. The use of the word 'And' is suggestive of a continuing dialogue, which after all it is, as the full poem traces his development as a poet by means of incidents from his early life. By establishing the scene for this incident, Wordsworth quickly draws us into his recreated personal memory. He uses both visual pictures and sounds to achieve a surprising depth of description in a very brief amount of writing. He also introduces the emotional aspect of this memory at this early stage. Wordsworth realised that memory is extremely important to human beings, not simply in the sense that we enjoy remembering factual details, but because memory allows us to recapture emotions from past situations. In this way, Wordsworth is able to feel again the 'rapture' that he experienced as a young boy. Similarly, he compares himself skating to 'an untried horse', in an effort to communicate both the physical and emotional freedom that he felt. The group of boys are described as 'imitative of the chase', not only to suggest that they skate in a group trying to catch a front-runner, but also to convey their natural spontaneity.

Just as Wordsworth links factual memory with emotional memory, so he joins what is seen with what is heard. The sense of hearing plays a vital role in memory. For instance, most people have a special piece of music that recalls a particular incident for them. Wordsworth uses sounds to add a greater depth to his description. The village clock; the hissing of the skates on the ice; the shouting of the boys; all are carried through the still, cold air and out from the page. This is not a silent world, but a world filled with movement and noise, just like our world today.

At this point, the skating boys are at the front of the description, with the world of Nature present but in the background. However, rather like a camera panning from the boys to the surrounding landscape, Wordsworth gradually shifts the descriptive focus more and more onto the countryside. He does this by using the echoes of the boys to lead us to the 'precipices', the 'leafless trees', the 'icy crag' and the 'far distant hills'. He looks up from the enclosed village to the limitless night sky; the 'cottage windows' give way to the 'stars' and the ' orange sky of evening'.

This outer movement reflects the inner alteration that occurs within the young Wordsworth in the course of the piece. Whereas previously his whole attention and being had been absorbed by the act of skating, gradually he becomes aware of Nature. He begins to physically separate himself from the other boys, so he 'retired into a silent bay', leaving 'the tumultuous throng'. The world of activity and sound fades into the background as Wordsworth's awareness of his natural surroundings increases. The boy who 'wheeled about' is now 'stopped short' by the awesomeness of the world around him. Finally his physical movement, which has been so much a part of this description, becomes overwhelmed by the greater movement of the Earth. By placing his emotional and psychological adjustment into a physical context, Wordsworth gives the whole experience a vividly dramatic effect.

Nevertheless, the final lines of the piece illustrate the limitations of the young Wordsworth. Although he becomes conscious of Nature, he is not yet able to understand the implications of this consciousness. He has not yet reached the mature perception of the Great Truths symbolised by Nature. At this point in his life, Wordsworth is not driven by Nature towards a significant moment. His reactions are limited, so that he simply 'stood and watched'.

## STYLE

'The Prelude' contains some of Wordsworth's most vivid and descriptive blank verse. Blank verse is unrhymed verse that is written in iambic pentameter. Iambic pentameter is a way of dividing up the metre, or rhythm, of a line of poetry. With iambic pentameter there are five divisions, called feet, in each line. In each of the feet there are two syllables, one weak and one strong. The opening line of this piece is a good example (the underlined syllables are strong):

And in/ the fros/ty sea/son, when/ the sun ...

*Alternatively*

Matthew Arnold commented on Wordsworth: 'It might seem that Nature not only gave him the subject matter for his poem, but wrote his poem for him.' Perhaps Nature wrote too much about itself in this piece. Should Wordsworth have edited some of his descriptions? Did he simply write a descriptive piece just to show off his abilities in this area, and then tack it on to a rather unbelievable incident from his youth just to give a point to the whole thing? Is it likely that a boy out skating and shouting with a group of friends, a boy who is having such a good time that he avoids going home, will suddenly go off on his own and look at the stars and the cliffs and think about the Earth going round?

# *To My Sister*

Text of poem: New Explorations Anthology page 30

BACKGROUND NOTE

This poem was written and published in 1798, when Wordsworth was twenty-eight years old. At this point he was living with his sister Dorothy and was working closely with Samuel Taylor Coleridge on the 'Lyrical Ballads'.

STRUCTURE

The poem consists of ten stanzas. Each stanza contains four lines with a rhyme scheme of *abab*. The final stanza largely repeats the fourth one, both for emphasis and to give a sense of unity to the poem.

A READING OF THE POEM

The first two stanzas of the poem show Wordsworth at his descriptive best. Within the restraints of four-line stanzas and a strict rhyme scheme, he manages to create a vivid and evocative description of 'the first mild day of March'. He appeals to the sense of sight, the sense of hearing and the sense of touch in order to give the scene depth and realism. He uses 'the very language of men', but in such a way that it is expanded in the power of its communication.

In the third stanza he addresses his sister, attempting to persuade her to spend the day outside. He tells her to change into her 'woodland dress', perhaps implying that she will be much more comfortable in this relaxed outfit rather than the more formal clothes that she wears indoors. He suggests that they will spend the day in 'idleness', so she should leave her book inside along with her indoor clothes. These ideas recur in the final stanza.

At this point, the poem changes from a simple description of a time and place to a reflection on the effects of Nature on Man. In this way, the moment becomes significant. Wordsworth describes these effects in the context of his group, but the implication is that the message applies to all men. The ordering of Time by a calendar is portrayed as arbitrary and restrictive, whereas the internal time that governs Nature is natural and positive. Wordsworth feels that by being outside, within Nature, Man opens himself to the Great Truths that Nature symbolises. Love, perhaps the greatest Truth of all, fills the natural world. Wordsworth does not simply mean that Spring is the time of growth and procreation in the natural world. Love, for him, is the instinct to exist in a positively creative way. It is an instinct that Man can all too easily lose by locking himself into the inside world of daily tasks, books and calendars. The spaciousness of the outside world fills and extends the very essence of Man. Then Man, in his turn, surrenders up something of his creativity to Nature. It is a mutually beneficial relationship that moves 'From earth to man, from man to earth'.

Just as Wordsworth sees a clear contrast existing between the inside and outside worlds, so he also views the way Man learns in each world as being distinctly different. In the inside world, learning is made up of 'toiling reason' for the intellect; but outside, learning becomes effortless and spontaneous. It is a complete experience for the mind and the body: 'Our minds shall drink at every pore'. Nature creates a situation where Man learns in a holistic way: that is, the learning becomes relevant to his very spiritual essence. What is absorbed outside, close to Nature, has a fundamental effect: 'We'll frame the measure of our souls:'. It works in a positive and constructive way, not only for the individual but for society as a whole, because it generates a willingness to be 'tuned to love'.

In the final stanza, Wordsworth once more repeats his request that Dorothy should change her clothes and leave her book, so that they can spend the day in 'idleness'. However, now that we have read the poem we, like Dorothy, fully understand just what Wordsworth is suggesting. We know exactly what 'idleness' means, so we can join Wordsworth and his sister in smiling at his gentle joke.

## STYLE

It is always important to remember that Wordsworth believed that poetry was created out of 'emotion recollected in tranquillity'. So although he places his poems in the present, and creates a sense of spontaneous immediacy, he is writing about an incident from the past. Wordsworth uses memory to recall this past incident and its accompanying emotions so that he can re-experience the moment in a new context, in 'tranquillity', and this enables him to draw out the depth of meaning that is embodied in the incident. In this way the moment becomes more significant. Therefore, with Wordsworth, spontaneity and immediacy are to be treated with caution!

## Alternatively

'It is possible enough, we allow, that the sight of a friend's spade, or a sparrow's nest ... might really have suggested to such a mind a train of powerful impressions and interesting reflections, but it is certain that to most minds such associations will always appear forced, strained and unnatural.'

So wrote Francis Jeffrey, a contemporary critic of Wordsworth. Is this a justifiable criticism of this poem and Wordsworth's other works on your course? Does he take incidents that may have a limited value and expand their relevance to such an extent that they are in continual danger of exploding; are they the poetic equivalent of an over-inflated balloon?

# A slumber did my spirit seal

Text of poem: New Exploration Anthology page 32

BACKGROUND NOTE

See the Background note for 'She dwelt among the untrodden ways'.

A READING OF THE POEM

The opening two lines of the poem appear to communicate an image that is readily understandable – that of Wordsworth falling into a sleep. He :depicts the condition as a pleasant one that has 'no human fears'. The first line reinforces this by its use of the 's' sound, giving a relaxed and sleepy quality to the words. His use of the past tense clearly indicates that this incident is a recollected one. However, with lines 3 and 4, the poem begins to move away from this apparent clarity. There is an underlying uneasiness as we encounter the puzzling 'She'. Who or what is 'She'? Could it be Wordsworth's 'spirit' of the first line, given a kind of timeless immortality by the protective 'seal' of sleep? Or does the 'She' refer to a separate person? By linking 'She' with the word 'thing', Wordsworth further confuses the matter. Can a 'thing' be human? The use of 'seemed' further increases this uneasiness. There is the strong implication that the ability of this 'She' to resist the effects 'of earthly years' was, in truth, only an appearance. Is there a haunting sense of disappointment, perhaps even distress, underpinning these words, although they are set in the past? Wordsworth deliberately leaves these questions hanging as he leads us into the second stanza.

The second stanza opens with an unsettling change of tense. We are now in the present. However, as the past was filled with an appearance of ability, so the present is filled with real inability. 'She' now has 'no motion', 'no force'; she is unable to hear or see. The image is clearly indicating a change in condition; but in what way and for whom? The negatives of 'no' and 'neither' suggest a ceasing of something that was present before. Furthermore, in spite of the overwhelming image of being unable to move, or hear, or see, there is a surprising lack of emotional reaction. Finally, Wordsworth describes an image that is stunningly vivid yet profoundly enigmatic. He seems to suggest that although 'She' is no longer able to actively move, 'She' is, nevertheless, still participating in movement: 'Rolled round'. 'She' has become part of the greater motion that propels our Earth through Time and Space. Whether this final image is to be understood as positively comforting, or negatively disturbing, is unclear. Reference to Wordsworth's poetic philosophy and his other works supports the view that Nature is a force for good in his world. However, because 'She' is never fully defined, because 'She' is altered in a fundamental yet unspecified way, because Wordsworth himself appears to be suspended in a world that is both conscious and unconscious, wakeful and sleeping, this last image neither clearly answers nor finally resolves the questions that were posed in the first stanza of the poem.

## Alternatively

It is significant that, here again, the female figure is viewed as in some way having the ability to connect with Nature in an instinctive and unconscious way, an ability that Wordsworth by implication felt that he lacked.

Samuel Taylor Coleridge guessed that this poem was written as an epitaph (words composed in memory of a person who has died), after Wordsworth had a premonition of the death of his sister Dorothy.

Given that the poem was published in a group dealing with the death of 'Lucy', it is tempting to view it as simply another aspect of Wordsworth's reaction to this event. Yet we have to pose the question whether the poem itself supports this interpretation. Indeed, should the meaning and relevance of a poem be dictated by its published context? Or should a poem be taken as a separate and distinct entity, with its own uniquely individual meaning? Does it matter when or where a poem is published, or what was happening in the poet's life at the time of its creation? By linking a poem to all these details are we simply taking the easy option and, although we may arrive at a satisfying explanation, have we sacrificed the essential quality that made it a poem in the first place? Wordsworth expressed the following view on this topic: 'Our business is with their books – to understand and enjoy them. And, of poets more especially, it is true – that, if their works be good, they contain within themselves all that is necessary to their being comprehended and relished....'

# Composed Upon Westminster Bridge

Text of poem: New Explorations Anthology page 34

## BACKGROUND NOTE

This poem was composed in 1802 and published in 1807 under the title 'Miscellaneous Sonnets'. Wordsworth subsequently increased the number of sonnets and rearranged their order. Although the sonnets deal with a wide variety of subjects, Wordsworth seemed to feel that they could be organised into a sequence.

## STRUCTURE

As with 'It is a beauteous evening', this is a Petrarchan sonnet. It is made up of an octet (eight lines) and a sestet (six lines). The rhyme scheme is *abbaabba,cdcdcd*. Wordsworth does not stick strictly to the general arrangement of having the octet descriptive and the sestet as a meditation on the description; he mixes description and meditation together throughout the sonnet.

## A READING OF THE POEM

The first line of this poem is deliberately designed to catch the reader's attention. By stating 'Earth has not anything to show more fair', Wordsworth creates a sense of expectancy and curiosity in the reader. He reinforces this in the following two lines, where he suggests that only a spiritually deficient person would not be affected by this scene. Not only does this reflect Wordsworth's belief that the appreciation of beauty involves the spirit of Man, but it also encourages the reader to read on. No one wants to be seen as being 'Dull...of soul'! The suggestion that the scene has 'majesty' contributes to this sense of expectancy. Rather like a DJ on 'Top of the Pops', Wordsworth has given the scene a terrific build-up.

In the second quatrain (four lines), Wordsworth sets about actually describing the scene. In a beautifully constructed phrase, he uses the vivid and significant image of 'a garment' to suggest the beauty of the City. Wordsworth employs the 'garment' image effectively to convey a number of levels of meaning. It implies the transitory nature of the beauty, in that Wordsworth is well aware that the quietness and tranquillity of the scene will not last; it has been put on, like a special outfit. The City, by its nature, is a place of noise and activity. Connected to this is the suggestion of illusion. A 'garment' is frequently worn to transmit a particular message about the wearer. Both of these meanings relate to Wordsworth's emotional reaction to the early-morning City. Although he is moved by the view, his reaction is ambiguous. His appreciation of the beauty of the City is very specifically linked to the particular moment when the City is quiet, deserted and therefore tranquil. However, once this moment passes, as it inevitably must, Wordsworth realises that he will no longer view the City as a thing of beauty. In fact, he will see it as ugly, chaotic and dehumanising. For an instant, the City is as beautiful as the countryside, but, unlike scenes from Nature, the beauty of the early-morning City has no permanence. Wordsworth's psychological acknowledgement and emotional awareness of this fact underpin his use of the image of the 'garment'. The words 'silent, bare' take on a resonance, coming as they do after this image. They fill the sweep of the City landscape as far as the distant fields and the domed sky. The 'silent, bare' City is, at this moment, able to 'lie open'. Its restricted confines become opened out and expanded. Even the physical appearance of the built environment is altered to 'bright and glittering', and, for this moment, the grimy air is 'smokeless'.

In the sestet (six lines) Wordsworth expresses the perfection and beauty of the early-morning City by comparing it to a country scene. This, in his view, is the ultimate comparison. In their deserted state, the 'ships, towers, domes, theatres, and temples' are as good as 'valley, rock, or hill'. Consequently the City, in this moment of 'natural' beauty, affects Wordsworth in a positive way. He feels a tremendous sense of tranquillity, 'a calm so deep'. This emotion is echoed by the movement of the river, that briefly flows undisturbed by busy river traffic. The very sound of the line 'The river glideth at his own sweet will' evokes a sense of peacefulness. However, the final two lines of this sonnet introduce a subtle, yet inescapable, feeling of unease. The use of the expression 'Dear God!' with its exclamation mark injects an emotional intensity at odds with the tranquil calm. At first, this appears to be Wordsworth just overdramatising the fact that 'The very houses seem asleep'. It is all rather reminiscent of the scene from 'The Sleeping Beauty' when the entire castle falls asleep under a magic spell. London is spellbound. But the final line communicates an image that is chillingly ambiguous, for 'all that mighty heart is lying still!' If we connect this to the sleeping houses, then it can be interpreted simply as a description of the sleeping City. However, the heart does not lie 'still' when the body is asleep; the 'heart is lying still' only when the body is dead. The pathos that Wordsworth feels because of his awareness of the transitory quality of this scene spills over into this final line. This beauty that affects him so deeply is tragically and inevitably limited, because it occurs for a brief and unrepresentative moment. Wordsworth does not regard the City in its entirety as beautiful, in the way that he views the whole world of Nature as representing beauty. The underlying sense of unease in the poem arises out of Wordsworth's awareness of the ambiguity in his reaction. For him, the City as a built environment is negative, because it separates Man from the positive influences of Nature. But Wordsworth has been stimulated to react positively to the City in the moment when Man is not in any way apparent in it. Wordsworth realises that once Man appears, the City will no longer be beautiful. Against this background of confusion, his assertion that he feels 'a calm so deep' has a hollow ring to it.

## Alternatively
This sonnet represents the intellectual and philosophical 'straightjacket' that Wordsworth created for himself. His insistence that Nature was infinitely good and beautiful, and a profoundly positive force on Man, compelled him to portray the constructed worlds of towns and cities as essentially bad and ugly and deeply negative influences on Man. By doing this, he restricted his creativity. He cornered himself into rejecting a large part of the human condition. As the critic Lionel Trilling commented about Wordsworth: 'To the ordinary reader he is likely to exist as the very type of the poet whom life has passed by, presumably for the good reason that he passed life by.'

# The Solitary Reaper
Text of poem: New Explorations Anthology page 36

## BACKGROUND NOTE
'The Solitary Reaper' was composed in November 1805 and published in 1807. Wordsworth was reading a friend's manuscript about a trip to Scotland, when one sentence triggered his memory of a solitary reaper from two years previously.

## STRUCTURE
The poem is made up of four stanzas, each consisting of eight lines. Interestingly, the first and fourth stanzas have the rhyme scheme *abcbddee*, while the second and third stanzas have a slightly different scheme of *ababccdd*. Equally noteworthy is the fact that Wordsworth opens the poem in the present tense, but closes it in the past tense.

## A READING OF THE POEM
Wordsworth commences this poem with a direct address in a conversational style of language. This suggests a sense of intimacy, in that we feel we are involved in an ongoing conversation. It also creates immediacy, because we are placed in the significant moment, with Wordsworth, observing the girl at work in the fields. With a few brief but well-chosen words, he conveys a picture of the worlds of Man and Nature existing in harmony: 'single in the field', 'solitary

Highland Lass', 'reaping and singing', 'cuts and binds the grain'. Yet the first stanza is not simply descriptive. The line 'Stop here or gently pass' introduces the concept of reaction to the reaper. It is just what this reaction is that really concerns Wordsworth. His emphasis on reactions to scenes separates him from the purely descriptive poems popular in his day. The choice of stopping or passing is decided by Wordsworth's image of the valley filled with the song. In such circumstances, only the 'Dull...of soul' would pass on.

The second stanza is taken up with two images of birds singing. The nightingale is used to introduce an exotic location, a 'shady haunt' set in the 'Arabian sands', while the cuckoo's environment is the wilds of the 'farthest Hebrides'. In eight lines Wordsworth sweeps us from the heat of the desert to the chill of the North Atlantic, not only to convey the unique quality that the Reaper's singing had, but also to communicate the emotional effect that this singing had on him. The nightingale sings 'welcome notes' to 'weary bands', just as the cuckoo breaks 'the silence of the seas' with his heralding of Spring. Both songs signal relief, comfort and hope in hostile settings. The implication is that the Reaper's song has the same effect on Wordsworth.

With the third stanza Wordsworth pulls us back to the scene described in the first. The question 'Will no one tell me what she sings?' is once again conversational; we are back in the significant moment, but only briefly. By asking this question Wordsworth propels us once more into the realm of reaction to the song. Different reactions to the song create different answers to his question. One listener might view it as being about 'old, unhappy, far-off things', while another may hear a 'humble lay'. Wordsworth answers his initial question with a series of other questions in an effort to convey a variety of equally valid reactions. His emphasis is on the effect of the song, not the song itself.

The final stanza reinforces this point with the phrase 'Whate'er the theme'. He focuses on the way that she sang, since it is this that haunts him. The Reaper sang in a manner that was unrestricted. It seemed to Wordsworth that 'her song had no ending'. This moment became significant for him because the commonplace and familiar activity of reaping coexisted with a uniquely special act of creativity that excited the human spirit. Wordsworth's reaction of standing 'motionless and still' suggests that his outer physical self became unimportant, as all his energies were directed internally to his spiritual reflex. Once this reflex had occurred, the moment of significance had been absorbed: 'The music in my heart I bore'; his energies were redirected once again and he 'mounted up the hill'. But the Wordsworth who climbed the hill was profoundly and fundamentally different from the Wordsworth who had come upon 'The Solitary Reaper'.

## STYLE

This is a lyric poem, because it seeks to communicate the emotional and psychological state of a single speaker. The lyric poem is not concerned with narrative (telling a story), nor is it dramatic, but these elements often occur in it. Wordsworth and his fellow Romantics were particularly fond of the lyric style, as it allowed them to express their uniquely personal responses to a variety of situations.

Wordsworth and Coleridge came up with the title 'Lyrical Ballads' for their collection of poems, and Wordsworth wrote a great many lyrical ballads in the course of his literary career. The ballad form can loosely be defined as having the following qualities: narrative, in that it tells a story; easily understood, as it comes from an oral tradition; dramatic, because it deals with an event; and impersonal, with no intervention on the part of the narrator. The uniting of the lyric and ballad forms was, in Coleridge's words, 'an experiment'. Just how experimental and revolutionary the results were is still a matter of debate among critics.

### Alternatively

The poet John Keats considered that Wordsworth suffered from 'the Wordsworthian or egotistical sublime; which is a thing *per se* and stands alone'. In other words, Wordsworth's Poetic Theory that 'feeling' gave importance to 'the action and situation' was just an excuse for him to describe, perhaps at too great length, his own emotions. 'The Solitary Reaper' is a perfect example of Wordsworth's exaltation of his own reactions. He might have been better advised to take off his jacket and help the girl, rather than to wallow in the self-indulgence of this emotional dissection.

# *The Stolen Boat (extract from* The Prelude*)*

Text of poem: New Explorations Anthology page 38

## BACKGROUND NOTE

'The Stolen Boat' is another extract from 'The Prelude'. It comes before 'Skating' in Book 1 of the fourteen 'Books'. See 'Skating' for further background notes.

## A READING OF THE POEM

Wordsworth opens the poem in a casual and relaxed mood. It has the feeling of a remembered tale from childhood, such as we have all been told by older adults. Initially, it appears that the reminiscence is about his trip in a small boat. Wordsworth simply recounts his actions of going to the boat, untying her and jumping in. Rather than provide a detailed description of the setting for this incident, he implies it by the use of such phrases as 'summer evening', 'willow tree' and 'rocky cave'. By his careful choice of descriptive phrases, Wordsworth effectively communicates the surroundings in six words.

However, a change in the mood of the extract is introduced by his comment, 'It was an act of stealth'. There is something confessional about his admission. This feeling is reinforced by the phrase 'troubled pleasure'. We now realise that the jaunt is not entirely innocent. Yet this mood change is fleeting; almost before we have fully noticed it, it has disappeared. In a beautiful description of the moonlight glittering on the watery disturbances left by the oars, Wordsworth shifts the focus away from any sense of unease. He leads us into the sheer physical delight that he feels as he rows the boat. He is doing it well and he knows it. The lines are filled with the young Wordsworth's elation and confidence; his strength and power seem to grow as he rows the boat skilfully. The boat moves easily like 'an elfin pinnace'. He plunges the oars into the water 'lustily' to propel the boat forward as naturally and gracefully as 'a swan'. Wordsworth and the boat are made one through his expertise.

Carried along with Wordsworth, we too skim the surface of the lake, until suddenly the mood changes with the appearance of 'a huge peak'. The description has echoes of the language of a child. The peak is 'huge' and 'black and huge'. Rather like a monster coming out of the shadows it 'upreared its head'. The sense of unease, previously only hinted at, returns with an overwhelming force. Wordsworth's rowing takes on an air of panic; he 'struck and struck again', the violence implicit in 'struck' emphasising how desperation has replaced his earlier confidence. The scene takes on the elements of a nightmare, with Wordsworth frantically trying to escape from the peak, while all the time the peak comes closer and closer until it blocks out the stars. The boy who had wielded the oars 'lustily' now turns the boat with 'trembling oars'. By using the word 'stole' to describe his return journey, Wordsworth fully exploits the word's various shades of meaning to communicate not only how he rowed and what he had done, but also how he felt. Like a wounded animal he retreats 'back to the covert of the willow tree'.

The significance of this moment affects the young Wordsworth deeply. He goes home a 'grave' and 'serious' boy. In the days following, he grapples with the implications of his experience 'with a dim and undetermined sense'. He is aware that the moment was significant, but as a child he is unable to rationalise and understand it. He is trapped in a world of 'huge and mighty forms' that haunt him 'by day' and fill his 'dreams' at night.

This extract shows Nature in a very different light from the way it is normally portrayed in Wordsworth's poetry. For Wordsworth Nature is a moral force, in that it encourages Man to live in a positive and creative way. Generally, this influence is shown occurring in a pleasant manner, as with 'It is a beauteous evening, calm and free', or 'To My Sister'. Learning from Nature is a happy experience. But here, Nature's moral force is exerted in such a way that it is an extremely unpleasant experience for the young Wordsworth. By stealing the boat, he violates positive and creative living, and because of that Nature expresses her disapproval. Wordsworth feels guilt, but is as yet unable to grasp the full implications of the actions of Nature. His youth places limitations on his intellectual, emotional and moral powers. Thus, he is sensitive to the alteration in the way that Nature presents herself to him, but because he is unable to recognise the lesson that is being transmitted, he is powerless to move on. Consequently, he remains swamped by the overwhelming force that was revealed to him in this alteration and by his own sense of uncomprehending guilt. Nature requires him to resolve what happened to him and why it happened, but the young Wordsworth simply cannot.

## Alternatively

William Empson believed that Wordsworth had 'no inspiration other than his use, when a boy, of the mountains as a totem or father-substitute.' In other words, Empson considers the guilt that Wordsworth experiences when the 'black and huge' peak confronts him as being indicative of a fear that he connected with his father. This fear arose from Wordsworth's feeling that his father's death was, in some unexplained way, a punishment. With his father's death, the young Wordsworth was forced into a state of solitude, both on a physical and emotional level, that he found frightening. In an effort to find some stability and comfort, he turned to Nature. Yet he was never able to eradicate his intense feelings of loss, nor to terminate his search for a parent figure.

# Tintern Abbey

Text of poem: New Explorations Anthology page 42

## BACKGROUND NOTE

Wordsworth composed this poem on 13 July 1798 and it was published later that same year. The full title gives the exact details of his situation at the time: 'Lines Composed a Few Miles Above Tintern Abbey, on Revisiting the Banks of the Wye During a Tour. July 13, 1798.' However biographical details, even when supplied by the poet himself, should always be treated with extreme caution.

## STYLE

In the 1800 edition of 'Lyrical Ballads', Wordsworth wrote of 'Tintern Abbey': 'I have not ventured to call this Poem an ode; but it was written with a hope that in the transitions and the impassioned music of the versification, would be found the principal requisites, of that species of composition.'

There has been considerable debate as to what Wordsworth actually meant by this statement. The Ode is related to the Lyric in that both are derived from Classical Literature. The Ode was considered to be a form of poetry composed for performance, while the Lyric was a personal style of expression. The Romantics took the Classical idea of the Ode form and reinvented it to suit their poetic ends. They retained the sense of flowing change both in rhythm and direction of thought and feeling, and the Ode's fusion of reflection and praise, questioning and earnest pleading. However, they infused it with a greater intensity of personal expression and applied it to a wider range of topics.

## A READING OF THE POEM

Wordsworth opens the poem with an apparently simple statement of fact, 'Five years have past'. However, there is a subtle ambiguity behind these lines. Wordsworth gives the impression that he is looking back to the past from the present moment. Yet we know Wordsworth believed that poetry was created by viewing a significant moment from a distance in time. So, the present moment that Wordsworth seems to be functioning in is in itself a moment from the past.

Despite this aspect, Wordsworth successfully creates a sense of intense immediacy. We are standing with him as he surveys the scene laid out below him. As we have seen previously, by his careful choice of descriptive phrases, Wordsworth is able to convey a rich setting in remarkably few lines. We too see 'the steep and lofty cliffs', the 'dark sycamore', 'these orchard tufts', and 'these pastoral farms'. Wordsworth controls this descriptive section of the poem with considerable skill. He enriches the visual picture by suggesting sound, the 'soft inland murmur' of the mountain streams. Similarly, we can almost smell the 'wreathes of smoke'. The introduction of the Hermit, a favourite Romantic image, carries suggestions of a man withdrawn from the outside world in order to connect with some greater Truth. These ideas recur later on in the poem.

Wordsworth has worked so hard in conveying this wonderful scene to us that we are perfectly willing to understand and accept his estimation of the influence that it has had on him, expressed vividly in three beautifully phrased lines:

> But oft, in lonely rooms, and mid the din
> Of towns and cities, I have owed to them,
> In hours of weariness, sensations sweet, ...

This is a deeply evocative image, one that is easily understood, since we all have mental pictures of treasured moments that provide comforting retreats in difficult times. But it is not just the imaginative conjuring up of this view that positively affects Wordsworth. He is convinced that his earlier interaction with this setting fundamentally affected his essence as a human being, by enabling him to develop 'that serene and blessed mood'. By this phrase, Wordsworth means the positive inner strength that pushes the human spirit towards what is right and good. For Wordsworth, it is this 'mood' that helps Man to live constructively within 'this unintelligible world'. It is this 'mood' that enables the human soul to encounter death without fear, because through death it will become 'a living soul' and will finally 'see into the life of things.' In the face of such impassioned writing, how can we not believe him?

Yet in the very next line Wordsworth introduces an element of doubt; after all, it could be 'but a vain belief'. He quickly dismisses the idea, almost too quickly perhaps. His images of the busy world are vivid and deeply disturbing with the 'joyless daylight', 'the fretful stir' and 'the fever'. We can all too easily visualise Wordsworth driven into illness by this world. Nor does it only affect him physically. Psychologically, it bears down on the very centre of his existence, 'the beatings' of his 'heart'. There is the strong impression that Wordsworth's speedy dismissal of his momentary doubt springs from his overwhelming need to believe that there has to be more to this world than 'joyless daylight'. The repetition of the phrase 'turned to thee' is filled with a terrible sense of need – a lingering echo from his parentless childhood?

Earlier in the poem, Wordsworth blended past and present; now, almost as a result of his emotional outburst, he joins past, present and future together in one breathtaking sweep:

> And now, with gleams of half-extinguished thought,
> With many recognitions dim and faint,
> And somewhat of a sad perplexity,
> The picture of the mind revives again:
> While here I stand, not only with the sense
> Of present pleasure, but with pleasing thoughts
> That in this moment there is life and food
> For future years.

For Wordsworth, there is a wonderful comfort in this disruption of the power of Time. When he visited Tintern Abbey five years previously, he recognised and mentally stored that significant moment. In the poem's present he is able to look on the wonderful scene again, to recognise and store a second significant moment. By doing this, he alters the original significant moment. In this way the past and present interact. In a similar way, Wordsworth connects the present with the future. As he looks on the expanse of countryside below him, he experiences the second significant moment. But he is also aware that he is storing up the information that will, when he mentally returns to it in the future, contribute towards a third significant moment. This, in turn, will deepen the two previous moments. As Wordsworth stands on the brink of this view, he exists in the past, the present and the future.

Wordsworth wants to make it clear that he was not born with these abilities fully developed. So he continues the poem with a brief history of how he, as an individual, came to be the poet who stands above Tintern Abbey. As a child, he loved to be outside experiencing Nature. But it was an unthinking form of experiencing; he 'bounded o'er the mountains'. He was completely taken up with the sensory experiences that Nature offered to him:

> The mountain, and the deep and gloomy wood,
> Their colours and their forms, were then to me
> An appetite;

But these sensory experiences were limited, for two reasons: firstly, he did not combine them with intellectualisation, and secondly, they were purely visual:

> A feeling and a love
> That had no need of a remoter charm,
> By thought supplied, nor any interest
> Unborrowed from the eye.

But, 'That time is past'. The mature Wordsworth may have lost the 'dizzy raptures' of his youth, but he has gained in that he can now experience Nature on a much more profound level:

> For I have learned
> To look on nature, not as in the hour
> Of thoughtless youth; but hearing oftentimes
> The still, sad music of humanity,...

He has come to understand that Nature is symbolic of a Greater Power:

> A motion and a spirit, that impels
> All thinking things, all objects of all thought,
> And rolls through all things.

For this reason, Wordsworth still loves Nature, just as he did when he was a child, but it is a more mature form of love for this his 'nurse', his 'guide', 'the guardian of my heart, and soul'. It is interesting to note the nurturing characteristics that Wordsworth attributes to Nature, given that many critics see his relationship with Nature as representing a search for the parent figures lost to him at an early age.

Indeed, Wordsworth's train of thought moves on to what was possibly his closest human relationship, his love for his sister Dorothy. References to Dorothy are frequent in his poetry, and in 'Tintern Abbey' he writes in a revealing way about her. He is absolutely clear that his relationship with his sister has been as fundamental to him as the one he shares with Nature. He recognises that even if he had not achieved his mature appreciation of Nature, he would still be happy at this moment because Dorothy is with him, she is his 'dear, dear Friend'. However, it is significant that Wordsworth describes this relationship with the focus very definitely on himself. Dorothy is a positive influence because she reminds him of what he once was. In her voice he hears the 'language of my former heart', and in her eyes he sees his 'former pleasures'. We have encountered the concept before that Dorothy, along with other female figures, is able, in some indefinable way, to connect with Nature at a level that Wordsworth finds impossible. Notably, Wordsworth generally represents Nature as female. He assures Dorothy that through their love of Nature, they will be empowered to withstand the negative and destructive influences of the world – the 'evil tongues' and 'the sneers'. Are these, perhaps, references to the critical reception his poetry received? Nevertheless, Wordsworth views himself as being united in a triangle of positive interaction, a 'cheerful faith', with his sister and Nature. This unity is so strong that it will not be broken by Time. He reassures Dorothy that, in the face of 'solitude, or fear, or pain, or grief' she will always be able to draw strength from this moment, but he connects this moment with himself. For although he implies that Dorothy is also able to experience Nature at a profound level – her mind is 'a mansion to all lovely forms' – he sees her 'healing thoughts' as coming from her memory of him, rather than the scene itself. He wishes her to remember him as a 'worshipper of Nature', one who loved Nature with a religious zeal. Finally, Wordsworth closes this poem with a series of images that have deep emotional resonances. There is the implication that his 'absence' and 'wanderings' do not merely refer to his travels, but are also suggestive of his emotional and spiritual wanderings. There is a moving intensity in the final image of Wordsworth himself, his sister Dorothy, and Nature in a close and intimate relationship:

Nor wilt thou then forget
That after many wanderings, many years
Of absence, these steep woods and lofty cliffs,
And this green pastoral landscape, were to me
More dear, both for themselves and for thy sake!

Perhaps the orphaned children did find a loving guardian to protect them after all.

TINTERN ABBEY AND WORDSWORTH'S POETIC THEORY

In 'Tintern Abbey', Wordsworth expressed many of the fundamental concepts that formed his Poetic Theory. Briefly, they can be summarised as follows:

1. Nature as a positive force on human emotions and spirit –    lines 25–30
                                                                lines 55–7

   See also Point 9.

2. Nature as a provider of order and coherence in the face
   of a disordered world –                                      lines 37–41
                                                                lines 155–9

3. Nature as an agency for spiritual growth –                   lines 43–9

4. The negative influence of the general world of men –         lines 38–41
                                                                lines 51–4
                                                                lines 128–34

5. The importance of memory –                                   lines 25–30
                                                                lines 55–7
                                                                lines 58–65
                                                                lines 137–42

6. The different ways that Nature can be experienced –          lines 67–105
                                                                lines 137–42

7. The paramount need to develop the senses –                   lines 106–8

8. Nature symbolising a Greater Truth –                         lines 88–102

9. Nature fulfilling a parental/guardian/comforter/educator
   role –                                                       lines 107–11
                                                                lines 122–34

10. The beauty of Nature –                                      lines 2–22
                                                                lines 67–79
                                                                lines 134–7

You may like to add other points to this list.

*Alternatively*
'The case of Mr. Wordsworth, we perceive, is now manifestly hopeless; and we give him up as altogether incurable, and beyond the power of criticism .... We really think it right not to harass him any longer with nauseous remedies, but... wait in patience for the natural termination of the disorder.'

This was written by one of Wordsworth's fiercest contemporary critics, Francis Jeffrey. Is 'Tintern Abbey' the ultimate in egotistical self-indulgence? Did Wordsworth function for so long in the rarefied world of his own self-centred Poetic Theory that he lost all touch with reality and, like a man who suffers from a fever, rambled through this poem in a confused and largely incoherent state?

## Wordsworth's poems in chronological order

| | |
|---|---|
| To My Sister | 1798 |
| Tintern Abbey | 1798 |
| She dwelt among the untrodden ways | 1799 |
| A slumber did my spirit seal | 1799 |
| The Stolen Boat | 1799 |
| Skating | 1799 |
| It is a beauteous evening, calm and free | 1802 |
| Composed Upon Westminster Bridge | 1802 |
| The Solitary Reaper | 1805 |

## Developing a personal response to William Wordsworth

1. What do you think of Wordsworth's Poetic Theory?
2. How did this Poetic Theory influence his writing?
3. Did he fulfil his own standards as set out in his Poetic Theory?
4. What themes recur in his poetry? Are they connected to his Poetic Theory?
5. Did the themes tell you anything about Wordsworth himself? Would you like him as a friend?
6. What aspects of Wordsworth's poetry did you like?
7. What aspects of Wordsworth's poetry did you dislike?
8. Did any of his poems stay with you in a lasting way? Why?
9. Has Wordsworth any relevance to the world of the twenty-first century?
10. Would you read more of Wordsworth's poetry? Why?

## Questions

1. Read 'She dwelt among the untrodden ways' and answer the following questions.
   1. (a) What impressions of Lucy and her life emerge for you from your reading of this poem?
      (b) Choose **two** images from the poem that especially convey these impressions to you and comment on your choices.
   2. (a) What is the poet's attitude to Lucy? Support your answer by reference to the words of the poem.

(b) Do you think you would have liked Lucy if you had met her? What words or phrases from the poem help you to decide?

3.  Answer **ONE** of the following (a), (b) or (c).

   (a) Choose from the following descriptions of Wordsworth's relationship with Lucy the one that is closest to your reading and explain your choice by referring to the words of the poem.

   Wordsworth and Lucy were in love
   Wordsworth did not really know Lucy
   Lucy was important to Wordsworth

   or

   (b) How would you describe the mood of this poem? What words or phrases in the poem convey this mood?

   or

   (c) From your reading of this poem what 'difference' do you think Lucy's death made to Wordsworth?

2.  Read 'It is a beauteous evening, calm and free' and answer the following questions.

   1.  (a) What sort of scene do you imagine from your reading of this poem?
       (b) Choose **two** phrases from the poem that especially convey this scene to you and comment on your choices.

   2.  Why do you think Wordsworth uses words connected with religion in this poem? Support your answer by reference to the text of the poem.

   3.  Answer **ONE** of the following (a), (b) or (c).
       (a) How is the Girl's reaction to the scene different from Wordsworth's?

       or

       (b) How does the fact that this poem is in sonnet form affect the way that the poem is written?

       or

       (c) Which do you think is more important in this poem, the description of the scene or the Girl's reaction to it? Or are they of equal importance?

3.  Read 'Skating' and answer the following questions.

   1.  (a) What impression of Wordsworth do you get from this extract?
       (b) What words or phrases from the poem help most to create this impression for you?
       (c) Do you think Wordsworth was a typical boy? Why?

   2.  How, in your view, does the poet convey the excitement of skating? Support your point of view by reference to the extract.

   3.  Answer **ONE** of the following (a), (b) or (c).
       (a) What is the tone of this extract? Does it change?

    **or**

    (b)  What is the point of this extract?

    **or**

    (c)  Choose a line from the extract in which the sound of the words adds to the meaning. Explain your choice.

4.  'In Wordsworth's poetry Nature is more than just a setting for his writing.' Discuss this view, supporting your answer by quotation from or reference to the poems you have studied.

5.  'Wordsworth's poems move from the highly personal to a wider relevance.' In your reading of Wordsworth's poetry did you find this to be true? Support your answer by quotation from or reference to the poems on your course.

6.  'William Wordsworth – A Personal Response'. Using the above title, write an essay on the poetry of Wordsworth, supporting your points by quotation from or reference to the poems on your course.

7.  'Memory is the cornerstone of Wordsworth's poetry.'
Discuss this view, supporting your answer by quotation from or reference to the poems you have studied.

8.  'Wordsworth's poems describe childhood in an unrealistic and idealised way.' Give your response to this point of view, with supporting quotations from or reference to the poems on your course.

9.  'William Wordsworth's poems constantly seek for meaning in a world that is unintelligible.' In your reading of Wordsworth's poetry did you find this to be true? Support your answer by quotation from or reference to the poems you have studied.

10. 'Fear, both explicit and implicit, plays a significant role in Wordsworth's poetry.' Discuss this statement, supporting your answer by quotation from or reference to the poems on your course.

# A short bibliography

Abrams, M.H., *Wordsworth – A Collection of Critical Essays*, New Jersey: Prentice-Hall 1972.

Arnold, Matthew, *Poetry and Prose*, London: Rupert Hart-Davis 1967.

Bourke, Richard, *Romantic Discourse and Political Modernity: Wordsworth, The Intellectual and Cultural Critique*, London: Harvester Wheatsheaf 1993.

Coleridge, Samuel Taylor, *Biographia Literaria*, London: J.M. Dent 1971.

Enright, D.J. and DeChickera, Ernst, *English Critical Texts 16th to 20th Century*, London: Oxford University Press 1971.

Hamilton, Ian, *Keepers of the Flame*, London: Pimlico 1993.

Hartman, Geoffrey H., *Wordsworth's Poetry 1787–1814*, New Haven: Yale University Press 1964.

Leavis, F.R. *Revaluation*, London: Penguin 1994.

Prickett, Stephen, *Coleridge and Wordsworth – The Poetry of Growth*, London: Cambridge University Press 1970.

Salvesen, Christopher, *The Landscape of Memory: A Study of Wordsworth's Poetry*, London: Edward Arnold 1965.

Schmidt, Michael, *Lives of the Poets*, London: Phoenix 1999.

Wu, Duncan, (editor), *A Companion to Romanticism*, Oxford: Blackwell 1999.

# 2   *Emily* DICKINSON

*John G. Fahy*

## An Enigmatic Life

The Dickinsons were prominent public figures. Emily's father, Edward Dickinson, was a well-known lawyer, with a great interest in education. For a time he was treasurer of Amherst College, which had been founded by Emily's grandfather, Samuel Fowler Dickinson. He served as state senator for Massachusetts, was elected to the US House of Representatives, and was instrumental in bringing the railway to Amherst. He is described by Emily's biographers as a somewhat severe and remote father, an interpretation based on her own letters, though she appears to have loved him, and she was devastated when he died.

The relationship between Emily and her mother, Emily Norcross Dickinson, does not appear to have been a very warm one either, as Emily mentioned in a letter to her literary guide and friend Thomas Wentworth Higginson: 'I never had a mother. I suppose a mother is one to whom you hurry when you are troubled.' In later life, however, she did become closer to her mother. It is worth remembering that the remoteness of parents was a feature of nineteenth-century child-rearing practice with the middle and upper classes; and Emily's childhood experiences may not have been that much out of the ordinary.

The family lived in half of the Homestead, an imposing brick house in Main Street, Amherst, built by Edward's father, who occupied the other half. In 1840 the grandfather sold out and moved away. Edward moved with his family to another part of Amherst until 1855, when he managed to buy back the entire house, and there Emily lived for the rest of her life.

In 1840 Emily was sent to Amherst Academy, a co-educational school offering a wide range of subjects, from classics to modern sciences. The principal of the school, Rev. Edward Hitchcock, was a well-known scientist. Emily developed a particular interest in biology and botany, which may account for the precision of her observations and the prevalence of natural imagery in many of her poems.

In 1847 Emily went to Mount Holyoke Female Seminary for further education, but was withdrawn after two terms because of poor health and possibly because of the overpowering religious ethos of the school. She had been expressing religious doubts even before she went there. Though she was a believer in God, she remained aloof from the religious fervour, in the form of religious revival meetings, sweeping through Amherst about this time.

## LIFE IN AMHERST

When her formal education finished, in 1847, Emily Dickinson seems to have lived a fairly normal life in Amherst, with some excursions to the cities (Boston in 1851, Washington and Philadelphia in 1855). In 1855 her mother, who had been in declining health, became seriously disabled. Emily and Lavinia, with the support of domestic help, took over the running of the household, and Emily began to develop that missing relationship with her mother – though with roles reversed, as she explained: 'We were never intimate Mother and Children while she was our Mother – but Mines in the same Ground meet by tunnelling and when she became our Child, the Affection came.'

In those days Emily's life was ordinary, her behaviour unremarkable. She went to church, walked her dog, wrote letters, did housework, and supported community events. In October 1856 she won a prize for her bread at the local cattle show and served as a member of the produce committee during the following year. In her garden she had the reputation of having 'green fingers'. Perhaps it was here that she first saw 'a Bird' come 'down the Walk' or encountered 'A narrow Fellow in the Grass' – though that was more likely to have occurred in the Dickinson meadow across the street.

In 1856 Austin joined the First Church of Christ, and also that year he married Emily's closest friend, Susan Gilbert. They built a house, the Evergreens, next door to the Homestead, and this was, at least at first, a place of much gaiety and entertainment, in contrast to the sombre austerity of Emily's own home. The happiness experienced by the young people was referred to by Kate Scott Anthon, a mutual friend, writing to Susan: 'Those happy visits to your house! Those celestial evenings in the library – The blazing wood fire – Emily – Austin – The music – The rampant fun – The inextinguishable laughter, The uproarious spirits of our chosen – our most congenial circle.'

Emily Dickinson was not short of friends and advisers at this time, though the relationships, particularly with her women friends, did not always remain untrammelled. The friendship with Susan Gilbert became somewhat strained after a number of years. In 1859 Emily met Kate Scott Anthon, a friend of Susan's, and considered her a close friend until 1866. Nor was she devoid of male company. Ben Newton, a law student of her father's, encouraged her reading and was considered by her 'a gentle, yet grave Preceptor'. Rev. Charles Wadsworth was her spiritual adviser for many years. Samuel Bowles, editor of the *Springfield Daily Republican,* was a close friend. The names of one or two other young men have been mentioned by scholars as possible recipients of her affections. After 1862 Thomas Wentworth Higginson became her literary guide and critic. Judge Otis Lord, a widower, wanted to marry her, and she seems to have cared deeply for him in the early 1880s until his death in 1884. And there was the unidentified man addressed as 'Master' in her letters and poems, whom she loved and who may or may not have been one of the acquaintances known to us.

As to her appearance, it is interesting to note how she described herself when asked by Higginson for a portrait: 'I had no portrait, now, but am small, like the Wren, and my Hair is bold, like the Chestnut Bur – and my eyes, like the Sherry in the Glass, that the Guest leaves.'

CRISIS AND WITHDRAWAL

There seems to have been some kind of emotional crisis in her personal life around 1861–63, the nature of which we can only guess at. The speculation is that she may have been rejected by, or may herself have rejected, the man she loved, perhaps the 'Master' of the letters and poems. The scholar Rebecca Patterson has put forward the thesis that Emily's friendship with Susan Gilbert and Kate Scott Anthon was lesbian in nature. The psychologist and critic John Cody came to the conclusion that her lover was fictional rather than factual and went on to discuss the question whether she suffered a nervous breakdown. He pointed out that certain poems give us a documented description of the inner processes experienced in a mental collapse (see 'A Funeral', 'After Great Pain', and 'The Soul'). In this regard Emily Dickinson is seen as the forerunner of modern women writers, such as Sylvia Plath, Margaret Atwood and Doris Lessing, who have dealt specifically with the experience of insanity.

Though the exact nature and cause of the experience are open to speculation and argument, Emily Dickinson seems to have undergone a psychological crisis in her early thirties, which resulted in a great outpouring of poetry (an estimated four to five hundred poems in 1862 and 1863) and led to her withdrawal from normal social life. Her biographer Richard Sewall goes to some lengths to demonstrate that this withdrawal was gradual, that she continued to see her family and close friends, and that she sent letters and presents and sometimes copies of her poems to friends and acquaintances. He argues that she withdrew to dedicate herself to her poetry.

This is an interpretation also strongly urged by Jerusha McCormack, who points to the withdrawal from society of other American writers of the time, such as Nathaniel Hawthorne and Henry David Thoreau. McCormack argues that Dickinson withdrew in order to master life, a process akin to Christian asceticism, except that she was not doing it for religious reasons. Her poems reflect this inner struggle to understand, to master and control circumstances, and she finally achieved mastery over life by rejecting it.

Her behaviour became noticeably more odd and eccentric. She became 'the myth' of Amherst, a lone woman dressed all in white who didn't meet strangers or even visitors, who spoke to friends from behind a half-closed door or shrouded in shadow at the head of the stairs, though she sent them in wine or fruit on a tray. She refused to go out. 'I do not Cross my Father's ground to any House or town,' she replied to Higginson's invitation to attend a lecture in Boston in 1869. But he made a trip to Amherst to see her in August 1870 and has left us (in a letter to his wife) an interesting impression of the poet.

I shan't sit up tonight to write you all about E. D. dearest but if you had read Mrs. Stoddard's novels you could understand a house where each member runs his or her own selves. Yet I only saw her.

A large county lawyer's house, brown brick, with great trees & a garden – I sent up my card. A parlor dark & cool & stiffish, a few books & engravings & an open piano – Malbone [Higginson's novel] & O D [Out-Door] Papers among other books.

A step like a pattering child's in entry & in glided a little plain woman with two smooth bands of reddish hair & a face a little like Belle Dove's; not plainer – with no good feature – in a very plain & exquisitely clean white pique & a blue net worsted shawl. She came to me with two day lilies which she put in a sort of childlike way into my hand & said "These are my introduction" in a soft frightened breathless childlike voice – & added under her breath Forgive me if I am frightened; I never see strangers & hardly know what I say – but she talked soon & thenceforward continuously – & deferentially – sometimes stopping to ask me to talk instead of her – but readily recommencing. Manner between Angie Tilton & Mr. Alcott – but thoroughly ingenuous & simple which they are not & saying many things which you would have thought foolish & I wise – & some things you wd. hv. liked.

In 1883 she visited her dying nephew, Gilbert, next door at the Evergreens and was ill for months afterwards. When she died, on 15 May 1886, on her own instructions her white coffin was carried across the fields to the churchyard rather than by the usual route of funeral processions. She was found to have left almost two thousand poems and fragments.

Modern writers on Dickinson tend to play down her oddness and in general paint a more rounded portrait of her personality. Margaret Freeman has written (in the introduction to *Emily Dickinson's Imagery* by Rebecca Patterson):

Scholarly research over the years has dispelled, once and for all, the popular myth of the reclusive nun, replacing it with a picture of a gifted, if eccentric, woman, witty but not pretty, fond of her family, her friends, her books, her plants, and her dog, a woman who in her adolescent years had all the nineteenth-century desires and expectancies of a healthy girl but who, for whatever reason, never married, who matured emotionally and intellectually through some crisis in her late twenties, and who had, above all else, a passion for poetry.

## Religion

Puritanism, with its strict religious outlook, was one of the most important formative influences on early white American culture. Its doctrines included belief in a severe and righteous God, belief that humankind was essentially evil and that only a tiny minority (the 'elect') were destined to be saved, and that individuals could do little about their fate, which was predetermined by God. This stern philosophy was given expression in a rigid everyday way of life. Strict sobriety, honesty and moral uprightness were required in public dealings, and a scrupulous examination of conscience was practised in private. All of life was seen as a preparation for the awful Day of Judgement (see 'A Fly').

Revivalist meetings provided some variation and were a feature of life in Amherst in the middle of the nineteenth century. At these, Baptist evangelists preached fiery emotional sermons on repentance and salvation. They taught that the individual, by repenting, could be saved.

Emily Dickinson was educated in the strict Puritan tradition of her time; but even as a young girl she seemed reluctant to commit herself completely. She wrote in 1846: 'I have perfect confidence in God and his promises and yet, I know not why, I feel the world holds a prominent place in my affections.' Some scholars argue that she could not bring herself to believe in the harsh doctrine that all those who were not of the 'elect' were to be damned. Others argue that she had a deep crisis of faith: that her empirical mind, focusing on the world as she experienced it, did not find much evidence of the divine in nature or other areas of life, that she found God remote if not deliberately perverse in not revealing himself (see 'Slant of Light'). Denis Donoghue argues that her rebellious spirit resisted having to believe in certain truths and refused to accept the discipline of doctrine.

At any rate, she seems to have withdrawn from the practice of orthodox Puritanism. Nor was she tempted by the more emotional Revivalists, though most of her family experienced a renewal of faith in the late 1840s and early 50s. She retained a belief in God and wrote many poems about faith, God, Heaven, and immortality. Yet her views were hardly orthodox. 'Let Emily sing for you because she cannot pray,' she wrote to a relative. Still, many find her songs or poems to be eloquent religious meditations. In general, it is difficult to decipher exactly what her religious beliefs were. But she certainly borrowed from her religious culture: themes and metaphors from the Bible and phrases and rhythms from the hymn books of Rev. Isaac Watts. She wrote many of her poems in the 'common metre' of the Psalms.

## Political agitation

The 1830s and 40s saw the beginning of the campaign for women's rights. In 1839 Margaret Fuller organised intellectual discussion groups for women in Boston, and this continued for some years; and in 1845 Fuller's influential feminist pamphlet, *Women in the Nineteenth Century,* was published.

The mid-century saw a flurry of political campaigns, for educational reform, for prison reform, for temperance reform. And there was the very divisive campaign for the abolition of slavery, one of the factors that led to the American Civil War (1861–65). Altogether it was a time of social ferment and political upheaval.

## Philosophical and literary milieu

Rationalism was a philosophy imported from Europe, from the eighteenth-century era of the Enlightenment. It put great faith in rational thought, the belief that humankind could be improved through rational thinking and scientific learning. All problems – social, religious, and moral – could be solved and society perfected through rational thought. This philosophy of human self-sufficiency fitted in well with the emerging American state.

In Europe, Rationalism was succeeded by Romanticism. The Romantics rejected reason, arguing that the way to truth was through the imagination and through intuition and feelings. There was great emphasis on the power of nature. For some Romantic poets, such as Wordsworth, nature revealed the divine. Romanticism also emphasised individuality. The rebellious individual was an icon. The American version of Romanticism was known as Transcendentalism.

### *Ralph Waldo Emerson (1803–1882)*

Philosopher, poet, and founder of the Transcendentalist movement, Emerson was the foremost literary figure of the era. Transcendentalism was a quasi-religious concept owing much to the Romantics and in particular to Wordsworth's reverence for nature. Each person's intuition and imagination led them to truth and to God, without the need for any particular religious practice or set of beliefs. The power of God existed in nature, and the intuitive soul sensed this and so came into contact with the divine. Emerson developed this concept in his essay 'Nature' in 1836. His 1841 volume of essays contains 'Self Reliance', with its now well-known provocative statements, 'Who so would be a man must be a non conformist' and 'A foolish consistency is the hobgoblin of little minds.' His 1844 collection of essays contains 'The Poet', in which he urges poets to write about America, 'our log-rolling, our stumps and their politics, our fisheries, our Negroes and Indians'.

## Walt Whitman (1819–1892)

Whitman did just that in *Leaves of Grass* (1855), a volume of poetry rooted in the life and characters of America. 'I have never read his book – but was told that he was disgraceful,' Dickinson said of his homoerotic verses, which shocked many at the time.

## Henry David Thoreau (1817–1862)

Thoreau described himself as 'a mystic, a transcendentalist, and a natural philosopher to boot'. He has become famous for *Walden, or Life in the Woods* (1854), describing a two-year experiment in self-sufficiency (1845–47), when he built himself a wooden hut on the edge of Walden Pond, Concord. In the book he describes his agricultural experiments, the wildlife, the visitors he had, and his neighbours. Thoreau developed an appreciation for the simplicity of the Native American way of life, as opposed to the materialism of white America at the time.

Emerson, Whitman and Thoreau represent the optimistic, positive face of American letters and exhibit an independence of mind and a self-sufficiency in outlook.

## Nathaniel Hawthorne (1804–1864), Herman Melville (1819–1891), Edgar Allan Poe (1809–1849)

Hawthorne, Melville and Poe might be taken to represent the pessimistic, negative outlook in American writing. All of them are preoccupied with evil, sin and the dark side of human nature.

Hawthorne was fascinated by sin, and his novel *The Scarlet Letter* (1850) is an examination of the nature of American Puritanism and the New England conscience. Dickinson certainly seems to have read his 1851 novel *The House of the Seven Gables* (see page 57). Poe, about whom Dickinson confessed not to have read enough, was fascinated by the macabre.

DICKINSON'S READING

We know from Rebecca Patterson that Emily Dickinson read widely, but particularly incessantly among the nineteenth-century English writers. The Brontës affected her deeply. She read *Middlemarch* and became fascinated by any biographical information that came to light on George Eliot. She read Dickens, valuing in particular *The Old Curiosity Shop* and *David Copperfield*. The poems of Elizabeth Barrett Browning and Robert Browning were also important to her. To a lesser extent she read the Romantics, Byron in particular.

She also read the contemporary American writers, notably Emerson, Hawthorne and Thoreau. Emerson she read as a young woman, and she was attracted by the mystical quality of his poetry. In 1850 she mentions 'the gift of Ralph Emerson's poems – a beautiful copy' received from her friend Ben Newton. Yet in 1857, when Emerson lectured in Amherst and stayed at the Evergreens with Austin and Sue, Emily did not attend. She read the local poet Helen Hunt Jackson, who urged her to publish her own poems.

Dickinson was steeped in the Bible, Shakespeare and Milton; but she also read less 'elevated' fare, for example *Kavanagh*, a popular romantic novel by Longfellow, which was secretly given to her by her brother, Austin, and created a family rumpus. She also read travel books, popular history, and journals such as the *Atlantic Monthly, Scribner's Monthly* and *Harper's Monthly Magazine*. Hers was a wide reading, but it was often indiscriminate.

Was this wide reading a recluse's substitute for life experience and so a vital element in the development of Dickinson's thought and poetry? Her life experience was not as limited as popular myth would have us suppose, but what she imbibed from her books and from her work in the garden was obviously important to her. But she didn't read to borrow or to compare. Reading was a stimulus for her own thoughts. It wasn't necessarily the great themes or the scope or the technique of a work that inspired her but, as Denis Donoghue points out, often just a line or a phrase. Little gems set her thinking.

> Her motive in reading other writers, great and small, was not to discover the variety and potentiality of the art she shared with them, but rather to find there a provocation for her own imagination. Sometimes a phrase was enough. She was deeply engaged by the Brontës, but on the other hand the abiding interest of Emily Brontë largely resolved itself in a magical line, 'Every existence would exist in Thee,' from 'No Coward Soul Is Mine'. The line is quoted three times in letters.

Two thousand poems

Because of Dickinson's method of arrangement and storage, among other factors, it is difficult to be certain about the dating of the poems or to suggest patterns or to talk about development in her poetry. But we can identify phases of writing.

## The early phase (up to 1858)

It is probable that Dickinson had been writing poems since her youth. What survives of her early work is relatively conventional poetry. Thomas Johnson, editor of the *Complete Poems*, thought it probable that in about 1858 she culled many of her earlier poems and transcribed those she decided to save.

## The middle phase (1858–65)

By 1858 she was writing poetry seriously. During this period she investigated themes of love, pain, absence and loss, doubt, despair, mental anguish, and other universal themes, and all in sparse poems of passionate intensity. Practically all the poems in the present selection are from this phase.

Thomas Johnson has described how the poems were handwritten in ink and stored in packets, each packet consisting of four to six sheets of folded paper held together with thread through the fold. These versions were fair copies or almost final drafts. 'Of the forty-nine packets, forty-six appear to include all the verses written between 1858 and 1865, the years of great creativeness.' 1862 seems to have been her most productive year, with over 350 poems. The packets constitute about two-thirds of the total body of her poetry.

From her entire output of about two thousand poems, only seven were printed during her lifetime. In 1861 the *Springfield Daily Republican*, edited by her friend Samuel Bowles, printed 'A Liquor Never Brewed', under the title 'The May-Wine'. In 1862 the *Republican* printed 'Safe in Their Alabaster Chambers'. Two more of her poems were published in 1864.

On 15 April 1862 Dickinson replied to an article advising young writers in the *Atlantic Monthly,* a literary magazine. The article was by Thomas Wentworth Higginson, an essayist, lecturer and former preacher, who was particularly interested in the status of women writers. She included four of her poems, asking his professional opinion, 'to say if my Verse is alive'. Higginson was a very traditional nineteenth-century critic and took issue with the odd and unorthodox qualities of her poetry and for this reason seems to have advised against publication. But he was not insensitive to this remarkable new talent. He recalled much later, in an article of 1891:

> The impression of a wholly new and original poetic genius was as distinct on my mind at the first reading of these four poems as it is now, after thirty years of further knowledge; and with it came the problem never yet solved, what place ought to be assigned in literature to what is so remarkable, yet so elusive of criticism.

The correspondence continued and grew into friendship; but Higginson printed none of her poems during her lifetime.

## The late phase (late 1870s and early 1880s)

This period contained a good many harsh and ironic verses.

### EDITIONS OF THE POEMS

After Dickinson's death her sister, Lavinia, found this great number of poems and set about having them published. She persuaded Mabel Loomis Todd, the wife of a professor at Amherst College, to prepare a selection. Todd, with the help of Higginson, selected 115 poems for publication; but the editors were concerned about her odd style, so they 'standardised' it, changing rhymes, regularising metre, even altering metaphors and sometimes the arrangement of lines. *Poems by Emily Dickinson* was published by Roberts Brothers of Boston in 1890, to a slightly baffled critical reception but good sales. Further selections were published in 1891 and 1896.

Todd published a selection of Dickinson's letters in 1894. But a dispute between Lavinia Dickinson and Todd resulted in a division of Emily Dickinson's unpublished works. The material in Lavinia's possession went to Susan and eventually to her daughter, Emily's niece, Martha Dickinson Bianchi, who issued another volume, *The Single Hound,* in 1914. This one had relatively few alterations from the originals. The material in Todd's possession did not see publication until 1945.

In 1955 an authoritative collection of Dickinson's work was prepared by Thomas Johnson. He issued a three-volume *variorum* edition (i.e. containing all known versions of each poem), *The Poems of Emily Dickinson,* published by Harvard University Press. The poems are dated but, as Johnson himself admitted, this is the result of educated guesswork. It is very difficult to be definite, since Dickinson never prepared the poems for publication, did not title them, and had the habit of binding poems from different years into the same packet. (There are different handwriting styles in some packets.)

In 1970 the Faber and Faber edition was published, in which Johnson selected one version of each poem as the probable original.

## *I taste a liquor never brewed*
Text of poem: New Explorations Anthology page 50

### BACKGROUND NOTE

A version of this poem was first printed in 1861 in the *Springfield Republican,* edited by Dickinson's friend Samuel Bowles. But it was entitled 'The May-Wine', some line endings were altered to get a more exact rhyme, and one line was completely changed. It is doubtful if this was done with the poet's consent.

### A READING OF THE POEM

This has been interpreted by some as primarily a nature poem, celebrating the simple home-grown joy of nature, a celebration of endless summer. The exuberance of nature is linked with the excitement of poetic inspiration.

But nature is more the stimulus than the subject of this poem. Nature provides the spur for excitement, good spirits, unrestrained joy. The poem is fundamentally a celebration of happiness and unqualified delight.

This has some of the elements of a romantic poem, with its sensitivity to nature and the strong sense of individualism shown by the rebellious speaker.

## THE ELEMENT OF FANTASY

The high spirits of this poem nudge it into the realm of fantasy. Susan Juhasz examines this pronounced element of fantasy in the poem. She comments on the childish air and the quality of make-believe it possesses. The riddle form of the first stanza enhances this atmosphere (what is the 'liquor never brewed'?). Real and imaginative experiences are compared in this fantasy world: real liquor to 'inebriate of Air'. It is a fantasy world where reality is stood on its head: lack of self-control is celebrated as virtue ('Seraphs swing their snowy Hats ... to see the little Tippler'); the drunken speaker seems to have a kind of superiority over the saints (is there a suggestion that their snowy hats would melt, while he can lean against the sun?); the saints are confined, perhaps imprisoned, while the drunkard is free; and time seems somehow to have been vanquished while the 'little Tippler' drinks on into eternity.

## THE HUMOROUS VOICE OF EMILY DICKINSON

### Comic effects

As well as the imaginative elements of fantasy, the poem features many of the more usual comic effects, such as exaggerated imagery – for example the metaphor of the flower as tavern and the bee as drunkard:

> When 'Landlords' turn the drunken Bee
> Out of the Foxglove's door –

or

> the little Tippler
> Leaning against the – Sun –.

The notion of the bee as tippler is maintained throughout the poem – reeling, leaning, etc. The ridiculous costumes ('the snowy Hats') add to the comic effect. The odd juxtaposition of the sacred and the profane is also comic (Seraphs, Saints and the Tippler). The alliteration ('Debauchee of Dew', 'Seraphs swing their snowy Hats') also contributes.

### Irony

A deeper humour is achieved through a pervasive sense of irony in the poem.

Given the poet's Calvinist background, the central metaphor of the drunkard is amusingly ironic. Her father was a strong advocate of the Temperance League. Perhaps Dickinson is exercising a delightful rebelliousness! To celebrate the riotous, even scandalous activities of the speaker in the common metre of church hymns is amusingly ironic. And there are ironies embedded in both imagery and language: the imprisoned saints contrast with the tipsy speaker at large, and also the fact that she uses the vocabulary of nature to deal with its opposite, timelessness.

## Wit
We have already noted the paradoxical riddle of the opening.

## Poem as parody
Juhasz, Miller and Smith (in *Comic Power in Emily Dickinson*) argue that this poem is a witty parody of Ralph Waldo Emerson's poem 'Bacchus'.
- Both poems compare poetic vision to the state of intoxication.
- The poems have a similar structure, beginning with a mystical reference to wine, going on to deal with concrete aspects of the world, and finishing with cosmic imagery.
- But Emerson's is a sombre, serious poem, where he forged links with Greek mythology and seems to have some affinity with eternal figures.
- Dickinson smirks at the sacred and deflates the notion of the serious poet.
- Dickinson's stance is outside the poem, smiling from a distance.
- The comic and fantasy elements of Dickinson's poem render a different tone.
  So there's a good case to be made that this is a conscious literary take-off by Emily Dickinson and as such is both effective and highly amusing.
  Here are some fragments of the Emerson poem for comparison.

> Bring me wine, but wine which never grew
> In the belly of the grape,
> Or grew on vine whose tap-roots, reaching through
> Under the Andes to the Cape,
> Suffer no savor of the earth to scape.
>
> Let its grapes the morn salute
> From a nocturnal root,
> Which feels the acrid juice
> Of Styx and Erebus;
> And turns the woe of Night,
> By its own craft, to a more rich delight.
> Wine which Music is, –

Music and wine are one, –
That I, drinking this,
Shall hear far Chaos talk with me;
Kings unborn shall walk with me;
And the poor grass shall plot and plan
What it will do when it is man.
Quickened so, will I unlock
Every crypt of every rock.

I thank the joyful juice
For all I know; –
Winds of remembering
Of the ancient being blow,
And seeming-solid walls of use
Open and flow.

# 'Hope' is the thing with Feathers

Text of poem: New Explorations Anthology page 52

[*Note: This poem is also prescribed for Ordinary Level 2005 exam*]

A READING OF THE POEM

This is one of Dickinson's 'definition' poems. She is exploring a psychological condition using a concrete analogy or metaphor. She has explored hope in other poems, variously describing it as 'a strange invention', 'a subtle glutton', and now 'the thing with feathers'. Through this bird metaphor she examines the various qualities and characteristics of hope, in so far as they can be described at all.

The association of hope with a bird is common enough in religious symbolism: the Spirit or divine inspiration is often represented as a dove. Dickinson maintains this spiritual aspect of hope ('perches in the soul'); but she is also at pains to establish its difference, its strangeness, its absolute otherness, in case we accept the bird analogy too literally. It is 'the thing' with feathers, a not quite definable quality of spirit. It is undemonstrative, unshowy, a silent presence ('sings the tune without the words'). It is permanent, perpetual, always there – a quality emphasised by Dickinson's unusual punctuation ('never stops – at all – '). That final dash might be taken to suggest that the process is continuing.

Characteristics of sweetness and warmth, very tangible qualities, are emphasised in the second stanza. Hope's indomitable nature and particular value in time of crisis are also stressed ('and sweetest – in the Gale – is heard').

The third stanza introduces something of a more personal experience of hope, with the introduction of the first person by the poet ('I've heard'). Again the value of hope in extreme circumstances is featured ('in the chillest land', 'on the strangest Sea'). Its absolute strength, its independence and the lack of demands it makes on its host body are emphasised.

> Yet, never, in Extremity,
> It asked a crumb – of Me.

For Dickinson, hope is an independent gift, a spiritual gift perhaps. It is delicate and fragile, yet strong and indomitable, and this paradoxical quality is reflected in the image:

> And sore must be the storm –
> That could abash the little Bird.

The tiny creature is not disconcerted or abashed by anything but the most dreadful of storms. There is also the suggestion that hope is a presence not easily defined ('the thing with feathers').

## Mood

Dickinson's poems are sometimes bleak affairs, examining such painful conditions as despair, alienation, mental anguish and unhappy love. But this is an exceptionally optimistic poem, which radiates a mood of buoyant self-confidence: 'I've heard it in the chillest land.' The optimistic tone is reflected too in the reference to music ('And sings the tune … Sweetest – in the Gale – is heard –') and warmth ('That kept so many warm'). The forward motion of the lines, with Dickinson's strange punctuation, also helps to suggest that this is a continuing state of mind, not just a temporary high point.

> And never stops – at all –

## Imagery

The poem is structured around the central metaphor of the bird as hope, and this is extended to feathers, singing, etc. Many of Dickinson's most startling metaphors and images consist of abstract and concrete elements yoked together, and we see this here in 'Hope is the thing …' It is as if by putting the two unlikely opposites together she is suggesting how really extraordinary is the virtue of hope.

# There's a certain Slant of light

Text of poem: New Explorations Anthology page 54

## A NATURE POEM

At a surface level this is a nature poem attempting to capture some of the essential features of winter: the lifelessness of winter afternoons, the slanting sunlight, etc. While the poet dwells on these outer manifestations, she is also aware that the essence of the season is experienced internally, in 'internal difference I Where the Meanings, are –'

The poem has a particularly narrow focus: a study of the light. The poet's view of it is startlingly different. She catches the commonly experienced painful discomfort of wintry sunlight that 'oppresses' but deepens it to 'Heavenly Hurt' and 'imperial affliction'. It becomes a visitation we must passively suffer ('it gives us' and is 'sent us of the Air'). It is not open to any influence or human control ('none may teach it – Any –'); rather is it seen as a teacher who makes the landscape listen. Its power and influence are reflected not only in that initial presence ('Shadows – hold their breath') but also in the after-effect: the landscape is changed ('like the Distance I on the look of Death'). With startling originality, the light is compared to a 'Seal', conveying all that artefact's paradoxical properties of being uncommunicative yet itself a token of communication. Even more unusually, she sees it as the 'Seal Despair', reversing the conventional interpretation of light as a sign of hope.

Altogether it is a most unconventional and unexpected view of light, and a particularly negative one. It is also worth noting that Dickinson seems more interested in the powerful effects of light – on the landscape and the speaker – and in its indefinable qualities ('none may teach it – Any – I 'Tis the Seal Despair') than in any description of the subject itself.

## POEM AS LANDSCAPE

The critic Judith Farr views this poem as a subtle word painting and explores it as a piece of visual art. She finds that it follows in the American landscape tradition, linking the sky with the earth. She also finds it in harmony with the artistic ideals of the famous nineteenth-century art critic John Ruskin, who advocated the creation of 'the mystery of distance' in landscapes and who also praised 'the unfatigued veracity of eternal light.' Do you find a sense of distance in the poem and an eternal significance? Would it be true to say that Dickinson is studying what Ruskin called 'the spirituality of atmospheric phenomena', in other words viewing nature as a reflection of the divine?

Perhaps; but her conclusions are far from the expected and the orthodox. To many nineteenth-century artists, such as the painter John Constable, for example, the sky was an affirmation of faith; but to Dickinson it is a sign of despair. The God behind nature in this poem smacks of cruel tyranny. The light is 'an imperial affliction', a vehicle of 'Heavenly Hurt', not a joyous divine revelation but 'the Seal Despair'. The simile of 'Cathedral Tunes' suggests the solemn weight of religion, particularly when coupled with 'Heft', with its connotations of heavy lifting. It suggests the 'difficulty of lifting up the heart', as Farr puts it, that is, the difficulty of belief, particularly at this death-time of the year.

It is a bleak landscape, devoid of any signs of a benign deity. The critic Barton St Armand called it 'the most lone of Dickinson's lone landscapes.'

## A POEM OF DESPAIR

In searching for the central core of this poem, some critics focus on the poet's feeling rather than the natural details and observations. In this reading, despair is seen as the central theme. This despair is brought about as the natural phenomenon, light, loses its orthodox meanings of illumination, insight and hope and becomes completely alien to the speaker. Denis Donoghue points out how Dickinson employs one of her common poetic techniques to effect this change. She begins with a neutral first line ('There's a certain Slant of light'), which is then exposed to alien associations, 'until it, too, is tainted and there is nothing left but the alien.' These are associations of oppression, the impossible weight of faith, etc. They are not visible but felt within. 'Heavenly Hurt' makes only an internal difference ('where the Meanings, are'). The feeling experienced by the poet is absolute, all-powerful, unshakable ('none may teach it – Any'). She groups the feelings and associations together under the seal or the sign of despair, which is likened to a divine pestilence, a punishment plague.

> An imperial affliction
> Sent us of the Air –

This affliction petrifies the landscape, making it appear a dead world in which the speaker, now alienated from God and nature, is marooned ('Shadows – hold their breath'). Even when the despair lifts, it leaves no relief but 'a memory of itself, looking now like the face of Death' (Donoghue). Donoghue points out that distance and death are frequently linked by Dickinson, especially in the love poems, where the distance of the absent lover is like death. So despair is experienced here as a sort of death, and it leaves its impression even when it lifts.

The speaker feels victimised, hurt, oppressed and afflicted by God. The poem is read as an accusation of divine betrayal, that God should allow such despair to happen. Certainly the image of God here is far from the conventional one of a caring and just being and seems more akin to the wanton, vengeful pagan gods of classical times. So this despair is occasioned by the poet's failure to find any comfort in the divine or the natural world.

## THE POET'S METHOD

Clearly this is not a conventional landscape representation, such as we might find in realistic visual art. Not only would we have great difficulty in isolating background, foreground, etc. but there is hardly a single concrete image, apart from 'Cathedral Tunes', which may have some resonance of real bells and perhaps the Seal image. But any attempt to give the latter concrete form is quickly dissipated by the accompanying abstract noun 'Despair'.

We are conscious, of course, that light is the poet's chief preoccupation, but the poem lacks a focus or centre of meaning, either in word or image. Even the subject, light, is not dealt with directly. It is contrasted or compared with more readily apprehended experience ('like the Heft | of Cathedral Tunes' and 'like the Distance | On the look of Death'). We are told what it is not ('none may teach it – Any'), and its effects are listed ('Landscape listens – | Shadows – hold their breath'). This circuitous approach to the subject means that all the discussion of meaning is on the periphery or borders of the subject, a technique described as 'negative definition' by the literary critic Cristanne Miller.

Perhaps it was this lack of definition in Dickinson's imagery and her circuitous approach to the subject that led Mabel Loomis Todd to consider this poem 'impressionistic' when she included it in the first edition of Dickinson's poems in 1890.

## PASSIVITY OF THE SPEAKER

The passivity of the speaker is another feature worth noting. We are aware of the powerlessness of the speaker, passively experiencing the oppression of the light:

> Heavenly Hurt, it gives us –
> We can find no scar,

The effect is to enhance further the power of the light. Its unreachable independence, its complete otherness is signalled in 'none may teach it – Any'.

# I felt a Funeral, in my Brain

Text of poem: New Explorations Anthology page 56

A READING OF THE POEM

This poem describes a psychological state. It depicts a condition of extreme anguish and mental disorder, a situation of psychological torment, where the speaker feels all the oppression and powerlessness of a helpless victim and ultimately collapses.

Mental breakdown is seen by the poet as akin to losing consciousness. The critic Judith Farr views this poem as a 'mindscape', which takes as its subject the death of consciousness. Indeed the narrative is so structured, describing the sensations experienced at different stages on the way to the loss of perception.

It begins with 'I felt' and finishes with the loss of all sensation, noting on the way the failure of the various senses and organs of perception. Farr notes how physiologically accurate this is, corresponding to the stages of an approaching faint. The dizzy spell is prefaced by a mental numbness (the 'treading – treading' of the 'Boots of Lead'). The ringing in the ears that precedes fainting is conveyed through the synaesthetic imagery of 'then Space – began to toll.' The fainting spell ('I dropped down, and down') and the sinking out of consciousness ('hit a World, at every plunge') concludes in the total loss of perception ('and Finished knowing – then –'). Yet the concluding dash might suggest survival of some kind, perhaps the continuity of intellect, as Farr suggests, somehow surviving to record the event.

It is worth noting that 'Brain', 'Mind' and 'Soul' were interchangeable terms for the nineteenth-century artist. Indeed an examination of the manuscript shows that Dickinson's first choice for 'Soul' in line 10 was 'Brain'. So this experience of traumatic collapse has both psychological and religious connotations.

Dickinson uses the structure of a funeral service and funeral imagery to convey her theme: the box, the mourners, the plank, the burial – all the paraphernalia of a funeral. But this is a most unreal funeral service. Normally the funeral is sombre, respectful and caring, and the ritual is designed to be comforting. But here the 'Box' is crudely impersonal and the ritual becomes a nightmare of unstoppable activity, as reflected in the grammatical structure of the poem ('till', 'when', 'till', 'then', 'again', 'then', 'then') and in the imagery of ceaseless activity ('to and fro', 'treading – treading', 'kept beating – beating'). Even the sounds of the funeral service are experienced as activity as well as sound ('Mourners ... treading', 'a Service, like a Drum – | Kept beating', 'lift a Box | And creak across my Soul | With those same Boots of Lead', 'then Space – began to toll'). There isn't a single still moment in the poem, except for the marvellous image of cosmic alienation in lines 15 and 16.

This unrelenting activity is experienced as oppression by the speaker, who is powerless to react and must suffer what is being done to her. As John Robinson says, she is using the funeral service to define herself as helpless victim. The sense of victimisation is further enhanced by the fact that what she suffers is only partially understood by her, though keenly felt and heard. The unreal strangeness of the imagery reflects the inscrutable nature of her sufferings ('a Service, like a Drum', 'all the Heavens were a Bell'). The unique vantage point of the speaker here, as she is being buried, graphically reinforces this notion of helpless victim. There is an element of gothic horror to this – a conscious victim being buried alive, and the sensationalism of 'creak across my Soul' and 'Boots of Lead'. All this adds to the quality of the mental trauma that is the poem's main theme.

Some readers feel that the main focus of this poem is the actual experience of death, rather than any metaphorical exploration of psychological death: that the poem enacts approaching death, loss of the senses, etc., and that the experience is given an extra frisson of horror through the speaker's unique vantage point from the coffin. Do you favour this literal interpretation? Perhaps it smacks too much of gothic sensationalism? Perhaps we can read the poem as addressing the issue of death in both the physical and psychological senses? What insights into death does the poem convey?

THEMES

- An enactment of mental breakdown, a depiction of the intense suffering of psychological disintegration
- The loss of order and meaning, intrinsic to breakdown: the sensation of tumbling through space, events have no properly understood cause, senses are confused, space tolls, a plank breaks, etc.
- A charting of the stages of death, the loss of sensation and perception
- The nature of the solitary soul, adrift in the universe:

  And I, and Silence, some strange Race
  Wrecked, solitary, here –

This is a vision of lonely suffering, interpreted by some as the effort of the soul to understand its place in the universe.
- Oppression: the poet as helpless victim, impotent sufferer
- Human alienation: the lack of control over the world or one's fate. The image of the living treated as if they were dead emphasises this extreme disunion between self and circumstances.

# A Bird came down the Walk

Text of poem: New Explorations Anthology page 60

Text of poem: New Explorations Anthology page 60

A READING OF THE POEM

This is a nature poem, but one with a difference, as Dickinson urges us to look closely at the detail, to explore beneath the surface and apprehend something of the essence of this creature – its natural elegance but also its essential oddity and difference.

The bird's crude predatory nature ('He bit an Angleworm in halves | And ate the fellow, raw') is combined with a sort of diffidence or politeness ('And then hopped sidewise to the Wall | To let a Beetle pass'). The more obvious creaturely qualities are present: the natural beauty of the 'Velvet Head' and the unrolled feathers, the prim, erratic bird-like movements ('He glanced with rapid eyes | That hurried all around'), and the natural caution of a wild creature ('like frightened Beads', 'like one in danger, Cautious'). But, above all, what is celebrated is the miraculousness of flight, as the bird blends into the elements, unifying air, water and light, displaying its mastery. The first striking metaphor sees the bird compared to a confident, relaxed rower, with the suggestion that the bird's natural element is the air ('home'). Naturalness is the paramount quality, as the comparisons emphasise the grace, elegance, lack of disturbance and perfect blend of creature and medium:

> And rowed him softer home –
> Than Oars divide the Ocean,
> Too silver for a seam

The playful summer gentleness of butterflies adds a romantic element. The synaesthetic fusion of water, air and light ('Banks of Noon') underlines the perfection of the movement and the lack of disturbance ('plashless as they swim'). This image has connotations too of youthful exuberance and joy, of summers spent swimming in the river.

Altogether, the poem celebrates the beauty of creatures, their mastery of the elements, but also their essential wildness.

POETIC TECHNIQUE

## Defamiliarising the familiar

In an effort to get us to look again, to see beneath the accepted, Dickinson gently shocks us into rethinking by 'defamiliarising' the familiar. For example, the bird, romantic instrument of song, symbol of poetic flight, is shown in all its awful naturalness as a greedy killer ('ate the fellow, raw'). Even the sound of the word 'raw' helps to reinforce the crudeness of the situation. But at a deeper level Dickinson alters the whole construction of reality, as in that final stanza, where the elements fuse together and time and space shift dimensions as the bird 'like a butterfly, swims, sails, leaps, flies, soars' (Juhasz, Miller and Smith). These critics use the term 'transformations' to describe this technique.

## Identifying with the subject

It is clear that at first Dickinson describes what she sees, though with her own particular slant. But then the speaker enters the picture and becomes more closely identified with the subject. Cristanne Miller explains how this identification is achieved through grammar and syntax, in a process she terms 'syntactic doubling'. Dickinson's compressed epigrammatical style of writing causes ambiguity, especially when 'using a single phrase to cover two non-parallel syntactic contexts' (Miller). For example, the middle line below could refer to either the first or third line:

> He stirred his Velvet Head
> Like one in danger, Cautious,
> I offered him a Crumb

The feelings of danger and caution are shared by both speaker and bird. This weakening of the distinction between the self and the other (or speaker and subject) is developed further in the climax of the poem, where the speaker half-creates what she sees and herself shares in the experience.

## Humour and wit

Juhasz, Miller and Smith examine the comic elements in this poem. The incongruities in the bird's behaviour are the most obvious expressions of humour: the natural carnivore's killer instinct exists side by side with a sense of civility and good manners ('an awareness of social etiquette from the raw worm eater'). Notice the irony of his guilt – the furtive shifting around in case his courteous behaviour is noticed! Juhasz, Miller and Smith also link the deeper transformations already mentioned to the anarchic transformations of cosmic vision, where reality is reconstructed in unaccustomed combinations, thereby producing laughter.

# After great pain, a formal feeling comes

Text of poem: New Explorations Anthology page 62

## A READING OF THE POEM

In the familiar Dickinson mode, this poem is a dramatisation of a feeling. The poet explores the effects of pain and grief on mind and body. The resulting state, that of 'formal feeling', is the focus of study here, and inertia, numbness, disorientation, mechanical activity and finally loss of all feeling are its main manifestations.

The 'formal feeling' is described through a series of analogies: the internal feeling is communicated through concrete images – of the body, of nature and of society. First the body's manifestations of this feeling are transmitted: those of nerves, heart and feet. These all display a stiff formality, a shocked lifelessness. The personified 'Nerves sit ceremonious, like Tombs,' are associated with the formal ceremony of death. For one critic (Susan Juhasz) this image conjured up a picture of polite but essentially inert old women at afternoon tea! The 'stiff Heart' has lost all trace of feeling, has become disoriented under the strain of suffering ('questions was it He, that bore, | And Yesterday, or Centuries before?'). 'The Feet, mechanical, go round': this is automatic behaviour, insensitive to surroundings ('of Ground, or Air, or Ought'). All these physical manifestations display a mindless formality, an absence of real feeling, an inert indifference brought on by suffering.

The 'formal feeling' is also communicated through analogies with nature ('a Quartz contentment'), crystallised like the mineral and sharing some of its properties, such as weight and brittleness. The dead weight of the depression is focused in space and time through the image 'Hour of Lead'. The feeling finally finds release in the more gentle but lethal analogy of snow, which initiates that final drift towards the death of the senses. For Dickinson, lack of feeling is symbolic of death, and here death is easeful, a gentle 'letting go'.

In essence, the poem deals with the after-effects of human pain: inertia, loss of feeling, and a numbness that is like the numbness of death.

But, in common with some other Dickinson poems, the ending is ambiguous. Because the poem is written in the present tense, we don't know if the experience is over and the speaker has survived it, or if it is continuing, or if it will be terminal. The final dash might suggest continuity. Either way, we are left with an awareness of a disembodied voice.

## POETIC TECHNIQUE

- This is a fine example of the 'analogical method' sometimes used by Dickinson. She often makes analogies between literal and metaphorical death. But here the internal feeling is called up through a range of external situations, as explained.

- Nouns are used as the focus for the effective metaphorical work ('Tombs', 'Stone', 'Lead', 'Snow'). As David Porter points out, they 'provide visual and tactile immediacy to the condition of paralysis brought on by grief'.
- We notice the technical language used to mechanise life and feelings ('the Feet, mechanical, go round', 'a Quartz contentment').
- A variety of sound effects contribute to the atmosphere of the poem: alliteration draws attention to the 'formal feeling'; the echoes of 'go round – of Ground' in stanza 2 underline the meaningless emptiness of the activity; the sound of 'stone' evokes a painful moan – indeed the proliferation of long *o* vowel sounds evokes the numbness and static fatalism of the feeling ('Tombs', 'bore', 'before', 'stone', 'Snow', 'go', and 'round', 'Ground', 'Hour').
- This is a dramatic enactment of feeling, using personification of Nerves and Heart and a vivid creation of concrete props to move it towards that inevitable climax.

POINTS OF COMPARISON WITH 'A FUNERAL'

Consider these points and decide which ones you think are particularly valid and can be substantiated easily from the texts:
- Both poems deal with extremes of feeling (anguish, pain, suffering).
- In both, the poet's self-image projected is one of helpless victim, oppressed, numb being.
- The speaker seems disconnected from order and meaning. The world of the speaker does not make sense.
- The speaker suffers mechanised repetition, an endless ritual of activity.
- The two poems follow the same narrative line: the mechanical activity, the weight of lead, the sense of numbness, and the final collapse.
- The human being exists at an intersection of time and space, but in these poems the connection is somehow missed and the speaker wanders off, lost in the universe.

# I heard a Fly buzz – when I died
Text of poem: New Explorations Anthology page 64

A READING OF THE POEM

This poem re-creates the drama of the deathbed scene, from the point of view of the dying or dead person, whose consciousness seems to have survived death and can therefore comment on the experience ('I heard a Fly buzz – when I died'). Dickinson focuses on the moment of death. She is fascinated by that moment of passage, the transition from life into eternity. She is probing the nature of death. 'What does it feel like to die? she is asking' (Richard Sewall, *The Life of Emily Dickinson*).

The moment is focused and dramatically prepared for. In the first stanza it is described as an isolated moment of calm 'between the Heaves of Storm', between the storm of living and 'the storm of dissolution', as Judith Farr puts it.

In the second stanza the family or watchers have got themselves under control and are almost holding their breaths for the final moment ('and Breaths were gathering firm | For that last Onset'). This is a bare, Calvinistic view of death, re-creating the awesome moment when the soul encounters the power and the majesty of God. 'That last Onset' suggests that, out of the smoke of the last violent battle of death, the king emerges, to whom the soul gives witness ('when the King | Be witnessed – in the Room'). The encounter with God is a formal moment of recognition and judgment, reinforced by the legal and religious terminology ('witnessed'). There are no angels here, no welcoming choirs, no rejoicing, no emotion even, just an intimidating encounter to give witness to one's life and deeds and to acknowledge the awful power of God.

So far the death scene is very much a managed ritual, ordered, controlled, orchestrated. She has tidied up all her legal affairs, given away little gifts and mementoes to friends ('willed my Keepsakes'). The legal language conveys an impersonal atmosphere ('witnessed', 'willed', 'Signed away', 'portion'). This is to be a controlled event.

The irony, of course, is that a mere fly, a household pest, can disturb this most significant moment. The fly is a grotesque intrusion, with its loudness, its aimlessness ('uncertain stumbling Buzz'), its associations with corruption and rot, and its confusing appearance, which is a fusion of sight and sound ('Blue … Buzz'). The fly has been interpreted in various ways, for example as a reminder of the disorder and confusion of life. Judith Farr sees in 'the stupid aimlessness … a suggestion of the puzzlement that is life'. Denis Donoghue suggests that it conveys alienation, that it represents 'all the remaining things … which detach themselves from the dying' ('There interposed a Fly … Between the light – and me … I could not see to see'). Perhaps we should consider it in the context of the tightly controlled and planned ritual. It disrupts the order, the ritual of the awesome moment. Here this grotesque fly might represent the dying person's loss of control, a final alienation from the puzzling, random, disordered world and a step that leads to the detachment that is death.

What is its significance at this juncture, as the soul is waiting for God? It certainly disrupts the solemnity of the moment. Does it go further and suggest that all that is real is the random disordered world and physical corruption, and that God and eternity are less certain? Beyond the presumption on Dickinson's part that some kind of consciousness survives the storm of death, there is no explicit reference to an afterlife here, no comforting glimpse of eternity. We are invited, certainly, to explore the contrast between the mundane and the divine. In fact the entire poem is structured on contrasts: the controlled scene versus the uncertainty of the fly; the dignified silence versus the incessant buzzing; human grieving versus religious expectation; the corporeal versus the spiritual; the tiny fly versus the majesty of God and the vastness of eternity. Yet this fly comes to dominate the poem and changes its focus. It steals the limelight from the 'King', leaves a question mark over the afterlife, and shows us the reality of death: as a loss of control, a failure of light, and a final alienation from the world.

## SOURCES

Emelie Fitzgibbon feels that Dickinson took the idea of the fly and the dying person from Hawthorne's novel *The House of the Seven Gables*. There the villainous governor dies alone sitting in a chair. The point of view of the narration alternates between that of the dying and dead governor and the outside narrator, until the fly is discovered:

> And there we see a fly – one of your common houseflies, such as are always buzzing on the windowpane – which has smelt out Governor Pyncheon, and alights, now on his forehead, now on his chin, and now, Heaven help us, is creeping over the bridge of his nose, towards the would-be chief magistrate's wide-open eyes!

In what ways do you think Dickinson's treatment of the scene is different from Hawthorne's?

## ELEMENTS OF THE THEME

The poem, as we have seen, is an exploration of the moment of death. Consider the following aspects of that theme; re-examine the text for any further suggestions it might provide on each.

- An exploration of the fading of consciousness and the senses
- The ritual of final leave-taking
- Death as a dramatic event
- The family or community aspect of death
- The awesome confrontation with God
- The loss of control
- The final alienation: the loss of understanding of the world, the failure to see any meaning in it
- The religious questions raised about the relative significance of the world and the divine.

IMAGERY

Dickinson relies on nature for much of her imagery (the storm, the light, the fly). It is her style not to elaborate on images, so the reader must explore for possible connotations.

The storm simile in the first stanza seems to link the room with the wider natural world, which has the effect of giving this single death scene a more universal significance. It may also suggest the inherent violence of death – death as a great storm of individual disintegration.

> The Stillness in the Room
> Was like the Stillness in the Air –
> Between the Heaves of Storm –

Dickinson identifies light with life, and the moment of death she associates with the failure of light. The possible significance of the fly has already been discussed. Dickinson's images are pared down even to single words, reduced to their essentials ('the Eyes around', 'and Breaths were gathering').

# The Soul has Bandaged moments
Text of poem: New Explorations Anthology page 66

## SOME READINGS OF THE POEM

This is one of the poems that can be read in a variety of ways: as a psychological insight into moods and mind, a 'mindscape' as it were; as a sexual statement; or as a reflection about creativity.

At the level of psychological exploration it deals with the different moods of the spirit, or 'soul'. In this case, great mood changes are evident, swinging between the mental paralysis and deep, shackled depression of stanzas 1 and 5 and the sheer elation of stanzas 3 and 4. To modern psychology, the violence and extreme nature of the change in moods might suggest manic depression.

In the first stanza the 'soul', or spirit, is portrayed as wounded, damaged, needing to be wrapped in self-protective and restraining bandages. In this shattered state the spirit is prey to all sorts of fantasies and nightmares, this time erotic in nature ('ghastly Fright … Salute her – with long fingers – Caress her freezing hair'). Why 'freezing'? Perhaps with fright, suggesting her attitude, frigid with fright? This is a grotesque parody of love.

> Sip, Goblin, from the very lips
> The Lover – hovered – o'er –

There is something decadent about the image of the Goblin replacing her lover, the spectre kissing the lips her lover worshipped so much that he merely hovered over them, feeling unworthy to kiss. The grotesqueness of the scene is reinforced by the juxtaposition of the delicate action ('Sip') with the hideous goblin. Perhaps there is also a hint of guilt as she recollects the delicacy and sensitivity of her lover, now, at the very moment that she accepts the goblin's advances. These images provide a frightening glimpse into the mind's darkness. They are images of truly gothic horror, demons from beyond the grave or, in this case, beneath the consciousness.

Stanzas 3 and 4 portray the opposite mood ('Escape – I when bursting all the doors'), unrestrained joy, the captive freed from depression, as the bee 'Long Dungeoned from his Rose' enjoys his sensuous liberty. The mood is equated with the joy of Paradise.

But even this elevation is fragile and dangerous ('she dances like a Bomb') and it is short lived. The spirit is again weighed down with shackles and staples, like a felon. The cycle of sinking and lifting moods begins again, and the knowledge that it is cyclical makes the weight of pain all the more poignant ('the Horror welcomes her, again'). Once again the inappropriate juxtaposition of 'Horror' and 'welcomes' gives us some indication of her confusion and despair.

The final line of the poem emphasises the essential loneliness of the condition, the social stigma attached to mental illness. It is not talked about in public ('not brayed of Tongue'). The connotations of brash, loud vulgarity in 'bray' suggest the discomfort any such talk would bring.

It has been suggested that this depression may be caused by failure in love and that a main theme of this poem is emotional loss, interrupted by brief glimpses of fulfilment in stanzas 3 and 4. There are cogent reasons to justify such a reading. The soul of the first line is wounded with disappointment in love. We have explored already the erotic and sensual nature of her nightmares. The elation too is of a sensual nature, as the bee sucks nectar from the rose and becomes delirious with pleasure. Noon probably symbolises the paradise of earthly love. Altogether, stanzas 3 and 4 paint a picture of sensual fulfilment. And when she is disappointed in love she feels guilty, like a criminal, a 'Felon led along', and she can no longer sing. Love's song no longer soars: there are 'staples, in the Song.'

Cristanne Miller classified the poem as one of Dickinson's 'rape poems'. The caressing figure enjoys complete control over her apparently helpless victim. Sometimes she responds ('Sip, Goblin'), but she eventually escapes from her tormentors. But there is a suggestion that this is a repeated sequence of events: capture, escape, recapture. This reading views the speaker as sexual victim.

The poem has also been read as a reflection on creativity, the failure of poetic inspiration and the great elation when it is rediscovered. The imprisonment is verbal; the loss is one of words rather than of physical liberty. The plumed feet (perhaps of Mercury, messenger of the gods) are shackled, poetic inspiration is imprisoned ('staples, in the Song'). However, this reading does not take account of the sensual and erotic element of the first two stanzas. If we are to incorporate the issue of creativity in a reading of the poem, then perhaps we should consider 'communication and the loss of it' as a suitable umbrella term. We could see the poem as dealing with communication at many levels: at the human sensuous level, at the level of creativity, and also at the level of mind where imagined horror is one of the mind's possibilities.

# I could bring You Jewels – had I a mind to

Text of poem: New Explorations Anthology page 69

# A narrow Fellow in the Grass

Text of poem: New Explorations Anthology page 71

[*Note: This poem is also prescribed for Ordinary Level 2005 exam*]

DICKINSON AND NATURE

Basically, this poem is concerned with Dickinson's attitude to nature, in particular her sense that the natural world was distinctly different. In this she differed from Emerson, who thought the entire world, human and non-human, was in harmony and could be known and understood by humankind. Dickinson is much more wary. She professes to have an amicable relationship with nature:

> Several of Nature's People
> I know, and they know me –
> I feel for them a transport
> Of cordiality –

This suggests a polite acquaintance more than any emotional attachment or real closeness. It displays a somewhat reserved sense of neighbourly tolerance for the Earth's creatures. But even that does not hold for this particular creature – the 'narrow Fellow'. Though there is some effort to personalise him – perhaps as a gentleman rider ('occasionally rides – you may have met Him') – and to refer to his likings ('a Boggy Acre'), the poet's basic reaction is one of unease. This shock on meeting is registered in the disjointed, awkward syntax, the faltering words of 'His notice sudden is.' We notice her feeling of threat coming through in the descriptions. Consider, for example, 'Whip lash'. It captures the speed, agility and wild unpredictability of the creature, but it also has connotations of sudden threat, injury, pain, lethal strike. And at the end of the poem she explicitly records her fear. She feels threatened to the marrow of her bones:

> Without a tighter breathing
> And Zero at the Bone –

For Dickinson, nature is to be treated warily. There are times when it is prudent to keep out of the way.

The method of her portrayal of the snake conveys how peculiar, mysterious and elusive nature is. In format, this is a sort of riddle poem. The snake is not named, indeed never fully seen, apart from the glimpse of 'a spotted shaft'. We just get clues to its passage – 'the Grass divides as with a comb ... and opens further on'. Its purpose or place in the scheme of things is beyond the speaker's comprehension. It just moves through the poem as a series of images. We never learn enough to understand its nature or even identify it. It makes occasional appearances that surprise or frighten. It is altogether outside everyday experience – totally other.

Her poetic method here reveals her attitude to nature. As Jerusha McCormack put it, 'Her method then, is not deliberately elusive, but an imitation of the bafflement she herself finds in the obscurity of natural things and their refusal to confess to significance. They might be mastered but they cannot be understood.'

## IMAGERY

There is an element of creative unexpectedness about Dickinson's imagery, for example in the depiction of the snake as an occasional rider or the bog as 'a Floor too cool for Corn'. This is a feature of her poetry in general.

The purpose of some of the imagery here seems to be an attempt to humanise nature (the narrow fellow 'occasionally rides'; 'Nature's People'), or it is an attempt to domesticate it ('the Grass divides as with a Comb'). The domestic and the strange are brought together. Again the natural is viewed in domestic terms, where the bog is seen as 'a Floor'. Ultimately this attempt to domesticate nature through the imagery fails, and the essential wildness of the snake reasserts itself in the image of 'Whip lash', conveying, as we saw, grace and agility, but also threat.

Dickinson's imagery is pared down to its simple essence in an image such as 'Zero at the Bone'. In a strange configuration of the abstract and the concrete she succeeds in finding expression for a primal inner terror.

# A brief overview of Dickinson's poetry

## THEMES AND TOPICS

This is a review of some themes and issues featured in this selection of Dickinson's poetry. Consider the ideas, then re-examine the poems mentioned for evidence to substantiate or contradict these interpretations.

### MINDSCAPES

Just as some poets are drawn to landscapes for their inspiration, 'mindscapes' are Dickinson's forte. Her most striking pictures are of inside the mind; she is primarily a poet of inner states. Consider the following aspects of her psychological explorations.

### Range of moods

She explores the full emotive range, from elation to deep despair. For example, consider the mood of giggling abandonment, the juvenile rebelliousness in 'A Liquor Never Brewed'. Notice the dangerous elation of 'she dances like a Bomb' ('The Soul'); the balanced self-confident optimism of 'I've heard it in the chillest land' ('Hope'); and the deep, unrelieved religious despair in 'Slant of Light'.

### Depression

Dickinson deals frequently with the numbness and the weight of depression. In 'After Great Pain' she explores the numbness, the lack of any emotion, occurring in the aftermath of suffering and pain. It is 'an analysis of the absence of feeling in those who have felt too much' (McCormack). It explores the 'Hour of Lead'.

The paralysis of depression is also touched on in 'The Soul'. She is very much aware of the social isolation and loneliness of the depressed person:

These, are not brayed of Tongue.

She deals with extreme mental pressure, with the breaking down of the mind into the emptiness of insanity.

And then a Plank in Reason, broke,
And I dropped down, and down – ['A Funeral']

She explores terror and dread and the obscene horrors the mind is capable of conjuring up, the 'ghastly Fright', the 'Goblin', the 'Horror' of 'The Soul'. There is also a hint of guilt in stanza 2. She has an intimate awareness of the wounded, damaged spirit.

## A dramatic rendering of mental states and processes
We are given an immediate, step-by-step view of the development of these traumatic mental states. It is as if we are watching a psychological drama, but inside the head. Consider the dramatic stages of 'A Funeral' or 'The Soul'. The use of first-person narrative, simple, dramatic verbs and staccato phrasing all contribute to the orchestration of this drama.

## The nature of consciousness
At the broadest level, Dickinson was fascinated by the nature of consciousness itself. Two aspects of it, feeling and knowing, are referred to in the exploration of psychic disintegration in 'A Funeral'. She dwells in particular on the loss of consciousness in that poem ('and Finished knowing – then') and also in 'A Fly'. In 'After Great Pain' consciousness is seen in terms of sensation and its loss:

> First – Chill – then Stupor – then the letting go –

## The fragile nature of the mind, the psyche under siege, the individual as victim
These are other aspects of this theme, hinted at throughout the poems. Which poems do you think best explore these issues?

## NATURE
### Admiration for nature
Dickinson's attitude to nature is quite complex. On the one hand she is full of admiration for the agility, the deftness and the beauty of nature's creatures. For example, the flight of the bird is awe-inspiring as he 'unrolled his feathers | And rowed him softer home.' The poet is moved by his beauty: 'he stirred his Velvet Head' ('A Bird'). There is an appreciation of the essential wildness and speed of the snake – 'Whip lash' – in 'Narrow Fellow'. As she says explicitly in that poem, she feels a certain 'cordiality' for 'Nature's People'.

Yet she is also aware of how different, how completely other, nature is. We notice this in a small way in 'A Bird', when she is shocked by the sudden realisation of his carnivorous nature, his essential bird quality.

> He bit an Angleworm in halves
> And ate the fellow, raw.

Likewise, the mysteriousness of the 'narrow Fellow', his essentially unknowable nature and the ever-present sense of threat he exudes, provoke in her 'a tighter breathing'. The sunlight in 'Slant of Light' loses its conventional associations and quickly becomes totally alien and oppressive.

So the human is sometimes cut off from nature, as the poet is from the bird:

I offered him a Crumb
And he unrolled his feathers ['A Bird'].

In spite of that, nature can be exotic, exciting, and full of romantic symbolism, as in 'Jewels'.

## Nature as metaphor

Dickinson uses nature motifs as metaphorical vehicles for her moods.

I shall not feel the sleet – then –
I shall not fear the snow ['Distrustful of the Gentian'].

The mood of playful drunkenness in 'A Liquor Never Brewed' is portrayed in natural terms: 'Inebriate of Air – am I'. And, in a startling departure from the expected, she uses light, stripped of its normal associations and invested with negative ones, as a medium for conveying her despair in 'Slant of Light'. She also uses natural phenomena in her definition poems, as one leg of the comparison. The concrete image from nature in 'Hope' is used as a metaphorical correlative for the abstract virtue.

## LOVE

### Hopeless longing

This selection of poems, for the most part, deals with the negative aspects and outcomes of love. Lost love, or the absent lover, features in such poems as 'The Soul' and 'Distrustful of the Gentian'. The yearning for love is strong in her poems, and this sometimes features as hopeless longing.

Hangs so distant Heaven –
To a hand below ['Distrustful of the Gentian'].

Is there a suggestion that love is always out of reach, that it is an illusion, that we have a great capacity for self-delusion in this respect?

### The effect of lost love

Consider the destructive effects of possible lost love in 'The Soul': depression, nightmares, sick erotic fantasies, guilt, and so on. Is she saying that the loss of love unbalances? Unbalanced, too, is the elation as she 'swings upon the Hours'.

## Romantic love

'Jewels' features something of the exotic and exciting feeling involved in romantic love: the gifts, the courtship, the exaggerated claims of 'Dower itself – for Bobadilo'. Love changes the perception, enriches the outlook, as in this colourful world of sights and smells. Simple, everyday things, such as the meadow flower, are viewed in a new light:

Never a fellow matched this Topaz –
And his Emerald Swing ['Jewels'].

## DEATH

### Re-enactment of actual death

Dickinson is fascinated by the deathbed scene, the moment of transition from life into death. Consider 'A Fly' and study the steps in the process; the fading of the light; the alienation or separation of the dying person from the things of life; the negation of order; the growing lack of comprehension of the world.

### Death as alienation from the world

Death is not merely a physical or biological process but an alienation of the consciousness from the world: see 'A Fly'.

### A Calvinist picture

The Calvinist austerity of death is shown in 'A Fly', where the emphasis is on the awesomeness of God as the king and on the last battle ('that last Onset'). It is a comfortless encounter, without a hint of angels or heavenly choirs or any of the trappings of a Catholic cosmology. Nor is there any view at all of the afterlife here. Does this suggest a failure of belief on the part of Dickinson?

### Other aspects of death

Other aspects not featured in this selection are the ease, the civility, the gentleness of it. See also the personification of death as a gentleman in a carriage in 'Because I Could Not Stop'.

### Technique of the surviving consciousness

Often the process of death is described by the speaker as if the consciousness somehow survived it and could relate the event. This gives us a dual perspective on death: that of the person undergoing it, and a more distant objective view.

## Metaphorical death

Dickinson does not always make a distinction between actual death and spiritual or mental death. Metaphorically, death is associated with despair, with separation, with depression. These states of mind are likened to the experience of death, as in 'the Distance on the look of Death' ('Slant of Light'). Burial is equated with mental breakdown in 'A Funeral', and the loss of feeling is described in terms of dying: 'First – Chill – then Stupor – then the letting go' ('After Great Pain'). Indeed this 'letting go' seems a welcome relief.

## Loss

Dickinson has been described as a poet of loss – lost love, lost sensation, lost sanity. Denis Donoghue said of her: 'in Emily Dickinson generally, experiences are more intensely apprehended just after their loss.' Which poems would you explore to examine this view of Dickinson?

THE RELIGIOUS ETHOS OF HER POEMS

### A view of Heaven

As we saw, Dickinson has not got an orthodox religious view. Heaven seems a very remote prospect: 'Hangs so distant Heaven – to a hand below' ('Distrustful of the Gentian'). Or Heaven is painted as an unrealistic pantomime where 'Seraphs swing their snowy Hats | and Saints – to windows run' ('A Liquor Never Brewed'). The afterlife here has been naturalised, but to the point of caricature. In a display of shocking originality, she manages to 'send up' Heaven!

### Religious despair

But she also feels the oppression of religion: 'the Heft of Cathedral Tunes' ('Slant of Light'). She suffers intensely from the internal scarring ('Heavenly Hurt', 'imperial affliction'). These she relates in a tone of bitter complaint and condemnation that God does not reveal himself through the world.

### The awesome Calvinist God

The final terrifying encounter with God, the king, at 'that last Onset' is one of the most poignant religious moments in this selection of poems. It points up Dickinson's view of humankind's insignificance before the divine, the awesome omnipotence of God, and the formal feudal nature of the relationship between God and humanity.

### The human being as victim

The helplessness of the human being is a motif running through many of the poems. We are unable to fulfil desire. Love is out of reach: frustration is the lot of the person ('Slant of Light', 'After Great Pain', 'The Soul').

## Religious oppression
The complete inability of the speaker to affect or influence the light in any way, even to understand it in the orthodox way, leaves one with a feeling of total impotence against heavenly oppression in 'Slant of Light': 'None may teach it – Any.' It is 'sent us', 'Heavenly Hurt', 'it gives us'; all these suggest the powerlessness of the victim.

### THE SPEAKER AS VICTIM
## A victim of mental frailty
Examine the breakdown of 'A Funeral'. Notice the robotic actions, the loss of human sensitivity and of motivation in 'After Great Pain', where 'the Feet, mechanical, go round.' The fragile mind is all too evident in 'The Soul', where the speaker is a mental victim, perhaps also a sexual victim ('too appalled to stir' or 'a Felon led along'). In 'Narrow Fellow' she is captive to her fear of nature, which induces in her 'a tighter breathing'.

## A victim of death
She is a victim of death, despite her attempts to control it in 'A Fly': 'there interposed a Fly … between the light – and me.'

Perhaps we can see her as dumb, a prisoner of language, unable to be creative, with 'shackles on the plumed feet, and staples, in the Song' ('The Soul').

Some critics feel that Dickinson deliberately sought out situations of oppression, that 'she cultivates the apprehension made possible by pain' (Denis Donoghue).

## Suffering and pain
Suffering and pain, whether mental or physical, are ever-present in Dickinson's poetry. Which poems do you think best exemplify this?

## Alienation
Alienation, from God and nature, are part of the suffering at the heart of Dickinson's poetry ('Slant of Light', 'Narrow Fellow').

### SOME TYPICAL MODES OF OPERATION IN DICKINSON'S POETRY
## Searching for meaning
Many of Dickinson's poems are struggling to find meaning in the experience being investigated, experiences such as the nature of hope; the feeling of

despair; the experience of breakdown; what it might be like to die; the essential nature of bird or reptile. Even the structure of some of the poems makes it clear that what is happening is an investigation, a struggle to name or master the experience. She uses analogies, similes etc. in an attempt to understand. She attempts to define abstracts in terms of concrete things ('"Hope" is the thing with feathers' or 'the Nerves sit ceremonious, like Tombs'). The bird's flight ('A Bird') is explored through the analogy with rowing. Mental breakdown is examined through the extended metaphor of a funeral ('A Funeral'). She is struggling to understand, using analogical terms.

Some of the poems are structured as riddles ('Narrow Fellow', 'Jewels'). Each of these is a circuitous exploration of a phenomenon that is gradually made clearer but is never fully named. Sometimes things resist being named. Sometimes, what at first appeared simple takes on an alien nature, and it becomes impossible for the poet to pin down its meaning accurately. Consider 'A Fly' and 'Slant of Light'. In the latter, the feeling of loneliness and hurt is brought out by the analogy with wintry sunlight, the coldness of winter afternoons, etc. However, the feeling is never fully comprehended but understood only in terms of its effects ('when it comes' and 'when it goes'). Yet she goes on, questioning and prodding at the meaning of things in an attempt to master their significance.

Some critics refer to the rhetorical quality of Dickinson's poems. Not only is she debating with herself, but she is using devices to argue and convince us of her position. We might consider the appeal to the reader (in 'Narrow Fellow'): 'You may have met Him – did you not.' Helen McNeil speaks of Dickinson's 'passionate investigation' and notices how, in a typical poem, she takes the reader through a sequence of rapidly changing images, exploring definitions that quickly break down, or veers off into unexpected surmises or more rhetorical investigation before ending, frequently, in an open closure. McNeil interprets that final dash as a graphic indication that the debate has not finished with the poem.

### Exploring transient states

Dickinson is fascinated by moments of change, the in-between condition: the point of breakdown ('and Finished knowing – then'); the moment of death ('I could not see to see'); the 'letting go' ('After Great Pain'). She explores the swiftly changing moods in 'The Soul'. Examining despair, she focuses on its arrival and departure.

> When it comes, the Landscape listens –
> Shadows – hold their breath –

When it goes, 'tis like the Distance
On the look of Death ['Slant of Light'].

There is a certain air of indeterminacy about her own attitude in some of the poems. She is unable to define her experience in 'Slant of Light', humorously vacillating in 'I could bring You Jewels – had I a mind to.' Despite her 'transport of cordiality' for nature, she is terrified by the 'narrow Fellow' ('Zero at the Bone'). John Robinson comments:

> She is a poet of passing away (death is one great form of this), of the elusive and the transient, and the fugitive, of what she called 'a quality of loss.' Her great brilliance is with this, and with the ominous, the vague, the threatening, the non-arrival, the not-quite-grasped, the not-quite-realised, the missing.

Which of these qualities do you think applies to the Dickinson poems you have read? Re-examine the poems for supporting evidence.

### Telling dramatic stories

For all the elusiveness of her subject matter and the circuitous nature of her poetic method, there is a strong narrative structure in many of Dickinson's poems. Most are told in the first person and constructed as reminiscent narratives ('A Funeral' and 'A Bird', 'A Fly', 'The Soul'). The poet takes us through a sequence of images, inside or outside the head, exposing us to a series of problems or confused feelings, which mostly lead on to a dramatic if sometimes inconclusive ending. This is the basic structure of story.

And they are dramatic. They deal with dramatic moments of discovery and insight ('A Bird', 'Narrow Fellow'); or they cover a personal crisis ('Slant of Light', 'A Funeral', 'After Great Pain'). Even death provides the ingredients for dramatic conflict, with 'that last Onset', 'the Heaves of Storm', and the dying person's struggle for control. Dickinson's technique of the 'divided voice' provides dramatic conflict in the narrative (i.e. the voice actually experiencing, which is separate from the voice outside the experience, the persona that has survived death or whatever). This is true in particular of 'A Funeral' and 'A Fly'.

### Offering a transformed view of the world

Dickinson disrupts and transforms our accepted view of things. 'She takes the normalising frames of our world and unhinges them, forcing them askew to make space for a joke, for a different take' (Juhasz, Miller, and Smith). We can see this in 'A Bird', where Dickinson disturbs our ordinary, somewhat clichéd view of nature. This is no sweet songbird, but a wild carnivorous creature:

> He bit an Angleworm in halves
> And ate the fellow, raw.

Yet at the same time we are expected to think of him as polite and gentlemanly, as he 'then hopped sidewise to the Wall | To let a Beetle pass.' But it is when she begins to describe his flight that we can no longer hold to our orthodox conception of bird or air.

> And he unrolled his feathers
> And rowed him softer home –
> Than Oars divide the Ocean,
> Too silver for a seam –
> Or Butterflies, off Banks of Noon
> Leap, plashless as they swim.

The elements mingle and the bird rows, leaps, flies, swims. What do the lines actually mean ('to row him softer home', 'Banks of Noon')? Juhasz, Miller and Smith say: 'You can see it, you can feel it, you get a shiver of delight every time you read it – but those lines of poetry do not make literal sense.' So what Dickinson has done is to evoke something outside our experience, create a new reality, a new construct. As readers we believe in it and enjoy it and in a certain sense we understand it, but it is not real. Yet we are willing to inhabit her transformed world.

Frequently she manages to disorient the reader, in little ways, through her word usage and stylistic devices. She confounds our normal expectations, for example, by substituting an abstract word for the expected concrete one. In 'A Funeral' she uses 'Space' instead of the expected 'bells' in the line 'then Space – began to toll.' But it carries the sense of emptiness brought on by depression and breakdown. This sensation is likened to the tolling of the death bell, and it resounds through the speaker's entire being. So, instead of the profound silence one might expect of emptiness we find a vibrating universe of sound in which the speaker is equally isolated and, if anything, more oppressed.

> As all the Heavens were a Bell,
> And Being, but an Ear.

Except that here, instead of the expected unfeeling state of numbness usually associated with depression, it is a state of hypersensitivity to the entire universe that isolates the speaker. And this sense of isolation from humanity is conveyed in that extraordinary image of herself and personified silence as a new race of beings in the galaxy.

And I, and Silence, some strange Race
Wrecked, solitary, here.

Once again we have entered Dickinson's new cosmic construct, unreal but rendered so convincingly that we have no difficulty inhabiting her transformed world.

Where else in the poetry do you find these radical transformations, and how are they achieved?

## In tones of seriousness and humour

The serious tones of Dickinson's poetry are patently obvious: the strong, confident tone of 'Hope'; the bleak and painful despair of 'Slant of Light'; the sense of oppression in 'A Funeral' and 'After Great Pain', and the sheer terror of 'The Soul'. Because of the peculiarities of her writing style – the punctuation, the truncated episodic imagery, the pared-down phrases, etc. – we are always conscious that these poems are crafted, and there is also an awareness of control and of some distance between the speaker and the feelings portrayed. So the tone is mostly one of controlled emotion, however powerful and painful.

There is a good deal of humour too, some of it bleak, some of it sheer slapstick. There is the dark, ironic humour of the fly – a mere house pest interrupting, and completely ruining, the solemnity and altering the focus of this most significant ritual. There is the grotesque humour in the figures of 'ghastly Fright' and the goblin in 'The Soul'. Perhaps it is more gothic horror than grotesque humour. But as well as the bleak humour we find a strain of literary humour in 'A Liquor Never Brewed', which is a parody of Emerson's 'Bacchus'. The fun in that poem is driven by sheer exuberance and can be seen in the extremity of metaphor she employs:

When 'Landlords' turn the drunken Bee
Out of the Foxglove's door.

There is a sense of comic rebelliousness in her caricature of Heaven, where 'Seraphs swing their snowy Hats,' etc. And there is a certain humour to be found in all her quirky, peculiar observations, such as the somewhat contradictory characteristics of the bird, as discussed earlier.

## Conciseness

Sparseness and economy of word and image are key features of Dickinson's poetry. For example, consider the preciseness of her descriptions in 'A Bird'. There is hardly a superfluous word, until she attempts to understand the nature of flight at the end. Consider also the precise details of the deathbed scene in 'A Fly'.

## The technical elements of Dickinson's style

### Punctuation

The most idiosyncratic feature of Dickinson's punctuation is undoubtedly her use of the dash. At first this was viewed as sloppy punctuation, indiscriminate, and just another example of her unpreparedness for publication. Then it was argued that the dashes had a rhetorical rather than a grammatical function. Because some of them were sloping in the original manuscripts it was felt that they might be hints for the pitch of a reading voice.

Nowadays readers accept them as a conscious feature of her punctuation, and they are seen as fulfilling a function somewhere between a full stop and a comma. It can be argued that a dash represents a long pause, linking what has gone before and what is to follow. It facilitates continuity and gives the impression of immediacy, i.e. that these ideas, fears, terrors or images are only just being processed by the mind. Reader and speaker are just now making these explorations and discoveries.

The dash fulfils a number of functions. The dash at the end of a poem might suggest continuity, that the debate is not finished, or that the consciousness somehow survives. We see this latter suggestion in 'A Funeral' ('and Finished knowing – then –'). There is a similar end to 'A Fly'. The dash affects the pace and rhythm of the line. It is used for very dramatic pausing, deliberately slowing the pace to correlate with the idea, as in 'First – Chill – then Stupor – then the letting go – ' ('After Great Pain'), though a combination of commas and consonants can slow a line equally well, as in 'Wrecked, solitary, here –' ('A Funeral').

Strategically placed dashes increase the sense of drama in 'The Soul' ('look at her – Salute her – with long fingers – caress her'). The tension of the awful moment is prolonged. The dash is used to isolate and emphasise when the fly interposes 'Between the light – and me – and then the Windows failed –' The speaker ('and me') is being graphically isolated and separated out for death. Altogether the dash functions as a very versatile form of punctuation.

### Capitalisation

Dickinson's capitalisation has been a source of much discussion and questioning. The eighteenth-century fashion of using capitals for the initial letter of all nouns had died out. Besides, she did not use a capital for every noun. So was her practice just a personal style, or had it a purpose? Present-day scholars feel that she used capitals for emphasis, drawing attention to words that carry the weight of the central imagery and meaning and so provide a line of emphasis through the poem. So we can view the capitalised words as stepping-stones through the meaning.

David Porter illustrates how this works by examining this first stanza of 'Slant of Light':

> There's a certain Slant of light,
> Winter Afternoons –
> That oppresses, like the Heft
> Of Cathedral Tunes –

'Slant of Light', 'Winter Afternoons', 'Heft' and 'Cathedral Tunes' carry the ideas in this stanza. The argument is then refined by the word 'certain', which denotes something special about the light, while 'oppresses' makes the emotional reaction specific.

'Slant of Light' and 'Winter Afternoons' give us the visual picture, the setting. 'Winter Afternoons' also carries an emotive significance: emotional cold, the dead season, emptiness and isolation, lifelessness leading to despair. 'Heft' and 'Cathedral Tunes' form the other part of the simile, linking the wintry emotion with a religious weight. In this way the capitalised words carry the visual, emotional and logical burden of the stanza.

Porter also suggests that the visual distinction of words by capital letters indicates that the meanings of these words have been enriched – that 'Winter Afternoons' denotes not only the scene but a range of sensuous suggestions (coldness, inactivity, whiteness) and also emotional responses (apprehension, meditation, isolation). We know that Dickinson relied greatly on the connotations of individual words and images; perhaps capitalisation was her way of signposting depth and richness, which readers must mine for themselves.

## Diction: Dickinson's use of words

- She uses words in a fairly straightforward way, without allusions or references, for the most part.
- Most noticeable is her tendency to mix the simple and the abstract: for example, in 'A Funeral' we get 'Funeral', 'Mourners', 'Service', 'Drum', 'Box', 'Bell', and then 'Being'.
- Probably the most important feature of her use of words is her reliance on the connotations, associations or suggestions of individual words to create layers of meaning. We have already considered the connotations of space and toll; another example worth considering is 'Seal' in 'Slant of Light'. A seal is a sign usually of authenticity or authority. Ironically, the divine sign here is not uplifting ('the Seal Despair'). It might also suggest a sealing off, that this state is unalterable, etc. Consider also a 'Quartz contentment'. This carries associations of coldness, the weight of despair, the immobility of rock, the glittering brittleness of quartz, etc.

- Some critics feel that the capitalisation encourages the reader to scrutinise these words for layers of meaning.
- She sometimes uses groups of words from a particular professional usage to create an effect. Consider, for example, the legal words in 'A Fly': 'willed', 'Keepsakes', 'Signed', 'portion', 'Assignable'. They suggest 'last will and testament' and accord precisely with the controlled, ordered atmosphere she wishes at her deathbed. She uses technical language to mechanise life in 'After Great Pain': 'mechanical', 'go round', 'a Wooden way'.
- One of the most fascinating and original but also exasperating facets of her diction is the development of a personal vocabulary. Some of these words, such as 'Circumference' and 'Experiment', originate from her interest in science at school, but she has endowed them with new, personal meanings. They have taken on some of the significance of a symbol, but unfortunately they do not always have the constancy of a symbol. Take, for example, her use of the word 'Noon', whose meaning varies throughout the poems. At times 'noon' and 'night' are interchangeable for 'life' and 'death'; but 'noon' has been used to suggest both immortal life and the timelessness of death. In this selection 'noon' is used to suggest playfulness, happy, excited activity, in the phrase 'Banks of Noon' ('A Bird'); but it is also used to suggest passionate love and sensual fulfilment in 'The Soul', as the escaped Bee is free to

> Touch Liberty – then know no more,
> But Noon, and Paradise.

There is a similar ambiguity and inconstancy in her use of colour. 'Red' mostly suggests life and blood. 'Green' is the colour of the grave. But there is ambivalence in her usage of 'blue'. It is used for the beloved and is the colour of the sky ('inns of Molten Blue'), but it is also used negatively, in the context of the fly, with the stumbling and failing of mind and consciousness for a theme.

## Imagery
- Emily Dickinson's poetry is primarily visual. Image follows image in a technique that might be seen as cinematic nowadays. Consider the sequence of images in 'A Bird', 'A Fly', 'The Soul', and 'Narrow Fellow'.
- Dickinson thinks in images. They are not ornamental: their function is to carry the thought of the poem. Examine the imagery in 'A Funeral': the treading mourners and the service 'like a Drum' carry the notion of being weighed down, oppressed, deprived of the ability to act, as does the image of 'Boots of Lead'. The 'Box', or coffin, suggests the confinement, the

claustrophobia of the condition and also suggests that depression is a sort of mental death. The imagery of the fourth stanza conveys the isolation of the speaker in cosmic terms (as already discussed: see page 51). Again a funeral image (uniting world and mind, concrete and abstract) provides the impetus for the mind's final plunge into chaos: 'a Plank in Reason, broke, and I dropped down, and down.'

- She uses similes and metaphors in an attempt to understand by analogy: 'I felt a Funeral, in my Brain'; 'Hope is the thing with feathers.' The investigation of the feeling of despair through an analysis of its symbolic correlative, the 'Slant of light', has been examined on page 48.
- Many of her most startling metaphors and images consist of abstract and concrete elements yoked together, such as 'a Plank in Reason', 'Zero at the Bone', 'Hope is the thing with feathers', etc.
- The metaphor poem 'Hope' resembles a particular kind of didactic metaphor, central to the tradition of Protestant preaching, indeed to all religious preaching. This was known as an 'emblem' and might be a picture or other religious object, from which meaning and a moral were elaborately constructed. Perhaps this is one of the bases for Dickinson's metaphorical style.
- Many of her images are pared down to a mere phrase, to their barest essential. This economy of imagery leads to a certain cryptic quality and often lends itself to ambiguity. But ambiguity was a conscious feature of her style. The reader is expected to work at these cryptic images, such as 'Zero at the Bone', 'Being, but an Ear', 'Banks of Noon', etc.
- We find a great range and variety of imagery in Dickinson, from the natural ('so bubble brooks in deserts') to the legal ('the Nerves sit ceremonious', 'the stiff Heart questions'), the military ('that last Onset'), the everyday (tankards, boxes, robbers), and the macabre ('ghostly Fright'). Much of her imagery comes from the natural world. Some comes from her own studies: references to geology, geography and biology. And some of it is obtained in her reading: the fly from The House of the Seven Gables, and jewels and spices and colours from her reading on explorations and scientific discoveries.

### Form and metre

The majority of Dickinson's verses are based on the hymn format and the ballad quatrain. They consist of quatrains with alternate lines of eight and six syllables. This was known as *common metre* in the hymn books (see page 38). For good examples of this examine 'Hope' and 'Slant of Light'. But notice that the metre is not always completely regular.

The ballad or hymn format suited her, as it satisfied her instinct for economy and it facilitated the tight constructions she was led to by her liking for definition, antithesis and paradox.

> 'Hope' is the thing with feathers –
> That perches in the soul –
> And sings the tune without the words –
> And never stops – at all –

There is a slight reminiscence of the hymn in her work, particularly in the tendency towards epigram and aphorism ('and sweetest – in the Gale – is heard'). The strong narrative line in her poems shows a similarity with the ballad. But she does not feel bound by a regular metre and displays the confidence and originality to vary it. Neither is she completely bound by the quatrain format. We find a six-line and an eight-line stanza in 'The Soul' and 'Narrow Fellow', respectively.

Altogether we find a flexible approach to metre and stanza, with a strong inclination to the ballad or hymn format that suited her.

### Rhymes and sounds of words

Again we find much flexibility and, some would say, originality. Though there is a deliberate intention to rhyme, quite a deal of it comes out as off-rhyme or half-rhyme, such as soul – all, storm – warm ('Hope'), Afternoons – Tunes ('Slant of Light'), fro – through ('A Funeral').

But she is interested in the music of words and manages to alliterate frequently, sometimes with comic results ('Debauchee of Dew'), sometimes poetic ('breathless Bee', 'bubble brooks'). The poems resound with internal musical echoes: 'Mourners to and fro', 'Being, but an Ear' ('A Funeral'); she is conscious of the onomatopoeic value of words in creating atmosphere: 'creak across my Soul', 'Space – began to toll.'

## *Developing a personal response to the poetry of Dickinson*

1. What issues did she write about? What insights did she give you into these issues?
2. About which themes, issues or topics did she make you think more deeply?
3. After reading her poetry, what understanding have you of her as a person – her preoccupations, interests, longings, fears, etc.?
4. What interested you most about her life and her writing?
5. Choose one poem that affected you deeply or said something important to you, and explain what you discovered.
6. What aspects of her particular style of writing appeal to you? Why?
7. In what ways is she different from other poets you have read?

8. What do you think Emily Dickinson's poetry has to offer to a young person today? Make a case for and also a case against reading her.
9. If you want to read more about her, try *The Life of Emily Dickinson* by Richard Sewall (Harvard University Press, 1974).

## Questions

1. List the main themes that preoccupy Dickinson in this selection of her poetry. Explore, in some detail, her views on any two of these themes.
2. How important is imagery in the poetry of Emily Dickinson? Explore:
   • the function of imagery in her poetry
   • the patterns you notice
   • the sources of the imagery
   • the range of the imagery.
3. Examine the depth of meanings provided by the imagery in any particular poem.
4. List the particular features of style you consider important in her poetry and explain the effects of any two features. Refer to the text to substantiate your views.
5. 'Emily Dickinson wrote about landscapes and mindscapes, and both terrains held pain and terror for her.' Consider Dickinson's poetry in the light of this statement.
6. 'Dickinson's poetry offers us a profound scrutiny of death and loss.' Would you agree? Substantiate your views, with reference to at least two of the poems.
7. 'Desolation, hopelessness and a fierce and frustrated longing arise from nearly every page' (John Cody). Would you agree with this reading of Dickinson's poetry?
8. But Dickinson also had a well-developed comic vision. Outline what you discovered about this often-neglected aspect of her poetry.
9. 'Dickinson's chief fascination is with passing moments and transition states.' Examine this aspect of her work in the light of the poems you have studied.
10. Do you think there is a disturbing tendency towards the macabre in Dickinson's poetry?
11. 'Emily Dickinson is a moody poet' (Denis Donoghue). Would you agree? Substantiate your views, with reference to the text.
12. 'Her main reaction to life experience is one of bafflement.' Comment on this in the light of the poetry you have read.
13. Emily Dickinson has 'a tendency to play up problems as if they were mysteries' (Denis Donoghue). Examine any two poems in the light of this view.

14. Do you find a dramatic quality in Dickinson's work? Support your views by reference to at least three poems.
15. There are two voices in many of Dickinson's poems: the suffering 'I' and a detached, observing persona who is outside the experience. What is the effect of this on the tone of the poems? Support your views with references to at least two poems.
16. How do you account for the elusive quality of her poetry? Examine both the abstract nature of the themes she investigated and the conciseness of her style.
17. 'The difficulty in Emily Dickinson's poetry has to do with the layers of meaning she constructs through the multiple connotations of words and images.' Investigate this aspect of her technique in any two poems you have studied.
18. Would you consider Emily Dickinson to be a religious poet? Explain your reasons with reference to texts.
19. Write about the 'snapshot brevity' of any three of her poems you have studied.
20. Examine 'A Funeral' as a typical Dickinson poem. Consider the experience investigated; the tone of the poem; the use of imagery and metaphor; the concentration of meaning; the dual perspective of the speaking voice; and any two features of the poetic format.

# Bibliography

Cody, John, *After Great Pain*, Cambridge (Mass.): Harvard University Press 1971.

Duncan, Douglas, *Emily Dickinson* (Writers and Critics Series), Edinburgh: Oliver and Boyd 1965.

Farr, Judith, *The Passion of Emily Dickinson*, Cambridge (Mass.): Harvard University Press 1992.

Fitzgibbon, Emelie, *York Notes on Selected Poems of Emily Dickinson*, London: Longman 1984.

Johnson, Thomas (editor), *Emily Dickinson: The Complete Poems*, London: Faber and Faber 1970.

Juhasz, Susan, *The Undiscovered Continent: Emily Dickinson and the Space of the Mind*, Bloomington: Indiana University Press 1983.

Juhasz, Susan, Miller, Cristanne, and Smith, M., *Comic Power in Emily Dickinson*, Austin: University of Texas 1993.

McCormack, Jerusha, 'Dying as an art: the procedures of Emily Dickinson's poetry', *ATE Journal*, no. 7, spring 1977.

McNeil, Helen, *Emily Dickinson* (Virago Pioneers), London: Virago 1986.

Miller, Cristanne, *Emily Dickinson: A Poet's Grammar,* Cambridge (Mass.): Harvard University Press 1987.

Patterson, Rebecca, *The Riddle of Emily Dickinson,* Boston: Houghton Mifflin 1951.

Patterson, Rebecca (editor), *Emily Dickinson's Imagery,* Amherst: University of Massachusetts Press 1979.

Porter, David, *The Art of Emily Dickinson's Early Poetry,* Cambridge (Mass.): Harvard University Press 1966.

Robinson, John, *Emily Dickinson* (Faber and Faber Student Guides), London: Faber and Faber 1986.

St Armand, Barton, *The Soul's Society: Emily Dickinson and her Culture,* Cambridge: Cambridge University Press 1984.

Sewall, Richard, *The Life of Emily Dickinson,* Cambridge (Mass.): Harvard University Press 1974.

Tate, Allen (editor), *Six American Poets, from Emily Dickinson to the Present: An Introduction,* Minneapolis: University of Minnesota Press 1969.

Weisbuch, Robert, *Emily Dickinson's Poetry,* Chicago: University of Chicago Press 1975.

# 3   *William Butler* YEATS

*John G. Fahy*

## *A literary life*

William Butler Yeats was born on 13 June 1865 at number 1 Sandymount Avenue, Dublin, a son of John Butler Yeats and Susan Pollexfen. John Butler Yeats originated from Co. Down, where his father was Church of Ireland rector and whose father before him had been rector at Drumcliff, Co. Sligo. The Butler part of the family name came from an eighteenth-century marriage to a relative of the Butlers of Ormonde, one of the oldest Anglo-Irish families. That marriage brought with it the more tangible asset of a few hundred acres of land in Co. Kildare, the rents from which continued to provide a measure of financial support for the family until it had to be sold in 1886.

John Butler Yeats had trained as a barrister before his marriage but decided to become an artist instead, and in 1867 the family moved to London so that he could study painting. This was the first move of a peripatetic childhood and youth for the young William, as the family moved from one house to another in London or between London and Dublin in pursuit of the father's artistic career, which never really became financially viable.

William was the eldest surviving child, followed by Susan Mary (called Lily), Elizabeth Corbet (called Lollie), and John Butler (Jack) – all born within six years of each other. Their mother, Susan Pollexfen, was the daughter of a wealthy merchant and shipping family from Co. Sligo; and when John Butler Yeats got into financial difficulties the family spent a good deal of time there, which the poet remembered with great affection. So a good deal of Yeats's childhood and youth was spent in an atmosphere of genteel poverty, supported by better-off relatives.

He was educated at the Godolphin School, London, 1875–80, the High School, Dublin, 1880–83, and the Metropolitan School of Art, Dublin, 1884–86. At first the young Yeats found it difficult to learn to read, and when by the age of seven or eight he still could not distinguish all the letters of the alphabet, his father is reputed to have thrown the reading book at him in a rage. In later life Yeats's spelling continued to be idiosyncratic, supporting the later conclusion that he suffered from dyslexia. As it was unlikely that he would pass the entrance examination for Trinity College, his father's old university, he was tutored to some extent by his father, who regarded himself as the young man's chief mentor, and was therefore largely self-educated. Consequently his acquaintances and readings assumed a very significant role in his development.

Among the people introduced to him by his father was the old Fenian John O'Leary, and this sparked off an interest in nationalism, particularly as a subject for poetry. He was influenced also by the writings of Douglas Hyde, Katherine Tynan, and Samuel Ferguson, as well as James Clarence Mangan's versions of Irish poems. But it was probably the histories and the fiction of Standish O'Grady that most impelled Yeats to investigate Irish mythology. At this time he was fascinated by the folk tales, fairy tales and supernatural beliefs found in Co. Sligo and Co. Galway, which resulted in the collection *Fairy and Folk Tales of the Irish Peasantry* (1888). He also wanted to reformulate in English the old Irish legends and so re-create Ireland's lost intellectual and cultural heritage. This found expression in his collection of poetry *The Wanderings of Oisín* (1889).

At this time also Yeats began to search for alternative philosophies to Christianity, such as Buddhism, magic, spiritualism and astrology. Influenced to some degree no doubt by his discussions with his friend George Russell, the poet, he began to explore mysticism and the occult, often through the practices of esoteric groups and cults. Among these were the theosophists (through whom he encountered the notorious Elena Blavatsky), who believed that knowledge of God could be achieved through spiritual ecstasy and direct intuition. He became involved also with the 'Hermetic Order of the Golden Dawn', a Rosicrucian order that practised ritual demonstrations of psychic power, which he joined in 1890. The Golden Dawn was based on the desire for alchemical change – the transformation of people into gods, the possibility of transforming the world. Yeats became quite dedicated to the practice of magic, believed in the evocation of spirits, and indeed was convinced that he himself was a magician.

Among the principal beliefs that he subscribed to were:
- that the borders of our minds are ever shifting and that minds can melt and flow into each other, creating a single entity or 'Great Mind'
- that there is a 'World Soul' or shared memory in nature
- that the Great Mind can be evoked by symbols, which Yeats introduced into poetry in order to access truths.

He learnt a great deal about symbolism from Shelley and Blake. Symbols reveal themselves in a state of trance. He felt that the purpose of rhythm in poetry is to create meditative rhythms in which the mind is lulled into a state of trance. So, when poetry is working well it operates like a mantra or chant, helping us to see past the ordinary. Yeats believed that 'simple' people (those who were considered fools), ascetics and women can see beyond modern culture into the world of magical truths.

Yeats also believed that Celticism was the remnant of a former world religion, that the occult is really the remnant of this old religion or magic, and that Ireland is the place where it can best be contacted. So Celticism and the occult are important and connected twin pillars of his poetic philosophy.

During the 1890s Yeats's poetry developed from simple pastoral poetry and verses about fairy tales to the use of cycles of mythology of Ulster and the Fianna. He introduced heroes from these tales into his poetry: Cú Chulainn, Méabh, Deirdre, and others. He began to use the Celtic material in a visionary way to create mystical poetry, which culminated in the volume *The Wind Among the Reeds* (1899).

Women were important in Yeats's life, and he had a number of troublesome and tempestuous love affairs. Of all the women he encountered two were to be most influential: Maud Gonne and Lady Augusta Gregory. The former, whom he met in the late 1880s, was the source of passionate romantic involvement and disappointment for him over the succeeding three decades; but she was also the inspiration for some of his work, such as the play *The Countess Kathleen,* was a frequent reference point in his poetry, and was the focus for some of his ideas on nationalism, women in politics, the aesthetic, ageing, and others.

He first met Lady Gregory in 1894, and from 1897 onwards her home, Coole Park, near Gort, Co. Galway, was a summer refuge from his somewhat nomadic life. As well as helping him collect folk tales she provided both psychological and financial support and the opportunity to meet other writers, such as George Russell, George Bernard Shaw, George Moore and Edward Martyn.

Lady Gregory, Yeats and Martyn were the principal co-founders of the Irish Literary Theatre. Their manifesto clearly outlines the driving philosophy and ambition of the movement.

> We propose to have performed in Dublin in the spring of every year certain Celtic and Irish plays, which whatever be their degree of excellence will be written with a high ambition, and so to build up a Celtic and Irish school of dramatic literature. We hope to find in Ireland an uncorrupted and imaginative audience trained to listen by its passion for oratory, and believe that our desire to bring upon the stage the deeper thoughts and emotions of Ireland will ensure for us a tolerant welcome, and that freedom to experiment which is not found in the theatres of England, and without which no new movement in art or literature can succeed. We will show that Ireland is not the home of buffoonery and of easy sentiment, as it has been represented, but the home of an ancient idealism. We are confident of the support of all Irish people, who are weary of misrepresentation, in carrying out a work that is outside all the political questions that divide us.

Eventually this movement led to the founding of the Abbey Theatre, Dublin, in 1904, where Yeats was manager from 1904 to 1910. But the public did not always appreciate the movement's artistic vision. There was adverse reaction to Yeats's play *The Countess Kathleen*; and in 1907 John Millington Synge's play *The Playboy of the Western World* sparked off riots in the theatre. Yeats was deeply disillusioned by this lack of understanding and aesthetic appreciation, a feeling that was deepened by the controversy over the Hugh Lane proposal. This disillusionment is reflected in his poetry *The Green Helmet* (1910), *Responsibilities* (1914), and *The Wild Swans at Coole* (1917). In contrast, his visit to Italy in 1907 with Lady Gregory and her son, Robert, pointed up the difference between the mob in Ireland and what it had been possible to create through aristocratic patronage in Florence and Ravenna.

The Easter Rising of 1916 forced Yeats to rethink his view of Irish society, as we see in the poem 'Easter 1916'. These years ushered in other decisive changes for Yeats. After a final round of marriage proposals to Maud Gonne and then to her adopted daughter, Iseult, he settled into marriage with Georgina Hyde-Lees on 20 October 1917. The marriage produced two children and much-needed domestic stability for Yeats. And, whether by chance or design, it also produced the 'automatic writing' created by his wife, who, while in a sort of trance, transcribed the words of certain spirit guides or instructors. This seemed to offer a new system of thought to Yeats, incorporating themes of change within a new view of history, which he developed in his book *A Vision* (1925).

The central idea of his philosophy was that civilisation was about to reverse itself and a new era of anti-civilisation was about to be ushered in. The signs of this were everywhere: in mass movements in Europe, in the rise of communism, fascism, etc. Yeats examined change against the backdrop of world history. In his review of history he noticed that certain eras favoured the development of human excellence in art and learning and also produced social harmony: Athens of the fifth century BC, Byzantium, the Italian Renaissance – all of which developed political culture and artistic culture and in general fostered human achievement, creating what Yeats termed 'unity of being'. These eras were separated by a thousand years, each reaching its peak about five hundred years after it replaced the previous 'millennium'. There were two main forces at work: what Yeats called 'anti-thetical' energies, which created this unity of being, and the opposite force, which he termed 'primary' energy. These two energies grew or waned in their turn over the course of each millennium.

Yeats represented this theory of change by the symbolism of the 'gyres', two interpenetrating cones (see page 101), one primary and the other anti-thetical, each growing or decreasing in strength as the centuries pass. He felt that his own time was now reaching the end of the primary gyre and that the growing violence on the Continent and in Ireland was an indicator of its imminent collapse, to be replaced by a new anti-thetical gyre. This is the philosophical background to the bleak view he took of the current fractious age in the volumes *Michael Robartes and the Dancer* (1921) and, in particular, *The Tower* (1928). See in particular his poems 'The Second Coming', 'Sailing to Byzantium', and 'Meditations in Time of Civil War'.

This philosophy, which had as its central belief the notion that the times were out of joint and that cataclysmic changes were about to happen, may help to explain Yeats's flirtation with extreme political philosophies and movements, for example his consideration of fascism, his exploration of the place of violence in politics, his scepticism about democracy and his preference for the political model of Renaissance prince – ruler (a model that cast the Anglo-Irish gentry in a similar role), and his engagement with theories of eugenics.

This search for solutions, for paradigms of thought and models for living, continued into the poet's old age, but it took more conventional forms in his volume *The Winding Stair and Other Poems* (1933). Here we find many elegies – to dead friends, to past times, and to other more unified eras, such as the eighteenth century, from which Yeats took his chief model, Jonathan Swift, whom he wished to emulate as poet – statesman.

Indeed, he was pursuing that ideal in his role as a senator in the new Irish Free State. He devoted much energy to his work in the new senate, which first sat on 11 December 1922 and of which he was a member until 1928. During 1923, for instance, he spoke nineteen times on such subjects as law enforcement, manuscripts, the Lane pictures, film censorship, and Irish, and he continued over the years to contribute on issues such as partition, divorce, and the new coinage. In 1922 the University of Dublin conferred an honorary doctorate on him, and he was similarly honoured by the Universities of Oxford and Cambridge in 1931 and 1933, respectively. But the crowning international recognition was the award of the Nobel Prize for Literature in 1923.

In the late 1920s and early 1930s Yeats experienced a number of health problems, and the family began to spend more time in the sunnier regions of southern Europe. The house at 82 Merrion Square, Dublin, was sold and exchanged for a flat in Fitzwilliam Square. In 1933 Yeats took himself out of the city altogether when the family took a long lease on a house, 'Riversdale', in Rathfarnham, 'just too far from Dublin to go there without good reason and too far, I hope, for most interviewers and the less determined travelling bores.' (See 'An Acre of Grass'.) But he continued to write, indeed with renewed vigour, and *New Poems* was published in 1938. His last public appearance was at the Abbey Theatre in August 1938. He died on 28 January 1939 at Roquebrune in the south of France; in 1948 his body was re-interred, as he had wished, in Drumcliff churchyard.

| PRINCIPAL VOLUMES OF POETRY | **Poems in this selection** |
|---|---|
| *The Wanderings of Oisín* (1889) | |
| *Crossways* (1889) | |
| *The Rose* (1893) | – 'The Lake Isle of Innisfree' |
| *The Wind Among the Reeds* (1899) | |
| *The Green Helmet and Other Poems* (1910) | |
| *Responsibilities* (1914) | – 'September 1913' |
| *The Wild Swans at Coole* (1917; second edition 1919) | – 'The Wild Swans at Coole' |
| | – 'An Irish Airman Foresees His Death' |
| *Michael Robartes and the Dancer* (1921) | – 'Easter 1916' |
| | – 'The Second Coming' |
| *The Tower* (1928) | – 'Sailing to Byzantium' |
| | – 'Meditations in Time of Civil War' |
| *The Winding Stair and Other Poems* (1933) | – 'In Memory of Eva Gore-Booth and Con Markiewicz' |
| | – 'Swift's Epitaph' |
| *A Full Moon in March* (1935) | |
| *New Poems* (1938) | – 'An Acre of Grass' |
| *Last Poems* (1939) | – 'Under Ben Bulben' |
| | – 'Politics' |

*Note:* The edition of the poems used in this anthology is *Yeats's Poems*, edited by A. Norman Jeffares (Basingstoke: Macmillan, 1989).

# The Lake Isle of Innisfree

Text of poem: New Explorations Anthology page 137

[*Note: This poem is also prescribed for Ordinary Level 2005 exam*]

This poem was written in 1888, when Yeats was living in London, where he was unhappy and homesick for Ireland. A somewhat altered version was first published in the *National Observer* in December 1890, to much acclaim; this really was the poem that first made Yeats's name. It is included in the collection *The Rose* (1893).

Yeats had been greatly influenced by the vision of self-sufficiency in nature found in Henry David Thoreau's book *Walden* (1854), which his father had read to him. And he too dreamed of living alone in nature in a quest for wisdom. This was a theme he explored not just in verse but in his prose writings also, an indication of the pervasive autobiographical nature of the quest. For instance, there are close similarities between this poem and the scenario in *John Sherman*, a novel Yeats had written in 1887–88, in which a young Sligo man who had left home in search of a fortune and was now homesick in London recalls an island on a lake where he used to pick blackberries. He dreams of returning there, building a wooden hut, and listening to the ripple of the water.

## YEATS'S VISION AND QUEST

The vision of self-sufficiency in nature obviously pervades this whole poem. However unlikely a scene, it shows the poet as rustic woodsman and gardener, writing in the first person, actually planning to build a simple, crude dwelling and attempting agricultural self-sufficiency. 'Clay and wattles' were the traditional rural building materials for centuries past. The hive and the bees suggest the simple sweetness and richness of life, as well as providing a natural musical ambience. Altogether the vision is one of idyllic rural primitiveness, with a hint of the hermit's ascetic: a life 'alone in the bee-loud glade'.

This is a romantic view of the human being in perfect harmony with nature, at one with its sights and sounds. It is an alluring picture, sensual even, where the feminised morning is draped in veils. But there is also a strange, slightly unreal quality about it. The light is different: noon is a 'purple glow'. The archaic language in the expression of 'midnight's all a glimmer' reinforces the strange, even magical nature of the atmosphere. For representative sounds Yeats chooses the simple, rhythmic, calming sound of lake water lapping and also the repetitive rustic sounds of the cricket on the hearth, a common feature of rural stories and tales. Co. Sligo is one of the few places in the country that provides an all-year-round habitat for the linnet, a small unspectacular bird that likes rough hillsides and uncultivated lands near the sea. With accurate recall, Yeats is celebrating the indigenous wildlife of the area. His vision of happiness is a romantic one – a simple, unsophisticated lifestyle in an unspoilt habitat, surrounded by the sights and music of nature. It is a picture full of the rich textures of colour, sound and movement, in total contrast to his present environment, that of the cold, colourless and lifeless 'pavements grey'. So in one sense the poem can be read as an expression of Yeats's romanticised and nostalgic yearning for his native countryside.

But it is also more than this. For it is no frivolous weekend in the woods that he is planning: it is rather a quest for wisdom, for deep, eternal truths – an attempt to see into the heart of things. This is the sentiment that comes across in the first line. The sound of water, one of the essential elements and a life force, haunts him and seems to suggest that only in nature will he find the truths of the heart. The ambiguity about whose heart is in question here further strengthens the connection between the poet's heart and the heart of the earth. This is a move he feels compelled to make, a compulsion. We can sense the strength of his resolve in the verbs 'I will arise' and 'I shall have'. But the biblical allusions underlying this expose even more complex layers of compulsion. The repeated 'I will arise' echoes the words of the Prodigal Son, who has wasted his inheritance, led a profligate few years in exile, and finally resolves to go home: 'I will arise and go to my father.' So the words of the poem carry great unhappiness, a sense of failure and loss, the loneliness of exile and separation and perhaps even a feeling of guilt or remorse. The phrase 'always night and day' could also be a Biblical allusion. St Mark's gospel (5:5) refers to a man possessed by an evil spirit who was freed from his torment by Christ: 'Night and day among the tombs and on the mountains he was always crying out and bruising himself with stones.' This allusion, if intended, hints at a somewhat manic compulsion and mental and spiritual turmoil, or at the very least a great discontent.

## THE MUSIC OF THE VERSE

The poet's feelings of unease and discontent and of being driven to take this course of action are hidden by the musical quality of the verse. Apart from the obvious repetitions of the end rhymes in alternate lines, there are subtle musical vowel repetitions throughout the poem. For example, there is a profusion of long 'i' sounds in the first stanza ('I', 'arise', 'Nine', 'I', 'hive') and a repetition of long 'o' and 'a' sounds in the final stanza ('go', 'low', 'shore', 'roadway', 'core' and 'day', 'lake', 'pavements', 'grey'). The repetition, particularly of long broad vowels, gives this a languidness and soporific calmness that belies the tension at the heart of it.

## ISSUES

Among the issues that preoccupy the poet here we might emphasise:
• the yearning for self-sufficiency in natural surroundings

- the search for truth, wisdom and peace
- the poet's discontent, which impels him on this quest.

# September 1913

Text of poem: New Explorations Anthology page 139

This poem was written in September 1913 and was first published on 8 September in the *Irish Times,* where it was entitled 'Romance in Ireland (on reading much of the correspondence against the Art Gallery)'. It was included in the volume *Responsibilities* (1914) under its present title.

YEATS AND POLITICS: SOME OF HIS VIEWS ON SOCIETY

At one level of reading this is just a political poem – an angry poetical response to a particular event in which Yeats was passionately involved. Sir Hugh Lane, a wealthy art collector (and Lady Gregory's nephew), had presented to the city of Dublin a unique collection of modern paintings, with the proviso that the city build a suitable gallery to house them. There were various suggestions for building a gallery, such as one on a bridge over the River Liffey; but the entire project became entangled in increasingly bitter public disputes about the location, the architecture, and particularly the cost. Yeats was furious about what seemed a mean-spirited, penny-pinching and anti-cultural response to Lane's generous offer. The opponents of the project drew attention to the poverty and slum living conditions that many Dubliners endured at the time and accused the proponents of the gallery of putting art before bread and also of an elitist arrogance typical of the Ascendancy class. The controversy developed strong overtones of class conflict and set Yeats thinking about the recent changes in Irish society.

The make-up of society, the need for particular kinds of people in a cultured society, and the responsibilities of particular classes – these were issues that had long preoccupied Yeats. In 1907, on the death of the old Fenian John O'Leary, Yeats wrote an essay entitled 'Poetry and tradition', in which he talks about the ideals that he and O'Leary had discussed and shared. Though the primary emphasis in the essay is on poetry and culture, the views reflect Yeats's notions of the ideal society.

> Three types of men have made all beautiful things. Aristocracies have made beautiful manners, because their place in the world puts them above the fear of life, and the countrymen have made beautiful stories and beliefs, because they have nothing to lose and so do not fear, and the artists have made all the rest, because Providence has filled them

with recklessness. All these look backward to a long tradition, for, being without fear, they have held to whatever pleases them.

So for Yeats, the really important constituents of society were the aristocracy, country people and artists. It should not surprise us that Yeats was bitterly disillusioned with the changes in society that were proceeding apace from the end of the nineteenth century and into the twentieth: changes in land ownership hastened the demise of the aristocracy; a new upper and lower middle class emerged. Yeats saw only a new Ireland of small shopkeepers, clerks and traders; and it is at this section of the new society that he directs his wrath in the poem.

In the main he makes two accusations. Firstly, their only preoccupations are making money and practising religion, as he ironically says:

For men were born to pray and save.

They are a money-grubbing and fearful people, tyrannised by their religion. And Yeats is revolted by this combination of materialism and religious serfdom; it is the antithesis of his Renaissance model of a cultured society, where art and literature are valued. Secondly, these small-minded, self-regarding, blinkered people are incapable of understanding the generosity of spirit and the self-sacrifice that motivated the patriots of old. Lines 25–30 can be read in this way. The selfless patriotism of the heroes of past time would now be misinterpreted by this unenlightened generation as love-crazed emotion merely to impress a woman.

You'd cry, 'Some woman's yellow hair
Has maddened every mother's son'

So the present generation and society are contrasted, most unfavourably, with previous generations.

It is worth exploring Yeats's notion of the heroic past and his view of the influential figures of romantic Ireland. They all were political rebels, risk-takers who tried and failed gloriously to free Ireland. They all were men of action, soldiers who willingly gave liberty or life for the cause: 'They weighed so lightly what they gave.' They were hugely energetic, forceful characters:

They have gone about the world like wind,
But little time had they to pray.

In particular, Yeats seems to admire their extraordinary selflessness and courage, their almost manic bravery: 'All that delirium of the brave'.

Yeats's thinking accommodated two sometimes conflicting notions of the heroic: the hero as representative leader of a people, and the hero as a solitary figure, often even in opposition to the people. There are elements of both notions here. There are some hints of their popular influence ('the names that stilled your childish play') and perhaps also in their willing sacrifice ('all that blood was shed'). But the overwhelming impression is that of the solitary figure, apart, different: 'they were of a different kind'; 'the wild geese spread | The grey wing upon every tide'; 'those exiles as they were | In all their loneliness and pain.' And it is this difference that gives them status in the poem. And, by implication, the present generation lack their qualities of nobility, courage, selflessness, and self-sacrifice for an ideal.

TONE

This poem is built on contrast – an extreme, somewhat simplistic contrast between a present and a past generation, or what Yeats sees as representative figures from these generations. The heroic past he idolises in tones of reverence and awe. There is a suggestion of their strange power in 'the names that stilled your childish play' and in the reference to their going 'about the world like wind'. He empathises with their loneliness and pain and inevitable fate:

> But little time had they to pray
> For whom the hangman's rope was spun,
> And what, God help us, could they save?

His undoubted admiration for their selfless courage is carried in 'They weighed so lightly what they gave' and in that 'delirium of the brave'.

In contrast, the new middle class is lampooned in the caricature of the shopkeeper as a kind of sub-human creature, fumbling, shivering, and certainly not capable of understanding more noble motives. The tone of savage mockery is often achieved by the use of irony – for example the perverse irony of 'What need you, being come to sense' – or the ironic statement of philosophy, 'For men were born to pray and save.' The bitter contempt is hammered home through the repetition of 'For this ... for this ... for this.' The sneer of disdain rings through these lines.

Altogether this is a poem exhibiting passionate but contrasting emotions.

SOME THEMES AND ISSUES

- Bitter disillusion with recent social changes
- Contempt for the perceived materialism and religious serfdom of the new middle class of business people
- Concerns for the well-being of a cultured society; concern for its lack of altruistic principles and generosity of spirit

- A particular view of Irish history as a history of courageous failure in the struggle for independence
- A nostalgic, romanticised view of Irish history
- Thoughts on patriotism and the notion of the heroic.

# *The Wild Swans at Coole*

Text of poem: New Explorations Anthology page 142
[*Note: This poem is also prescribed for the Ordinary Level 2005 exam*]

The poem was written in 1916 and first published in the *Little Review* in 1917, and it is the title poem of the volume *The Wild Swans at Coole* (1917).

This poem is structured as a retrospection by Yeats as he records how his life has changed since he first stayed at Coole Park during the summer and autumn of 1897 ('the nineteenth autumn'). It is important to be aware that this is an artistic construction, because in reality his state of mind had changed very little. Though he chooses to say that he was more carefree ('trod with a lighter tread') at that earlier period, probably for aesthetic purposes and to set up a contrast, in fact he had been in a state of mental and nervous exhaustion during that visit in 1897. His love affair with Diana Vernon had just ended. He was 'tortured with sexual desire and disappointed love', and, as his diaries reveal, 'It would have been a relief to have screamed aloud.'

In the summer of 1916, the year the poem was written, Yeats went to France to Maud Gonne, the great, omnipresent, passionate love of his life for the previous quarter of a century. Her husband, Major John MacBride, had been shot for his part in the Easter Rising. She was working as a volunteer nurse with the war wounded, and Yeats once again proposed marriage to her. On her refusing for the last time he contemplated the possibility of marriage with her adopted daughter, Iseult. Possibly it was this turmoil and the disparity in their ages that set him thinking of time, age and immortality, the death of love or the possibility of its being eternal. But this is one instance where a biographical approach does not help very much, as the poet orders and alters events and ideals to suit an artistic construction rather than any actual reality.

When Iseult finally refused him in 1917 he married Georgina Hyde-Lees and bought a tower-house, Thoor Ballylee, not far from Coole in Co. Galway.

## THEMES AND ISSUES

This poem, as Yeats's literary biographer Terence Brown says, 'sets a mood of autumnal introspection'. In a certain sense it is quite a personal poem, in which Yeats, at fifty-one, unmarried and alone despite many passionate love affairs, takes stock of his emotional situation. Primarily he laments the loss of youth, passion and love. He regrets the loss of his carefree youth, 'trod with a lighter tread', however inaccurate this nostalgia is. Now his 'heart is sore'; he is a man broken-hearted, discontented, emotionally unsatisfied. He no longer has what the swans appear to have – youthful passion.

> Unwearied still, lover by lover ...
> Passion or conquest ...
> Attend upon them still.

And he has not got unchanging or constant love, while 'their hearts have not grown old'. Above all else, the poet seems to resent the loss of passionate love in his life; we cannot mistake this yearning in the many references to hearts, lovers, passion and conquests.

The loss of love is just one aspect of Yeats's general sense of regret here, which concerns ageing and the passage of time. Indeed he seems to have been ambushed by time – the nineteenth autumn 'has come upon me' – and is forced to accept that 'all's changed'. His awareness of this and his resentment are accentuated by the seeming immortality of the swans: 'Their hearts have not grown old'. By implication we sense the poet's yearning for changelessness, for immortality.

Yet another kind of loss is hinted at here: the possible loss or diminution of the poetic gift, insight or vision. Perhaps that is what he fears at the end of the poem, in that final plaintive image: that the poetic sight or vision will have deserted him and passed to others. For him, the swans are in some way a manifestation of his poetic vision. So we can see that he explores
- the personal loss of youth, passion, and love
- the consequences of ageing
- the passage of time and the yearning for changelessness and immortality
- the loss of poetic power and vision – the sense of failure.

IMAGERY AND SYMBOLISM

The entire poem is structured around the swans, real and symbolic, which have particular significance because they appear to have defied time for the past nineteen years. They give the illusion of immortality: 'Unwearied still ... Passion or conquest ... attend upon them still.' Our rational mind tells us that of course they may not be exactly the same swans; but the poet glosses over and even builds further on this poetic illusion. He concentrates our attention on the patterns they establish, patterns that will survive even though they may die. These 'great broken rings', the spiral imagery they create, are similar to the 'gyres' or cones of time (see page 101) that Yeats saw as the cyclical pattern behind all things, time and eternity. So there is a hint of the eternal about the spiral imagery the swans establish. Also, they link the water to the sky, link earth and heaven; and so in a way they are both mortal and immortal. The swans provide an exciting, vibrant, multi-layered symbolism, but they are also hauntingly and accurately described as real creatures. The real power and energy of the movement is evoked by the breathless enjambment of the lines and by the use of sinuous and muscular verbs and adverbs:

> All suddenly mount
> And scatter wheeling in great broken rings
> Upon their clamorous wings.

The swan imagery carries great resonances and symbolic value in the poem; but there are other images also that add to the richness of texture. The 'woodland paths' can be either the straight paths of the intellect or the winding paths of intuition. Whatever symbolic weight they carry they are dry here, in keeping with the themes – lack of passion and creativity. The trees, a great symbol of permanence for Yeats, are in the ageing cycle of their lives, as is the poet.

Three of the four symbolic elements are used in the poem: earth, air and water. Only fire is not used, indeed is conspicuously absent. The suggestion is that this is more than just a poem, that it carries elements of magical divination. Even the musical image 'The bell-beat of their wings above my head' reinforces this sense of the magical. And of course Yeats believed in and practised magic. Our sense of this is strengthened further by an exploration of the degree of patterning in the poem. Notice how the swans on the lake take to the air and finish by drifting on the still water again – creating a perfect round or circular pattern. Consider the pattern of antitheses in the poem – between the swans and the speaker and between the poet now and the poet nineteen years ago. And, as the critic Donald Stauffer points out, the essential pattern is a contrast of moods, something experienced only by humans. The essential contrast in the poem is that between transient humanity and eternity.

All in all, there is a richness of imagery and symbolism here that can be enjoyed and appreciated at many levels.

STRUCTURE

There is a gradual opening out of both the voice and the vista as this poem progresses. Stanza 1 just paints the picture, unemotionally and accurately, as any ornithologist or naturalist might do. From this very anchored and particular opening we go to the poet's personal reminiscences in the second and third stanzas, before moving on to more generalised speculative philosophising in the fourth stanza. The final stanza opens up unanswerable questions, speculating on the future, leaving us with the possibility of a completely empty final scene, a blank canvas. The future is as unclear and ungraspable as that final question – incidentally the only question in the poem.

The poem goes from the particular to the general and then to the entirely speculative. Beneath the tranquillity of the imagery, the languidness of language, and the sounds of the words, the ideas of the poem are tightly linked and structured. Notice how images or ideas are picked up from one stanza to the next, and so the stanzas are chain-linked.

The first stanza ends with the enumeration of 'nine-and-fifty swans', and the second stanza takes up the count.

> The nineteenth autumn has come upon me
> Since I first made my count;

Stanzas 2 and 3 are linked by the poet's looking: 'I saw ... I have looked'. At the end of stanza 3 he remembers or fancies his carefree 'lighter treat' of nineteen years earlier. Stanza 4 opens with the still 'unwearied' creatures.

The fifth stanza picks up phonetically on the word 'still', and, though semantically different, it provides a phonic linkage. There is of course the imagery link also, where swans 'paddling in the cold | Companionable streams' of the fourth stanza are picked up in the fifth stanza as they 'drift on the still water'.

# An Irish Airman Foresees his Death

Text of poem: New Explorations Anthology page 145

This poem was one of a number written by the poet for Robert Gregory, Lady Gregory's son, including 'Shepherd and Goatherd' and 'In Memory of Major Robert Gregory'. Yeats saw Gregory as an educated aristocrat and all-round Renaissance man ('Soldier, scholar, horseman, he'). He was also an energetic boxer and hunter and a painter who designed sets for Yeats's own plays. The poem was written in 1918 and first published in the second edition of *The Wild Swans at Coole* (1919).

## CRITICAL COMMENTARY

At one obvious level of reading, this is a type of elegy in memory of the dead man. But it is a variation on the form, in that it is structured as a monologue by the dead man rather than the more usual direct lament by a poet, praising the person's good qualities and showing how he is much missed, and so on.

It makes an interesting contribution to war poetry in its attempt to chart the motivation and psychological state of the volunteer. What strikes one immediately is not just the fatalism – he knows his death is imminent – but the bleakness of his outlook on life, his disenchantment with living, despite his privileged background.

> The years to come seemed waste of breath,
> A waste of breath the years behind ...

In contrast, the war seemed an adventure, an 'impulse of delight', a 'tumult in the clouds'. The poem captures well the excitement and exhilaration felt by many a volunteer. As Ulick O'Connor put it (in *The Yeats Companion*, 1990), 'There can seldom have been a better summing up of the sense of elation which the freedom to roam the uncharted skies brought to the young men of Gregory's pre-1914 generation.'

Yet the decision to volunteer was not a heady, emotional one. The poem stresses the thought and calculation brought to the decision. The concept of balance is repeatedly stressed:

> I balanced all, brought all to mind ...
> In balance with this life, this death.

He was not carried away by the emotion of enlistment meetings ('Nor public men, nor cheering crowds'). He was not moved by any sense of 'duty' or 'patriotism'; neither was there conscription in Ireland ('Nor law, nor duty bade me fight'). These 'nor – nor' negatives of the rejected motives are balanced against the excitement of action. The general picture is of a young man who has chosen, after careful consideration, this path of action, almost indeed chosen his death.

This heavy sense of fatalism is most obvious in the opening lines. But there is never a sense in which this fatalism is merely weak surrender or opting out. He accepts his fate, he goes consenting to his death, but more like one of Homer's heroes. Yeats gives Gregory Homeric stature by allowing him to choose a heroic death; and this gives meaning to an otherwise meaningless conflict. The airman feels none of the great passions of war, neither patriotic love nor hatred of the foe:

> Those that I fight I do not hate,
> Those that I guard I do not love;

Further, he does not think the war will make a whit of difference to his own countrymen:

> No likely end could bring them loss
> Or leave them happier than before.

But it is the self-sacrificing death, 'this death' freely chosen, that raises the young man above the events of his time and confers particular significance on him. The awareness of impending death also brings this moment of insight, this clearness of vision that allowed him to evaluate his past life and contemplate a possible future as a country landowner – all of which he rejects for the 'tumult' of action.

So, as a war poem, this is an interesting, personal, even intimate approach, charting the thoughts and motivation of this young man. But it has a more general aspect also. Gregory may be seen as representative of all those young men of talent who were cheated of their promise by the slaughter of the First World War.

We have already mentioned that Yeats saw Gregory as the all-round Renaissance man – in other words, an educated man and person of culture as well as a man of action. Yeats had felt that the 'lonely impulse of delight' was what differentiated the artist from others, that the artistic impulse was essentially lonely and solitary. Here we see this artistic impulse motivating a man of action, who is essentially instinctive rather than intellectual. Yeats felt that the impulse was sometimes hampered in the artist, who often thought too much. So the later Yeats began to champion the non-intellectual hero and the instinctive man; the sportsman and the adventurer are given the status of mythic figures. The airman Gregory is essentially a solitary figure, like other mythic figures created by Yeats, such as the 'Fisherman'.

Some critics read this poem as a classic statement of Anglo-Irishness as Yeats saw it. In later life Yeats used to talk about the 'Anglo-Irish solitude'. Is there a sense here of not quite fully belonging to either side, of being neither fully committed English nor unreservedly Irish? There is certainly a sense of emotional distance on the part of the subject, both from those he guards and those he fights. Though he has an affinity with Kiltartan's poor ('my countrymen'), he is aware that the war and his involvement in it will have no impact on their lives. In general, the feeling one gets is of some detachment from the events in which he participates, and this could be read as a metaphor for 'Anglo-Irish solitude'.

# Easter 1916

Text of poem: New Explorations Anthology page 148

On Monday 24 April 1916 a force of about seven hundred members of the Irish Volunteers and the Irish Citizen Army took over the centre of Dublin in a military revolution and held out for six days against the British army.

At first the rising did not receive widespread support; but the British military authorities regarded it as high treason in time of war, and the subsequent systematic executions of fifteen of the leaders between 3 and 12 May brought a wave of public sympathy and created heroes and martyrs for the republican cause.

Though Yeats's poem was finished by September 1916 and a number of copies had been printed privately, it was not published until October 1920, when it appeared in the *New Statesman*. It is included in the volume *Michael Robartes and the Dancer* (1921).

## THE NATIONAL QUESTION: YEATS'S POLITICAL VIEWS

Yeats spent a good deal of his time in England during his early life, but he felt that the English understanding of the Irish was stereotypical and condescending. One of his main ambitions was to help change Ireland's view of itself through a revival of its unique cultural identity. He had denounced the English government of Ireland, and his refusal of a knighthood in 1915 is a statement of his political stance. Yet his view did not prevent him living there, and indeed he was in England when the Easter Rising took place.

This ambiguity was further complicated by Yeats's arrogant and scathing dismissal of the current generation of Irish people as ignoble, self-focused, materialistic and priest-controlled, who were totally incapable of the idealism or courage necessary for heroic leadership and personal sacrifice. These views he had expressed very trenchantly in 'September 1913'.

The Rising took Yeats by surprise and blew some serious holes in his thinking. Firstly, he now had to rethink his public stance and views on the new Irish middle class. These people had been prepared to give their lives for an ideal. Yeats had been quite wrong. Secondly, though he was disgusted, like most people, at the savagery of the executions, he began to realise that the establishment's brutality had created martyrs, had transformed ordinary men into patriots with a strange new unchallengeable power. Perhaps Pearse's idea of a blood sacrifice was correct. Yeats had to rethink the place and value of revolutionary determination. So Yeats had to work out how this cataclysmic change had occurred in Irish society – 'all changed, changed utterly'.

## A READING OF THE POEM

Though it may not appear on the surface to be a questioning poem, this work is really an attempt to answer or clarify a great number of questions that the 1916 Rising stirred up in Yeats's mind, an attempt to come to terms with:
- how everything had changed
- how wrong he had been
- how ordinary people had been changed into heroes
- the deep structure of change in society, the mysterious process, a kind of fate that directed and powered change (Terence Brown puts it eloquently: 'It seeks to penetrate beneath the appearance of history to comprehend the mysteries of destiny.')
- the place and functioning of revolutionary violence in the process

- the change in his own position: how to resolve his own complex and contradictory feelings towards this violent process.

The diplomatic difficulty of having to recant his views on Irish society Yeats faced honestly and generously in the first section of this poem. Technically he achieved this by structuring the poem as a *palinode* or recantation of his opinions in the earlier 'September 1913'. Re-creating the drab, unexciting milieu of pre-revolution evenings, the poet acknowledges his own blindness and failure to engage with these people in any depth:

> I have passed with a nod of the head
> Or polite meaningless words,
> Or have lingered a while and said
> Polite meaningless words,

He confesses to his own unpleasant, condescending mockery ('a mocking tale or a gibe …') and his belief that all the pre-1916 organising was mere comical posturing:

> Being certain that they and I
> But lived where motley is worn …

He includes himself ('they and I') in this attempt at identification.

He spends the second section looking again at these people that he knew, as he needs to understand how they have changed. They are still the flawed characters he remembers: Constance Markievicz wasted her time in misplaced volunteer work ('ignorant good-will') and became a shrill fanatic ('nights in argument … voice grew shrill'); MacBride he thought 'a drunken vainglorious lout' who 'had done most bitter wrong' to Maud Gonne and Iseult. These are very ordinary, fallible, flawed and unlikely heroes.

Furthermore, the impression Yeats perceives is not one of energetically active heroes, but rather the passive recipients of this mysterious change. MacDonagh 'might have won fame in the end'. MacBride 'has resigned his part | In the casual comedy'. This smacks of an unknown actor giving up his part in an inconsequential work. The impression given is of relatively insignificant lives, out of which MacBride 'has been changed in his turn'. Note the passive voice: the change was effected on him, rather than by something he did, and it happened 'in his turn'. He waited his turn – perhaps a reference to the executions. Is Yeats saying that it was the executions that effected this change, transformed everyone utterly, and gave birth to this terrible beauty? That it was not due to the nature or any action of heroes?

Another aspect of these patriots that Yeats refers to is their feminine qualities. 'What voice more sweet' than Constance Gore-Booth's (in younger days)? MacDonagh's thought is 'daring and sweet'. Even MacBride has his passive side. So there is a sensitivity about these people that balances their more aggressive and masculine qualities, also referred to.

It is this softer, feminine quality in man and woman that is destroyed by fanaticism, something Yeats explores in the third and fourth sections. But first it is worth noticing the feminine aspect of the new order. This utter transformation of the social and historical reality is imagined as a new birth; but Yeats is so disturbed and confused by it that he can only describe it in paradoxical terms as a 'terrible beauty' – something that is partly feminine, aesthetically pleasing, sexually alluring even, but also carries suggestions of terror and of destructive power. This magnificent image carries all Yeats's confusions and contradictory feelings about the dramatic change.

In the third section he explores how change is effected. Only a stone, usually taken as a metaphor for the fanatical heart, can change or trouble the course of a stream, and it can achieve this only at a price. The heart will lose its humanness:

> Too long a sacrifice
> Can make a stone of the heart.

In the 1909 *Journals* Yeats had already written about the effects of political fanaticism on Maud Gonne, in metaphors akin to those used here:

> Women, because the main event of their lives has been a giving of themselves, give themselves to an opinion as if it were some terrible stone doll ... They grow cruel, as if in defence of lover or child and all this is done for something other than human life. At last the opinion becomes so much a part of them that it is as though a part of their flesh becomes, as it were, stone, and much of their being passes out of life.

In this third section Yeats is exploring the dangers of fanatical devotion to a cause or ideal, and he represents this metaphorically as the conflicting forces between a stone and a stream.

The living stream is marvellously evoked. It is a picture of constant change, the flux of natural life and bursting with energy. The seasons are changing 'through summer and winter'; the skies change 'from cloud to tumbling cloud'; all is life and regeneration, as 'hens to moor-cocks call'. It is full of transient animal and human appearances, as they slide or plash or dive. And all this activity happens 'minute by minute'. Against this stream of ever-changing energy and life is set the unmoving stone, the fanatical heart. It is not difficult to conclude that the weight of the poet's sentiment is with the living stream rather than the unmoving stone. And yet out of this confrontation is born the 'terrible beauty'.

There is no easy answer to the conflicts posed by the poet. And indeed he seems to weary of the dialogue and of this dialectic in the fourth section. Having concluded that prolonged devotion to an ideal is dehumanising –

> Too long a sacrifice
> Can make a stone of the heart.

– he seems to accept the necessity of it and at the same time wishes for an end, in that sighing plea: 'O when may it suffice?'

The first seventeen lines of this fourth section are structured in questions – rhetorical questions, or questions that cannot be answered – thereby revealing the poet's uncertainties about the validity of the entire process of revolution and change. There is a kind of shocked vulnerability about the poetic voice here, a realisation of helplessness as all the doubts flood in with the questions: Are they really dead? Was it necessary if England intended to grant home rule after the war? What if they were just confused and bewildered by an excess of patriotism? There is an awareness that some things cannot be answered, that some of this mysterious dynamic of change cannot be understood – 'That is Heaven's part.' And the poet adopts a soothing mother's voice and persona, murmuring 'As a mother names her child'.

But then he seems to shake off the uncertain and shocked voice and finds a new assurance for that very definite confident ending. Why is this? Terence Brown believes it has to do with the magical significance of the poem, deliberately created by Yeats. He suggests that the poem is a 'numerological artefact', based on the date when the rising began: 24 April 1916. There are four movements or sections, with the following numbers of lines in each: 16, 24, 16, 24. It is suggested also that Yeats intended this to be a verse of power, a magical recitation, seen in for example 'I number him in the song'; 'I write it out in a verse.' Certainly there is a surge of powerful assurance in those final lines, whether we read them as a litany of respectful remembrance or an occult incantation.

> I write it out in a verse –
> MacDonagh and MacBride
> And Connolly and Pearse
> Now and in time to be,
> Wherever green is worn,
> Are changed, changed utterly:
> A terrible beauty is born.

# *The Second Coming*

Text of poem: New Explorations Anthology page 154

This poem was finished in January 1919, to a background of great political upheaval in Europe: the disintegration of the Austro-Hungarian, German and Russian empires, and uprisings and revolution in Germany and Russia. The events in Europe are most likely to have prompted the speculation that 'mere anarchy is loosed upon the world'; but as the poem was not published for twenty-two months, in the *Dial* of November 1920, it came to be read as a reaction to the atrocities of the War of Independence in Ireland. It is included in the volume *Michael Robartes and the Dancer* (1921).

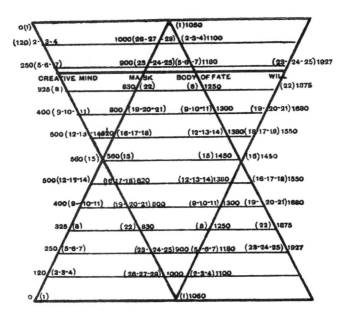

## YEATS'S OCCULT PHILOSOPHY AND THEORIES OF HISTORY

Yeats was deeply interested in the patterns of history. He was also engaged in the study and practice of the occult and maintained regular contact with the spirits. These 'spirit communicators' helped him develop a cyclical theory of change in history, which is outlined in *A Vision* (1925). He used geometrical forms to express abstract ideas; and the concept of 'gyres' or cones representing time zones is one of these. In this poem the reference is to a single gyre or inverted cone. But the full representation of the gyres consists of two interpenetrating cones, expanding and contracting on a single axis. These represent the contrary forces, always changing, that determine the character of a person or the culture of a particular phase in history. There are particularly significant moments both for individuals and in historical time when the dominant influence passes from one gyre to its contrary. In history, he believed, this can happen every two thousand years. Hence the reference to 'twenty centuries of stony sleep' that preceded the Christian era, which is now waning and giving way to a new and antithetical era.

In its Christian interpretation, the 'Second Coming' refers to the prediction of the second coming of Christ; in Yeats's occult and magical philosophy it might also refer to the second birth of the Avatar or great antithetical spirit, which Yeats and his wife felt certain would be reincarnated as their baby son, whose birth was imminent. In fact the child turned out to be a girl, dashing that theory.

In this poem the hideous 'rough beast' that 'slouches towards Bethlehem to be born' is suggestive of the Anti-Christ, that legendary personal opponent of Christ and his kingdom expected to appear before the end of the world. See, for example, the Book of Revelations (chapter 13) on the portents for the end of the world:

> And I saw a beast rising out of the sea, with ten horns and seven heads, with ten diadems upon its horns and a blasphemous name upon its heads. And the beast that I saw was like a leopard, its feet were like a bear's, and its mouth was like a lion's mouth. And to it the dragon gave his power and his throne and great authority. One of its heads seemed to have a mortal wound, but its mortal wound was healed, and the whole earth followed the beast with wonder. Men worshipped the dragon, for he had given his authority to the beast, and they worshipped the beast, saying, 'Who is like the beast and who can fight against it?'

A READING OF THE POEM

This poem reflects Yeats's interest in historical change and his real fear that civilisation would break down and be replaced by an anti-civilisation or an era of anarchy. This was sparked off in part by his disgust and revulsion at what was happening in European politics and history around this time (1919). But, as we have seen, he was also preoccupied with patterns in history and immersed himself in the occult, with signs, portents, astrological charts and spirit communicators, and had developed a cyclical theory of change in history, which was represented graphically by the 'gyre' symbol.

So this poem deals with the turbulence of historical change; but what is particularly exciting is the enormous perspective that the poet takes. Time is not counted in years or decades but in millennia; and it is this vast perspective that is both exhilarating and terrifying.

## First section

Essentially what is happening here is that Yeats is exploring the breakup of civilisation in metaphorical language. The falcon, that trained bird of prey, cannot hear the falconer and is reverting to its wild state. The falconer has also been interpreted as a representation of Christ, and so the image has been read as representing the movement of civilisation away from Christ. This dissipation is happening within the framework of its allotted time span, at a point within the gyre, representing the present. Yeats is bringing a critical philosophical viewpoint to bear on the social and political structures. He suggests that there is failure at the very heart of society, presumably in human beings themselves: 'things fall apart; the centre cannot hold. Instead of clear-sighted vision and forward progress there is this confusing circular movement, an out-of-control centrifugal force that threatens to send everything spinning away in disorder. In this chaos human beings are changing, becoming ignoble and destroying innocence: 'The ceremony of innocence is drowned.' People either have no convictions at all or are irrationally and passionately committed to causes; they have become either cynics or fanatics.

> The best lack all conviction, while the worst
> Are full of passionate intensity.

This first section embodies this very tension in its structure. Consider how the ideas are set up as opposites: centre – fall apart; falcon – falconer; indifference – intensity; innocence – anarchy. This polar oppositional tension is seen in the terrifying image of 'the blood-dimmed tide … loosed … innocence is drowned.' This sinister image has connotations of the great flood and its destruction of the world, but might also suggest a ruthless cleansing or purging. The repetition of 'loosed upon' and 'loosed' might suggest a savage wild animal, at the very least the 'dogs of war'. The circular imagery creates a sense of continuous swirling movement. Look at the repetition of *-ing*: 'turning, turning, widening'. There is a sense of a world out of control, of inevitable disaster.

Really it is the force of the imagery that carries the ideas in this section. Consider the falconry image. This was the pastime of kings and lords, so the image carries associations of an aristocratic life, civilised living, affluence. We know how much Yeats valued civilised living. Falconry was a 'noble' pastime, requiring skill and patience. Now this trained bird of prey is reverting to its wild state – a metaphor for the destruction of civilised living. It would also carry religious overtones and signal the breakdown of ordered religious systems. The falcon has also been interpreted as symbolic of the active or intellectual mind, so the breakdown of intellectual order might be signalled as well. Either way the image suggests dissolution in a number of different spheres and levels.

The second graphic image, of the 'blood-dimmed tide', has already been explored for its layers of suggestiveness. Its general impact is powerful, both visually and intellectually: innocence is drowned in a sea of blood. This is the ultimate nihilism, a world without justice, reason or order. Note Yeats's emphasis on the 'ceremony' of innocence. The rituals of civilised living will also be destroyed, of course.

The final image of the section, though somewhat ill defined, is a political one, suggesting that fanatical people have now got all the influence and are in power. The general impact of the imagery is one of frightening and irrational disorder and breakup in life and society.

## Second section

Yeats begins by casting around for a reason for the breakdown of civilisation, and the possibility of a second coming together with the end of the world suggests itself as the only one great enough to cause this. 'Surely the Second Coming is at hand.' But it turns out not to be the Second Coming of Christ as foretold in the Gospels but rather the emergence of the Anti-Christ that Yeats imagines, an Anti-Christ who embodies the absolute reverse of the Christian era, which is now drawing to its end in the gyre of time. This rough beast, a nightmare symbol of the coming times, signals the end of this era, with its values and order.

Again, the image of this rough beast carries all the ideas about the new era. It is a 'vast image', overwhelming and troubling. It is a horrific hybrid of human and animal – suggesting unnatural times, such as foretold in the Book of Revelations. Its blank gaze suggests no intelligent sight or understanding; indeed it is as 'pitiless as the sun', incapable of empathy or feeling. The qualities it conjures up are gracelessness and brutishness: 'moving its slow thighs ... Slouches towards Bethlehem to be born'. The final paradox is explained by the fact that its era has already begun, overlapping with the demise of the Christian era, so it is moving into position to initiate the new age or be born. The paradox further emphasises the antithetical nature of the coming age: how totally contradictory or opposite it is. There is something blasphemously shocking in the idea of the beast being born at Bethlehem. The nugget of insight gained by the poet out of this horrific vision concerns the nature of time and changing eras. He realises that eras have come and gone before, and that the advent of the Christian era must have been as troubling to the previous age.

> Now I know
> That twenty centuries of stony sleep
> Were vexed to nightmare by a rocking cradle.

# Sailing to Byzantium

Text of poem: New Explorations Anthology page 156

This poem was written some time in the autumn of 1926 and is the opening poem in the collection *The Tower* (1928).

## A READING OF THE POEM

Writing for a radio programme in 1931, Yeats outlined some of the preoccupations of his poetry at that time, in particular the spiritual quest of 'Sailing to Byzantium':

> Now I am trying to write about the state of my soul, for it is right for an old man to make his soul [an expression meaning to prepare for death], and some of my thoughts upon that subject I have put into a poem called 'Sailing to Byzantium'. When Irishmen were illuminating the Book of Kells and making the jewelled crosiers of the National Museum, Byzantium was the centre of European civilisation and the source of its spiritual philosophy, so I symbolise the search for the spiritual life by a journey to that city.

So this poem is structured, as he says, in the shape of a journey – more of a quest, really – with a tightly argued personal commentary by the poet. The main theme surfaces immediately in the first stanza. With that strong, declamatory opening he renounces the world of the senses for that of the spirit and the intellect, the timeless.

> That is no country for old men. The young
> In one another's arms ...

Notice the perspective ('that'): he has already departed and is looking back, not without a little nostalgic yearning for the sensuality of youth. The sensual imagery of lovers and the teeming rich life of trees and seas, the athletic vigour of the hyphenated words ('the salmon-falls, the mackerel-crowded seas') and the sensual 'f' and 's' sounds of 'fish, flesh or fowl' – all used to describe the cycle of life in the flesh – would strongly suggest that he does not renounce it easily. Indeed this ambiguity is carried in the paradox of 'those dying generations', with its linking of death and regeneration.

The importance of the spirit is re-emphasised in the second stanza as the poet asserts that it is the soul that gives meaning to a person: 'An aged man is but a paltry thing ... unless | Soul clap its hands and sing.' And art enriches the soul, teaches it to sing: 'studying | Monuments of its own magnificence,' i.e.

works of art inspired by the spirit. Byzantium, as a centre of religion, philosophy and learning and also of a highly formalised art, is the ideal destination for the intellectual and spiritual person. In 'A Vision' (1925) Yeats wrote about the harmoniousness of life in fifth-century Byzantium: 'I think that in early Byzantium, maybe never before or since in recorded history, religious, aesthetic and practical life were one.' He had visited Ravenna in 1907 and when he composed the third stanza probably had in mind a mosaic on the wall of S. Apollinore Nuova showing martyrs being burnt in a fire.

Addressing these sages or martyrs directly in the third stanza, he entreats them to traverse history in the gyre of time, come to him and teach his soul to sing. He wants them to 'make' his soul, as he said, to purify it, separate it from emotions and desires and help it transcend the ageing physical body:

> Consume my heart away; sick with desire
> And fastened to a dying animal
> It knows not what it is …

These lines betray a seriously troubled state of mind. Central to the conflict is a dualist view of the human being as composed of two radically different and warring elements: body, and soul or spirit. Yeats values one element – the soul – imaged as singer and bird but is filled with self-disgust and loathing for his ageing body, imaged as a dying animal, not even dignified as human, that has entrapped the soul.

This confusion is evident even in the ambiguity of language here, in for example 'sick with desire'. Is he sick because of the desires of the flesh he cannot shake off, or does the desire refer to his spiritual aspiration, which continues to elude him? This acute existential conflict has led to a loss of spiritual identity: 'It knows not what it is'; hence his emotional entreaty to the sages to 'gather me | Into the artifice of eternity'.

It is worth exploring the richness of this ordinary language here. By using 'gather me' the poet is acknowledging how fragmented and scattered his condition is and how he needs both direction and comfort; it is as if he needs to be embraced, gathered in arms. Ironically, he wants to be gathered into the coherence and timelessness of art – 'the artifice of eternity'. It is through this transition that he will find immortality. But the language carries hints of ambiguity, even about this much-desired goal. 'Artifice' refers primarily to a work of art, but it can also mean 'artificiality'. Is this the first hint that this great quest might be flawed?

Still he begins the fourth stanza with great confidence that art holds the answer to the problem of mortality. 'Once out of nature' he will be transformed into the perfect work of art and so live on. The golden bird is ageless and incorruptible and will sing the song of the soul. The final irony, though, is that the song it sings is about the flux of time, 'what is past, or passing, or to come'. There is no perfect solution after all.

## THEMES AND ISSUES

Discuss these and see if you can justify each from the evidence of the poem.

- Yeats in old age is attempting to develop his spiritual side. It is a poem about the values of the soul as against the world of the senses.
- It is an attempt to escape the harsh reality of old age and death through the immortality of spiritual things and of art.
- The view of the human being portrayed is that of a fractured, divided entity in an uncomfortable state of war between the spiritual and the physical.
- It is a meditation on the nature of art and its importance to humanity.
- It delivers fine insights into the nature of Byzantine imagination and culture.

## STRUCTURE

As befits the theme of conflict, the ideas and images in this poem are developed in a series of *antinomies* or contrasts. In the very first line youth and age are set opposite each other: 'That is no country for old men ...' While youth is imaged in those wonderful scenes of sensuous life in the first stanza, age is realised in the scarecrow image – 'a tattered coat upon a stick' – with all its suggestions of fake outward show, a grotesque parody of the human being and the sense of powerlessness and indignity. The body is imaged as a dying animal, while the soul is imaged as a priceless golden bird, singing.

The mortality of life is contrasted with the timelessness of art. The teeming sensuality of Ireland is set against the culture of Byzantium, with its religious ethos ('holy city'; 'God's holy fire'), its reputation for learning and philosophical thought ('O sages'), and its artistic achievement ('artifice'; 'a form as Grecian goldsmiths make | Of hammered gold and gold enamelling', etc.). These conflicts reflect the internal struggle, the yearnings and the reality within the poetic persona here.

Yet the struggle is smoothed over by the grace and elegance of the language used. There is a regular pattern of end-rhymes or sometimes half-rhymes, which gives the verses a musical ease. Yeats also uses a rhythmic phrasing, often grouping in lists of three, which has magical significance as well as producing a rhythmic rise and fall: 'fish, flesh, or fowl'; 'Whatever is begotten, born, and dies'; 'unless | Soul clap its hands and sing, and louder sing'; 'Of what is past, or passing, or to come'. We might also notice other rhetorical qualities, such as the strong, declamatory opening, the rhetorical plea to the sages, indeed the strong, confident, first-person voice of the poet all through. These sometimes belie the conflicts and uncertainties at the heart of the work.

## *The Stare's Nest by My Window*
Text of poem: New Explorations Anthology page 160

FROM 'MEDITATIONS IN TIME OF CIVIL WAR'

'Meditations in Time of Civil War' is quite a lengthy poem, structured in seven sections. Apart from the first, composed in England in 1921, it was written in Ireland during the Civil War of 1922–23 and was first published in the *Dell* in January 1923. It is included in the volume *The Tower* (1928).

In the poem as a whole, Yeats explores aspects of the Anglo-Irish ascendancy tradition: its origins and heritage and his own sense of sharing in the values of that tradition, particularly those of continuity, culture, and family line. Conflict too was a necessary element of that planter culture, and now he is brought face to face with the violence of the Civil War and must re-evaluate his own role in the continuing tradition of history.

Images of houses and building provide one of the unifying metaphors and themes throughout this poem. Yeats acknowledges the violence out of which the great Anglo-Irish culture was built:

> Some violent bitter man, some powerful man
> Called architect and artist in, that they,
> Bitter and violent men, might rear in stone
> The sweetness that all longed for night and day.

His own house in Co. Galway, Thoor Ballylee, was originally a defensive fifteenth-century tower. He acknowledges proudly that conflict is part of his tradition; he wishes that his descendants too will find 'befitting emblems of adversity'. So in section V, when a band of Irregulars calls to his door, he experiences a certain envy of the men of action. Perhaps it is the graphic details of that war in section VI that led to a reappraisal. The terrifying vision of the nightmarish destruction of civilisation in section VII throws him back to thinking on his own role as poet in his isolated tower.

Yeats wrote the following description of the genesis and context of section VI:

> I was in my Galway house during the first months of civil war, the railway bridges blown up and the roads blocked with stones and trees. For the first week there were no newspapers, no reliable news, we did not know who had won nor who had lost, and even after newspapers

came, one never knew what was happening on the other side of the hill or of the line of trees. Ford cars passed the house from time to time with coffins standing upon end between the seats, and sometimes at night we heard an explosion, and once by day saw the smoke made by the burning of a great neighbouring house. Men must have lived so through many tumultuous centuries. One felt an overmastering desire not to grow unhappy or embittered, not to lose all sense of the beauty of nature. A stare (our West of Ireland name for a starling) had built in a hole beside my window and I made these verses out of the feeling of the moment ... [here he quoted from 'The bees build in the crevices' to 'Yet no clear fact to be discerned: come build in the empty house of the stare.'] ... That is only the beginning but it runs on in the same mood. Presently a strange thing happened. I began to smell honey in places where honey could not be, at the end of a stone passage or at some windy turn of the road, and it came always with certain thoughts. When I got back to Dublin I was with angry people who argued over everything or were eager to know the exact facts: in the midst of the mood that makes realistic drama. (From *The Bounty of Sweden*)

A READING OF THE POEM

At one level, this poem is an attempt to balance the horrors of war with the healing sweetness and regenerative power of nature. As Yeats himself saw it, 'Men must have lived so through many tumultuous centuries. One felt an overmastering desire not to grow unhappy or embittered, not to lose all sense of the beauty of nature.' The brutality of war is graphically represented here:

Last night they trundled down the road
That dead young soldier in his blood ...

The onomatopoeic sound of 'trundled' carries suggestions of some primitive war machine or evokes the tumbrels and savage excess of the French Revolution. There is none of the traditional respect for a dead enemy here, but rather the ferocity of civil war enmity in the indignity with which the dead solder was treated – 'trundled ... in his blood'. The bees are evoked as an antidote to this savagery. They may symbolise patience and creative force, as opposed to the destructive forces round about. They bring sweetness, healing and the richness of life. These may also be a classical allusion to Pomphyry's bees, who visited the world to perform tasks for the gods. So the bees could be seen as a manifestation of the divine in the world. Whether they evoked for Yeats the simple beauty of nature or carried more complex connotations, his plea to them is a desperate plaintive cry. That cry for healing and for natural regeneration of life echoes through that repeated refrain at the end of each stanza, culminating in the final direct personal address, 'O honey-bees'. There is honest emotion here.

But this is more than simply a reaction to a specific event. Taken in the context of the poem as a whole, we could read this section as a metaphor for Yeats's own life situation and that of his traditional class, the Anglo-Irish ascendancy. The tower-house, once a fortified planter house, used as a place of both safety and dominance, is now a place of 'loosening masonry'; the structures of that colonial past are crumbling. The Yeatses' isolation in the tower during that particular fortnight is symptomatic of the isolation and uncertain future of the entire minority but once-powerful class.

> We are closed in, and the key is turned
> On our uncertainty.

This is not just physical imprisonment but a mental segregation, a way of viewing themselves as different, distinct and separate – a cultivated isolation. The key has been turned from the inside. The physical barriers of stone or wood accord with the mental barriers created by class and outlook, so that we are acutely aware of how introverted and cut off the poet is. Yet there is a hint in the first stanza that some sweetness can come with the ending of his self-isolation:

> My wall is loosening; honey-bees,
> Come build in the empty house of the stare,

Or is this just a vain hope?

In the final stanza he faces up to the illusions on which his philosophy is based and which are explored in the rest of the poem: that sweetness and beauty might grow out of bitter and violent conquest, that conflict and a life of adversity could be a glorious thing. These are the fantasies that sustain his class outlook and for which he now indicts himself. The consequence has not been beauty but self-brutalisation.

> The heart's grown brutal from the fare.

He strips away any delusions of superiority or righteousness as he admits that negative emotions are strongest.

> More substance in our enmities
> Than in our love.

It is as if the violence outside has forced him to confront the past violence of his own class, in an honest moment of shared guilt. This is a critical moment of bleak insight, yet one that he attempts to balance with the final plea: 'O honey-bees' – a plea for sweetness and healing at a time of pain, for order in a time of chaos.

IMAGERY

Images of houses and buildings dominate this poem; but they are either abandoned, like the house of stone, or destroyed by violence ('a house burned'), or are gradually crumbling away in time ('loosening masonry'; 'My wall is crumbling'). They are symbols of a way of life being destroyed; or else they are isolating and self-imprisoning:

> We are closed in, the key is turned
> On our uncertainty.

Any building done is for destructive and disorderly purpose: 'A barricade of stone or wood'. So the poet's plea, while romantic and positive in outlook, is rather pathetic in the context. Only the bees and birds may build where the once-powerful colonising class raised great edifices.

# *In Memory of Eva Gore-Booth and Con Markiewicz*

Text of poem: New Explorations Anthology page 162

This poem was written in the autumn of 1927, was first published in 1929, and is included in *The Winding Stair and Other Poems* (1933). Constance Markievicz had died in August 1927, her sister Eva the previous year.

A READING OF THE POEM

This is one of Yeats's poems of age, the reverie of an old man addressing the now-dead companions of his youth: 'Dear shadows ...' It is very much a retrospective piece, viewing life from the perspective of the end. Yeats avoids sentimentality, opting instead for retrospective judgments, assessing the significance of their lives. He felt that they had wasted their lives. Constance Markievicz's years of political agitation for socialist and republican ideals he dismisses as dragging out lonely years – 'Conspiring among the ignorant' – while Eva's social and women's suffrage work is merely 'some vague Utopia'.

To understand this harsh condemnation of what to us seem idealistic and committed lives we need to take the poet's value system into account. His view was that the Anglo-Irish ascendancy class, with its wealth and great houses, had a duty to set an example of gracious and cultured living; this was its value for society. As the critic Alasdair MacRae says, 'The graciousness of accustomed affluence, the unostentatiousness of inherited furnishings and family traditions, what he saw culminating in courtesy, appealed to Yeats and he considered Eva and Con along with Maud Gonne as betraying something precious and feminine.' Yeats's idea of beauty is linked to the feminine. The image of feminine beauty he creates here is exotic. The silk kimonos give a hint of eastern mysteriousness, while the comparison with a gazelle suggests both a natural elegance and a certain wild, unknowable quality. And the two sisters are a decorative part of the big-house scene, a house that is elegant, imposing, a symbol of Anglo-Irish achievement and cultured way of life. It is primarily this image and what it symbolised that Yeats is nostalgic for: it is not the people he missed in the first instance but the house and the cultured dinner-table conversation!

> Many a time I think to seek
> One or the other out and speak
> Of that old Georgian mansion, mix
> Pictures of the mind, recall
> That table and the talk of youth ...

Yeats's negative retrospective judgments are not so much the bitter rantings of an old man but rather what he saw as a failure to fulfil an inherited role in society.

But this has some of the more usual features of an 'age' poem – the contrast of youth and age. The 'two girls in silk kimonos ... one a gazelle' become 'withered old and skeleton-gaunt'. It is interesting that old bodies are rarely beautiful for Yeats: he is repelled and disgusted by physical ageing. We are made aware of the ravages of time very early on in the poem, right after the first four lines of that beautiful limpid opening, and it comes as quite a shocking contrast:

> But a raving autumn shears
> Blossom from the summer's wreath.

Autumn is 'raving', mad, hysterical, out of control, and the sharp-edged onomatopoeic sound of 'shears' conveys its deadly potential. Even summer carries the seeds of death in its 'wreath'.

Out of this retrospection Yeats attempts to distil a certain wisdom about life. This philosophy he sets down in the second section. In a more kindly address to the 'dear shadows' he presumes they now agree with him about the vanity of all causes and all zeal, irrespective of rightness:

All the folly of a fight
With a common wrong or right.

And, secondly, he knows that the great quarrel is with time, destroyer of innocence and beauty. He reflects on the vanity of it all, as it will end in a great apocalyptic conflagration, which will consume not just all they've built – great houses or mere gazebos – but all the anguished decisions of their lives. All is vanity before the end.

## TONE

At times he manages to be gently nostalgic, such as at the beginning and end of the first section. But he can be very censorious about lives wasted in political agitation. And he seems quite excited by the possibility of the great final conflagration. This is communicated by the energy and repetition of strong verbs (strike, strike, climb, run) and by the repetition of phrases ('strike a match').

## THEMES AND ISSUES

- What is a worthwhile way to live life?
- The vagaries of life, the imperfections
- Is it all vanity? What is the point of it all?
- The real enemy is time.
- Contrasting youth and age.

## RHYMES AND RHYTHMS

Though Yeats imposes a quatrain rhyming scheme, *abba,* on the poem, he does not structure the thought in quatrains, apart from the first four lines. The first section, for instance, is structured periodically in groups of 4, 5, 4, 7. So the thought structure provides a sort of counter-rhythm to the rhyming structure and gives it a conversational naturalness.

This naturalness is emphasised by the use of off-rhymes rather than full rhymes, for example south – both, wreath – death, ignorant – gaunt, recall – gazelle. Some could argue that the imperfect rhyme befits the theme – the imperfections of life. The rhythmic quality of the language is achieved partly through repetitions: repetitions of phrases such as 'And bid me strike a match', but more obviously with the repetition of the well-known refrain 'Two girls ...' However, the tone of the second repetition differs markedly from the first, because of the context, where it now carries all the bleak irony and the disappointment of hindsight.

The structure of this poem is almost unnoticed, so deftly is it done. It opens with 'The light of evening', proceeds to the darkness of 'Dear Shadows', and erupts again into the final apocalyptic inferno of the end of time. It begins with youth and ends with death; it opens with the great house of Lissadell and ends with a fragile gazebo.

## Swift's Epitaph

Text of poem: New Explorations Anthology page 166

[Note: This poem is also prescribed for Ordinary Level 2005 exam]

Begun in 1929 and finished in September 1930, this was first published in the *Dublin Magazine* in the winter of 1931. It is included in the volume *The Winding Stair and Other Poems* (1933). The poem is essentially a translation, with some alterations, of the Latin epitaph on Jonathan Swift's memorial in St Patrick's Cathedral, Dublin.

Hic depositum est Corpus
JONATHAN SWIFT S.T.D.
Hujus Ecclesiae Cathedralis
Decani,
Ubi saeva Indignatio
Ulterius
Cor lacerare nequit.
Abi Viator
Et imitare, si poteris,
Strenuum pro virili
Libertatis vindicatorem.
Obiit 19º Die Mensis Octobris
A.D. 1745. Anno Aetatis 78º.

Here is laid the body of
JONATHAN SWIFT, doctor of sacred theology,
dean of this cathedral church,
where savage indignation
can no longer
rend his heart.
Go, traveller,
and imitate, if you can,
an earnest and dedicated
champion of liberty.

He died on the nineteenth day of October
AD 1745, in the year of his age 78.

Jonathan Swift (1667–1745) was dean of St Patrick's Cathedral, Dublin. Poet, political pamphleteer and satirist, he was the author of such famous works as *The Drapier's Letters, A Modest Proposal, A Tale of a Tub,* and *Gulliver's Travels.* Politically conservative, Swift voiced the concerns and values of Protestant Ireland with an independence of spirit and a courage that Yeats admired greatly. Swift's writing made him enemies on all sides, but this isolation endeared him even further to Yeats, who often spoke admiringly of 'Anglo-Irish solitude'. Yeats thought of Swift as a heroic figure, an artist – philosopher who, despite the conflicts of his personal life, served liberty by speaking out in his writings and freeing the artist from the tyranny of the mob. He ranked Swift together with Berkeley, Goldsmith and Burke as one of the intellectual founders of the Anglo-Irish tradition.

Yeats's play *The Words upon the Window Pane* (1930) explores some of the conflicts of Swift's life.

A FREE TRANSLATION

Among the chief interests of the Yeats poem are the significance of the changes he made. For instance, 'Swift has sailed into his rest' is much more confident, energetic and vigorous than the original. It sounds more like a victorious progress, while being at the same time a gentle and graceful journey. There are also clearer overtones of a spiritual afterlife – 'his rest' – where the original merely notes the depositing of the body!

He retains the famous reference to *'saeva indignatio'* (savage indignation), which was the driving force of Swift's satirical work, and the reference to his capacity for empathy and for being affected by the injustices and miseries he encountered ('cannot lacerate his breast'). The challenge to the observer is stronger than in the original – to imitate him 'if you dare' rather than 'if you can'. And the traveller is described as 'world-besotted', worldly, lacking in spiritual values and outlook. The implication may be to enhance, by contrast, the unworldly qualities of Swift (which would be somewhat at variance with the facts). Yeats also retains the epithet noting Swift's defence of liberty, a philosophy they shared.

In general it might be said that Yeats has nudged the epitaph more in the direction of a eulogy. And there is more transparent emotion and admiration in the Yeats version.

# An Acre of Grass

Text of poem: New Explorations Anthology page 168

This poem was written in November 1936 and first published in *New Poems* (1938).

A READING OF THE POEM

This poem is quite a remarkable response to old age and thoughts of death. The first stanza captures the shrinkage of an old person's physical world in the twilight years. With the ebbing of physical strength his world is reduced to the gardens of his house, 'an acre of green grass | For air and exercise'. The final two lines of the stanza are a marvellous evocation of the stillness, isolation and sense of emptiness that can be experienced at night by the wakeful elderly, a feeling carried in part by the broad vowel rhymes 'house – mouse':

> Midnight, an old house
> Where nothing stirs but a mouse.

He could easily resign himself to restfulness and silence. 'My temptation is quiet.'

But this old man, this poet, needs to write, to continue to find new truths, and he knows that neither a 'loose imagination' – an imagination that is not disciplined by the structure of writing – nor any ordinary observation of everyday occurrences will deliver up any significant truths.

> Nor the mill of the mind
> Consuming its rag and bone,
> Can make truth known.

Real creativity needs something more, like mystical insight; and that comes only through really passionate endeavour or frenzy. Hence his prayer, 'Grant me an old man's frenzy.' That frenzy or madness produced insight and truth for King Lear at the end of his life; and mystical visions, which some interpret as madness, produced the beautiful wisdom of William Blake's poetry. Even at the end of his life, Yeats knows the huge transforming energy necessary to forge new insights and truths, and he faces up to it.

> Myself I must remake

What courage for a person in his seventies!

Yeats had been reading Nietzsche's *The Dawn of Day*, about people of genius who can distance themselves from character and temperament and rise above the weight of personality like a winged creature. Yeats had used Nietzsche's ideas to develop his theory of the Mask: he felt the need to continually transform himself. And this is the ideology driving this poem – the need for transformation in order to achieve new insights and truths. So the poet must discard the persona of dignified old man and remake himself as a wild, mad prophet-like figure, such as Timon or Lear or Blake, and that will bring the searing vision, the 'eagle mind' 'that can pierce the clouds'. This is a poet's fighting response to old age and approaching death. It may remind us of Dylan Thomas's later 'Rage, rage against the dying of the light.'

THEMES AND ISSUES

Explore the following ideas, and expand on each with reference to what you find in the poem.

- A response to ageing: refusing to accept a quiet retirement; summoning reserves of energy to continue working; aware of the huge demands, yet praying for the chance.
- The process of creativity: the ordinary imagination processing or milling everyday events is not sufficient; a frenzy or madness is necessary in order to see things differently or see into things; the after-truths or insights are all-consuming; the power of that insight can 'pierce the clouds' and 'shake the dead'.
- The poet's need for continued transformation. Is it comfortable being a poet? Is it worth it?

# *Politics*

Text of poem: New Explorations Anthology page 170

A READING OF THE POEM

We know that Yeats had intended that the volume *Last Poems* should end with 'Politics'. It is suggested that it was written as an answer to an article that had praised Yeats for his public language but suggested that he should use it more on political subjects. If so, then this is written as a mocking, ironic, tongue-in-cheek response. The speaker affects the pose of a distracted lover who is too preoccupied with the woman to give any attention to the political chaos of European politics of the mid-1930s: Franco, Mussolini, etc. He is little concerned for these earth-shattering events, dismissing them casually in a throw-away comment:

And maybe what they say is true
Of war and war's alarms ...

We can almost see the shrug of indifference.

But the mask of the dispassionate observer slips in the final two lines as his passionate yearning breaks through and we realise that the 'she' is probably 'Caitlín Ní Uallacháin' – Ireland. So we understand Yeats's mocking response to those who have not understood one of his major poetical preoccupations.

The regularity of the four-stress lines alternating with three-stress lines and the simplicity of alternative end-line rhymes, together with the simplicity of the language, give the impression that this is lightweight verse. But, as with all good satire, we are lulled into a false sense of security until the final punch is thrown.

# From 'Under Ben Bulben'
Text of poem: New Explorations Anthology page 172

## SECTIONS V AND VI

The final draft of this poem is dated 4 September 1938, about five months before the poet's death. Parts of it were published in 1939.

### BACKGROUND AND CONTEXT

Some acquaintance with the poem as a whole is necessary for an understanding of the context of sections V and VI. It is recommended that you read through all six sections.

'Under Ben Bulben' can be seen as Yeats's poetic testimony, an elegy for himself, defining his convictions and the poetical and social philosophies that motivated his life's work.

Section I incorporates the two main belief systems that informed his poetry: the occult philosophy, and folk beliefs and traditions.

Section II features another aspect of his belief system: reincarnation.

Section III suggests that poetic insight is born out of moments of violence; that violence and conflict can be invigorating.

Section IV outlines what he considers the great tradition in art, from Pythagoras through Egyptian and Greek sculpture to Michelangelo's Renaissance.

In Sections IV and V Yeats urges all artists, poets, painters and sculptors to do their work in this great tradition of art, to promote the necessary heroic images that nourish civilisation. Specifically, he had in mind the forms of the perfected human body as the necessary poetic inspiration, a concept linked to his ideas on eugenics (the pseudo-science of improving the human race through selective breeding). Yeats had joined the Eugenics Society in London in 1936 and became interested in research on intelligence testing. During 1938 he worked on a verse tract on this topic, published as *On the Boiler* (1939). Convinced that eugenics was crucial to the future of civilisation, he wrote: 'Sooner or later we must limit the families of the unintelligent classes and if our government cannot send them doctor and clinic it must, 'till it gets tired of it, send monk and confession box.'

Section VI of 'Under Ben Bulben' rounds his life to its close and moves from the mythologies associated with the top of Benbulbin to the real earth at its foot, in Drumcliff churchyard.

A READING OF THE POEM

## Section V

This is Yeats's advice to Irish poets concerning the model or tradition they should follow. And the model he recommends is a new, composite one, attempting to fuse together two cultural traditions, those of peasant and aristocratic cultures.

> Sing the peasantry and then
> Hard-riding country gentlemen ...

The former is the Irish tradition of folk and fairy tales and fantastical mythology; the latter is the Anglo-Irish cultural tradition, which Yeats traced back to the 'other days' referred to, the eighteenth century and the intellectual contribution of Swift, Berkeley, Goldsmith and Burke. He valued this tradition for its spirit of free enquiry, its sense of order and the example of gracious living it produced in Georgian mansions and fine estates. To this fusion he adds the religious tradition as worthy of celebration ('The holiness of monks'), followed immediately by 'Porter-drinkers' randy laughter', which rather devalues the former. Perhaps it's meant to be ironic. The Irish nobility are worthy of celebration, even though they 'were beaten into the clay | Through seven heroic centuries'. So heroic defeat is a fitting subject.

But once again Yeats scorns the present generation. Physically they do not conform to the traditional model of aesthetic beauty ('All out of shape from top to toe'). With an arrogance derived from the reprehensible theories of eugenics, he scorns their low intelligence and inferior lineage:

> Their unremembering hearts and heads
> Base-born products of base beds.

That arrogant tone continues, to end in that triumphant note – 'Still the indomitable Irishry.' The trouble with this poem is that it is so 'well made' – the rhythms of the language, the regular metre, the alliterative repetitions, the graphically grotesque imagery, etc. – that it can distract us from the seriously questionable class and racist attitudes.

## Section VI

This section is beautifully structured, like a film shot. Opening with a long shot of the mountain, the camera draws back and focuses on the churchyard, panning by the church and the ancient cross until it finishes with a close-up of the epitaph cut in limestone. The effect is of a closing down of Yeats's life, a narrowing-in to death. Many of the important elements of Yeats's life are here: the mythology and folklore associated with Benbulbin; the sense of ancestry, family and continuity provided by the rector; and the continuity of cultural tradition in the 'ancient cross'. No ostentatious marble tomb or conventional tired phrases are permitted, but rather a piece of indigenous material, local stone, to carry his epitaph.

This is a curiously impersonal epitaph, neither celebrating the person's virtues nor asking remembrance or recommending the soul to God: rather it is a stark piece of advice that the challenges of life and death should not be taken too seriously but should be regarded with a certain detachment. It is his final summation, that all the great issues merely come to this.

## Developing a personal understanding

1. Select the poem by Yeats that made the greatest impact on you, and write about your reaction to it.
2. What issues raised by the poet did you think significant?
3. On reading this selection, what did you find surprising or interesting?
4. What impressions of Yeats as a person did you form?
5. What questions would you like to ask him?
6. Do you think it important for Irish pupils to study Yeats?
7. What do you find difficult about the poetry of Yeats?
8. What do you like about his poetry?

## Overview

On each point, return to the poem for reference and further exploration.

YEATS AND THE NATIONAL QUESTION

Among the issues explored by the poet under this heading are the following:
- the heroic past; patriots are risk-takers, rebels, self-sacrificing idealists who are capable of all that 'delirium of the brave' (see 'September 1913')
- how heroes are created, how ordinary people are changed ('Easter 1916')

- the place of violence in the process of political change; the paradox of the 'terrible beauty' (see 'September 1913', 'Easter 1916', and 'Meditations in Time of Civil War')
- the place of 'fanaticism' and the human effects of it—the 'stone of the heart' (see 'Easter 1916', 'September 1913', 'In Memory of Eva Gore-Booth and Con Markiewicz')
- the force of political passion (see 'Easter 1916', 'Politics').

YEATS'S NOTIONS OF THE IDEAL SOCIETY

- The vital contribution that both the aristocracy and artists make to society; the importance of the Anglo-Irish tradition in Irish society (see 'September 1913', 'In Memory of Eva Gore-Booth and Con Markiewicz', 'Meditations in Time of Civil War', 'Swift's Epitaph', 'Under Ben Bulben').
- His contempt for the new middle class and the new materialism (see 'September 1913').
- Aesthetic values and the place of art in society (see 'Sailing to Byzantium', 'Under Ben Bulben').
- The yearnings for order and the fear of anarchy (see 'Meditations in Time of Civil War', 'The Second Coming').
- His views on the proper contribution of women to society (see 'In Memory of Eva Gore-Booth and Con Markiewicz', 'Easter 1916').

THEORIES OF HISTORY, TIME AND CHANGE

- His notion of thousand-year eras, 'gyres', etc. (see 'The Second Coming').
- The world and people in constant change and flux (see 'The Second Coming', 'Easter 1916').
- Personal ageing, the transience of humanity (see 'The Wild Swans at Coole', 'An Acre of Grass').
- The yearning for changelessness and immortality (see 'The Wild Swans at Coole', 'Sailing to Byzantium').
- The timelessness of art, or the possibility of it (see 'Sailing to Byzantium').

CONFLICTS AT THE CENTRE OF THE HUMAN BEING

- The conflict between physical desires and spiritual aspirations (see 'Sailing to Byzantium').
- The quest for aesthetic satisfaction (see 'Sailing to Byzantium').
- The search for wisdom and peace, which is not satisfied here (see 'The Lake Isle of Innisfree').
- A persistent sense of loss or failure; loss of youth and passion (see 'The Wild Swans at Coole'); the loss of poetic vision and insight (see 'An Acre of Grass').

## General questions

1. Select any major theme explored by Yeats and outline his treatment of it.
2. Review critically any poem by Yeats that you considered interesting.
3. 'Yeats displayed great reverence for the past but little respect for his own time.' Consider the truth of this statement in the light of the poems you have examined.
4. 'W.B. Yeats explored complex issues of national identity with great honesty.' Discuss.
5. Having read his poetry, what do you think Yeats chiefly valued in life?
6. 'Yeats's poetry is fuelled by conflict – conflict between past and present, youth and age, mind and body.' Explore this view of his poetry.

## Bibliography

Brown, Terence, *The Life of W.B. Yeats,* Dublin: Gill and Macmillan 1999.

Cullingford, Elizabeth, *Yeats: Poems, 1919–1935* (Casebook Series) Basingstoke: Macmillan 1984.

Cullingford, Elizabeth Butler, *Gender and History in Yeats's Love Poetry,* Cambridge: Cambridge University Press 1993.

Donoghue, Denis (editor), *W.B. Yeats: Memoirs,* London: Macmillan 1972.

Ellman, Richard, *The Identity of Yeats,* London: Faber and Faber 1968.

Ellman, Richard, *Yeats: The Man and the Masks,* Oxford: Oxford University Press 1979.

Foster, R.F., *W.B. Yeats: A Life, vol. 1: The Apprentice Mage,* Oxford: Oxford University Press 1997.

Harwood, John, *Olivia Shakespear and W.B. Yeats,* Basingstoke: Macmillan 1989.

Hone, Joseph, *W.B. Yeats,* Harmondsworth (Middx): Pelican Books 1971.

Jeffares, A.Norman, *W.B. Yeats: Man and Poet,* London: Routledge and Kegan Paul 1966.

Jeffares, A.Norman, *W.B. Yeats: The Poems,* London: Edward Arnold 1979.

Jeffares, A.Norman, *W.B. Yeats: A New Biography,* London: Hutchinson 1988.

Jeffares, A.Norman (editor), *Yeats's Poems,* Basingstoke: Macmillan 1989.

Jeffares, A.Norman, and MacBride White, Anna (editors), *The Gonne – Yeats Letters, 1893–1938,* London: Hutchinson 1992.

Kelly, John (editor), *The Collected Letters of W.B. Yeats* (three vols.), Oxford: Clarendon Press 1986, 1997, 1994.

Kinahan, Frank, *Yeats, Folklore and Occultism,* Boston: Unwin Hyman 1988.

MacRae, Alasdair, *W.B. Yeats: A Literary Life,* Dublin: Gill and Macmillan 1995.

Martin, Augustine, *W.B. Yeats,* Gerrards Cross (Bucks): Colin Smythe 1983.

Smith, Stan, *W.B. Yeats: A Critical Introduction,* Dublin: Gill and Macmillan 1990.

Tuohy, Frank, *Yeats,* London: Macmillan 1976.

Yeats, W.B., *A Vision* [1925], London: Macmillan 1937.

Yeats, W.B., *Autobiographies: Memoirs and Reflections,* London: Macmillan 1955.

Yeats, W.B., *Mythologies,* London: Macmillan 1959.

Yeats, W.B., *Essays and Introductions,* New York: Macmillan 1961.

# 4  *Thomas Stearns* ELIOT

*John G. Fahy*

## *Timeline*

| | |
|---|---|
| **September 26, 1888** | Thomas Stearns Eliot is born in St. Louis, Missouri. |
| **1906–1909** | Undergraduate at Harvard. Becomes interested in the symbolists and Laforgue. |
| **1909–1910** | Graduate student at Harvard. Studies in France and Germany. 'Prufrock' is completed but not published. |
| **1911–1914** | Graduate student at Harvard. Begins work on the philosophy of Francis Herbert Bradley. |
| **1914–1915** | Study in Germany stopped by war. Moves to Oxford. Short satiric poems. 'Prufrock' is published in Chicago, June 1915. Marriage to Vivienne Haigh-Wood, July 1915. |
| **1915–1919** | Eliot has many different jobs, including teaching, bank clerk and assistant editor of the literary magazine *Egoist*. |
| **1915–1916** | Teaching and doing book reviews in London. Bradley thesis is finished. |
| **1915** | Eliot moves to London. |
| **June 1917** | *Prufrock and Other Observations* is published. |
| **1917–1920** | Works in Lloyd's Bank. Many editorials and reviews. Writing of French poems, quatrain poems. |
| **1921–1922** | London correspondent for *The Dial*. |
| **1922–1939** | Founder and editor of *The Criterion*. |
| **1922** | 'The Waste Land'. Eliot wins Dial Award for *The Waste Land*. London correspondent for *Revue Française*. |
| **1925** | Senior position with publisher Faber & Faber. |
| **1927** | Eliot is confirmed in the Church of England and becomes a British citizen. |
| **1927–1930** | *Ariel Poems*. |

| 1940–1942 | 'East Coker', 'The Dry Salvages' and 'Little Gidding'. |
| 1943 | 'The Four Quartets'. |
| 1947 | Death of Eliot's first wife, Vivienne Haigh-Wood, after long illness. |
| 1948 | King George VI awards the Order of Merit to T.S. Eliot. Eliot is awarded the Nobel Prize in Literature. |
| 1957 | Marries Valerie Fletcher. |
| 1958 | *The Elder Statesman*. |
| January 4, 1965 | T.S. Eliot dies. |

# *The Love Song of J. Alfred Prufrock (1917)*

Text of poem: New Explorations Anthology page 204

THEMES/ISSUES AND IMAGERY

## Title

This is, perhaps, one of Eliot's most striking titles. Yet the poem is neither a song nor a traditional, conventional expression of love. Neither is J. Alfred Prufrock a conventional name for a love poet. It is more evocative of a respectable small-town businessman. (In fact, there was a furniture dealer named Prufrock in St Louis when Eliot lived there.)

The name can be seen as mock-heroic, if not comically ridiculous, in the circumstances of the poem. Indeed 'Prufrockian' has entered the language as an adjective indicative of a kind of archaic idealism which is paralysed by self-consciousness. The rather self-conscious 'J.' before Alfred recalls Mark Twain's distrust of men who 'part their names in the middle'.

Overall the incongruity of associations between the two halves of the title prepares us for the tension developed in the poem.

## Epigraph

A literal translation of the epigraph reads:

> *'If I thought that my answer were to one who might ever return to the world, this flame should shake no more; but since no-one ever did return from this depth alive, if what I hear is true, without fear of infamy I answer you.'*

The passage is from Dante's *Inferno*, XXVII, lines 61–66, in which Guido de Montefeltro, tortured in hell for the sin of fraud, is willing to expose himself to Dante because he believes that the poet can never return from the pit of hell to the world. In Eliot's poem, too, the speaker tells of himself, because he feels his audience is also trapped in a hell of its own making. This is so since he is speaking to himself.

The use of the extract from Dante's *Inferno* also suggests that the lovesong is not sung in the real world, but in a 'hell' which is the consequence of being divided between passion and timidity.

## Lines 1–12

Most critics agree that the 'you and I' of the first line are two sides of the same personality, the ego and alter ego, as it were. Thus the poem is an interior monologue, an exposure of the self to the self. However, the reader is, of course, free to think that it is he who is being addressed, as the self he addresses may be in all of us.

At any rate, the character Prufrock is struggling with the idea of asking the 'overwhelming question' of line 10.

The poem opens with a command to accompany him, presumably to the room of line 13. However the air of decisiveness collapses immediately with the simile of describing the evening (line 3). This image may be quite striking but it does not give us an immediate visual image. Rather, it reveals a great deal about Prufrock's psychological state. He is helpless – 'etherised'.

The setting of these opening lines is evening or twilight — a sort of halfway period, neither night nor day. This enhances the theme of indecision.

The description of what appears to be the seedy side of the city in the next four lines is presented in a series of quite sordid images. They may indicate the pointlessness of Prufrock's search. His emotional numbness would appear to have led him to unsatisfactory sordid sexual relations in the past, in 'one-night cheap hotels'. The image of the 'sawdust restaurants with oyster-shells' suggests the vulgarity of these encounters, while also introducing sea imagery, which is a feature of the poem.

These seedy retreats show the tiresome, weary nature of city life. So the streets are compared to 'a tedious argument | Of insidious intent'. Thus Prufrock's encounters and perhaps life itself are seen as mechanical and repetitive and characteristic of an inner sickness. Such an area and such a lifestyle naturally lead to 'an overwhelming question'.

Prufrock is unwilling to face this question. It remains isolated and hidden within, and the 'you' is told not to ask. Thus we are beginning to see the depiction of a melancholic character who cannot satisfy his desires.

## Lines 13–14

This room would appear to be Prufrock's destination. The women are satirised and seen as quite pretentious. Their 'talking of Michelangelo' as they 'come and go' is made to seem quite trivial and empty-headed. This is suggested by the jingling rhythm and rhyme.

The subject of their conversation, Michelangelo, is the great sculptor of heroic figures. This is a figure to whose magnanimity and greatness Prufrock could not possibly aspire. So how could the women find him (Prufrock) interesting, even if their knowledge is limited and their talk pretentious? Prufrock is a most unheroic figure.

## Lines 15–22

There is a fusion of imagery here. The fog which surrounds the house (presumably the house which contains the room) is described in terms of a cat. This essentially metaphysical conceit suggests the theme of unfulfilled promise. This is seen in particular by the fact that the action leads to sleep.

Cats, it must be noted, have been traditionally associated with sexuality and so much of the imagery here may also suggest unsatisfied desire.

The image of the fog serves another purpose. It may convey blurred consciousness or vision, a constant theme in Eliot's poetry. Thus on a wider note, through the imagery of the poem and the character of Prufrock, Eliot is speaking of the degenerated vision and soul of humanity in the twentieth century.

## Lines 23–34

Time is one of the important themes, not only of this poem, but also of Eliot's poetry generally. Prufrock takes great comfort in time, repeating rather hypnotically, 'There will be time'.

There will be time to 'prepare a face' against the exposure of the true self, or 'To prepare a face' to make small talk over 'a toast and tea', and to 'murder and create' reputations or characters in a gossipy fashion, perhaps.

This unexciting prospect, with its mundane 'works and days of hands' merely leads him back to the question, which he puts off because of his timidity and hesitancy. The sarcasm of lines 32–33 emphasises the avoidance of decision. The play on the words 'vision' and 'revision' adds further emphasis to this.

And all this anxiety and procrastination doesn't lead to some momentous event, but merely to taking 'toast and tea'. The element of mock-heroic is clear.

## Lines 35–36

The repetition of lines 13–14 here underscores the tediousness of the women's talk. It further emphasises Prufrock's limitations and how he is inhibited and perhaps intimidated by so-called social discourse. It, together with the reference to Hamlet later, represents the greatness of the past in contrast to the modern world.

## Lines 37–48

Here Prufrock speculates on the women's view of his physical self. The 'prepared face' is no protection against the pitiless gaze of the women. The time for decisive action may be at hand, yet he wonders if he dares. He fears a rebuff and even if he retreats – 'turn back and descend the stair' – he may still seem absurd. He is aware of his unheroic appearance. He is growing bald and 'his arms and legs are thin!' He dresses well – albeit in a very conventional manner – possibly to compensate for these physical shortcomings, and indeed his attractive clothes may be part of his mask – his need to make an appearance.

His doubts are expressed in obvious hyperbole – 'Do I dare | Disturb the universe?' How could *he* possibly disturb the universe? The possibility may lie in the immediate sense of the 'universe' of his own world or in his realisation that even trivial human actions may have immeasurable consequences. This self-conscious awareness precludes his taking any decisive action. Emotionally, at least, Prufrock is impotent.

## Lines 49–54

Here Prufrock puts forward the first of three arguments against deciding the overwhelming question. Again, Prufrock is hesitant to act due to the limitations of his inner self. He lacks self-confidence due to the sterility and meaninglessness of his life – which is merely an endless round of 'evenings, mornings, afternoons'. The line 'I have measured out my life with coffee spoons' not only epitomises the repetitive tedium of his everyday existence, but may also suggest a desire to escape the pain of living via the use of a stimulant.

How could he, Prufrock, challenge the meaninglessness of such a life? Such a challenge would be presumptuous.

## Lines 55–61

His second argument is presented here. He is afraid of being classified and stereotyped 'in a formulated phrase' by the perhaps contemptuous looks of the women. He recoils from the absolute horror of being pinned down and dissected like an insect in some biological experiment. He has a phobia of being restricted, linked perhaps to a fear of emasculation. So how could a man with such fears risk, or presume, to expose himself to further ridicule? The image of the 'butt-end' of a cigarette to which he compares his life suggests further self-disgust.

## Lines 62–69

His third argument against deciding the overwhelming question is presented here. He cannot ask the question because he is simultaneously attracted and revolted by the physicality of women.

The ideal perfection of 'Arms that are braceleted and white and bare' develops into the physicality of '(But in the lamplight, downed with light brown hair!).' The sense of the ideal becoming real reflects his being overwhelmed at the prospect of turning desire into action.

The altered but effectively repeated question of 'And should I then presume?', reflecting his insecurity, suggests an apparent increase in tension towards a sense of impending climax. Yet he cannot conceive any formula for his proposal – 'And how should I begin?'

## Lines 70–74

Prufrock offers a possible preface or preamble to his question. He wonders if he should mention that he is aware of a different type of world from that known by the women in the room – the seedy world of lines 4–9 recalled in the imagery here. This awareness may be his justification for asking the question. He knows more, but the fact that he poses the preamble in the form of a question suggests uncertainty as to its relevance.

Again the imagery suggests he is a passive observer, not an active participant. Failure to address the overwhelming question leads, as in line 10, to a trailing off into silence indicated by the three dots.

This section ends with his wish to be something like a crab. This sea imagery in fact is reduced to 'claws'. Thus Prufrock seems to wish to dehumanise himself completely, to become a thing of pure action without self-awareness – living, yet mentally inanimate; to be in a place where he can survive in the depths and yet avoid the pain of living. Obviously this is the very opposite of Prufrock's true situation.

## Lines 75–88

This section must be seen as a form of reverie. It is also the turning point of the poem.

Having previously seen the fog as a cat (lines 15–22), Prufrock now sees the afternoon as such. All the tensions up to now are resolved, not in action but in images of inaction and weakness. The afternoon/evening/cat 'sleeps', 'malingers', 'Stretched on the floor'. The sense of being etherised (line 3) is recalled.

The triviality of Prufrock's existence is seen in the mock-heroic rhyming of 'ices' and 'crisis'. This prepares us for Prufrock's efforts to put himself in a heroic perspective. However, his greater sense of personal inadequacy won't permit him to sustain the comparison with St John the Baptist. The ironic discrepancy between John the Baptist and Prufrock is heightened by the self-mockery of '(grown slightly bald)'. Prufrock's head would simply look absurd. He is aware of this and immediately denies the possibility of heroic status for himself – 'I am no prophet' (line 84). The continuation of this line can be read as 'it doesn't really matter' or 'I'm not important.' Either way it is an acknowledgement of his own inadequacy.

The final image in this section is of the eternal Footman. This is Death personified. Even death is laughing at him, but the image also suggests that the servants of the polite society hosts whom he visits do not take him seriously. He feels he is the butt of their jokes. To both death and the ridicule of servants, the profound and the trivial, Prufrock admits his fear. It is too late for him to act. Fear is his reality.

## Lines 89–115

Prufrock's speculation on whether forcing the crisis, asking the overwhelming question, would have been worthwhile reads like an excuse for inaction. He is rationalising his failure.

He names again the trivial aspects of his polite environment, recalling earlier lines (49–51, 79). However, now the 'you and I' of line 1 are very much part of the trivia of this environment. They are 'Among the porcelain, among some talk of you and me'. Perhaps he cannot accept that any significant action can take place in this type of environment. He is afraid of being misunderstood. What would he do if his 'overwhelming question' should meet with an off-hand rejection like:

'That is not what I meant at all.
That is not it, at all.'

The fact that these lines are repeated shows the extent of his fear.

Two references in this section suggest that Prufrock continues to compare himself to those of heroic status.

Line 94 is a reference to Andrew Marvell's poem 'To His Coy Mistress' in which the poet urges his beloved to enjoy immediate sexual union with him as a sort of victory over time. Prufrock's inaction is the antithesis of this.

Both men by the name of Lazarus in the Gospels were figures of triumph over death: one, the brother of Martha and Mary, by being recalled to life by Jesus; the other, a poor man, by gaining Heaven – unlike the rich man, Dives.

Prufrock fears that even the most profound knowledge may be decorously, but casually, rejected.

Essentially Prufrock's fear here is of never being able to connect emotionally with another person. The gulf between human beings inner selves cannot be bridged. This has him cry out in frustration:

It is impossible to say just what I mean!
(line 108)

The possibility of the insensitive comprehension of the other exposes his own sensitivity. It is 'as if a magic lantern threw the nerves in patterns on a screen' (lines 109–110). Thus throughout this section women again appear as catalysts to Prufrock's inadequacy and inferiority.

## Lines 116–124
Here Prufrock settles for a less than heroic version of himself. He recognises that any further heroic action would be absurd. He may have something in common with Shakespeare's Prince Hamlet, for he too was indecisive, but any direct identification would be ridiculous.

Rather, he sees himself as a Polonius figure – an advisor to kings – or even a lesser person. The theatrical imagery of lines 117–119 suggests a bit player. Prufrock has become consciously unheroic. In lines 119–124 he is quite self-deprecating, reducing himself eventually to the level of a wise Fool. A passage that begins with 'Hamlet' ends with 'the Fool'.

However, there is the possibility, with the capitalisation of 'the Fool', that Prufrock does not see himself as any old fool, but perhaps akin to the Fool in Shakespeare's *King Lear* – a wise fool who utters uncomfortable truths, which powerful people would prefer not to hear. Maybe this is Prufrock's final fantasy.

## Lines 125–136
A world-weariness introduces this section. This in effect becomes a process of dying, until 'we drown' in the last line.

He does, however, make a decision in line 126 – to 'wear the bottoms of my trousers rolled'. The triviality of the decision, in contrast to the 'overwhelming question', suggests his resignation to a trivial existence. This decision is followed by two further trivial questions, which underscore the point. Parting his hair may hide his bald spot. Eating a peach may be the riskiest behaviour he will ever again indulge in.

This hopeless, empty existence has him resort to the beach. Sea imagery throughout the poem (lines 7, 73–74) has suggested some alternative lifestyle – some hope of avoiding the pain of consciousness.

The mermaids of line 129 symbolise a sort of idealised erotic beauty similar to the arms in line 63. But Prufrock realises that this is only a fantasy, a dream. He has been deluding himself. His realisation of this is expressed in the simple bathos of line 130: 'I do not think that they will sing to me.'

Yet delusions are hard to let go and he asserts the existence of the mermaids, of the erotic ideal, in a defiant final cry (lines 131–133).

But he has 'lingered in the chambers' of his world of ideal relationships and heroic actions for too long, perhaps. The dream is unattainable. The use of 'we' here is not just the 'you and I' of line 1, but also the universal plural. All of us can get lost in our reveries, until we are called to reality by other human voices

– a reality where 'we drown'. All struggle is ended and we accept the death of our inner selves.

## LANGUAGE, TONE AND MOOD

The irony inherent in the title has already been described. It is the self-irony of Laforgue, adapted to a dreadful seriousness. The poem is a tragic comedy, the epitaph sets the mood.

The lyricism of the opening is appropriate to a love-song, but it collapses almost immediately in the simile of Line 3. The simile is quite comically inappropriate for a love-song but is tragically appropriate for the hapless Prufrock and his situation.

The repetition of 'Let us go' suggests that he is already faltering.

The sibilant sounds which dominate the opening sequence underscore the seedy imagery and the sense of being 'etherised'. This is continued into the simile of 'like a tedious argument'. These sounds combined with the rhyming couplets do give a lyrical or musical effect, but also enhance the sense of ennui.

The dramatic pause indicated by the three dots in line 10 emphasises Prufrock's tragic flow and reinforces the bathos.

This bathos is further felt in the jingling rhythm and rhyme of lines 13–14: 'In the room the women come and go | Talking of Michelangelo.'

The fog/cat passage (lines 15–22) is also dominated by sibilant sounds which enhance the tone. These sounds are in contrast with the more cacophonous lines 23–34 which follow.

The fog/cat metaphor is in effect a metaphysical conceit. It is a flight of fancy, a sort of *jeu d'esprit*. Adding to the sensual sibilant sounds is the use of the letter 'L', often seen as the liquid letter, enhancing the sinuous movement of the fog.

The solemn incantatory tone of lines 23–34, echoing the Old Testament speaker in Ecclesiastes, contributes to the mock-heroic element of the poem, which is further added to by the pun on 'revisions' (lines 34 and 48).

Unlike the contrasts in the Book of Ecclesiastes, the opposing forces here do not show a sense of balance or equilibrium, but add to the confusion. The repetition of lines 13–14, which are in danger of becoming a refrain, emphasises the sterility and shallowness of the modern human condition, as mentioned above.

The constant repetition of rhetorical questions is a feature of the next several sections:

'Do I dare?'
So how should I presume?
And how should I begin?

These suggest a tone of uncertainty and underscore the sense of inaction.

The dominant verbs of lines 58–61 – 'formulated', 'sprawling', 'pinned', 'wriggling' – suggest not only the fear of individual inadequacy, but also a sense of being a victim.

His self-contempt, and possibly anger, are seen in the mixture of sibilants and cacophonous consonants in lines 73–74:

I should have been a pair of ragged claws
Scuttling across the floors of silent seas.

The ridiculous rhyming of 'ices' and 'crisis' (lines 79–80) has already been alluded to for its mock-heroic, satiric effect. The same effect is achieved with the rhyming of 'flicker' and 'snicker' in lines 85 and 87. The pathetic admission of:

I am no prophet – and here's no great matter;
I have seen the moment of my greatness flicker,

is reduced to a snort of mockery with the word 'snicker'.

The note of tragic satire is also in the bathetic joke on his 'head (grown slightly bald)' and the prophetic Biblical echoes of:

'I am Lazarus, come from the dead,
Come back to tell you all, I shall tell you all' –
(lines 96–97)

The broad vowels here remind us of one crying in the wilderness and being ignored.

The tone changes in the last section. Now that he acknowledges that 'It is impossible to say just what I mean!', and the 'overwhelming question' is gone, the poem settles down to a lyricism which merely flickered earlier. The use of alliteration, assonance and onomatopoeia in lines 131–136 both intensifies the description and underscores the tone and mood:

I have seen them riding seaward on the waves
Combing the white hair of the waves blown back
When the wind blows the water white and black.

We have lingered in the chambers of the sea
By sea-girls wreathed with seaweed red and brown
Till human voices wake us, and we drown.

The reference to Prince Hamlet does not seem pedantic, given the tone of this section. The rather comic bewilderment of:

Shall I part my hair behind? Do I dare to eat a peach?

helps to raise our sympathy for him. Thus both the 'serious' references and the mocking tone serve to emphasise the comic-tragedy of Prufrock's situation.

Overall, the poem is quite fragmented, full of quickly changing images – aural, visual and tactile – presented in a cinematic, stream-of-consciousness style, reflecting both his character and situation.

## THE CHARACTER OF PRUFROCK

- He is consciously unheroic.
- Melancholic and contemplative
- Feels inferior, inadequate and inhibited
- Fears rejection
- Both attracted to and threatened by women
- Women fall short of his idealised vision.
- Cannot find a language in which to express himself
- Indulges in escapist fantasies to avoid despair
- Indecisive, self-contemptuous and sees himself as a victim
- In a 'hell' – the consequence of being divided between passion and timidity – his tragic flaw
- A sensitive man in a psychological impasse
- An ageing romantic, incapable of action
- Tormented by unsatisfied desire
- A comic figure made tragic by his acute self-awareness
- The poem gives us not only the thoughts and feelings of Prufrock, but also the actual experience of his feeling and thinking.

## PRUFROCK'S PROBLEMS WITH LANGUAGE

- Much of the meaning of the poem arises from its form: the digressions, hesitations, references, all suggest Prufrock's inability to express himself.
- Language regularly fails him. The first section never arrives at the question.
- Prufrock struggles with his own inarticulateness – 'Shall I say?' 'It is impossible to say just what I mean!'
- The failure of his love-song is also a failure to find a language in which to express himself.
- The fragments that make up the poem are essentially a collection of potential poems, which collapse because Prufrock cannot express his 'overwhelming question'.
- He is not included in the mermaids' song.
- Human voices suffocate and drown him.

## MAIN THEMES

- Indecision

- Confronting the difficulty of action
- Time
- Emotional impotence
- The obduracy of language
- Superficiality and emptiness
- The hidden and isolated inner self
- The limitations of the real world
- Dying – spiritually, mentally, physically – death in life
- The movement in the mind.

MAIN IMAGES
- Sordid, seedy city life
- Fog/cat
- The room of pseudo-gentility
- Sea imagery – shells, crab, mermaids
- Cultural imagery – Michelangelo, John the Baptist, Lazarus, Hamlet
- Hair, clothes
- Coffee, tea, cakes and ices.

# *Preludes (1917)*

Text of poem: New Explorations Anthology page 212

*[Note: This poem is also prescribed for the Ordinary Level 2005 exam]*

INTRODUCTION

The 'Preludes' present us with urban scenes where what is seen reflects a particular state of mind. For the deeply disillusioned young poet they illustrate the ugliness, decline, emptiness and boredom of modern life.

The city here is effectively the same as that described by Prufrock in the 'Love Song of J. Alfred Prufrock'. It is a sordid world of deadening monotony and empty routine. The time sets of the poem – evening, morning, night and day – reinforce the feeling of tedious monotony.

The title 'Preludes' can be seen as a reference to this sequence of evening, morning, night and day. They, as it were, are a 'prelude' to more sameness in the purposeless cycle of life.

'Preludes' could also point to the musical or lyrical effects in the poems.

As is usual with Eliot the poetry here is fragmented, full of quickly changing images – visual, aural, tactile and olfactory – in what is often described as a cinematic style. In what is essentially also a stream-of-consciousness style, Eliot takes us on a journey through the senses and the minds of his observers.

A READING OF THE POEM

## Section I

Here the 'winter evening' is personified as it 'settles down' in a way reminiscent of the fog/cat in 'The Love Song of J. Alfred Prufrock'.

Olfactory images and tactile images abound – 'smell of steaks', 'burnt-out', 'smoky', 'grimy', 'withered leaves about your feet', the showers 'wrap' and 'beat' – leaving a sense of staleness and decay. This is compounded by the image of cramped apartments in 'passageways'.

'The burnt-out ends of smoky days' is a visual image that reminds us of Prufrock's 'butt-ends of my days and ways' and also evokes a sense of weariness and disgust.

Adjectives such as 'withered', 'broken', 'lonely' and 'vacant' suggest the decay and isolation of city life, while the insistent beating of the rain adds to the misery. The visual image of the uncomfortable and impatient cab-horse completes the picture of dreariness.

The isolated last line of this section: 'And then the lighting of the lamps', suggests that something dramatic might be about to happen. But nothing does. The opening words 'And then' are not a prelude to drama, but rather a closing in of the night.

Thus the imagery of the section evokes the speaker's mood. The reader can imagine him trudging home through the wet misery of a winter's evening, surrounded by withered leaves and discarded newspapers and inhaling the burnt and musty smells of his living quarters. What else could he be but depressed by it all? The feeling of a numb, aimless, struggle in an ugly, sterile environment suggests a mood of spiritual and mental decay.

## Section II

Like 'evening' in the first section, 'morning' is here personified. It is as if the monotonous time-sets were living an independent life from the actors in this tedious drama of life.

Olfactory and tactile images – 'smells of beer', 'sawdust-trampled street', 'muddy feet that press', 'coffee-stands' – again suggest a sense of staleness and decay. Words such as 'trampled' and 'press' add to the mood of oppressiveness.

Individual life is submerged in the city and by the onward march of time and what emerges is a mass conformity and uniformity:

> One thinks of all the hands
> That are raising dingy shades
> In a thousand furnished rooms.

This sense of sameness and monotony is also suggested by:

all its muddy feet that press
To early coffee-stands.

Eliot regularly depersonalises the character of individuals to show the mechanical nature of their lives. Here people are reduced to 'hands' and 'feet', invoking something living yet spiritually inanimate. Life has become an enslavement to pressure – the pressure of time, crowds and gulped-down coffee.

For Eliot this morning rush to work is a masquerade. It is an act put on by all the 'feet' and 'hands' to give their lives some meaning. The poet is suggesting that behind all the mad masquerade of activity there is a paralysis of the metaphysical, as people's lives are constituted solely by their mundane masquerades.

## Section III

The third section illustrates physical inaction as a woman (the 'you' of the poem) struggles to wake and sluggishly prepares to get out of bed, where during the night she fitfully dozed.

Her uncomfortable sleepless night is caught in the verbs of the first three lines – 'tossed', 'lay', 'waited', 'dozed', 'watched'. She is trapped between sleep and wakefulness which allows her imagination to wander randomly:

... revealing
The thousand sordid images
Of which your soul was constituted;

Thus her paralysis, just like the city's, is also a paralysis of the metaphysical. She is quite inert, apart from throwing the blanket from her bed.

As is typical of Eliot, we are again presented with a character's state of mind. The woman cannot sleep and when she dozes her semi-conscious mind projects, like a film on a screen, her interior self which 'flickered against the ceiling'. These 'sordid' images reflect not only her degradation, but are symbolic of the degenerated consciousness and spirit of mankind in the twentieth century. As a projection of the twentieth century she is more passive and vulgar than the woman in 'A Game of Chess'.

When morning arrived, its light 'crept up between the shutters', almost as if it were an unwelcome intruder, while the sparrows are stripped of all beauty by being heard 'in the gutters'. Her vision of the street is not clarified. It is again blurred – a vision that is hardly understood. Both woman and street appear earthbound – she is supine in bed while the personified street is 'trampled' in both Sections II and IV.

The feeling of degradation and disgust is continued in the last four lines of this section. Eliot again depersonalises the character of the woman to portray this. She is dehumanised into bodily parts – 'hair', 'feet', 'hands' – to evoke the image of a living person who is spiritually inanimate, just as in Section II.

The sense of disgust is more intense here, however. Her hair is artificially curled with paper, her feet are unhealthily 'yellow' and her hands are 'soiled'. This is quite unlike the meticulous image of Prufrock in the 'Love Song of J. Alfred Prufrock'. He may be ridiculous. She is repulsive. The capacity for spiritual growth is non-existent.

## Section IV

This final section in this poetic sequence reveals the speaker more fully. Like the woman in Section III whose soul's images are 'flickered against the ceiling', his soul is also mirrored upwards. But the skies on which it is stretched are not attractive. They 'fade behind a city block'. Indeed, the image is rather tortured – 'His soul [is] stretched tight', reflecting the tension and strain of urban life. The passing of the hours – 'At four and five and six o'clock' – merely reflects the tense tedium and emptiness of his existence.

Eliot again dehumanises and depersonalises individuals to show the mechanical nature of city life – 'trampled … feet', 'short square fingers', 'and eyes'. Their daily routine consists of 'newspapers' and 'pipes' and being 'Assured of certain certainties'. Thus the human reality of the street reveals itself as neither conscious nor aware of its own insecurities and sordid dilapidation. The poet sees these people as living lives of drudgery, whose 'conscience' has been 'blackened'. This is a valueless, dreary society, which is now menacingly seen as being 'Impatient to assume the world.'

In one of those abrupt shifts for which he is famous, Eliot suddenly reveals himself in a moving, pathos-filled quatrain:

> I am moved by fancies that are curled
> Around these images, and cling:
> The notion of some infinitely gentle
> Infinitely suffering thing.

What saves the poet from being swamped by his disgust for modern life is his clinging to a belief in 'some infinitely gentle | Infinitely suffering thing'. This is, perhaps, indicating his move towards Christianity as a source of order and veneration.

However, in an equally abrupt shift he returns to cynicism and encourages us to laugh at, and not sympathise with, the human condition:

> Wipe your hand across your mouth, and laugh

The emptiness in life and the struggle for survival is suggested in a simile which underscores the horrific drudgery of deprivation:

> The worlds revolve like ancient women
> Gathering fuel in vacant lots.

The process of dying, which is prevalent among most, if not all, of the characters in Eliot's poetry, is dramatically evident here also.

## LANGUAGE AND MOOD

Lyrical devices are common throughout.

The monotonous metre of the first section emphasises the drudgery and oppression of these mean streets. Most lines have four iambic stresses, while the others have two. This is in keeping with the image of trampling feet in Sections II and III and, matched by the inexorable flow of time, emphasises the general weariness of moods.

The emphatic rhymes equally convey the sense of oppression. This is particularly the case with the rhyming couplets – 'wraps – scraps' and 'stamps – lamps'.

The insistent beating of the rain is further emphasised by the use of alliteration:

> The showers beat
> On broken blinds...

while the impatience of the horse is intensified by alliteration and the strong iambic rhythm:

> And at the corner of the street
> A lonely cab-horse steams and stamps.

Earlier in this section the use of alliteration and consonance furthers the sense of decay and staleness. The use of sibilant 's' sounds is particularly effective in this:

> The winter evening settles down
> With smell of steaks in passageways.

Thus, in keeping with the musical note of its title, the poet uses lyrical devices to emphasise his themes and underscore imagery and mood.

While Section I is generally composed of end-stopped lines, Section II is composed of lines which run on. This use of enjambment serves to convey a sense of movement – the movement of 'muddy feet' on a 'trampled street'. It also emphasises the pressure of time.

The use of synecdoche, in which a part is substituted for the whole, has been alluded to earlier for the way in which it depersonalises individuals and emphasises monotonous conformity:

One thinks of all the hands
That are raising dingy shades
In a thousand furnished rooms.

While Eliot favoured *'vers libre'*, he does use rhyme to draw attention to or satirise a situation, as we saw in Section I. The rhyming of 'consciousness' with 'press' and 'masquerades' with 'shades' here underscores the theme of pretence; the desire to put on an act to give life some meaning. It also intensifies the mood of oppression.

Overall in this section there is a strong sense of contrast between the descriptions of movement and the sense of spiritual paralysis.

The essentially passive nature of the verbs used at the beginning of Section III reflects her supine state and degenerated consciousness.

The repetition of 'And', which introduces three lines, intensifies the experience of dull monotony, while the almost onomatopoeic effect of the rhyming couplet, 'shutters...gutters', reflects the lack of lyricism in the perceived sound of the sparrows. The result is particularly satiric.

The monotonous metre evident in the earlier part of Section IV emphasises the drudgery and oppression of this city's life, just as in Section I. The movement of these first nine lines underscores the repetitive routine. They go on and on.

The abrupt shift from the third to the first person in the tenth line dramatises the poet's revelation of himself and his feelings. The strong iambic metre is also relaxed, suggesting a sense of release from tension and strain.

The sense of pathos inherent in these lines is lost in another abrupt shift in the last three lines to a mood of deep cynicism. The simile is intensified by the word choice – 'ancient', 'vacant' – and the slowing down of the rhythm.

MAIN THEMES
- incessant toil and suffering
- the decay and isolation of twentieth-century life
- time
- death-in-life
- life is mundane, monotonous, repetitive, mechanical.
- paralysis of the soul/consciousness
- a journey through the mind and senses.

MAIN IMAGES
- the street
- the woman
- food and drink
- body parts
- the detritus of the street

- masquerades
- rapidly changing images – visual, oral, tactile, olfactory – cinematic style.

# Aunt Helen (1915)

Text of poem: New Explorations Anthology page 216

## INTRODUCTION

This is one of those poems in which Eliot outlines his impressions of genteel society in Boston, to the inner circle of which he was introduced through his uncle.

What the philosopher Santayana referred to as its cultural deadness and smug righteousness left this society open to satire. In this poem Eliot comments on its manners and mores, while also suggesting the emotional and spiritual shallowness behind its conventional beliefs and culture. Aunt Helen is a symbol of a world that ought to be mocked. Eliot himself called it a world 'quite uncivilised, but refined beyond the point of civilisation'.

## A READING OF THE POEM

The poem is written in the imagist style. The satiric meaning of the poem, therefore, has to be inferred from the few concise detailed images.

The personal note of the first line is quickly dropped in favour of Eliot's usual device of the detached observer. The banal tone borders on that of a newspaper reporter as a series of apparently objective details are given.

She lived 'in a small house' – a large one would have been vulgar. 'Near a fashionable square' further suggests a genteel refinement. Living *in* the square would be too ostentatious.

The rather contrived and archaic-sounding line 3 conveys the fastidious nature of Miss Helen Slingsby and her self-contained little world: 'Cared for by servants to the number of four.'

Lines 4 and 5 have a satiric edge, which is devastating in its implications. The 'silence at her end of the street' is what is expected out of respect for the dead person. However, the 'silence in heaven' conveys the full contempt of the poet for Aunt Helen's self-serving lifestyle. Faced with this, Heaven has nothing to say. Eliot's contempt is not surprising when one considers how he was raised in a religious environment that promoted unselfish service to the wider community's needs.

The observance of conventions that indicate respect for the dead is also seen in line 6: 'The shutters were drawn and the undertaker wiped his feet –'

However, the dash at the end of the line is almost a challenge to the reader to see the gesture as one of rejection. The reader is reminded of Christ's advice to followers concerning those who reject His and their values – to shake the dust of their towns from their sandals.

The deadpan sarcasm of line 7:

> He was aware that this sort of thing had occurred before

reduces the death of this privileged lady to the commonplace. Aunt Helen's death is being dismissed as 'this sort of thing'.

Her decorous but distorted sense of values is seen in the next line:

> The dogs were handsomely provided for,

The implied criticism of such values controls our response to line 9, which evokes laughter rather than sympathy. Perhaps the poet is also implying that her values don't survive her any longer than the life of a parrot.

The lifeless, artificial, materialistic world in which she lived is seen in:

> The Dresden clock continued ticking on the mantelpiece,

and when we read that the servants resort to behaviour which Aunt Helen would not have tolerated, disregarding both her property and her values, laughter entirely replaces sympathy. The servants' behaviour is not a perversion of ancient values, but a release from their artificial confines.

However, even though we do laugh at and reject Aunt Helen's self-centred values, we are also left with a slight sense of distaste at the vulgarity of the final lines. Satire has not entirely reversed our sense of pathos.

The student may wish to compare Miss Helen Slingsby with the portrayal of women in 'A Game of Chess' and in 'Preludes'.

LANGUAGE AND TONE

The flat, banal tone has been alluded to already. This banal style of narration undermines the seriousness with which Aunt Helen viewed herself and the trivialities that surrounded her.

However, the reader might declare the ultimate tone of the narrator to be quite serious and reject its apparent levity; but, as F.R. Leavis has pointed out, 'It is as necessary to revise the traditional idea of the distinction between seriousness and levity in approaching this poetry as in approaching the metaphysical poetry of the seventeenth century.'

A few random rhymes do little but emphasise the overall absence of lyricism, thus reflecting the general dullness of Aunt Helen's life. Indeed, some lines read almost as prose. This is particularly so of lines 6 and 7. This adds to the sense of boredom and staleness.

The reader could not be blamed for believing initially that this poem is a sonnet. It has the general appearance of one. However, if it does then Eliot is perhaps mocking the attitudes and expectations of the reader, for this is a very distorted 'sonnet', being 13 lines long, with little rhyme and varying rhythm patterns. Thus, this distortion may reflect not only Aunt Helen's distorted values but the reader's also. Satire works in a number of ways.

The contrast between the behaviour of the footman and housemaid and that of Aunt Helen might also be said to add to the humour and introduces a slightly risqué, if not entirely vulgar element.

Finally, Eliot the dramatist is very much in evidence in this poem. Apart from his ability to create a comic type with a few strokes of his pen, he has also created a time and place and most especially, perhaps, he has mimicked the pompous tone of Aunt Helen. Thus quite ordinary words and phrases, such as 'a fashionable square', and 'this sort of thing' echo the bourgeois speech of Miss Helen Slingsby.

The reader will have to decide whether Aunt Helen's life was a tragedy or a comedy.

## Main themes
- criticism of cultural deadness and self-righteousness
- emotional and spiritual shallowness
- distorted values
- time.

## Main images
- silence
- the undertaker
- the dog and the parrot
- the Dresden clock
- the servants.

# A Game of Chess (extract from The Waste Land II, 1922)

Text of poem: New Explorations Anthology page 218

## Themes, issues and imagery

'A Game of Chess' is section II of Eliot's best-known long poem, 'The Waste Land'. This was first published in 1922 and quickly and enduringly became synonymous with the poet himself.

Just like the full poem, 'A Game of Chess' can be read on the level of a narrative or in its more complicated form, when an understanding of the many references helps to universalise the themes and issues. This use of references concurs with Eliot's belief, expressed in an essay published in 1919 called 'Tradition and the Individual Talent', that literary tradition does not just belong to the past but should be used by the poet to express himself more completely. This allows Eliot to overtly contrast the marvels of the past with the squalid nature of the present. 'A Game of Chess' is an example of this, where the first 33 lines describe, amongst other things, past grandeur, while the rest of the poem depicts the present.

'A Game of Chess' describes the stunting effects of improperly directed love or of lust confused with love. The poem is constructed as an apparent contrast between the class, wealth and education of the characters in the first part and the lower-class female characters in a pub at closing time. A closer reading will suggest that the differences are superficial in comparison with the fundamental similarities.

The title of the poem is taken from a play by Thomas Middleton (1580–1627), where the action is played out like moves in a game of chess. This play is a political satire which created a furore at the time and which Eliot has described as 'a perfect piece of literary political art'. Middleton's greatest tragedy, *Women beware Women*, is also in Eliot's mind here. In this play a young woman is raped while her mother, downstairs and quite unaware of what's happening, plays a game of chess. The allusion to the rape of Philomel by Tereus, as told in Greek legend, is symbolised later in the poem. All of this is related to the principal theme of the section: the theme of lust without love.

The opening lines place a woman in a room that has been described as full of 'splendid clutter'. This room, or more precisely a rich lady's boudoir, is surrounded by symbols of our cultural heritage. The extreme lavishness of the boudoir is stressed by evoking the opulence of legendary queens like Cleopatra, Cassiopeia, Dido and Philomel.

These opening lines also reflect Enoborbus's description of Cleopatra's ceremonial barge in Shakespeare's *Antony and Cleopatra*. Cleopatra is famous for her love affairs with powerful Roman generals such as Julius Caesar and Mark Antony. However, Eliot substitutes 'chair' for 'barge', thus evoking the Andromeda legend and the story of Cassiopeia, which are also 'waste-land' tales. Lavish wealth is suggested by 'burnished throne', 'marble', 'golden'. The carved Cupidons on the glass standards suggest possible shameful love affairs.

The 'sevenbranched candelabra' (line 6) adds to the richness of the room while evoking further historical and cultural references. The seven-branched candelabra suggests the Jewish Menorah, which in turn reflects a religious sanctuary and the laying waste of much of Judaic culture over the centuries. The candelabra may also be a reference to the constellation of the Seven Sisters (the Pleiades), which is next to the Cassiopeia constellation. Thus the richness of description also becomes a richness of reference.

This superabundance of rich visual details continues. There are glittering jewels, 'satin cases', 'ivory and coloured glass'. However, the greater the accumulation the greater the confusion in the reader and the less sure we are of what we are seeing or sensing. The woman's perfumes are strange and synthetic (line 11) and they 'lurked' in her vials, suggesting perhaps something illicit or at least decadent. Words such as 'unstoppered' and 'unguent' add to the sense of decadence, as does a phrase like 'drowned the sense in odors' (line 13) and thus the reader also is left 'troubled, confused'.

'The air | That freshened from the window' (line 13–14) doesn't really freshen the room, but stirs the odours into 'fattening the prolonged candle-flames'. Thus the sense of a stifling, decadent sensuality, or indeed sexuality, is further enhanced.

The 'laquearia' (line 16), which is a panelled ceiling, also holds a reference to Virgil's Aeneid, to the scene in Carthage where Queen Dido gives a banquet for her beloved Aeneas. He will eventually desert her. This reinforces the theme of misplaced love.

The patterns on the ceiling continue the notion of almost divine decadence. The colours are rich; the scale is huge and the associations are deliberate. The 'sea-wood' can be linked with the dolphin, which in early Christian times was a symbol of diligence in love, and the word 'framed' prepares us for the pictorial representation of the Philomel story. Even as he introduces the story, Eliot reinforces the theme and tone with a reference to Milton's 'Paradise Lost'. The picture was like a window opening upon 'a sylvan scene', but this sylvan scene is the one which lay before Satan when he first arrived at the Garden of Eden. Thus sexual corruption is introduced in a deceptively beautiful scene. 'The change of Philomel' is a euphemism for what really happens – the violent rape of this girl. The reader is troubled by such violence occurring in such a beautiful place. The story of Philomel, which Eliot takes from Ovid's *Metamorphoses*, is continued in lines 24–27. The barbarity of the sexual violence done to Philomel by King Tereus of Thrace (who was married to Philomel's sister Procne) is compounded by the cutting off of her tongue. Zeus, the king of the gods, took pity on Philomel and turned her into a nightingale – the 'nightingale' of line 24. This classic tragic story is given further voice in this room of the present. The theme of rape, the most immoral and improperly directed love/lust, forces us to react and to see its significance in the 'present' of the poem.

The violated Philomel, her tongue cut out, still manages to express her sorrow in inviolable voice when, as the nightingale, she fills all the desert with song. Perhaps this expresses Eliot's own wish to fill the wasteland, or desert, with song.

However, this may not be possible, for even the sound of the nightingale – the 'Jug Jug' of line 27 was a conventional Elizabethan method of expressing birdsong – becomes merely salacious in the modern world 'to dirty ears'. The move in line 26 from the past tense 'cried' to the present tense of 'pursues' underscores this more prurient perspective.

Lines 28–31 return to a description of the room. The other decorations, presumably outlining scenes from our cultural inheritance, are dismissed as 'withered stumps of time'. The poet is scornful of those who possess but do not appreciate such riches. This further suggests modern people's failure to come to terms with this same cultural inheritance. These 'stumps of time' then, ironically, no longer speak to us, despite being 'told upon the walls'. Perhaps, the 'stumps of time' may also evoke Philomel's stump of a tongue.

The image of the woman brushing her hair in lines 32–34 suggests a nervous person under considerable emotional strain. The rather surreal image of her hair glowing into words suggests her hypersensitivity and her tense speech, while 'savagely still' suggests a truly neurotic silence.

Lines 35–62 are made up of a dialogue between this woman and a male protagonist. The lines between the quotation marks represent the woman's words. The man's are not given quotation marks. Perhaps he is silent; his answers to her questions being unspoken thoughts. Thus the episode is not, perhaps, a full dialogue: just an exchange of sorts, indicating an emotional and communicative stalemate.

While the staccato rhythm of the woman's utterances reveals her nervous tension, the substance suggests her state of purposelessness. The dialogue, if such it be, pivots around aimless questions and nervous imperatives. The answers of the protagonist indicate that his is as desperate a situation as hers is. However, his is a calmer, more resigned despair. He may be in a psychological Hell ('rats' alley') but he is aware of alternatives. He quotes from Shakespeare's *Tempest*: 'Those are pearls that were his eyes.' This suggests the possibility of transformation. Indeed, in *The Tempest* two lovers play a game of chess that may be linked with genuine love.

However, the sardonic counter-perspective immediately intrudes with 'that Shakespeherian Rag' of line 52, an American hit tune of 1912. The words 'elegant' and 'intelligent' deny in this context both true elegance and true intelligence, and perhaps the possibility of finding the true nature of either in this room with these people, despite the grandeur of the room itself.

The overall sense of purposelessness is reinforced by the woman's final questions and the answers to them. Water, which is normally a symbol of life giving, is here without potency. In fact it must be avoided by using a closed car.

The pub scene, apparently set in a working-class urban area from the tone of the narrative, opens in line 63. Much of the essential nature of this scene is its vocalness. We, the readers, have the experience of eavesdropping on a bar-side monologue. The speaker of the narrative is a woman. The difference in class between her and the woman of the earlier lines is quite apparent. There is a sense of immediacy in the setting, with the woman recounting a dialogue between herself and another woman, Lil, some time earlier. The barman's words, in capitals, break into the narrative contributing meanings to the narrative not recognised by its narrator.

The theme of the past haunting the present is again immediately identifiable, as are those of sterility, lust without love, spiritual/emotional illness and emptiness and intimations of mortality and the role of women. The sense of a Waste Land is acute: not the waste of war's destruction, but the emotional and spiritual sterility of modern man.

In a society where appearance means everything, Lil is told to smarten herself up for her husband Albert, who is returning from war. Lil is criticised for looking old before her time (line 82). Indeed Albert had criticised her some time earlier, presumably when he was on leave, and had given her money to get a new set of teeth. She, however, had used the money to procure an abortion (line 85).

The sympathy of the narrator lies with Albert – the 'poor Albert' of line 73 who will want 'a good time' after his four years in the army. Albert may even 'make off' with those who will give him a good time if Lil doesn't.

Lil, meanwhile, is told to smarten up; that she 'ought to be ashamed ...to look so antique' and that she is 'a proper fool'. Little sympathy is had for her nearly dying in pregnancy (line 86) and a fatalistic attitude is held towards the sexual demands of her husband (lines 90–91). The vulgar insensitivity of it all can be compared to the fate of Philomel in the first section, while the use of the word 'antique' (line 82) also reminds us of the imagery of the first section. In this outline of Lil's life, social satire is in effect evoking sympathy.

The narrative is not concluded. It is disrupted by closing time and there is the suggestion of the speaker leaving the pub (line 98). Time is running out for the characters in the narrative, reinforced by the urgent, constant calling of 'Hurry Up Please It's Time'. Their farewells fade into the Shakespearian final line, drawing us back to one of those stumps of time – Ophelia's madness and her drowning. This reference adds a sense of dignity to the narrative, while also universalising the themes of misplaced love and destruction.

## LANGUAGE, TONE AND MOOD

As said, Eliot's poetry is essentially dramatic – from conflict to characterisation, from action to dialogue, from plot to imagery. The student may be well advised to search for examples of these dramatic elements.

The language in 'A Game of Chess' both reflects and is part of the essential drama of the poem. The diction and syntax of the first section reflect the description of the room. Thus words used to describe the 'props' of the dramatic setting could well describe the style also – words such as 'burnished', 'synthetic', or 'rich profusion'. Archaic and artificial-sounding words such as 'Cupidon', 'unguent' and 'laquearia' add to this sense of an urgent, forced style. Overall, the feeling is one of claustrophobia, a sense of being trapped, or 'prolonged' in this gorgeous, cluttered room. The long sentences add to this feeling. (The first sentence is nine lines long.) Similarly, the various subordinate clauses within these long sentences contribute to the sense of being 'troubled, confused'. The lavish opulence of the room and the language in which it is described thus creates a feeling of unease.

In the same way there is a glut of active verbs and participles from lines 14–34, almost hypnotising the reader and stifling a response.

At times, however, the language is wonderfully economic. 'Sad light' (line 20) and 'And still she cried, and still the world pursues' beautifully combine both description and emotion.

However, on other occasions the deliberate literariness of the lines hides the brutal reality. This is the case with the description of the rape of Philomel. The rather lofty, Miltonic tone of:

> Above the antique mantel was displayed
> As though a window gave upon the sylvan scene

tends to obscure what is actually happening in the picture. The euphemisms used, 'The change of Philomel' and 'So rudely forced', tend to lessen the enormity of the sexual violence. Thus the sense of sexual decadence is evoked.

The poet's scornful reaction to such opulent decadence is seen in lines 28–29:

> And other withered stumps of time,
> Were told upon the walls ...

The cold brevity of these lines is in sharp contrast to the aureate earlier descriptions. This economy of expression continues in line 30:

> Leaned out, leaning, hushing the room enclosed.

Here the strained repetitiveness of the line prepares us for the strained emotions of the woman introduced in line 35, while the word 'enclosed' confirms for us the claustrophobia of the room.

The woman's speech reflects her neurotic state. The repetition of one word from earlier on in the line at the end of three of the lines – 'Speak.' 'What?' 'Think.' – emphasises the neurotic state.

The repetition of 'nothing' from lines 44–50 reflects not only the emotional vacancy of the man, but also suggests that this vacancy reverberates in her mind as well. An emotional stalemate is the result.

The unnaturalistic rhythm of the woman's speech, with its deadening, repetitive, nervous questioning, is counterpointed by the smooth rhythm of the quotation from Shakespeare's *Tempest* (line 49). However, the irony here is further compounded by the vulgar ragtime rhythm of 'that Shakespeherian Rag –'

The diction and syntax of the speaker in the pub scene is essentially that of urban English working class. In tone it is an abrupt shift from that of the woman in the room. The word 'said' is repeated some fifteen times in a gossipy fashion. This not only realistically reflects the rhythms and patterns of speech of the working class, but also adds a certain prayer-like intonation.

The barman's sonorous 'HURRY UP PLEASE IT'S TIME' both breaks into and breaks up the speaker's narrative, adding levels of meaning not intended by the speaker. Its repetition contributes to the urgency of the narrative, even introducing a comic quasi-apocalyptic tone.

The quotation from Shakespeare's *Hamlet*, which ends the passage, has Ophelia's lingering farewell remind us that the time is indeed out of joint. Ophelia's words, which rise out of the mêlée of farewells in lines 100–101, enhance the pathos of these people's lives and remind us again that the past does indeed haunt the present and that music may be made out of suffering.

## MAIN THEMES

- the marvels of the past contrast with the squalid nature of the present.
- the past haunts the present.
- the stunting effect of improperly directed love/lust
- lust without love
- sexual corruption may be deceptively beautiful
- the desire to fill the wasteland with song
- modern people's failure to come to terms with their cultural heritage
- the emotional strain of modern life
- sense of purposelessness in modern life
- intimations of mortality.

## MAIN IMAGES

- opulent luxury of the room
- rape of Philomel
- nervous gestures of the woman
- the story of Lil and Albert
- the landlord crying 'Time'.

# *Journey of the Magi (1927)*

Text of poem: New Explorations Anthology page 224

This is the first of the Ariel Poems, a set of poems which, beginning in 1927, the year in which Eliot joined the Anglican church, were published by Faber &

Faber as a sort of Christmas card. Both this poem and 'A Song for Simeon' (1928) refer specifically to the birth of Christ.

The Magi were the three wise men or kings – commonly, but not scripturally, known as Balthazar, Caspar and Melchior – who journeyed from the east to pay homage to the newly born baby Jesus, according to the gospel of St Matthew 11: 1–12. However, Eliot's inspiration comes not from this well-known gospel story alone but also from a sermon preached by Lancelot Andrews, Bishop in Winchester, on Christmas Day 1622, which Eliot quotes in his 'Selected Essays'. The first five lines of the poem are a direct quotation from this sermon by Lancelot Andrews.

The poem is essentially a dramatic monologue spoken by one of the magi, who is now an old man, recalling and reminiscing on the journey he and his companions made to witness a Birth. Thus the poem is concerned with a quest and those travelling must traverse a type of wasteland to reach the promised land. The Magi's journey is challenging, painful and difficult. It involved giving up old comforts, certainties and beliefs so that it became a 'Hard and bitter agony for us'. Reaching their destination doesn't lead to any great sense of achievement or celebration. Instead the narrator is unsure of the significance of what he has seen. 'It was (you may say) satisfactory.' The narrator remains disturbed and bewildered as he returns to the 'old dispensation' which he and his companions now find strange. He longs for death now, so that he can achieve new life.

The poem can be seen as an analogy of Eliot's own agonising spiritual journey. The quest for a new spiritual life involves rejecting the old life with its many attractions. Thus, the Birth also includes a death; the death of the old way of life. Such a journey involves doubt, regrets and lack of conviction. Maybe 'this was all folly.' This tone of uncertainty leads us to appreciate that rather than asserting his beliefs Eliot is expressing his willingness to believe, which is his present spiritual condition.

THEMES AND ISSUES

The poem is a dramatic monologue in which the magus, the narrator, tells of his and his companions' experiences in their journey to the birth of Christ. The opening five lines are an abbreviation of Andrew's sermon as mentioned above, which Eliot includes as part of the magus's narration.

The journey undertaken is one from death to life. It begins in 'The very dead of winter.' The hardships endured represent the sacrifice the magi must make in order to achieve new birth. Also, before there is a birth there must be a death of the old life.

The hardships undergone include not only the weather and trouble with their camels, but also major regrets for what is left behind:

The summer palaces ... the silken girls bringing sherbet.
(lines 9–10)

These real attractions cannot be easily overcome.

Exactly how tough the journey was is seen in the sequence from line 11 to line 16. The increasing torment outlined in the matter-of-fact descriptive statements here is made all the more effective by the repetition of 'And ...' The hostility of various communities, symbolic of a disbelieving world, leads them 'to travel all night'. Adding to their discomfort is the realisation that the hostile unbelievers may be right – 'That this was all folly.' (line 20)

The next section, beginning at line 21, seems at first to confirm the death-to-life theme. It is 'dawn'; there is 'a temperate valley', 'a running stream and a water-mill beating the darkness' – all of which can be seen as birth images. However, ambiguity and uncertainty quickly return. The 'three trees' are reminders of the Crucifixion of Christ, as are the 'Six hands ... dicing for pieces of silver' (line 28). These, coupled with the negativity of the horse galloping away, 'the empty wine-skins' and 'no information', can be seen as furthering the theme of death. However they may also suggest the interrelation between death and birth. Christ's incarnation leads inexorably to His Crucifixion, just as His Crucifixion leads to eternal life.

Ambiguity can also be seen in what should be the joyful climax of the journey and confirmation of belief. However, this is not so. The intense anticipation and anxiety of 'not a moment too soon' is immediately followed by the uncertain reticence of

it was (you may say) satisfactory. (line 32)

No description of the Birth or the One who was born is given.

This sense of uncertainty turns to a degree of confusion in the last section, as the magus tries to work out the meaning of what he saw. Maybe like the knight meeting the Fisher King in the Holy Grail legend, he has failed to ask the right question. While he is convinced that it was significant – 'And I would do it again' (line 34) – and is anxious that no part of his narrative should be overlooked:

... but set down
This set down
This: ...
(lines 34–36)

the Birth doesn't seem to have been what he expected. He 'had thought they (birth and death) were different', but 'this Birth was ... like Death, our death.' (lines 39–40).

So the Magi return to their kingdoms but feel alienated among their own people. They must continue to live amidst the old way of life – 'the old dispensation' (line 42) – while not believing in it. So their Birth remains a bitter agony while they wait for 'another death' (line 44). Another death is required – the magus's own, or perhaps Christ's – before he can enter a new life.

## IMAGERY AND SYMBOLISM

The whole poem is structured around a journey, both real and symbolic. The journey as recalled by the magus is one from death to birth, the imagery of which suggests the inner struggles of the narrator and his companions.

The journey begins at 'the worst time of year' with 'The ways deep and the weather sharp' and ends in 'a temperate valley ... smelling of vegetation'. The symbolic movement from death to life is clear. Paradoxically, however, there is also a movement from life to death. Here 'The summer palaces ... And the silken girls bringing sherbet' represent the old life. The travellers make their way through a wasteland of 'cities hostile and the towns unfriendly', until in the valley there is a symbolic death of the old life as the 'old white horse galloped away'. Some critics have seen references to the Fisher King myth in the journey and its symbols.

The second stanza contains a series of death and birth images. 'Dawn', 'temperate valley', 'vegetation' can be seen as birth images, while water is universally acknowledged as symbolising life. However, a flowing river or stream is also a traditional poetic symbol of the passing of time. The action of the 'water-mill' can be seen as beating the darkness of time.^ There then follow a series of images foreshadowing the well-known imagery surrounding Christ's death. The 'three trees on the low sky' reflect the three crosses on the Hill of Calvary. The 'hands dicing' suggest the Roman soldiers dicing for Christ's clothes and the 'pieces of silver' remind us of the thirty pieces of silver that Judas was paid for his treachery.

The 'white horse' can be seen as an ambiguous image. It may symbolise the life-giving triumphant Christ of the Book of Revelations (VI: 2, 19:11). However, as the horse is said to be 'old' and since it 'galloped away' it may also represent the collapse of paganism, 'the old dispensation' of line 42.

## LANGUAGE AND TONE

As befits a dramatic monologue the language reflects not only natural speech patterns, which catch the rhythms of speech, but also a particular voice – the voice of the magus, at times both reminiscent and complaining:

> Then the camel men cursing and grumbling
> And running away, and wanting their liquor and women.

Here the emphasis falls into a natural pattern of speech and voice inflection. The prayer-like, incantatory tone also befits both the speaker and the theme. The strong repetition of 'And' in the first two sections reflects this. Overall the purposefully ambiguous symbols and images introduce a tone of uncertainty.

The opening paraphrased uncertainty of Lancelot Andrews' sermon sets the tone of desolation and the bitter environment of the first stanza. The quotation also serves a second purpose for Eliot. It incorporates the poem into a particular tradition. Thus it serves a similar function to the quotation from Dante at the beginning of 'Prufrock' and is part of his efforts to create a synthesis between past and present.

The remainder of the first stanza is quite vitriolic in tone, as the magus criticises both his predicament and his previous life. This criticism is coupled with a tone of regret,

> The summer palaces on slopes, the terraces,
> And the silken girls bringing sherbet.

The sensual sibilant 's' sounds of these lines underscore what is being regretted. A tone of contempt can be seen in the ever-expanding criticism of the remainder of the first stanza.

The second stanza suggests a tone of nostalgia as the magus remembers his arrival at 'a temperate valley'. Then the last three lines of this stanza culminate in an understatement: 'it was (you may say) satisfactory.'

The word 'satisfactory' as seen, reflects the ambiguity and uncertainty of the magi's reaction. Perhaps, they are not completely aware of its relevance. The word is given particular emphasis by the expression in parentheses preceding it and by its irregularity with the set rhythm of the line.

This tone of uncertainty is continued in the next stanza and develops into a tone of anxiety and of urgency:

> ... but set down
> This set down
> This: ...

The dislocation and repetition of these lines emphasise this residual tone of uncertainty and urgency. The run-on line:

> ... this Birth was
> Hard and bitter agony for us, ...

creates a similar tone of anxiety and perhaps even of self-pity.

The poem ends in a conditioned statement:

> 'I should be glad of another death',

perhaps expressing a tone of resignation.

## Main themes

- the Birth of Jesus Christ
- a quest/journey as an analogy of spiritual searching
- lack of conviction/uncertainty/alienation
- birth entails death
- the need for suffering in order to attain a new Birth.

## Main images

- a journey
- a Wasteland of 'cities hostile'
- death and birth images
- biblical images.

# *Usk (extract from* Landscapes III, *1935)*

Text of poem: New Explorations Anthology page 226

## Introduction

This is one of Eliot's five 'Landscape poems', three of which are based in America, one in Wales and one in Scotland.

This poem resulted from a ten-day holiday taken by Eliot in Wales in 1935.

In keeping with the term 'Landscape' the poem is a suggestive or evocative sketch in which the poet can be seen as an artist/painter. Like the other 'Landscape' poems, this poem consists of scenes and perceptions of deep significance in the development of Eliot's thinking. In particular, the 'Landscape' poems are definitive pointers in terms of Eliot's developing religious and poetic sensibilities, which are further explored in the 'Four Quartets'.

In this sense, although listed under *Minor Poems*, there is nothing minor about the significance of these poems. Indeed, taken as a sequence of five poems, we can see that Eliot is again evoking drama here, as he did in 'The Wasteland' and in the individual quartets of 'Four Quartets'. The sequence of five is in keeping with the number of acts required by Aristotle for tragic drama. Shakespeare also adhered to this. So both 'Usk' and 'Rannoch' can be seen as two acts in a drama outlining the relationship between human beings and the natural world. As number III, Usk marks a climax in the sequence.

## A reading of the poem

'Usk' is a pastoral poem in both senses of the word, i.e. it is descriptive of the countryside and is also spiritually instructive.

The opening of the poem is abrupt, sudden and in the imperative mood. The reader is being instructed:

> Do not suddenly break ... or
> Hope to find ...
> ... do not spell

We are being told *not* to seek images such as 'the white hart', 'the white well', the 'lance'. These are evocative of the classical Arthurian/Celtic legends. As such they are also evocative of the countryside.

Thus Eliot is suggesting that in such a landscape we should not conjure up the past or any notion of romantic fantasy. This he dismisses as 'Old enchantments.' He tells us to 'Let them sleep.' As a sort of second thought he allows us to '"Gently dip, but not too deep"'.

However, having been instructed *against* something we are now instructed *towards* something. Our relationship with the landscape should not be escapist or full of romantic fantasy, but should be such as to lead us *towards* the spiritual.

In a prayer-like incantation, he tells us to 'Lift your eyes'. We are being sent on a more active spiritual journey – a pilgrimage – 'Where the roads dip and where the roads rise'.

Here we are to seek 'The hermit's chapel, the pilgrim's prayer' which, although conventional images of the spiritual, will not be found in any conventional setting but 'Where the grey light meets the green air'.

A spiritual home will be found in something that is neither human nor animal. Indeed it may not be found in the natural landscape at all, but in the eternal continuum of light and space, i.e. 'Where the grey light meets the green air'.

There is a note of hope here that is not found in 'The Love Song of J. Alfred Prufrock', 'Preludes' or 'A Game of Chess'. It echoes that tiny note of hope, which is to be found in 'The Journey of the Magi' and marks a shift towards a spiritual solution for Eliot in the face of life's difficulties.

USE OF LANGUAGE

The language suggests a certain sense of detachment on the part of the poet. The poem reads as advice to others from someone who has already reached a conclusion or discovered a position with which he is happy. Even though this is a description of a place, the poet is not part of the place. This can be seen as a type of metaphysical detachment.

The negative imperatives and the cacophonous alliterative sounds of the first line introduce us to the poet's attitudes towards the 'Old enchantments.'

These same imperatives also evoke that sense of self-assured, commanding authority we associate with metaphysical poets such as the seventeenth-century poet, John Donne.

In keeping with this robust style the rhythm is quick and irregular. This lively, almost bounding style is furthered by the use of alliteration and repetition in many of the lines. The rhythm, like the road, dips and rises. The use of enjambment, or run-on lines, in the second part of the poem in particular, and the quite intense rhyme, also add to the sense of insistent energy.

The incantatory tones of some of the imperatives have been alluded to already. In fact the tone of the whole poem can be found in the three dimeter lines:

> Hope to find ...
> Lift your eyes ...
> Seek only there ...

The dramatic exhortational tone of an Old Testament prophet is clear and in keeping with one aspect of the pastoral theme.

Finally, the choice of colours in this landscape 'painting' suggests both a sense of peace and invigoration. 'White' is bright, while 'grey light' evokes images of a chill, bracing wind, and 'green' is traditionally seen as a natural, soothing colour. The sense of peace is also evoked by the choice of individual words such as 'sleep', 'gently', 'dip' and 'prayer'.

## MAIN THEMES

- A pastoral poem in both senses
- Avoid the 'old enchantments'
- Seek the spiritual
- A journey.

## MAIN IMAGES

- Medieval romantic fantasies – 'hart', 'well', 'lance'
- The road
- 'The hermit's chapel'
- 'Grey light', 'green air'.


# Rannoch, by Glencoe (extract from Landscapes IV, 1935)

Text of poem: New Explorations Anthology page 228

[Note: This poem is also prescribed for the Ordinary Level 2005 exam]

'Rannoch' is the fourth in the five-poem sequence, 'Landscapes'. (See Introduction on 'Usk'.)

A READING OF THE POEM

The poem explores the relationship between human beings and the natural world. Like 'Usk' it is a pastoral, in the sense of being both a description of a countryside and also containing a message. It may suggest elements of a pastoral elegy to some readers.

In many ways this poem is a stripping away of the idyllic, idealised Golden Age pastoral to reveal a landscape of famine and war.

The poem opens with two death-in-life images – 'the crow starves', 'the patient stag | Breeds for the rifle.'

They are the distressing results of the capacity of humans to condition the landscape. This is a barren landscape full of death. Here all creatures feel constricted and oppressed:

... Between the soft moor
And the soft sky, scarcely room
To leap or soar.

The softness here is not of ease or comfort, but a reflection of the sense of oppression. Sky and moor practically meet. If all relationships need space and time, then failure is inevitable here due to a distinct lack of space. This landscape is a burden.

Erosion is the norm here – 'Substance crumbles'; everything is suspended 'in the thin air' of the inexorable movement of time – 'Moon cold or moon hot.'

This psychological topography allows no means of escape. 'The road winds' without apparent purpose. Instead we are offered a journey through 'listlessness', 'languor' and 'clamour'. The sense of direction and invigorating movement evident in 'Usk' is totally absent here. We are stuck in the wretchedness of history and its endless cycles: 'ancient war', 'broken steel', 'confused wrong'. These are the relics of embattled lives, before which the only appropriate response is silence. These old rivalries will not be resolved because 'Memory is strong | Beyond the bone.'

In this landscape of memory where 'Pride snapped', the 'Shadow of pride is long'. In 'the long pass' of a lifetime, there will be no resolution, no reconciliation – 'No concurrence of bone.' This is because even though pride is humiliated (snapped), it holds onto its shadow.

Unlike 'Usk' this poem offers no religious perspective, no sense of hope and direction between life and death – only a sense of 'betweenness', where we are biologically fated to evoke old rivalries. They are of the bone and 'Beyond the bone'.

Living in a state of betweenness, the rational aspect of ourselves is lost amidst the 'Clamour of confused wrong', almost indifferent to suffering, including our own. As is common in Eliot's poetry, the human in its non-rational state is symbolised in animal imagery. Here the human is seen as 'crow' and 'the patient stag' awaiting their fate. They are as unable to understand what they had been reduced to as are the inhabitants of the city street in the 'Preludes'.

The existentialist awareness and its agony are to be found in the speakers and the readers of these poems.

The tragedy of 'Rannoch' may be alleviated by the hope of 'Usk'. However, 'Usk' is not a solution but an indication of the journey that must be taken. But 'Rannoch' is the tragedy that may prevent 'Usk'.

## THE USE OF LANGUAGE

This is a dysfunctional landscape and the poet's use of language reflects that.

The end-of-line neatness of strong rhyme and natural pauses in 'Usk' is absent. Instead we are presented with a rather discordant structure. A line or lines run on, only to finish abruptly in the middle of the next line.

There is an emphasis on alliteration, in keeping with Eliot's admiration of medieval English.

This, however, does nothing to even out or smooth the lines. Rather the effect is insistent, if not altogether frenzied when combined with the stutter-like rhythm. This nervous, stutter-like effect is added to by actual close word repetition. All of this creates an unease and a tension in the reader.

Rhyme, where it does exist, is internal or slightly off end – e.g. 'wrong', 'strong' and 'long' and 'sour', 'war'. Again this adds to the sense of a discordant structure.

The sense of constriction explored in the imagery of the first four lines is also present in the language. In the second sentence:

> Between the soft moor
> And the soft sky, scarcely room
> To leap or soar.

there appears to be no room for a main verb.

We are also presented with an anagram as a type of rhyme, i.e. 'moor' and 'room'. The 'moor' turns on itself to become 'room', emphasising the constriction and oppression and becoming an analogy for the retracing and restating of grievances in a closed system of confused wrongs and strong memories.

## MAIN THEMES
- death in life
- time
- impact of human beings on the natural world
- war, destruction and erosion
- unresolved rivalries.

MAIN IMAGES

- the crow and the stag
- moor and sky
- winding road
- (images of) war
- bone.

# East Coker IV (extract from The Four Quartets, 1940)

Text of poem: New Explorations Anthology page 230

## INTRODUCTION

This short piece is part of 'East Coker', the second of 'The Four Quartets'.

'The Four Quartets' is seen by many critics as the most important work of Eliot's career. Helen Gardner has called them Eliot's masterpiece. The new forms and ideas with which he experimented in the 'Landscape' poems ('Usk', 'Rannoch') are developed fully in 'The Four Quartets'.

In keeping with the musical title, the structure of the 'Quartets' is symphonic and thus extraordinarily complex – a complexity which may not trouble the student here.

Time is again one of the central themes – in particular its constant change in contrast with unchanging eternity. The philosophical considerations of the contrast between the real and the ideal, the human and the spiritual, explored in his earlier poetry, are again evident here.

'East Coker' takes its name from the village in Somerset, England, from which Eliot's ancestors emigrated to America. 'East Coker' is concerned with the place of mankind in the natural order of things and with the notion of renewal. This theme of rebirth, which is also found in the 'Journey of the Magi', is part of the spiritual progress of the soul. The soul must yield itself to God's hands and die in order to be born again. Indeed the soul must first suffer in order to be capable of responding fully to God's love. St John of the Cross calls this 'the dark night of the soul'. The saint's writing on this has influenced Eliot here.

## A READING OF THE POEM

The poem, written for Good Friday 1940, sees Eliot at his most symbolic and a reading of the poem is, in effect, an interpretation of this symbolism.

The poem is a metaphysical one, structured around metaphysical conceits and paradoxes similar to those which may be found in the poetry of the seventeenth-century poet, John Donne. It lies in the tradition of seventeenth-century devotional verse, such as that of Donne, Herbert and Vaughan.

The 'wounded surgeon' is Jesus Christ, whose suffering and death on the Cross, and whose subsequent Resurrection, ensured mankind's redemption.

The 'wounded surgeon' will cure the soul of its sickness: 'the distempered part'. The surgeon's knife, 'the steel', which operates, or 'questions', is God's love. This is in keeping with St John of the Cross's 'The Dark Night of the Soul', which has influenced Eliot here.

The soul is not unaware of God's love operating on it. It feels 'The sharp compassion of the healer's art'.

The oxymoron that is 'sharp compassion' suggests the idea of a necessary evil, i.e. in order to be cured the soul must suffer first. Suffering is a means of grace. This is 'the enigma of the fever chart'. A physical evil can be seen as a spiritual good. Thus the metaphysical paradox is 'resolved'.

The beginning of the second verse continues this notion of suffering as a means of grace. Thus, 'Our only health is the disease'.

The concept of a hospital is continued with the image of 'the dying nurse'.

'The dying nurse' is the Church – 'dying' in the sense of the common fate of mankind. The Church's role is not to placate or please us, but to remind us firstly of 'Adam's curse', which is never-ending toil and suffering, similar to the vision of mankind's daily life in the 'Preludes'. The Church's second role is to remind us that, 'to be restored, our sickness must grow worse', that is, that it is only through the fullest suffering that we can be fully cleansed or cleared of our sickness/evil.

The 'hospital' concept is continued in the third stanza. 'The whole earth is our hospital' in the sense that it is here we can learn the value of suffering and can be cured of our sickness. The 'ruined millionaire' is Adam, whose endowment brought sin into the world – Adam's sin is Original Sin in Christian belief. The 'paternal care' is that of God, under Whose care we would be privileged to die, if we do well as 'patients' in this world. The word 'prevents' is used in its seventeenth-century sense, meaning to go before us with spiritual guidance. God will help us by guiding us towards repentance. The second and modern meaning of 'prevents', that is to stop or frustrate, is also appropriate. God stops our lives everywhere through death.

The notion of cure is continued in the fourth stanza. The cure is a fever one – because 'to be restored, our sickness must grow worse', as stated in the second stanza. The purgation, or cure, must move from a purgation of the flesh, burning away all the sickness and impurities of the flesh, until it ascends to a purgation of the mind:

> If to be warmed, then I must freeze
> And quake in frigid purgatorial fires

The essence of a breaking cold/hot fever, the body shivering and sweating as it rids itself of disease, is achieved here.

The flames of purgation Eliot calls roses, the symbol of both human and divine love. Roses and thorns are also the emblem of martyrdom. So suffering is seen as the basis of the cure – a thorough penitential suffering.

The fifth stanza opens with an image of the 'wounded surgeon' again. It is Jesus Christ on the Cross, whose suffering leads to our Redemption. The image also evokes the Eucharist, the central act of worship for Christians. It may also evoke the need for suffering in ourselves, so that we too will be cured.

The image of flesh and blood is continued in the next two lines in Eliot's criticism of our blindness. We like to think that there is no need for humility and penance with our ideas of our own importance – 'we are sound, substantial flesh and blood'.

The adjectives 'sound, substantial' suggest that we rely too much on the physical, the materialistic.

However, Eliot recognises that behind our materialism, we innately acknowledge our need for repentance and the grace of God. This is why 'we call this Friday good.'

USE OF LANGUAGE

In this poem Eliot has revived the metaphysical poem. He uses many of the features we associate with the seventeenth-century poetry of Donne, Herbert and Vaughan.

In line with metaphysical poetry there is a strong sense of argument throughout the poem. The argument, as outlined above in the READING OF THE POEM, is that we need to reject the demands of the body and achieve redemption through curing its ills. Pain and suffering are means towards achieving redemptive grace or enlightenment.

This argument is presented throughout a series of metaphysical paradoxes, e.g.

> The 'wounded surgeon' will cure us
> 'sharp compassion'
> 'the enigma of the fever chart'
> 'Our only health is the disease'
> 'to be restored, our sickness must grow worse.'
> 'if we do well, we shall | Die'
> 'If to be warmed, then I must freeze'
> 'frigid purgatorial fires'
> 'in spite of that, we call this Friday good.'

Many of these are examples of what is known as metaphysical wit, which is renowned for its clever but serious, incisive, challenging and intelligent puns and paradoxes. The wit of the last stanza in particular removes any sense of emotional religiosity and serves to intensify the devotional mood.

A conceit is an elaborate, sustained comparison. These were much used by the seventeenth-century metaphysical poets. Eliot, in keeping with this, uses conceits in this poem. The 'wounded surgeon' is an example, as are seeing the earth as a hospital and the notion of the fever cure.

The meaning of symbols used is explored above in READING OF THE POEM. However the student should be aware that symbolism is as much a use of language as it is an exploration of meaning. Such usage invigorates both language and meaning.

Similarly, Eliot's precision of language adds depth to the meaning of both individual words and the poem as a whole. His use of the word 'prevents' in the third stanza is an example of this.

Examples of metaphysical wit are seen in the last stanza, in the evocative fused imagery of the first two lines in particular.

Eliot 're-invented' the alliterated four-stress line commonly found in medieval English. This poem generally follows their pattern, with quite strong medial pauses: e.g. 'The **wound**ed **surg**eon **plies** the **steel**' or 'Be**neath** the **bleed**ing **hands** we **feel**'.

However, this kind of verse can become monotonous. Eliot's genius was to apply the pattern with sufficient flexibility to avoid monotonous rigidity.

W.B. Yeats once said that rhythm in poetry should be used 'to prolong the moment of contemplation'. Perhaps we can say this of both the rhythm and the strong, definite rhyme patterns in this poem.

MAIN THEMES
- the idea of necessary evil – a physical evil may be a spiritual good.
- suffering as a means of attaining grace/redemption
- the purgation of evil
- the caring love of God
- growth towards a new life.

MAIN IMAGES
- the wounded surgeon
- concept of a hospital
- the nurse
- the ruined millionaire – Adam
- play of opposites – 'frigid fires'
- the Cross
- the Eucharist.

## T.S. Eliot – An Overview

Not even the most learned critic has said that Eliot's poetry makes easy reading. Yet of all twentieth-century poets he is perhaps the most rewarding. No other poet has better expressed the social condition and psychological state of modern man.

While Eliot's poetry can be read with pleasure at first sight, a full understanding will not come immediately. This is so because quite often, instead of the regular evocative images other poets use, Eliot presents us with a series of literary and historical references. Eliot himself insisted that the reader must be prepared to answer the call for knowledge which poetry demands. Indeed if the reader does persevere, then he/she will be rewarded with a use of symbolism and allusion, and an experimenting with the language and form of poetry, which deepen and intensify the experience of reading it. He/she will feel what Eliot himself called the 'direct shock of poetic intensity'.

### INFLUENCES AND THE 'MODERN MOVEMENT'

The 'Modern Movement' is that which effected a revolution in English literature between 1910 and 1930. As the leading poet in the movement, Eliot brought about the break from the poetic tradition of the nineteenth century. Apart from some notable exceptions, such as Hopkins and Hardy, poetry in English had become degenerate in both taste and theme. It appealed to the imperialist prejudices of a smug, self-complacent audience, convinced of its own superiority in just about everything. Poetry flattered rather than educated.

Eliot's achievement, in both his poetry and his critical essays, was in founding new criteria of judgement on what constitutes poetry.

Similar revolutions were happening in the other arts. James Joyce revolutionised prose writing, as did Pablo Picasso painting and Igor Stravinsky music. The First World War (1914–1918) also helped. At first poetry was used for propaganda. Rupert Brooke's saccharine war sonnets were enthusiastically received. However, as the war dragged on public perception was forced to change, as Wilfred Owen and Siegfried Sassoon wrote of the revolting horrors of war. Owen insisted that poetry need not be beautiful, but it must be truthful.

One aspect of the revolution that Eliot effected was the introduction to English of a style of poetry that is known as 'Symbolism'. When he arrived at Oxford in 1914, Eliot brought with him a deep love and admiration for the French nineteenth-century symbolist poets. These included Charles Baudelaire and Jules Laforgue. Eliot's debt to these poets is extensive – from diction to creative remodelling of subject matter, from tone to phrasing.

Eliot adapted from Charles Baudelaire (1821–1867) the poetical possibilities of addressing 'the more sordid aspects of the modern metropolis'. Examples of these are seen in 'Preludes' and in 'The Love Song of J. Alfred Prufrock'.

From Laforgue (1860–1887) he adopted a tone of mocking irony and despair. Eliot said he owed more to Laforgue 'than to any poet in any language'. Laforgue was a technical innovator. He pioneered '*vers libre*', or free verse, which Eliot also adopted. '*Vers libre*' is verse freed from rigid, conventional forms of regular rhyme and rhythm. Instead Laforgue, and Eliot, use odd or irregular rhyme with varying rhythms to enhance both the theme and tone of the verse. Examples of these can be found throughout Eliot's poetry.

Laforgue also developed a sort of dramatic monologue, a stream-of-consciousness or interior monologue, as it is better known. Eliot adapted this method also, as can be seen in 'The Love Song of J. Alfred Prufrock' and 'Journey of the Magi'. However, Eliot developed the method to a further degree in the distancing and the self-mockery of the dramatic personae of his poems.

Eliot also admired many of the seventeenth-century English poets, seeing in them the emotional intensity and intellectual precision he found in the French Symbolists. Eliot saw a similarity between the seventeenth and twentieth centuries, in that both centuries experienced the disintegration of old traditions and the arrival of new learning. He particularly admired what came to be known as the Metaphysical Poets and felt that John Donne was closer to him in spirit than most other English poets. Eliot shares with Donne an often robust style, with colloquial language mingling with intellectual language. Like Donne, Eliot's poems contain a sense of argument, unexpected juxtapositions and eclectic references, demanding an intelligent attention from the reader. Even a cursory glance at 'A Game of Chess' or 'The Four Quartets' will confirm this.

However, it was the Italian poet Dante (1265–1321) who was the greatest influence upon Eliot. He saw Dante as greater even than Shakespeare, seeing the Italian poet expressing 'deeper degrees of degradation and higher degrees of exaltation'. The presence of Dante in Eliot's verse extends beyond the epigraph in 'The Love Song of J. Alfred Prufrock' to a recreation of the whole experience of his verse. The hell or purgatory in which both Prufrock and the women in 'A Game of Chess' live reflects this.

Eliot first met Ezra Pound in 1915, another great American poet and critic, who subsequently had a profound influence on Eliot's development both as a poet and as a literary critic. It was through Pound that Eliot came to be influenced by the so-called imagist school of poetry. Imagism promoted the use of common speech in poetry, a complete freedom in subject choice, accuracy, concentration and precise description. The reader need only look at the 'Preludes', 'Rannoch, by Glencoe' or 'Aunt Helen' to see how true all of this is of Eliot's poetry.

THEMES

As said above, Eliot lived in a period that saw the disintegration of old traditions and beliefs and the arrival of new learning and new experiences. As a poet then, he had to find a different way of addressing the new. Pound's famous phrase 'Make it new' was a rallying cry to those who wished to tackle themes relevant to their own experience. For Eliot, this was as much a recovery of a lost tradition in poetry as it was a revolution. Thus we find in Eliot's poetry a *contemplation of the past and an examination of the new* in relation to the past. 'Journey of the Magi' is one such poem.

While Eliot made poetry new, it didn't mean that he approved of everything that was new in contemporary life. On the contrary, there was his belief that much in modern life was a betrayal of civilised values. His poetry is full of his sense of disgust for urban society. 'The Love Song of J. Alfred Prufrock' and 'Preludes' are two such poems. *Modern urban life*, for Eliot, *is an emotional and cultural wasteland*, a world of thoughtless self-gratification and deadening purposelessness. The modern city is a symbol of the nightmare of human decadence. This view is explored in particular in 'Preludes' and 'A Game of Chess'.

This particular notion of *meaningless existence* expands into the wider theme of *death-in-life* and *life-in-death*. Twentieth-century man may be condemned to a living death, but redemption can be achieved. For Eliot this is the answer to how we should live: that is, we need to die to the old life in order to be born into the new. Humanity needs to *journey in search of its spiritual well-being*. This may involve *suffering* but the cure is at hand. The 'Journey of the Magi', 'Usk' and 'East Coker IV' explore these themes. To redeem itself and construct a new life for itself, humanity must face a painful readjustment of its values and attitudes. Death accompanies a new Birth. Joy follows.

Much of the above reflects Eliot's own *spiritual journey* and his conversion to Anglicanism in 1927. Anglicanism, or more particularly Anglo-Catholicism, appealed to his need for orthodox theological dogma and for an emotional, mystical spirituality.

His conversion to Anglicanism was also a consolation to him during the nightmare that was his first marriage. This too was a living death. His marriage with Vivienne Haigh-Wood may explain the most persistent *personal theme* underlying Eliot's poetry i.e. the *sexual*, whose erotic note is as often as not linked with regret, disappointment, frustration and longing. 'The Love Song of J. Alfred Prufrock' explores this theme most strongly. At the centre of Prufrock's purgatory is a *confusion between love and sexual gratification*. Prufrock is both attracted to and repulsed by women. The theme of *appearance and reality*, or the *real and the ideal*, is explored in Prufrock's love-song, where his fear of women who 'fix you with a formulated phrase' is contrasted with his idealised vision of womanhood as 'sea-girls wreathed with seaweed red and brown'.

Eliot's *portrayal of women* is said to be critically and tortuously realistic, reflecting his attitude towards *human relationships* in general. The girl in the 'Preludes' is physically repulsive and, while the woman in the first part of 'A Game of Chess' may be attractive, she is an emotional wreck. The second part of 'A Game of Chess' explores the tragedy resulting from casual relationships. Miss Helen Slingsby, in 'Aunt Helen', is his 'maiden aunt', whose social foibles suggest a fastidious but repressed character and whose mores are flamboyantly rejected by the behaviour of the footman and maid after her death.

For Eliot, though, it is only the *beauty of divine love* that makes sense of all human relationships. In the 'Preludes' he declares:

> I am moved by fancies...
> The notion of some infinitely gentle,
> Infinitely suffering thing.

'The Journey of the Magi' too can be seen as an exploration of divine love or as a struggle to understand the Incarnation of Christ, that moment when divine love made itself manifest.

This theme of *divine love* is made all the more clear in 'East Coker IV', where Christ himself is seen as suffering and dying in order to be reborn. Divine love is linked inextricably with the theme of a journey through suffering to a rebirth.

The Incarnation took place in a moment of time, a moment when historical time and the timelessness of God's eternity met. Eliot's exploration of *time* is central to his poems. It is part of his effort to make sense of life. This is seen in 'Journey of the Magi'.

In 'The Love Song of J. Alfred Prufrock', time is seen as inexorably repetitive, a process which leads ultimately to decay. In the 'Preludes' time is a burden, whose rhythmic patterns beat out the tedium of urban life. Time destroys 'Aunt Helen's' passion for order and restraint, while the result of man's behaviour in times past is seen in 'Rannoch, by Glencoe', where both man and animals are stuck in the wretchedness of history.

## IMAGERY, SYMBOLISM AND ALLUSION

While all of the above are dealt with in specific detail in the discussion of the individual poems, a few general points may be useful for the student also.

Eliot's use of *imagery is eclectic*, that is he drew inspiration from a wide tableau of human experience and did not limit himself to nature as a source, something which had become so much a part of the later Romantics. Under French influence and his admiration for seventeenth-century English poets, Eliot trawled widely to ensure an intellectual sharpness and an emotional intensity in his poems.

Much of the meaning and the power of Eliot's poetry lie in his use of images and symbols. *Sordid, seedy images of city life* appear again and again, from 'The Love Song of J. Alfred Prufrock' to 'Preludes' to 'A Game of Chess'. Even in 'Journey of the Magi', cities are seen as 'hostile'. Such use of significant imagery becomes, with repetition, a symbol. It evokes particular ideas and emotions. This is in keeping with Eliot's rather notorious view that poetry communicates before it is understood. Thus the suggestiveness of imagery and symbolism become part of the excitement of discovery when reading Eliot's poetry.

Similarly *journeys, a street or road are common images* throughout Eliot's poetry. These are seen in 'Journey of the Magi', 'Preludes', 'Usk' and 'Rannoch, by Glencoe', for example. These images also become symbolic, evoking Eliot's search or quest for meaning in life, culminating in his achievement of a satisfactory religious perspective.

However, individual images can also be symbolic. Eliot, for example, uses *animal imagery* to reflect the human in its non-thinking, non-rational state. Hence the use of the crab image/symbol in 'The Love Song of J. Alfred Prufrock'. The 'crow' and 'the patient stag' play similar roles in 'Rannoch, by Glencoe'.

Similarly, Eliot's use of *body parts as images*, as in 'Preludes', 'The Love Song of J. Alfred Prufrock' and 'A Game of Chess' becomes symbolic of the depersonalisation, stereotyping and conformity of modern urban society.

Similarly also, the *images of clocks* and the references to *time* from 'Aunt Helen', to 'Preludes' to 'A Game of Chess' and 'The Love Song of J. Alfred Prufrock', can become a symbol of individual transience and the urgency for renewal.

The student should be particularly aware of Eliot's abrupt transitions in imagery and of his use of images other than visual images. 'Preludes', for example, explores *aural, tactile and olfactory images* in quickly changing, cinematic-style sequences.

Eliot is the most erudite of poets. He was widely read in *everything from literature to history, from psychology to anthropology, from psychology to philosophy*. This is in keeping with his passion not only for self-discovery, but also for discovering the nature of twentieth-century man. Hence his use of allusion is his way of exploring intellectual traditions and expressing himself more precisely.

In this way, his use of allusion is not just an ostentatious *reference to literary history*, for example, but is a way of making a tradition alive again, while also focusing the present situation in that tradition. So, his epigraph in 'The Love Song of J. Alfred Prufrock' both recalls Dante's work and places Prufrock in an urban Hell. Thus, his allusions universalise his themes and the situations in which his characters' personae exist.

Sometimes his allusions come in the form of more *indirect quotation*, as in his reference in 'The Love Song of J. Alfred Prufrock' to Andrew Marvell's poem 'To His Coy Mistress', or in his references to Hamlet and Lazarus. *Direct quotation* of Shakespeare also takes place in 'A Game of Chess', while indirectly Thomas Middleton, Virgil and Milton are alluded to. All such references and allusions help to build up the picture which tells us some universal truth.

The detailed notes on each poem explain the significance of these allusions and references.

VERSE STRUCTURE

In keeping with the French Symbolists' '*vers libre*', or free verse, Eliot broke with the regular forms and structures of his immediate predecessors. The suggestiveness of his imagery and symbols demanded that the structures of his verse should be equally suggestive.

If Eliot's imagery often consists of *abrupt transitions*, so also does his verse structure. The structure often reflects both themes and imagery. Thus the *irregular juxtaposition of lines of different length* in 'The Love Song of J. Alfred Prufrock' reflects the agitated nature of Prufrock, while the regularity of lines 23–34, reflect the incantatory tone of the lines. Similarly, the *short lines 33–35* in 'Journey of the Magi' reflect the anxiety of the magus that no part of his narrative should be overlooked.

Eliot also composes his lines to suggest *the natural speech patterns and rhythms of contemporary speech*. This is particularly true of the pub scene, which opens in line 139 of 'A Game of Chess'. The direct speech rhythms of the female narrator give a sense of immediacy to the tone and themes. Into these speech patterns Eliot introduces *colloquialisms and even slang*. The lines do indeed reflect speech patterns, but they also satisfy a metrical pattern.

At times Eliot *repeats particular words and phrases to give a prayer-like or incantatory tone*. This may also effect a reflective mood. This is seen in 'Journey of the Magi' with the strong repetition of 'And'. The strained repetitiveness of lines in 'A Game of Chess' and in 'The Love Song of J. Alfred Prufrock' reflects the nervous tension of the speakers.

*Rhyme* is used for particular effects in Eliot's poetry. The jingling rhyme of the couplet referring to Michelangelo in 'The Love Song of J. Alfred Prufrock' reflects the shallowness of the women and the mock-heroic tone. Rhyme is used in the 'Preludes' to create a *lyrical effect* in keeping with its title. Both the rhythm and rhyme use in 'East Coker IV' are 're-inventions' of Medieval English verse, which W.B. Yeats, for one, believed helped 'to prolong the moment of contemplation'.

*Eliot's interest in music* is seen not only in many of the titles of his poems – e.g. 'The Love Song of J. Alfred Prufrock', 'Preludes', 'The Four Quartets' – but *in the very structures of the poems and his use of language*. Some of the verses of 'The Love Song of J. Alfred Prufrock' are composed of single sentences, whose repetitiveness not only reflects the tedium of Prufrock's life but give a symphonic effect. The heavy stressed *rhythm* of the 'Preludes' suggests the fatigue of the city's inhabitants, while the lyrical sibilant 's' sounds of lines 9 and 10 of 'Journey of the Magi' evoke the sensuality of the life being left behind. The robust rhythm of 'Usk' suggests the invigorating landscape and underscores the commanding authority of the imperative verbs. The musicality of 'East Coker IV' has been referred to already.

## Eliot – A dramatic poet

As can be seen in his poems, Eliot excels in creating characters whose situations reflect the universal condition of man.

Eliot's greatest *verse drama* is, without doubt, 'Murder in the Cathedral', but many of his poems are verse dramas in themselves. The use of *internal monologue*, or stream-of-consciousness speech, is a particularly effective device in *creating drama* in verse.

'The Love Song of J. Alfred Prufrock' has all the elements of drama. The main character is in *conflict*, within himself and with society in general. In his monologue he develops his conflict and demonstrates his *character*, while also creating both the characters and speech of others. Characters are placed in *particular times and places* where the drama unfolds. A *plot*, or storyline, is developed and comes to a conclusion. The reader, (or audience), becomes interested in the fate of this character – one who reflects the reader's own predicament, perhaps. Overall, *dialogue* is either direct or implied, advancing the plot and enhancing the reader's understanding of the character.

In this way, 'Aunt Helen', 'Preludes', 'A Game of Chess' and 'Journey of the Magi' are also verse dramas. The pub scene in 'A Game of Chess' is a dramatic reflection of the world in miniature. The student may enjoy reading it out loud in 'an appropriate accent'.

Many of Eliot's poems are 'spoken' by created personae or else detached observers. The latter, as in 'Preludes', has been called a cinematic style. For the student interested in film these may prove especially rewarding. It may also be worth noting how many of Eliot's characters are grotesque in the literary sense. In Prufrock, Miss Helen Slingsby and the women in 'A Game of Chess', Eliot has created characters as memorable as those of Shakespeare or Dickens.

## Questions

1. Write a personal response to the poetry of T.S. Eliot. Support your answer by reference to the poetry of Eliot that you have studied.
2. 'The poetry of T.S. Eliot appeals to modern readers for various reasons.'

Write an introduction to Eliot's poetry in which you suggest what these reasons might be.

3. Imagine you have been asked to give a reading of T.S. Eliot's poetry to your class. What poems would you choose and why would you choose them?

4. Suppose someone told you that he/she found T.S. Eliot's poetry too obscure. Write a response to this person in which you outline your understanding of Eliot's poetry.

5. What impression did the poetry of T.S. Eliot make on you as a reader? In your answer you may wish to address the following:
   • your sense of the poet's personality
   • his major themes
   • the poet's use of imagery and language
   • the poem/poems that appealed to you most.

6. 'Eliot's major achievement is as a verse dramatist.'
   Write out a speech you would make to your class on the above topic.

# *Bibliography*

Gardner, Helen, *The Art of T.S. Eliot*, Faber and Faber: London 1985.

Moody, A.David, (editor), *The Cambridge Companion to T.S. Eliot*, Cambridge: Cambridge University Press 1994.

Braybrooke, Neville, (editor), *T.S. A Symposium for His Seventieth Birthday*, Garnstone Press: London 1958.

Donoghue, Denis, *Words Alone: The Poet T.S. Eliot*, Yale University Press 2000.

Steed, C.K., *The New Poetic: Yeats to Eliot*, Pelican Books 1967.

Herbert, Michael, *T.S. Eliot Selected Poems*, York Notes, Longman York Press 1982.

Southam, B.C., *A Student's Guide to The Selected Poems of T.S. Eliot*, Faber and Faber: London 1968.

Press, John, *The Chequer'd Shade: Reflections on Obscurity in Poetry*, Oxford University Press: London 1963.

Leavis, F.R., *New Bearings in English Poetry*, Pelican Books 1972.

^ If the 'water-mill' represents Christ then 'darkness' could represent death which Christ conquers by the Resurrection. On the other hand the water-mill could represent the superior forces of those in the world who put Christ to death.

# 5  Patrick KAVANAGH

*John McCarthy*

## Kavanagh Overview

Kavanagh was born on the 21st of October 1904, in the village of Inniskeen, Co. Monaghan. His father was a shoemaker and had a small farm of land. Kavanagh received only primary school education and at the age of thirteen, he became an apprentice shoemaker. He gave it up 15 months later, admitting that he didn't make one wearable pair of boots. For the next 20 years Kavanagh would work on the family farm, before moving to Dublin in 1939. From his early years on, he was a man who was out of place. When in Monaghan Kavanagh was a dreamer in a world of realists who were concerned with what seemed to him to be the mundanities of life. In Dublin he stood out as the man up from the bog, who didn't understand the complexities of city life. He was seen as gauche and unrefined. Ironically in Monaghan he was seen as effeminate for having an interest in poetry.

Kavanagh's interest in literature and poetry marked him out as different from other people in his local place. In a society that was insular and agricultural, a man's worth was measured by the straightness of the furrow he could plough, rather than the lines of poetry he could write. Kavanagh's first attempts to become a published poet resulted in the publication of some poems in a local newspaper in the early 1930s, and in the publishing of his autobiographical novel, *Tarry Flynn*, in 1939. Urged by his brother Peter, who was a Dublin-based teacher, Kavanagh moved to the city to establish himself as a writer. At that time, the Dublin Literary Society was dominated by an educated Anglo-Irish group with whom Kavanagh had nothing in common; among them were Oliver St John Gogarty and Douglas Wylie. They saw Kavanagh as a country bumpkin and referred to him as 'that Monaghan boy'.

Kavanagh's early years in Dublin were unproductive as he struggled for recognition. In 1947 his first major collection, 'A Soul for Sale', was published. These poems were the product of his Monaghan youth. In the early 1950s Kavanagh and his brother Peter published a weekly newspaper called 'Kavanagh's Weekly'; it failed because the editorial viewpoint was too narrow. In 1954 Kavanagh became embroiled in an infamous court case. He accused 'The Leader' newspaper of slander. The newspaper decided to contest the case and employed the former Taoiseach, John A. Costello, as their defence counsel;

Kavanagh decided to prosecute the case himself, and he was destroyed by Costello. The court case dragged on for over a year and Kavanagh's health began to fail. In 1955 he was diagnosed as having lung cancer and had a lung removed; he survived, and the event was a major turning point in his life and career. In 1958 he published 'Come Dance with me Kitty Stobling'. In 1959 he was appointed by John A. Costello to the faculty of English in UCD. His lectures were popular, but often irrelevant to the course. In the early 1960s he visited Britain and the USA; in 1965 he married Katherine Maloney. He died in 1967 from an attack of bronchitis. Kavanagh's reputation as a poet is based on the lyrical quality of his work, his mastery of language and form and his ability to transform the ordinary and the banal into something of significance. He is an acute observer of things and situations, and this allows him to make things that may seem ordinary and unimportant into something deserving of a place in poetry.

He is constantly using his work to make sense of the natural world, be it in Dublin or Monaghan. More importantly, Kavanagh is always trying to assess his own place in this world. He often approaches a poem from a point of doubt, where he is unsure about where he belongs, and uses the poem to come to a resolution. The best example of this is in the poem 'Epic'. He is also trying to praise God and Nature in his poems. Indeed his Monaghan poems are not so much about the area, but about how it affects him and his work. It would not be unfair to say that Kavanagh is very self-obsessed. But on the other hand, he is writing about what he knows best.

## Technique and Style

### LANGUAGE

In attempting to create a sense of the mystery and magic of a child's mind, Kavanagh's use of language is a vital ingredient in his work. He uses words in a new fashion. He fuses words together, such as 'clay-minted' and most famously 'leafy-with-love'. These phrases and words give extra energy to his poetry and provide it with vigour.

### IMAGERY

Kavanagh's use of imagery is a very important aspect of his language. In 'Advent' he alludes to the Nativity: '...old stables where Time begins'. In 'Inniskeen Road' he refers to Alexander Selkirk. Colloquial language is an intrinsic element of Kavanagh's style. His phraseology is conversational and many of his phrases owe their origin to his Monaghan background: 'Among simple decent men too who barrow dung...'; 'he stared at me half eyed'; '...every blooming thing'.

## Structure – Form

The poems on the course display Kavanagh's ability in the sonnet form, which is a structural feature of 'Inniskeen Road', 'Advent', 'Lines Written...' and Canal Bank Walk'. In 'Inniskeen Road', Kavanagh combines features of the Petrarchan and Shakespearean forms. Stanzaic pattern reflects the Petrarchan subdivision of a sonnet into an octet and a sestet. In the octet a picture is painted by the poet and the problems are posed. The poet's own personal response is contained in the sestet. The opening stanza can be subdivided into two quatrains, each containing a separate picture of Monaghan life. The sestet also can be divided into a quatrain and couplet, therefore mirroring the Shakespearean division into three quatrains followed by a rhyming couplet. The rhyme scheme of the poem is also Shakespearean: *abab, cdcd, efef, gg*. 'Advent' represents Kavanagh's particular use of the sonnet form. The poem is an amalgam of two sonnets, and the stanzaic pattern is neither Petrarchan nor Shakespearean. The opening two stanzas each contain seven lines, with the third stanza representing an entire sonnet. The division of the sonnet into two septets is unusual and Kavanagh formulates a rhyme scheme to parallel this: *aabbccbd, aab, aacc*. Stanza three is again different as Kavanagh reverts to the Shakespearean rhyming technique: *abab, cded, fgfg, hh*. The thought pattern of the third stanza follows that set out by the opening two stanzas, with a natural pause occurring at the end of the seventeenth line. The reason why Kavanagh does not create a fourth stanza is that the rhythm of the third one reflects the excitement that he associates with having rediscovered '...the luxury of a child's soul'. The three stanzas in the poem reflect the three stages in Kavanagh's bid to regain this position – penance, forgiveness, grace.

'Canal Bank Walk' is written in the traditional 14-line sonnet form with no stanzaic separation. In this poem, Kavanagh combines both the Petrarchan and Shakespearean sonnets, using the same methods as in 'Inniskeen Road'.

'Lines Written...' is fashioned completely in the Petrarchan style. Both the thought pattern and the rhyming scheme follow an octet–sestet sublimation.

'Memory...' and 'On Raglan Road' are reminiscent of ballad technique in that they each feature four-line stanzas; however, Kavanagh doesn't stick rigidly to the rhyming schemes of the ballad, displaying again his ability to individualise a fashion or feature.

## Religion

Religion is a dominant feature in Kavanagh's poetry, both as a theme and as a source of imagery. Religion features thematically in 'Advent', 'Canal Bank Walk' and in a minor way in 'Stony Grey Soil'. 'Advent' derives from religion in both its theme and its main source of imagery. The theme of the poem is penance–forgiveness–grace, which reflects the Catholic church's seasons of

Advent, the Nativity and the beginning of the new church year. Kavanagh formulates his wish to return to the state of innocence as a child within the imagery of religion, using original sin to represent acquired knowledge, penance as a main act of contrition and the grace of the forgiven soul as the newly required state of innocence. In 'Canal Bank Walk' the theme is one of redemption reflecting baptism, as Kavanagh draws analogies between the waters of the baptismal font and the water of the canal.

RURAL AND URBAN

Although Kavanagh arrived in Dublin in 1939, leaving behind his sixteen acres of stony grey soil, it was not until the mid-1950s that his adopted city provided the environmental background to his work. The summer of 1955 and the banks of the Grand Canal in Dublin are the time and place which moved Kavanagh to write 'Canal Bank Walk' and 'Lines Written...'.

Kavanagh's attitude to the environment changed dramatically following his operation for lung cancer. He said, 'As a poet I was born in or about 1955, the place of my birth being the banks of the Grand Canal.' This new appreciation of the environment, his vision of Eden, is evident in his novel *Tarry Flynn*, where he wrote: 'O the rich beauty of the weeds in the ditches, Tarry's heart cried: the lush Nettles and Docks and tuffs of grass. Life pouring out in critical abundance.' In the novel he also wrote, 'Without ambition, without desire, the beauty of the world pared in thought his unresting mind.' These two sentences describe exactly the moods of Kavanagh in 'Canal Bank Walk' and 'Lines Written...' Here the environment is glorified in a pantheistic manner. Kavanagh uses hyperbole and many neologisms in an attempt to demonstrate the magnificence of Nature, as experienced by the innocent mind of a child or of the poet reformed to the state of grace. The opposing attitudes expressed by Kavanagh to the environments of Monaghan and Dublin reflect more on his state of mind than on the environments themselves. In 1963 he did recognise the beauty of the Monaghan countryside:

> Thirty-years before, Shank Duff's water-fill could of done the trick for me, but I was too thick to realise it.

## Bibliography

PRIMARY SOURCES

| | |
|---|---|
| Ploughman and other poems | 1936 |
| The Green Fool | 1938 |
| The Great Hunger | 1942 |

| A Soul for Sale | 1947 |
| Tarry Flynn | 1948 |
| Recent Poems | 1958 |
| Come Dance with me Kitty Stobling | 1960 |
| Self Portrait | 1964 |
| The Complete Poems | 1972 (Posthumous) |

SECONDARY SOURCES

| John Nemo | *Patrick Kavanagh* |
| Alan Warner | *Clay is the Word* |
| Antoinette Quinn | *Patrick Kavanagh: Born Again Romantic* |
| Peter Kavanagh | *Sacred Keeper* |
| Anthony Cronin | *Dead as Doornails* |

# *Inniskeen Road: July Evening*

Text of poem: New Explorations Anthology page 234

Kavanagh self-visualises himself in this poem. The poem is all about him, even though he spends over half the poem appearing to be concerned with others. In the poem Kavanagh attempts to describe where he sees his position in society; this question is central to all of his work. His position is at best on the fringes of the society he chooses, and at worst completely outside it and isolated. Another question central to Kavanagh's work is: where does he want to be? Is this role, as the outsider looking in, one that he has decided suits him? Does he need the tension of being different to stimulate his work?

The poem may or may not be based on a real event, but the first thing that Kavanagh does is make everything seem real. He does this by giving us real places and time. The poem's title presupposes a reality. It is 'Inniskeen Road', not a road in Monaghan. It is 'July Evening', not some time in his youth. Kavanagh seems to be looking for sympathy in this poem, and by making things real he adds to this emotional appeal. He even mention's 'Billy Brennan's barn', which is a real place owned by a real person. The premise is that if Kavanagh is using fact here, then everything else that he says must also be true.

In fact the truth may matter little, and what may be most important in this poem is how Kavanagh sees himself and how he wants to be seen.

This part is simple. To Kavanagh, he is *'l'étranger'*. He is the outsider who can observe his own community's actions from the inside, yet still look objectively. The major question for a reader is, 'Is Kavanagh objective enough?' The answer to this question must be 'no'. Even when he's outside the action of the poem, his observing is still central to the poem.

## WHAT DOES KAVANAGH SEE?

He sees society passing him by. He sees local people passing him by on the way to a dance. They don't look at him or stop to talk to him. They are in 'twos and threes'; he is on his own. They are on their way to something too important. This is a regular occurrence.

> There's a dance in Billy Brennan's barn tonight.

This is not *the* dance. It's just *a* dance. It is a regular thing that he takes no part of. It appears he never will. The alliteration in this line suggests optimism and a childlike sense of fun, and these sit uneasily with Kavanagh. The alliteration of the B's is inapposite with the spat-out sounds of desperation that come in the final stanza.

Kavanagh sees a means of communication that he does not understand. He hears 'half-talk' and 'wink and elbow language'. This frustrates him. He is not allowed to be part of this society. There is even a hint of knowingness and sexuality in this way that people are communicating.

As full of people and life and communication as the first quatrain was, the second quatrain is quickly depopulated. Kavanagh spends four lines telling us that there is nobody to be seen. Even the coded language he complained about in lines three and four is gone for there is:

> ... not
> A footfall tapping secrecies of stone.

As much as he complained about the people passing him by, he seems to feel that it was better than the silence.

This quatrain is full of the language of spy movies. It is almost like a scene from the movie *The Third Man*, with its silence and secrets and footfalls and shadows. Again there is a frustrated isolation evident here. Kavanagh is convinced that he is incapable of decoding the language and the nuances that these people use.

In the sestet, Kavanagh gets to the nub of the matter. The people that populated the octet are gone and now he turns to himself. He addresses his audience in an aggressive and prosaic manner. He is direct and uncompromising in the first two lines. He then makes direct reference to a much older poem by William Cowper, 'Verses supposed to be written by Alexander Selkirk'. Cowper's Selkirk has the following to say:

> I am monarch of all I survey.
> My right there is none to dispute;
> From the centre all round to the sea,
> I am lord of the fowl and the brute.
> O solitude! Where are the charms

That sages have seen in thy face?
Better dwell in the midst of alarms
Than reign in this horrible place.

Kavanagh takes these sentiments and adapts them to his own situation. He is more concerned with the bogs and farms of county Monaghan than with a deserted island where Selkirk was supposed to have been abandoned. He nevertheless shares the sentiment that his 'gift' brings bitter fruits with it. Is this too extreme a metaphor? Selkirk was abandoned and left on a deserted island. In circumstances beyond his control, he had to live the life of a hermit on a deserted island, with no hope of communicating with anybody for years. Kavanagh is in self-enforced exile, unless you submit to his own theory that he has no choice but to be a poet, and to be a poet meant exiling himself from the society that he felt closest to. The irony is that he still needs to write about these people and include them in his poetry. There is a complete contradiction between trying to stay away from these people and still writing about them centrally.

He finishes his rant with the wonderful pun on the curse 'blooming thing'. The double meanings are a euphemism for 'bloody' and another word for 'growing'. If he says 'bloody', you can understand this: he is angry at his exile. If he is talking about 'growth', then he is saying that there is room for growth in a land where there should not be hope for any type of growth, an area 'Of banks and stones ... '; maybe this is like his poetry, an area were he sees little of hope, but that little amount of hope is enough for a poem to grow.

## LANGUAGE, STRUCTURE AND SOUNDS

Kavanagh works within the confines of the sonnet and this seems to suit his purpose well. The structure moves from the first quartet, which is well populated, to the second quartet where everybody is now off the road and in the barn, presumably enjoying themselves. The sestet brings us Kavanagh and allows him to pontificate on what all this means to him.

The rhyming sequence is *abab cdcd efefgg*. The effect of this is a highly exalted poetic sense. By working with a Shakespearean structure, he seems to imply a sense of accuracy and truth, that everything that is reported is correct.

The sonnet's sense of false balance is also used well. There is no 'I' in the first eight lines, yet it dominates the sestet.

The prominent sounds in the poem suggest anger and bitterness. The heavily prominent 'B' sound at the beginning is spat out like an unwanted taste by his use of alliteration. Importantly, he brings this sound back right at the end of the poem, when he writes about '... every blooming thing.'

# Epic

Text of poem: New Explorations Anthology page 236

This poem has a grandiose title, a grandiose first line and an even more grandiose last sentence. Kavanagh's favourite poetic theme has always been poetry and the role of the poet. He is constantly self-conscious. Often in his poetry he will use a specific real event from his own life or the lives of the people who surrounded him in order to make a more direct point about poetry, the job of the poet or aesthetics.

In this poem he uses a real incident: a row between two families over a plot of land. In the notes to the collected poems, Kavanagh's brother Peter gives the background to the incident:

> I recall the row over the half a rood of rock in 1938. The row was temporarily settled when the contestants agreed to arbitration by the local schoolmaster who was also unofficial surveyor. Neither side was fully satisfied and the row smouldered for some years. Today all the surrounding farms including the disputed rock are owned by the same farmer.

Kavanagh starts the poem in what might seem to be an ironic mood. Words such as 'important places' and 'great events' can hardly be appropriate when referring to something as trivial as a dispute between two families over a 'half a rood of rock' or 'iron stones'. But when relativity kicks in, then these retrospectively trivial occurrences can seem gigantic to the protagonists. This, according to Kavanagh, is the stuff of poetry. This is where his concerns are, because this is where his people's concerns are. The 'Munich Bother' might as well have been happening on another planet as far as the Duffys and the McCabes were concerned. It would be easy for Kavanagh to mock or patronise these people, but he doesn't. Or at least he doesn't any more. Kavanagh admits that he was:

> ... inclined
> To lose my faith in Ballyrush and Gortin

But he was inspired by a fellow artist, the great Greek poet Homer, whose 'Ghost came whispering to my mind'. Kavanagh says that if it was good enough for Homer and Greece, then it must be good enough for himself and the parishes of County Monaghan.

In the action of the poem, Kavanagh sets up a drama between the two sides and reports about it directly to us. He even tells us what each side said. The fierceness of the dispute is typified by the warlike declaration of 'Damn your soul'.

He shows us one of the protagonists stepping on the disputed land and declaring a new border between the families – the iron stones being like Hitler's Iron Cross.

It then looks as if he is delving into farce, as he compares this dispute with one of the twentieth century's most important events, the beginning of World War Two. He even dismisses this event as 'the Munich bother'.

When he finally decides on which one was more important, he says he has changed his mind. He tells us that once he dismissed the local matter, but then after he did some reading of Homer's 'Iliad' (and more importantly, E.V. Rieu's biography of Homer), he came to change his mind.

In Kavanagh's poem 'On Looking into E.V. Rieu's Homer' he describes the Greek poet's vision:

> For only the half-god can see
> The Immortal in things mortal.

And later he observes of Homer:

> The intensity that radiated from
> The Far Field Rock – you afterwards denied –
> Was the half-god seeing his half-brothers
> Joking on the fabulous mountain-side.

In 'Epic' he is talking to Homer to justify the idea that nothing is beyond a poet's telling of it. A literary classic may begin in a simple local event, but it is the poet's telling of it that makes it immortal. It is not the event but the reporting of the event that gives immortality. By proposing this thesis Kavanagh makes this not a poem about a local dispute, but a poem about poetry itself.

Kavanagh's ego comes through twice. First of all he shows no shyness in comparing himself with Homer. Remember that this poem was published in the early 1940s, before Kavanagh's reputation was in any way established in the way it is today. To compare himself with one of the most important poets of all time seems incredibly presumptuous. He also seems to compare a poet with a God in this poem and in the other Homer poem. He says that a poet is a creator of worlds. There may be some sense to this; a poet does have control of the world that he reports on. He is allowed to influence his readers' thoughts. It seems that Kavanagh is acknowledging the importance of this role. He is saying that what a poet reports on will last and become important.

At the end of the poem the reader is left to wonder whether the events are important or not, because Kavanagh uses those events to make a point about poetry itself, rather than the events the poem is describing.

# Shancoduff

Text of poem: New Explorations Anthology page 238

[*Note: This poem is also prescribed for the Ordinary Level 2005 exam*]

According to the critic Antoinette Quinn, 'Shancoduff is a north-facing hill farm depicted at its wintry worst, frostbound, starved of grass, swept by sleety winds.' Yet this is a love poem to it.

Kavanagh had a love–hate relationship with the countryside of his youth. One of his most famous poems is 'Stony Grey Soil'. In that poem the poet accused the area where he was reared of burgling 'his bank of youth'. He describes the area as being one that is lifeless and soulless, and he questions how he managed to survive in a place where even plant life struggled to maintain an existence. Yet in this poem his attitude is different; he is more interested in finding the good in his 'black hills'. He turns any notion of something negative into something positive. He transforms the faults of Shancoduff in the same way that a lover transforms his partner's faults into something to be loved. The immediate question that must be asked is: Why would anybody write a love-poem to Shancoduff?

The answer must be because the hills are his. He claims ownership four times. He calls them '*My* black hills' twice in the first verse, and then '*My* hills' and '*my* Alps' in the second. Possession of this land is obviously very important to Kavanagh. After all, they are 'eternal'. Shancoduff will last long after he has gone and more importantly, they will still be there after the people who sneer at them are gone. He also personifies them. They are given a personality like a lover would have. The hills can 'look', they are 'incurious', they are 'happy', they 'hoard'.

Kavanagh relishes their drabness. Anything that might be confused as being something negative can be construed into a positive: for example, the fact that the hills are so incurious or inactive that they can't even be bothered to look at the sun. This is seen as a good thing when Kavanagh compares it with the fate of Lot's wife, who was turned into a pillar of salt for looking back as she left Sodom and Gomorrah.

Kavanagh puts a lot of emphasis on the local place names. He lists them with pride: Glassdrummond, Rocksavage, Featherna Bush; these are as important as the Alps. The names themselves have mythic qualities. They sound tough and treacherous. They have a resonance of something from an action movie, in which a hero stands proud above the hills. They all have a grandness granted to them by being multisyllabic.

Kavanagh's own importance in the poem is also highlighted here as the person who has:

> ... climbed the Matterhorn
> with a sheaf of hay for three perishing calves.

This act itself seems heroic, as if he had climbed the most dangerous mountain face in the world – whereas all he has done is walk up a hill to feed the cows. This use of hyperbole shows the love that Kavanagh has for this place. The rebellious nature of the hills is also shown as they refuse to conform to the usual structures of nature. They are oblivious to the changes in the seasons and the weather. Their immortality is stressed by the fact that they are unchanged by the travails of time  Springtime cannot catch up with them as his

> ... hills hoard the bright shillings of March
> While the sun searches in every pocket.

The poem turns at this point; the poet has come to the realisation, albeit after being told, that his mountains are not the glorious thing of beauty that he may have thought they were. The farmers who are in a more sheltered, wealthier place sneer at him. Even though his hills are personified with their 'rushy beards', nobody else declares them worth looking after. When he is acknowledged as a poet, it is almost done as a form of derision. A poet may be someone who is seen as poor.

Kavanagh departs with a rhetorical question that is forced on him by the comments of the other men. This affects him deeply, just as if his wife or lover were to be described as ugly or disgusting. He asks himself: 'Is my heart not badly shaken?' The love that he felt for  the hills is broken by the piece of reality forced on him.


# *The Great Hunger*
Text of poem: New Explorations Anthology page 240


'The Great Hunger' could well be Kavanagh's most important work; the format of the poem is certainly the most unique and ambitious. One of Kavanagh's biggest influences (although their subject matter was often completely different) was the English poet W.H. Auden. Auden was one of the best and most frequent practitioners of the long poem. 'The Great Hunger' is quite different from Auden's dramatic poems, or his 'Letter to Lord Byron' or 'New Year Letter', which are meditations on a specific time. Even poets who were in turn influenced by Kavanagh, like John Montague and Seamus Heaney, knitted together a series of poems to make up 'The Rough Field' and 'Station Island' respectively. This long poem is almost divided as a novelist would divide a book into chapters, with different parts coming together to give us a more rounded view of the life, times and opinions of Patrick Maguire.

Kavanagh takes on a narrative structure in this poem. The narrative allows him to use a cinematic technique to develop the central character in the poem. 'The Great Hunger' is focalised completely around the character of Patrick Maguire. It allows us to see what he sees, feel what he feels and hear what he says and hears. However, it also allows us some time to look at Maguire objectively.

Kavanagh seems to be on a voyage of discovery in this poem, and he seems to be enjoying bringing his reader with him. He uses a 'cinematic technique' to do this, by helping the reader to visualise what's going on as it happens. He is always shifting the angle, even though we are constantly viewing the character of Maguire. In the middle of the first section he reaffirms this by imploring the reader to:

> Watch him, watch him, that man on a hill whose spirit
> Is a wet sack flapping about the knees of time,

This poem sees Kavanagh with his most negative attitude towards his own background. The poem begins with lifelessness and a sense of biblical foreboding where the Word is not made Flesh, a symbol of the beginning of Life. Instead all is turned to where Death exists. We are pointed to where the dead go; in Kavanagh's landscape we begin with a lack of life.

> Clay is the word and clay is the flesh.

It is already obvious that this terrain that Kavanagh is about to map out is one that sees little chance for hope. When we see the

> ... potato-gatherers like mechanised scare-crows move
> Along the side-fall of the hill –

it feels like being stuck in a purgatorial vision from Dante. Then Kavanagh gives his instruction and his despair as he asks:

> If we watch them an hour is there anything we can prove
> Of life as it is broken-backed over the Book
> Of Death?

There appears to be no hope in this landscape at all. There appears to be no sympathy between the inhabitants of the landscape, between wind and worms and frogs and seagulls. And then he gets to the question that must be asked: why write this poem? What is the point in examining this seemingly desolate terrain? He tells us that he is searching for the 'light of imagination'. He is searching for something worth searching for.

He finds what he is looking for in a character who seems different from the other bleak people who live on the terrain. The rest of this first section of the poem attempts to show us Patrick Maguire. Kavanagh promises us a view of his life:

Till the last soul passively like a bag of wet clay
Rolls down the side of the hill,

This life is in a terrain where accuracy and intent are dismissed, things seem to happen with routine – but if they don't, it doesn't seem to matter too much. Kavanagh litters this early part of the poem with places where the plough missed, dogs lie lazily and horses pull rusty ploughs. This languorous air seems to suit Maguire, or at least that's the impression that he likes to give. He shrugs off the idea that experience of a broader life would be preferable – but the narrator of the poem tells us differently when he tells us that Maguire 'pretended to his soul'. Maguire convinces himself that children would only get in his way and be a nuisance even more than crows are. There is a sense here of regret; that something is missing from his life.

Central to this is the idea that Maguire is married to the land. The land dominates his life: he is in love with it and he hates it. He is committed to it, but the commitment may be too much. It is causing a deficit in other areas of his life. The narrator shows us Maguire bent among the potato fields, turning over the clumps of root. He asks *the* most important question: 'What is he looking for there?' The answer tells us that Maguire is a man lost; a man who thinks he is in control of his own life and destiny, but isn't. We know this from his answer: 'He thinks it is a potato, but we know better ...' This seems like condescension from the omniscient narrator, but we now get a chance to examine Maguire in his own voice. The narrator is almost saying to us, 'If you don't believe what I'm saying, then listen for yourself.'

At this point the narration changes to allow us to listen to Maguire. When we hear him speak, he sounds like a man in charge of his own affairs. He is giving instruction to his workers, he is ordering people to 'move', 'balance', 'pull', 'straddle'. He is a man in touch with Nature:

The wind's over Brannagan's, now that means rain.

He is capable of planning for the future:

And that's a job we'll have to do in December,

and capable of getting angry when he sees 'Cassidy's ass'.

So perhaps he is not the solitary stand-still figure that we saw in the first 40 lines. But if we believed that thesis, then the narrator brings us back to earth by putting Maguire back in the 'cloud-swung wind'. He is married to the land: a man who is living his life for the future not of his children, but of the crops that will grow in his fields even when he:

> Is spread in the bottom of a ditch under two coulters
> crossed in Christ's Name.

This poignant vision of his own future, as no future at all, is even more depressing with the symbol of the Cross being represented by two parts of a plough. There is also the element of martyrdom here. He has sacrificed his own life for the good of others.

We are shown his distance from a regular youth by the way he sees girls of his own age. If they laughed, they laughed at him. When they screamed, he regarded them as animals. He knew that life was showing him a difficult path ahead, and it seems that perhaps he was aiming for it.

The next piece, from lines 67 to 79, is probably the most harrowing of the poem. Maguire seems depressingly regretful here; he is not able to shake 'a knowing head | And pretend to his soul'. He acknowledges that he is trapped by his undying commitment to the land; he knows that there is no easy way out from here, but that perhaps there was a time when a way out was possible. He sighs in despair twice: 'O God if I had been wiser!' The only thing that lifts him temporarily from his despair is the knowledge that he could be part of a bigger picture, that he and his life are part of Nature and God's will, because 'God's truth is life', even the hardship that he has to endure. The trick that Maguire has learned is to find ways of coping with Nature. He has taught himself compensatory skills, such as when to avoid life's obstacles, when to avoid climbing over boulders that will make him bleed.

The poem begins its end with universal natural images – the sun, rain, wind, light – blending in with more local, specific images like Donaghmoyne and Brady's farm, reinforcing the earlier thesis that 'God's truth is life,' no matter where it is.

Finally an invitation is issued to look at the beginnings of this story (we have already seen the end). The narrator asks us to detach ourselves and listen to the grim story that he wants to tell.

It must be remembered that this poem is part of a larger piece. There are dominant themes in the poem of self-sacrifice and of the relationship between man and Nature, and more specifically of the relationship between man and The Land. It would be wrong, however, to see this poem as one of Kavanagh's lyric poems, that have an exact structure and a single dominant theme. It is more wide ranging in its scope and aspirations. It genuinely attempts to provide a truthful, honest and – most importantly – full picture of a man at a particular time. By doing that Kavanagh gives us an insight into a whole society. He is presenting a vivid portrait of rural Ireland in the prewar years by focusing us on the character of Patrick Maguire.

# A Christmas Childhood

Text of poem: New Explorations Anthology page 245

[*Note: this poem is also prescribed for the 2005 Ordinary level exam*]

In 'A Christmas Childhood', Kavanagh seems to be very conscious of his voice and the voice that he is using in the poem. Kavanagh adopts an innocent, naïve attitude in this poem and that seems to be central to both the style and the substance. It is the merging of what he is saying and how he is saying it that gives the poem real quality. It uses simple, direct language and this simplicity is also important in what the poet is attempting to say. It is, however, in this reader's eyes a poem of two halves, to use the football cliché. Indeed it was originally published as two separate pieces, the first part being published in 1943, and what is now the second part a full three years earlier. This reader feels that the later addition was unnecessary.

## Part I

The poem begins with a simple description of a potato field, where one side was in the sun and was beginning to thaw out. The other side was still frozen over and 'white with frost'. Nature dominates everything; it takes over and liberates inanimate objects. The paling-post that was once merely supporting a fence now sends music out through it:

> And when we put our ears to the paling-post
> The music that came out was magical.

The way that nature attacks all the senses is important to Kavanagh. He goes through sight, taste and hearing in order to give us a holistic vision of how the Christmas spirit invades everything.

He then inserts an 'over-the-top' repetition of his emotions. Hyperbole pervades this part, with even the fence providing 'magical' music. He continues with this mixture of the simple and the marvellous when comparing a gap of light with 'a hole in Heaven's gable.' Even an apple tree reminds him of the temptation of Adam.

The death of innocence, and a longing to return to innocence, is a familiar theme in Kavanagh's poetry and it is reinforced here. The world has taken him, like Eve took Adam from what he supposed was a better life:

> O you, Eve, were the world that tempted me
> To eat the knowledge that grew in clay
> And death the germ within it!

He then sets up the second part of the poem by leaving us tranquil symbols of the 'gay garden that was childhood's', the most important being the final image:

'Of a beauty that the world did not touch.'

There is a longing here to return to a better time for himself. That time is when people were more dependent on Nature. This closer interaction with Nature is epitomised and made clearer by the amount of religious imagery that runs through the first section. There is plenty of religious imagery present, such as 'Heaven's gable' and Eve and the apple. The time was more sacred to Kavanagh; he saw it as a time that was also good and holy.

## Part II

The second part of the poem continues with the religious imagery, making striking comparisons between an Irish town and Bethlehem with its 'stars in the morning east'. There is a genuine excitement pervading this part and it is less diluted by adult knowingness than the first part was. There are simple descriptions of what was going on in his childhood, and this allows him to retain an attitude of childlike wonder. The voice in the second half of the poem is certainly more full of clarity.

The setting for the second half of the poem is almost completely outdoors, and this natural open setting allows him to go from the local to the universal – or even biblical – with ease. There is a seamless intertwining of the personal and the public. Again, the significance of the fact that the father was playing his music outdoors cannot be underplayed. He finds harmony with Nature and allows it to influence his playing. The stars manage to recognise his father's music and are so captivated that they decide to dance to it.

Rapidly Kavanagh brings us back to his own townland and remarks on the unspoken signs between the families. Where in 'Epic' he describes local rivalries, here the unspoken language of music is a uniting force as 'his melodion called | To Lennons and Callans.' Kavanagh remarks that he 'knew some strange thing had happened.' The harmonising power of his father's music is highly significant when one reflects on the first verse, where the music from the paling-post is described as magical.

His mother's daily ritual of milking the cows becomes inspired by 'the frost of Bethlehem'. The religious imagery continues here. Bethlehem brought new hope to Christians, and this time of year, with its sense of a new start, also suggests rebirth. Nature in the form of ice and wind and the water-hen is recalled. It is the sense of 'wonder of a Christmas townland', where even the dawn is personified and winks, which makes this poem one of the most beautiful that Kavanagh wrote. Yet again he tries to show how the senses are affected: sight with the 'child-poet (who) picked out letters'; the sound of the melodion and of when:

A water-hen screeched on the bog,
Mass-going feet
Crunched the wafer-ice on the potholes,

In the sixth verse he shows exquisite skill at mixing the northern constellation Cassiopeia with 'Cassidy's hanging hill', using run-through lines with clever use of alliteration to expose the child's sense of awe at Christmas. This also introduces the religious notion again and suggests the Eastern Star that guided the Three Wise Men towards the birth of Christ; instead, the stars guide people towards his father's house.

There is one wise man who proves his intelligence by commenting on the poet's father's fiddle playing. His father is working just like Nature, when the inanimate is brought to life as the man says, 'Can't he make it talk.'

Pleasant childhood memories of Christmas are exposed graciously throughout the poem: his father's way of making the melodion talk, his mother's commitment to the daily work on the farm, his presents, and an overall satisfaction that Nature had provided all of these things.

## *Advent*

Text of poem: New Explorations Anthology page 248

'Advent' is a poem made up of two sonnets. The sonnet itself is a structure that gives way to easy division. It is usually divided into an octet followed by a sestet. Kavanagh abandons this convention in the first sonnet, dividing his sonnet into two even halves of seven lines each. It is no coincidence that in this poem he seeks an equality. (That initial octet is often divided into two quatrains.) So the idea of stitching two separate sonnets together should immediately suggest some sort of linear progression of ideas. Kavanagh does that in this poem. The journey that he decides to adopt is a peculiar one;  he sets out his new poetic manifesto in this poem. To do so, he decides that in order to go forwards, he must first go back. The poem was originally called 'Renewal', and to this reader that title was certainly a more direct approach.

The poem starts with a world-weary reminiscence to somebody familiar:

We have tested and tasted too much, lover

He then returns to an earlier poem, 'A Christmas Childhood'. In that poem he states:

The light between the ricks of hay and straw
Was a hole in Heaven's gable.

Here he points out that you can overexpose yourself. He decides that it is more worthwhile to search for the minutiae of life than for true wonderment. So he has to go back to real basics in a genuine and ascetic way, because 'Through a chink too wide there comes no wonder.'

He advocates returning to simple sustenance, because he feels that this will garner a truer sense of spiritual purity. When he talks about penance he attributes no negativity to it, but rather sees it as part of a process towards self-fulfilment. He promises himself that he will give back the negativity of useless knowledge. Experience for its own sake is not enough for him now – just as it wasn't when he was younger. Back then he did not appreciate it:

> The knowledge we stole but could not use.

In the second half of the first sonnet he spells out his own poetic manifesto. He needs to return to a state where he finds wonder in simple things. He makes a list of the lifestyle he has abandoned, and he obviously feels that he has suffered from being without this feeling. He wants to have his spirit shocked; he needs to feel a 'prophetic astonishment'. If he can find these things again, then he will have a poetic rebirth.

It is all very well Kavanagh talking about these things; the proof will come in whether or not he puts them into practice.

> And the newness that was in every stale thing
> When we looked at it as children.

Kavanagh uses hyperbole again and again in his poems, to great effect. So when he talks about 'the spirit-shocking | Wonder in a black slanting Ulster hill', the sense of uniqueness is certainly very heightened, even though it seems mundane now. He is longing for a time when these hills were comparable to the Alps. It is perception that is important here, and the ability to see things as though for the first time. Again Kavanagh is never content with dealing with one of the senses, just in case we might think that sight is the only sensation that is allowed to be heightened. To a child, even what is heard seems different. What can seem now to an adult like 'the tedious talking | Of an old fool' can be relayed to the child as 'prophetic astonishment'.

The imagery that he uses in the poem is one clear indication that he is capable of doing this. He uses apparent opposites to achieve it. When he breaks a paradox he sets out his poetic philosophy, so he can reconcile 'newness in every stale thing', 'astonishment in the tedious talking of an old fool ...', and he can find 'old stables where Time begins'. This brings to mind a connection reminding us that Jesus himself was born in a an 'old stable'. There is a strong note of caution here: don't take things like 'bog-holes, cart-tracks, old stables' for granted.

The second sonnet allows Kavanagh to say what he's going to do about all of this. He is saying that the poetry is dependent on his attitude. If he opens himself to a new way of reacting to Nature, then the poetry will come to him. There is a lot of emphasis on faith and fate in the second verse; he seems determined to change his ways now. He says, 'We'll have no need to go searching', or he insists we don't have to listen for it: 'We'll hear it ....' It is almost as if the hearing is enough and that the hearing will come naturally, too. If he gives way to God.

Where this new inspiration comes from is an important element. It will be in simple places and from simple people doing simple things, such as:

> ... in the whispered argument of a churning
> Or in the streets where the village boys are lurching.

And especially:

> Wherever life pours ordinary plenty.

This shall be reward in itself. The inspiration will come to him. Indeed, too much analysis by him could destroy the beauty of the act. He makes this clear when he insists to his lover:

> Won't we be rich, my love and I, and please
> God we shall not ask for reason's payment,
> The why of heart-breaking strangeness ...
> Nor analyse God's breath in common statement.

This is a Catholic poem, accepting without question God's goodness and simplicity, and Kavanagh insists that 'pleasure, knowledge and the conscious hour' should be 'thrown in the dust-bin'. He must open himself to the glory of God and constantly praise the vision that he has been given.

The poem is partly an obituary for the past, and partly an incantation to a new celebratory aesthetic. Kavanagh says that by learning the lessons of self-sacrifice and rebirth that are taught during Advent, he will re-emerge reinvigorated and more in understanding with Christ, like a 'January flower.'

# On Raglan Road

Text of poem: New Explorations Anthology page 250

*Note: This poem is better known as a song, made most famous by Luke Kelly of the Dubliners. It is worth the reader's effort to hear a recorded version of this song.*

This is a love poem. In itself this is rare in Kavanagh's poetry. It is a love poem tinged with regret. Kavanagh sometimes prided himself on his innocence in his poems; indeed, in a number of them he advocated a sensibility that encouraged it. In this poem he expects the reader to see him as completely naïve.

He begins the poem with a specific place. This is very similar to many of his poems. Of the poems in this anthology, however, this is the first poem set in Dublin rather than in Monaghan. When Kavanagh names a place he does so not only because

> Naming these things is the love act,
> ['The Hospital']

but also because the naming of these places helps to ground the poems. It allows the reader to believe them and him. The perception may be that if this is a real place and time ('an autumn day'), then it must be true.

From the beginning of the poem, Kavanagh puts himself in the place of an innocent who has been dragged into a situation that he did not want but could not avoid. Kavanagh sees the inevitable pitfalls ahead but cannot resist. He admits that he

> ... knew
> That her dark hair would weave a snare that I might one day rue;

He acknowledges that he 'saw the danger', yet still walked into her path. Indeed, the image created by Kavanagh of himself is of an innocent hypnotised by a Medusa-like creature who forces him to do her will. Kavanagh admits to giving in to temptation, but like Othello he only admits in his own way that he 'did not love too wisely but too well'. He says that he '... loved too much and by such and such is happiness thrown away.'

The Queen of Hearts image is a curious one. There is an element here that suggests Kavanagh was gambling and it didn't pay off. He certainly didn't end up 'making hay'. He seems to be complaining that the woman was too quiet and spent her time doing homely things, rather than making hay with him.

In the third verse he declares that he gave and she took. This may seem like an arrogant attitude to a contemporary reader:

> I gave her gifts of the mind I gave her the secret sign that's known
> To the artists who have known the true gods of sound and stone
> And word and tint.

He declares that he has brought her to Parnassus and has given her that which every intelligent person would want: an insight into his mind. He was even gracious enough to name her in some of his poems. What more could any woman want?:

> I did not stint for I gave her poems to say
> With her own name there ...

He does this even though she may have ruined his talent and killed the sunshine that should have fallen on him:

> ... her own dark hair like clouds over fields of May.

In the fourth verse Kavanagh sees his 'ex' and rationalises why she would turn away from him. He comes to the final damning conclusion that she did not deserve his love. He describes himself as an angel and his ex as a gargoyle. The angel made too much of a sacrifice, by trying to love somebody so base that they are made of clay. The net result of this encounter has been inevitable; the angel was injured:

> ... I had wooed not as I should a creature made of clay –
> When the angel woos he'd lose his wings at the dawn of day.

As a poem, 'On Raglan Road' is certainly presented from the poet's point of view. Should he be expected to give more balance? He is not writing a piece of journalism. Poetic licence with the truth is allowable, but it is important to see that this is one side of the argument and maybe Kavanagh loses some of the impact that he might have had.

Some of the imagery that Kavanagh uses is worth remarking upon. He seems to be referring to himself in a passive mode and as somebody who is angelic and taken by Nature, whereas the woman in the poem is associated with darkness: 'her dark hair', 'a deep ravine', 'Clouds over fields of May', 'made of clay'.

The long, winding lines of the poem are often associated with poetry written *as gaeilge* and they fit in with many of the poems written in the bardic tradition. Many of these poems were also about women, but saw a woman in a vision poem and as someone who was pure, representing Ireland to the poet and encouraging him to eulogise rather than lament (although Kavanagh's lament seems to be more for himself). These long lines fit into the pattern of the song-line; they flow dreamily and sweetly.

He uses a lot of mid-line rhyme in this poem, too, which also encourages a lament-like atmosphere. There are examples of this all the way through the poem. In the first verse: 'hair' and 'snare' and 'grief' and 'leaf'. In the second verse he uses 'ravine' and 'seen', 'hearts' and 'tarts' and 'much' and 'such'. The third verse has 'mind' and 'sign', 'tint' and 'stint' and 'there' and 'hair'; while finally the fourth has 'street' and 'meet', 'me' and 'hurriedly', 'wooed' and 'should' and 'woos' and 'lose'.

# The Hospital

Text of poem: New Explorations Anthology page 252

This is yet another sonnet, obviously Kavanagh's favourite form; yet again its content is what makes this sonnet different from other poets' versions of the same form. This is a love poem. That must be clear from the fact that he uses the word 'love' or 'lover' five times in the space of the five sentences that make up the poem. The main question that should be going through the reader's mind is: why would anybody want to write a love poem to a building? For it is the building that he is in love with, not what has been done to him within the building. He does not seem to be writing a poem about being grateful for being cured. He seems to be referring in this paean to just the hospital itself. Or is he yet again writing a poem about poetry?

The octet begins in a matter-of-fact manner. There is nothing austere or profound about this place. It is not a miraculous healing place; it is a 'functional ward'. It seems incredibly uniform and without personality:

> ... square cubicles in a row
> Plain concrete, wash basins –

Immediately it is dismissed as 'an art lover's woe'. Surely a poet should know something about art. Is his dismissal a contradiction, or does he hate art? Not only is the room drab, but also the other occupants are not exactly people to be revered. Rather than populate his hospital with healing angels, Kavanagh inserts a 'fellow in the next bed (who) snored'.

Kavanagh uses that first quatrain to describe the place. The next two lines explain the motivation for his love. There is nothing that cannot be loved. He reassures himself that by loving something:

> The common and banal her heat can know.

There is nothing that cannot be used as a subject for poetry; this is the essence of much of Kavanagh's work. The same theme is directed at us in 'Epic' or in 'Shancoduff'. It is not enough just to write about them, however. It must be done well and in a proper poetic genre. Therefore it is also not enough to 'just love' the Hospital: it must be done with passion, as he tells us about 'her heat'.

This poem was written during a period of transition for Kavanagh. It is one of the first of his poems that was written during what is known as his Canal Period. It is appropriate, therefore, that just as his period of illness led him to a new period of poetic freedom, then he should also point out that the hospital is not just the building itself, but outside there is 'the inexhaustible adventure of a gravelled yard.' He doesn't tell us what the adventure is, but he tells us some of the things that go on there.

He then goes on to tell us what type of things have not just happened, but have existed. Kavanagh by naming them in his poem has now given them immortality. They exist outside themselves now. They exist in his poem; this is the love that he can give to them. Indeed he sees it as his duty to name them. The naming is an act of love; it is personal and intimate between Kavanagh and the hospital.

He is giving it a life 'out of time'. He feels it is important to give immortality to that which has affected him. Because he has been affected by a particular place or situation, he feels that he has a duty to explain about it and to give it life. Places are the lifeblood of his poetry; he always names them. The venues of his life make up the different stages of his life – his time in Monaghan, his illness in the hospital, and afterwards his time at the Grand Canal.

The time that he spent in the Rialto Hospital was obviously a very important time for him. It did mark a turnaround in his poetic oeuvre. This poem is important for him because it is a time when he began to have a self-realisation about his own future, and about the direction in which his poetry should go.

# Canal Bank Walk

Text of poem: New Explorations Anthology page 254

If in 'Advent' Kavanagh was looking for a renewal of his way of looking at things, he seems to have found it in this sonnet. He found his spiritual renewal, or rather it found him, when he fell ill in 1955. This poem was written during his convalescence. As his health was improving, Kavanagh became more and more grateful for his gifts and for life itself. This poem is a clear celebration; indeed, one critic has described it as a hymn. It is not perhaps a hymn to God, but to the world that God has created. This is important in the overall context of Kavanagh's new poetic philosophy. He felt that poetry was a gift, and he believed that poets had a duty to use that gift.

The predominant images in the poem are natural ones, and he starts with a beautifully crafted neologism: 'leafy-with-love' gets the mood of the poem right almost immediately. This place, after all, is a little piece of the country in a city setting. The area and the canal are inspiring him to do the 'will of God'. When the poet says that God would wish him to wallow, he does not mean that he should lie and do nothing, but rather that he should cherish and enjoy the glory of being with nature and that he should celebrate it fervently.

Kavanagh sees redemption coming with water and he wishes to grow 'as before'. The image of the stick represents himself 'immobilised and helpless, but radiant'. His new way of living will be populated by romance and he wants to feel comfortable with Nature, as the couple on the bench do. He wants to use the energy of moments such as these and to add 'a third | Party to the couple kissing on the old seat'. But he wants to be infused with the knowledge that Nature will have a controlling influence. His poetry will take off into a different sphere of thought and it will be 'Eloquently new and abandoned to its delirious beat.'

The sestet is a prayer that reaches out for inspiration and like 'Lines written ...', it reaches out with a poetic invocation to Nature to allow him to become a better poet and to envelop his senses. It is when surrounded by Nature that he can paradoxically be most free. Kavanagh wants to be both enraptured and encaptured. He expects Nature to do this to him; all he has to do is to submit to it.

What he desires is to abandon himself to another power which will allow him to become a medium for the glory of Nature:

> Feed the gaping need of my senses, give me ad lib
> To pray unselfconsciously with overflowing speech

Kavanagh has needs in this poem, just like a baby might have. The 'new dress woven' is like a baptismal gown that will bring him and his poetry to a place where his spiritual and poetic rebirth can take place.

The rhythm and structure of the poem suggest fluidity and use enjambment or 'run-on lines', subtle rhyme and assonance to produce an incantation that flows like the canal which he describes.

There are a lot of differences between this poem and 'Advent'. They are both about the importance of being grateful to God; the difference between them is simple. 'Advent' urges a sense of solemn ascetic devotion, whereas 'Canal Bank Walk' is in favour of a more glorious outpouring of emotion where the poet is urging himself to praise God in a more open and vigorous manner. The verbs that Kavanagh uses are much more aggressive: 'enrapture', 'encapture', 'gaping'. He wants to lose control here, rather than keep things under control like he did in 'Advent'. He feels that the qualities of the water can have an invigorating effect on him, just as they did on Jesus when he met John the Baptist.

# Lines Written on a Seat on the Grand Canal, Dublin
## 'Erected to the Memory of Mrs Dermot O'Brien'

Text of poem: New Explorations Anthology page 256

'Lines Written ...' is the second of the Canal poems, and is a plea from the heart for poetry to be given the tribute that he feels it deserves. There are some questions raised by the idea of such a poem in the first place. The first one is: does a poet deserve commemoration in the first place? To answer this we must understand Kavanagh's ideas behind the role of a poet. The second obvious question is: why set the poem on a seat overlooking a canal? The third is: why does he leave the subtitle in?

## A READING OF THE POEM

To answer the last point first, he seems to admire the idea of having a seat as a memorial. He thinks it is a good idea, so he includes it in his poem. He also includes it perhaps to instigate an idea of mortality in the reader of the poem. This poem may be seen as the poet's requiem for himself. It is worth it, at this point, for the reader to re-read the poem in that context.

The poem begins in a gloriously poetic manner; the first word is the declaring 'O'. The 'O' sets up an intensely poetic mood. If it is left out, what difference does it make? One of the effects it definitely has is that it sets up the poem as a grand exercise. We have seen in Kavanagh's poems up to this point that he likes using simple, even colloquial language, but this declaration is something new and unusual for him. There is also a sense of death in this opening phrase, and Dr Antoinette Quinn has remarked that the opening and its mirror phrase at the end 'frame the sonnet like a black mourning border'. This introduces an element of finality in the poem again and goes back to the inscription on the seat.

So Kavanagh continues through the poem and reflects that the place for people to remember him should be where there is water. Water suggests life, but it also suggests birth and in the Christian tradition it suggests rebirth. A rebirth of the imagination was important to Kavanagh's poetic thesis. He felt that a poet should not just accept what he could see, but should constantly re-inspect his perception of what was seen to be present.

It is Kavanagh's belief that a poet should seek out the wonder of the ordinary that brings him to see the water as something that was capable of many lives: and perhaps so, too, a poem can have many different readings for its readers. The idea of a simple lock in Dublin roaring like Niagara Falls is a use of hyperbole that backs up Kavanagh's belief that perception and attitude are everything. If you wish to see the Niagara Falls, you can. The inspiration that comes from this sight is what is important to him. Kavanagh also wants this attitude to be his legacy to other poets:

> No one will speak in prose
> Who finds his way to these Parnassian islands.

Nature and the seemingly banal as muse is an important theme in Kavanagh's work. He uses an image that was previously used in 'Advent' and 'Shancoduff', where light can find its way through any hole and bring life to a place where previously it was thought that there was none. In 'Advent' we are told:

Through a chink too wide there comes in no wonder.

Here we are reminded that:

Fantastic light looks through the eyes of bridges –

Hyperbole is used throughout this poem. His references to Parnassus, Niagara and 'fantastic light' are in an exaggerated manner, and now Athy is a place where mythologies are born.

He siphons this hyperbole by coming back at the end of the poem with a simple, modest, heartfelt plea that we would not commemorate him with a 'hero-courageous | Tomb – just a canal-bank seat for the passer-by.'

This poem is Kavanagh's last great poem, and it is entirely appropriate that in it he tries to find a place for himself in the whole scheme of the world. He desperately seeks a return to the natural world of his youth – the difference being that he is now in a position to enjoy what he sees and what goes on around him. He has found modesty in this poem, not just with God, because he had found that already; he has found his place among regular people and seems to be much more aware that this is where life is at its most vibrant. Seeing things becomes very important to him here. He wants to acknowledge the greatness and majesty of the ordinary things that go on around him. By recognising them, he makes things seem far more magnificent. He transforms the Grand Canal into Parnassus quite naturally, because this is the place that transforms him and gives him his inspiration. This inspiration to his art is awe-inspiring to him, and it is for that reason that he feels free to make the comparison.

Again it is the sense of place that influences Kavanagh. In the Gaelic tradition 'Dinnseanchas' is the term given to the poetry written about a sense of place. In this tradition, the act of describing a place left behind was very important to the poets. In Kavanagh's case, he tries to bring his craft a bit further. He has already acknowledged the influence that County Monaghan and the past have had on him, for better or for worse; now he wants to pay tribute to his present.

# 6 Séamus HEANEY

*John G. Fahy*

## Nobel laureate

Séamus Heaney was born on 13 April 1939, the eldest of nine children. Mossbawn was the family farm at Bellaghy, County Derry; here he attended Anahorish primary school from 1945 to 1951. He went as a boarder to St Columb's College, Derry, from 1951 to 1957, and it was during this time that his four-year-old brother, Christopher, was killed in a road accident, an experience that generated the poem 'Mid-Term Break'.

Heaney went on to study at Queen's University, Belfast, and graduated in 1961 with a first-class degree in English language and literature. He then took a Teacher Training Diploma at St Joseph's College of Education and went to teach in St Thomas's Intermediate School in Ballymurphy, Belfast, from 1962 to 1963. The headmaster there was the short-story writer Michael McLaverty, who encouraged Heaney to write and introduced him to the work of Patrick Kavanagh.

From 1963 to 1966 Heaney taught at St Joseph's College of Education, and it was during this time that he became involved with Philip Hobsbaum's 'Group'. This was a self-critical poetry workshop founded by the Queen's lecturer that included many emerging talents, such as Michael Longley, James Simmons and Stewart Parker.

In 1965 Heaney married, and in 1966 he succeeded Hobsbaum in the English Department at Queen's.

| PRINCIPAL VOLUMES OF POETRY | Poems for study |
|---|---|
| *Death of a Naturalist* (1966) | 'Twice Shy' |
| | 'Valediction' |
| *Door into the Dark* (1969) | 'The Forge' |
| | 'Bogland' |
| *Wintering Out* (1972) | 'The Tollund Man' |
| *North* (1975) | 'Mossbawn: (1) Sunlight' |
| | 'A Constable Calls' |
| *Field Work* (1979) | 'The Skunk' |
| | 'The Harvest Bow' |
| *Sweeney Astray* (1983) | |

*Station Island* (1984)
*The Haw Lantern* (1987)
*Seeing Things* (1991)                    'Field of Vision'
                                      'Lightenings VIII'
*The Spirit Level* (1996)            'St Kevin and the Blackbird'

## Publication of 'Death of a Naturalist', 1966

Heaney's first volume of poetry, *Death of a Naturalist*, was published in 1966. Filled mostly with the characters, scenes, customs, flora and fauna of the countryside that formed him, this volume explores Heaney's cultural and poetic origins. Poems such as 'Digging', 'Follower', 'Churning Day', 'Ancestral Photograph' and 'The Diviner' honour his rural roots as they celebrate ancestral and family skills, diggers of turf, makers of butter, ploughers of fields and diviners of water, and show a people living in a close and almost spiritual relationship with the earth. Dominant among these is the larger-than-life heroic figure of his father. In describing them, and keenly aware that he is breaking with this tradition, Heaney seems to be at the same time defining his own space as a writer.

> But I've no spade to follow men like them.
> Between my finger and my thumb
> The squat pen rests.
> I'll dig with it.
> ['Digging']

His writing and his development as a poet, which is inspired by his sense of place, is really an adult version of childhood exploration.

> As a child, they could not keep me from wells
> And old pumps with buckets and windlasses.
> I loved the dark drop, the trapped sky, the smells
> Of waterweed, fungus and dark moss.
>
> Now, to pry into roots, to finger slime,
> To store big-eyed Narcissus, into some spring
> Is beneath all adult dignity. I rhyme
> To see myself, to set the darkness echoing.
> ['Personal Helicon']

Many of the poems in this volume deal with childhood and coming of age. 'The Barn' and 'An Advancement of Learning' are an invitation into childhood terror (fear of the dark and of rats). 'Death of a Naturalist', 'Blackberry Picking', 'The Early Purges' and 'Mid-Term Break' explore loss of innocence and a growing awareness of sex, decay, cruelty and death. Two poems ('At a Potato Digging' and 'For the Commander of the *Eliza*') deal poignantly with race memory, exploring the horrors of the Great Famine.

Towards the end of the volume there is a scattering of love poems celebrating his relationship with his wife, to whom this volume was dedicated. 'Twice Shy' and 'Valediction' are from this series.

The book brought instant recognition and praise for Heaney, the Somerset Maugham Award in 1967, and the Cholmondeley Award in 1968.

# *Twice Shy*

Text of poem: New Explorations Anthology page 319

This love lyric explores the thrilling tension and conflicting emotions experienced in the early stages of a love relationship. It deals with the almost paradoxical nature of the feelings involved: a wariness, a nervousness, an uncertainty, but accompanied also by excitement, a sense of thrill and the stir of deep feelings. The nervousness is born not so much out of fear of expressing love –

> Not to publish feeling
> And regret it all too late –

– but out of a fear of trusting the feelings, a cynicism born of experience:

> Mushroom loves already
> Had puffed and burst in hate.

Perhaps there is a cynical aphorism implicit in the title, i.e. once bitten, twice shy. But this reservation is balanced by a giddy excitement:

> We thrilled to the March twilight
> With nervous childish talk:

– imagery suggestive of romantic birdsong. There is also tension between the surface casualness, even falsity, of the conversation –

> Preserved classic decorum,
> Deployed our talk with art.

– and the real and powerful feelings underneath:

Still waters running deep
Along the embankment walk.

The conflict of feeling is encapsulated in the images of falconry:

But tremulously we held
As hawk and prey apart,

and

So, chary and excited
As a thrush linked on a hawk,

Is there a suggestion here that love is dangerous, that it can mean exposure to pain, indeed be a fatal attraction? Certainly there is a suggestion that love is a primitive instinct and the lover a hunter. The strength, the sheer drawing power of the emotion is obvious: it is a 'vacuum of need'.

So this poem works at the level of feeling, faithfully recording the emotions experienced; but we are also aware of the poet simultaneously analysing and reflecting on these feelings, which gives it a detachment, a perspective – feelings balanced by thought.

## IMAGERY

Heaney uses imagery from nature – river, birds, mushrooms – almost in a symbolic way, to convey the complexity of feelings in this poem. 'Still waters running deep' suggests powerful hidden currents of human emotion. 'Mushroom loves', with their sudden, silent appearance, fragile transitory nature and tendency to sprout in unlikely places, even in poor soil, carries a great deal of comment on immature, adolescent love affairs. Perhaps this is expecting too much from a single image. Is the relevance of the swan to this theme too obvious, with its romantic associations of fidelity, pairing for life, a bird of calm, dignified exterior but hidden motions under water?

We have already commented on the connotations thrown up by hawks and thrushes and the implications for the nature of the relationship. Perhaps it is worth looking at the manner in which the hawk image is introduced in the second stanza. In a most unusual simile, dusk is first compared to a backcloth, suggesting that the episode has all the high drama and unreality of a badly staged play. Then this shimmering backdrop takes on the tremulous hovering of a hawk, beautiful but lethal. This startling complexity of image associations has all the cleverness and excitement of a traditional *conceit* – a metaphorical comparison that appears on first reading to be more startling than accurate.

Certainly the imagery here is concentrated and striking, but you must decide for yourself whether you think it apt.

The principal tone communicated by this poem is one of tension, shifting between wariness and excitement, as we have seen. The nervousness is conveyed in the structure of the poem. The short three-stress lines are crammed with movement and energy, which suggests a tautness of control, feelings barely held in check ('Traffic holding its breath', 'dusk hung', 'shook', 'tremulous', 'hanging deadly'). Most of the six-line rhyming stanzas are structured as single sentences, which serves to draw out the tension. Stanza 3 is a good example of this.

Tension is also communicated through the imagery, as examined. Do you find any intimacy in this poem, any personal feeling as appropriate to a love poem, or do you think that the obvious crafting and heavily symbolic use of imagery gets in the way of real feeling? Perhaps the short lines encourage pithy sayings and aphorisms, rather than sincerity and depth of feeling?

# *Valediction*

Text of poem: New Explorations Anthology page 321

This love poem deals with the effects of separation on the writer. He uses the conceit of a ship at sea to communicate his feelings of inner turmoil.

The poem focuses on the writer's psychological state rather than on the relationship. Feelings of emptiness, turmoil and disorder are expressed in quite a logical, narrative, almost prosaic style. The first three lengthy sentences are each stretched across five short lines. At first a rhythm is set up, which is then abruptly derailed as each sentence finishes at the beginning of a new line. Towards the end of the poem the rhythm becomes even more disjointed. Sentiments are uttered in short, staccato bursts of phrases, attempting perhaps to reflect the poet's confused state.

> Need breaks on my strand;
> You've gone, I am at sea.

How effectively it succeeds is open to debate. Indeed some critics feel that this is a very artificial love poem, never really allowing the reader to share the intimacy. John Wilson Foster (in *Critical Quarterly,* 1974) expressed his reservations as follows:

> The love poems in *Death of a Naturalist* are placed coyly at the end of the book and they are, moreover, removed in a metaphysical style from

immediacy of feeling. 'Valediction'; 'Scaffolding'; 'Poem for Marie'; and 'Honeymoon Flight' are all conceits and while clever and even beautiful (for example, 'Scaffolding') keep the reader outside the taut, stave-like lines of their stanzaic compounds.

Do you think his comments are justified in relation to both 'Valediction' and 'Twice Shy'?

## 'Door into the Dark', 1969

*Door into the Dark,* Heaney's second volume, was published in 1969. While the first volume dealt in the main with childhood, coming of age and the poet's relationship with the somewhat heroic figure of his father, this volume deals with more adult relationships. It focuses in particular on the joys, grief and social role of women as mothers and partners, in such poems as 'The Wife's Tale', 'Cana Revisited', and 'Elegy for a Still-Born Child'.

A series of poems – 'Rite of Spring', 'Undine', 'Outlaw', and 'A Lough Neagh Sequence' – celebrate the teeming fertility of nature. A couple of poems – 'The Forge' and 'Thatcher' – hark back to the themes of the first volume in the celebration of local skills and in the poet's discovery in them of metaphors for his own craft. But the poet's Irish focus broadens out from local considerations to a more general awareness of Irish geography, history and archaeology in such poems as 'The Peninsula', 'Whinlands', 'The Plantation', 'Shoreline' and 'Bogland'.

# The Forge

Text of poem: New Explorations Anthology page 322

THEME

At one level this might be read as another descriptive poem celebrating local craftsmanship (such as that of the diviner, thatcher and digger already mentioned) and exploring cultural roots, a nostalgic poem of social history. Such a reading leaves one unsatisfied, an outsider rebuffed by an inarticulate and rude, if talented, smith.

The real subject of this poem is the mystery of the creative process. The work of the forge serves as an extended metaphor for the beating out of a work of art, the crafting of poetry. The reader, like the speaker in this case, is outside, peering in at the mystery. One can catch glimpses of beauty in the making ('The unpredictable fantail of sparks') or hear snatches of its elegant sound (the 'short-pitched ring' or the 'hiss'), but the secret of its construction remains a mystery, inaccessible to the non-artist. Just as in 'The Diviner', the onlookers can see the event but cannot themselves perform it or even understand it.

Creativity is a fabulous process, the stuff of legend, of mediaeval romance. The anvil is a horned 'unicorn'; but it is also a sacred process, and the smith is its high priest:

> at one end square,
> Set there immovable: an altar
> Where he expends himself in shape and music,

The making of art is not the exclusive preserve of intellectuals and the 'chattering classes' but can be born of even the uncouth and uncommunicative ('hairs in his nose, | He leans out ... grunts and goes in').

Art is not necessarily anchored to the here and now. The artist withdraws from the modern world to create ('He ... recalls a clatter | Of hoofs where traffic is flashing in rows ... grunts and goes in, with a slam and flick | To beat real iron out ...').

So the poem deals with the mystery and the sacredness of art and at the same time puts before us the ordinariness of the artist.

Origins of the image

This is probably based on Heaney's experience of a real forge – Devlin's forge at Hillhead, not far from Mossbawn, where the Heaneys first lived during the poet's youth. From this forge he borrowed the anvil to lend realism to his part as a blacksmith in a Bellaghy Dramatic Society production about the 1798 Rising. So the ordinary bric-a-brac of life is endowed with metaphysical meaning and poetic significance by the writer.

But the image has literary echoes also. Smiths featured in the work of Gerard Manley Hopkins, a poet much admired by Heaney. Hopkins uses the smith as a symbol of human strength, beauty and Christian courage in 'Felix Randal' and as a metaphor for God in 'The Wreck of the *Deutschland*', where he sees the God-smith forging humankind to what shape he wills.

> With an anvil-ding
> And with fire in him forge thy will
> Or rather, rather then, stealing as Spring
> Through him, melt him but master him still.

Joyce too, through Stephen Dedalus, utters that famous arrogant statement of artistic *raison d'être* in *Portrait of the Artist as a Young Man,* where he resolves to 'forge in the smithy of my soul the uncreated conscience of my race'.

So for Heaney the forge had both a strong physical and a literary presence.

## IMAGERY AND SOUND

All the imagery in this poem is generated by the forge and its surroundings. The discarded bric-a-brac ('old axles and iron hoops rusting') recalls the real disorder out of which true beauty is created. The unexpected glory of sparks ('The unpredictable fantail of sparks') provides the only flash of colour in the otherwise Stygian gloom.

Darkness is the predominant backdrop colour here. In fact a number of poems in this volume – 'The Outlaw', 'Gallarus Oratory' and 'The Forge' – feature dark places, enclosed spaces that, paradoxically, are places of great energy and creativity, whether biological, spiritual or artistic. Here too the dark is seductive and creative, enticing and explosive. Would you agree with the critic who said that Heaney here presents 'an image of the poet as master of the powers of darkness'?

The central image is the anvil, which Heaney allows to have a couple of different implications, associating its horn with the mythical beast of mediaeval romance and its square end with a religious altar. So both the romantic and the sacred aspects of creativity are fostered.

Sound is an essential feature of pictorial composition for Heaney. At a conscious level we are aware of the musical quality of the verse, the onomatopoeic 'ring', 'hiss', 'slam' and 'flick', and the alliteration of 'grunts and goes'. But there are also subterranean musical echoes within words, which provide a background resonance. For example, the flat *e* and *a* sounds in 'somewhere', 'square' and 'altar' focus on the weight of the anvil and its central importance.

## FORM

The poem is structured as a Petrarchan sonnet, with the octave devoted to the forge and the sestet providing a shift in focus to the smith. This division allows the anvil as 'an altar' to be emphasised at the pivotal point of the poem. Other than that it is not technically effective as a sonnet: the pentameter rhythm is uneven, and the rhyming scheme is irregular (*abba cddc efgfeg*), with the sestet most uneven. Some of the rhymes are off-rhymes rather than true. One could see this as a failure of technique, a lack of verbal sophistication; or could one see it as a naturalness that fits the often conversational rhythms of language ('He leans out on the jamb, recalls a clatter | Of hoofs ... ') and the rough subject?

# *Bogland*

Text of poem: New Explorations Anthology page 324

<small>BACKGROUND AND CONTEXT</small>

In the autumn of 1968 the Heaneys spent some time with the painter T.P. Flanagan and his family at McFadden's hotel in Gort an Choirce, Co. Donegal. Poet and painter wandered the landscape, stopping at times to sketch or view. They were careful to keep separate and independent their reactions to the landscape, the painter reluctant to show Heaney even the outline of his sketches, lest they should influence and colour the poet's own individual, authentic approach to the subject. Heaney dedicated 'Bogland' to T.P. Flanagan.

In *Preoccupations: Selected Prose, 1968–1978*, Heaney gives us some more information about the genesis of this poem and the significance of bog for him.

> I had been vaguely wishing to write a poem about bogland, chiefly because it is a landscape that has a strange assuaging effect on me, one with associations reaching back into early childhood. We used to hear about bog-butter, butter kept fresh for a great number of years under the peat. Then when I was at school the skeleton of an elk had been taken out of a bog nearby and a few of our neighbours had got their photographs in the paper, peering out across its antlers. So I began to get an idea of bog as the memory of the landscape, or as a landscape that remembered everything that happened in and to it. In fact, if you go round the National Museum in Dublin, you will realise that a great proportion of the most cherished material heritage of Ireland was 'found in a bog.' Moreover, since memory was the faculty that supplied me with the first quickening of my own poetry, I had a tentative unrealised need to make a congruence between memory and bogland and, for the want of a better word, our national consciousness. And it all released itself after 'We have no prairies ...' – but we have bogs.
>
> At that time I was teaching modern literature in Queen's University, Belfast, and had been reading about the frontier and the west as an important myth in the American consciousness, so I set up – or rather, laid down – the bog as an answering Irish myth. I wrote it quickly the next morning, having slept on my excitement, and revised it on the hoof, from line to line, as it came ...
>
> Again, as in the case of 'Digging', the seminal impulse had been unconscious. What generated the poem about memory was something lying beneath the very floor of memory, something I only connected with the poem months after it was written, which was a warning that older people would give us about going into the bog. They were afraid we might fall into the pools in the old workings so they put it about (and we believed them) that

there was no bottom in the bog-holes. Little did they – or I – know that I would filch it for the last line of a book.

A number of poems in *Door into the Dark* deal with local landscape – 'Whinlands', 'The Plantation', 'Shoreline' and 'Bogland'. There is a similarity of approach to the theme, in that the poet is delving into the past history of the place and also making connections with modern society, perhaps attempting to find a universal significance in the landscape. 'Bogland' is the clearest of these poems.

BOGLAND: OUR NATIONAL CONSCIOUSNESS

As he said himself, Heaney thought of bogland as the memory of the landscape, a landscape he viewed poetically as somehow incorporating national consciousness. Here he has forged a metaphor to explore 'Irishness'. In this poem the bog is, first of all, a repository of history. It preserves and gives back heritage ('the skeleton of the Great Irish Elk | Out of the peat'). Also, it yields up some mysteries:

Butter sunk under
More than a hundred years
Was recovered salty and white.

Notions of superstition and magic were associated with the burial of butter in bogs, adding another layer of complexity to this newly excavated consciousness. Myth and folk knowledge too are part of it ('The bogholes might be Atlantic seepage'). Tales to frighten children still resonate in the adult consciousness ('The wet centre is bottomless'). So the bog is the repository of our history, of memories of myth and magic, of folk fears – all of which go to make up identity, what we are, how we still think and feel. Heaney is attempting to deal with buried memory, with the dark areas of the human psyche, the Cyclops-like grotesqueness in all of us. The bog is the door into this dark.

But Heaney is dealing also with tribal consciousness, race memory. The contrast with the American prairies helps to define this. The prairie view opens out before a person, providing opportunities, offering possibilities of new achievement, of expansion. In contrast, the Irish landscape limits the view, restricts human possibilities.

Everywhere the eye concedes to
Encroaching horizon,

Is wooed into the cyclops' eye
Of a tarn.

It draws us downwards, inwards and backwards through history. Is Heaney adverting to the inward-looking nature of the Ulster mind, aware, as one critic put it, 'that Ulster is not a place of expanding frontiers'? Certainly the process of uncovering the consciousness involves going down and down, excavating layers of history and past experience, uncovering the psychological profile of Irishness.

> Our pioneers keep striking
> Inwards and downwards,
>
> Every layer they strip
> Seems camped on before.

These pioneers uncover past magnificence that is grandly out of place and functionless today (the great elk has become 'An astounding crate full of air'), along with the magic, the superstition and the folk fears. But the poet is aware too of the depth and complexity of national consciousness, that the full truth may be unreachable ('The wet centre is bottomless'). So, through the metaphor of bogland, the poet has created a metaphysical description of Ireland and is, as Edna Longley said, ready to 'pioneer the frontiers of Irish consciousness'.

## THEME

The poem is making a statement about the complexity of the Irish mentality, with its layers of race memory, its sense of heritage, myth and magic, its introspection, its fluid, shifting consciousness ('Melting and opening underfoot'), which ultimately may be impossible to define fully.

## IMAGERY

The central metaphor is that of bog, with all the connotations that that image can hold about Irishness. We have already examined its main facet: as repository of a heritage. But even more interesting from a psychological point of view is its delicate nature: the surface is a thin, delicate layer for living on, 'crusting | Between the sights of the sun.' Underneath this is a soft, moving, volatile mass, an apt parallel for the unconscious mind. It is gentle and placid ('The ground itself is kind, black butter'). It has not got the hardness of coal; rather it is a flabby consciousness, an all-enveloping softness that embraces 'the waterlogged trunks | Of great firs, soft as pulp.' The bog is feminine, all-embracing, welcoming.

Eyes and sight feature prominently, appropriate to the notion of search in the theme ('big sun', 'everywhere the eye concedes', 'sights of the sun'). But the most arresting sight reference is to 'the cyclops' eye', an image that makes naught of time, linking us immediately to the classical world. Perhaps more significant are the associations thrown up by the image of misshapen man, grotesque humanity. It is through this singular and unnatural vision that the past is viewed.

Everywhere there is water or hints of it (the tarn, waterlogged trunks, bogholes, Atlantic seepage, the wet centre that is bottomless).

But the most astonishing image, with all the excitement of a conceit, is forged out of the great Irish elk as 'An astounding crate full of air.' The heritage, while exciting, does not sit easily in today's world and almost defies description.

Altogether, the poem is threaded together on memorable natural images full of significance to the theme.

FORM

The poem is written in thin, unrhymed four-line stanzas. The short lines force a tightening of expression, where ideas are communicated in short bursts of phrases, concentrated but unpolished.

> The ground itself is kind, black butter,
>
> Melting and opening underfoot,
> Missing its last definition
> By millions of years.

At times, as with the last line quoted, the language is casual, almost colloquial.

## Publication of 'Wintering Out', 1972

Heaney's third volume of poetry, *Wintering Out,* was published in 1972. The terms 'wintering out' and 'winterage' are used in farming to describe the custom of putting mature cattle onto a sheltered area of dry land with relatively good grass. This is often at some distance from the main farm, where they would be expected to survive the winter with no extra feeding and with little supervision. It was a sort of seasonal exile for animals. The term 'wintering out' was also used in connection with the seasonal movement of migrant farm labourers, and it is in this context that the term is used in the poem 'Servant Boy'.

The year 1969 saw riots, bombs and sectarian killings in Northern Ireland. The Provisional IRA became a powerful force, and the British army was deployed on the streets. Yet at this stage, Heaney hardly ever addresses these contemporary political issues directly. Instead he makes a journey back into the past, exploring Ireland's past and also the remote past of prehistoric humans. So he concentrates on the origins of the conflict: the sense of linguistic and cultural difference; the history of conflicting classes; an exploration of the traditions, history and sense of identity of his own clan, the Northern Catholics.

For example, in 'Bog Oak', through the metaphor of the title, he can revisit the native dispossessed of the seventeenth century. In 'Gifts of Rain' he tries to forge links with the watery landscape of his birth and establish a sense of his own identity. 'The Last Mummer' points up the clash of cultures and signals the death of the old ways. And there are many poems exploring the meaning of place-names and, in so doing, exemplifying the linguistic dispossession of the Irish: poems such as 'Anahorish', 'Broach', 'Toome', and 'Traditions'.

'The Other Side' is one of the few poems in *Wintering Out* that deals directly and personally with the issue of religious and cultural difference in present-day society. Directness and immediacy are achieved by dramatising the issues and objectifying them in the uneasy relationship between the poet's family and a Presbyterian neighbour. Once again Heaney is focusing in on the local scene, the small picture; but by examining the microcosm he gives us an insight into the larger scene, the relationship between the two cultures. Differences in outlook, self-image and modes of language, as well as in religion, are explored.

In 'The Tollund Man' he finds an oblique way of examining the sacrificial killings, the power of religion and the deadly demands of myth in our society. But this examination is carried out at one remove, with the voice of the anthropologist or historian for the most part. It is as if the present is too raw to be viewed directly.

Part 2 contains some more personal and emotive poems: exploring the sadness behind the celebration on his 'Wedding Day', recording painful separation in 'Mother of the Groom', and a string of poems featuring isolated, unappreciated, tragically unhappy female figures: 'A Winter's Tale', 'Shore Woman', 'Maighdean Mara', 'Limbo' and 'Bye-child'.

# *The Tollund Man*

Text of poem: New Explorations Anthology page 327

BACKGROUND AND GENESIS OF THE POEM

We have seen Heaney's fascination with local landscape, in particular bogland, and his use of it as a metaphor to explore the nature of Irish consciousness. He seemed more reluctant to explore the contemporary visible expression of that consciousness in the explosion of political violence in 1969. But in that year the chance discovery of a book, *The Bog People: Iron Age Man Preserved* by P.V. Glob, a Danish archaeologist, seemed to provide a new poetic impetus for Heaney to continue exploring the past, and at the same time it provided a historical perspective and parallels with which he could confront the present Troubles.

Glob's book is concerned with the perfectly preserved bodies, dating from the Iron Age, discovered this century in Danish bogs. One of these is 'Tollund Man', discovered in 1950 in western Denmark by two turf-cutters. The man was naked, except for a cap and belt, with a noose around his neck (a 'torc' in the poem). It is presumed that he had been put to death in a fertility rite as an offering to the Earth Mother, the fertility goddess Nerthus, and buried in her bog, which preserved his body.

Glob's book was fascinating for Heaney, as it dealt with many of his poetic obsessions and themes, such as landscape, history, myth, sexuality and violence. The poet was moved particularly by the photograph of Tollund Man. His first reaction was one of recognition, familiarity across the ages. 'The Tollund Man seemed to me like an ancestor almost, one of my old uncles, one of the moustached archaic faces you used to meet all over the Irish countryside,' he said in an interview (with James Randall, in *Plough Shares*, vol. 5, no. 3, 1979). This empathy, this sense of instant familiarity, almost of family feeling, gives a great intimacy to the poem.

But, more importantly, the image of Tollund Man, a symbol of humans sacrificed to dark forces and the needs of community, provides a link to the present-day Troubles. Heaney had been searching for 'images and symbols adequate to our predicament'. In October 1974, in a lecture entitled 'Feeling into Words' given at the Royal Society of Literature, he explained the connections – political, religious and social – that Tollund Man established for him across the Dark Ages.

> From that moment [the outbreak of violence in 1969] the problems of poetry moved from being simply a matter of achieving the satisfactory verbal icon to being a search for images and symbols adequate to our predicament. I do not mean liberal lamentation that citizens should feel compelled to murder one another or deploy their different military arms over the matter of nomenclatures such as British or Irish. I do not mean public celebrations or execrations of resistance or atrocity – although there is nothing necessarily unpoetic about such celebration, if one thinks of Yeats's 'Easter 1916'. I mean that I felt it imperative to discover a field of force in which, without abandoning fidelity to the processes and experience of poetry as I have outlined them, it would be possible to encompass the perspectives of a humane reason and at the same time to grant the religious intensity of the violence its deplorable authenticity and complexity. And when I say religious, I am not thinking simply of the sectarian division. To some extent the enmity can be viewed as a struggle between the cults and devotees of a god and a goddess. There is an indigenous territorial numen, a tutelar of the whole island, call her Mother Ireland, Kathleen Ni Houlihan, the poor old woman,

the Shan Van Vocht, whatever; and her sovereignty has been temporarily usurped or infringed by a new male cult whose founding fathers were Cromwell, William of Orange and Edward Carson, and whose godhead is incarnate in a rex or caesar resident in a palace in London. What we have is the tail-end of a struggle in a province between territorial piety and imperial power.

Now I realise that this idiom is remote from the agnostic world of economic interest whose iron hand operates in the velvet glove of 'talks between elected representatives', and remote from the political manoeuvres of power-sharing; but it is not remote from the psychology of the Irishmen and Ulstermen who do the killing, and not remote from the bankrupt psychology and mythologies implicit in the terms Irish Catholic and Ulster Protestant. The question, as ever, is 'How with this rage shall beauty hold a plea?' And my answer is, by offering 'befitting emblems of adversity'.

Some of these emblems I found in a book that was published in English translation, appositely, the year the killing started, in 1969. And again appositely, it was entitled *The Bog People*. It was chiefly concerned with preserved bodies of men and women found in the bogs of Jutland, naked, strangled or with their throats cut, disposed under the peat since early Iron Age times. The author, P.V. Glob, argues convincingly that a number of these, and in particular the Tollund Man, whose head is now preserved near Aarhus in the museum at Silkeburg, were ritual sacrifices to the Mother Goddess, the goddess of the ground who needed new bridegrooms each winter to bed with her in her sacred place, in the bog, to ensure the renewal and fertility of the territory in the spring. Taken in relation to the tradition of Irish political martyrdom for that cause whose icon is Kathleen Ni Houlihan, this is more than an archaic barbarous rite: it is an archetypal pattern. And the unforgettable photographs of these victims blended in my mind with photographs of atrocities, past and present, in the long rites of Irish political and religious struggles. When I wrote this poem, I had a completely new sensation, one of fear. It was a vow to go on pilgrimage and I felt as it came to me – and again it came quickly – that unless I was deeply in earnest about what I was saying, I was simply invoking dangers for myself. It is called 'The Tollund Man' ...

And just how persistent the barbaric attitudes are, not only in the slaughter but in the psyche, I discovered again when the frisson of the poem itself had passed, and indeed after I had fulfilled the vow and gone to Jutland, 'the holy blisful martyr for to seke.' I read the following in a chapter on 'The Religion of the Pagan Celts' by the Celtic scholar Anne Ross:

Moving from sanctuaries and shrines ... we come now to consider the nature of the actual deities .... But before going on to look at the nature of some of the individual deities and their cults, one can perhaps bridge the gap as it were by considering a symbol which, in its way, sums up the whole of Celtic pagan religion and is as representative of it as is, for example, the sign of the cross in Christian contexts. This is the symbol of the severed human head; in all its various modes of iconographic representation and verbal presentation, one may find the hard core of Celtic religion. It is indeed ... a kind of shorthand symbol for the entire religious outlook of the pagan Celts.

My sense of occasion and almost awe as I vowed to go to pray to the Tollund Man and assist at his enshrined head had a longer ancestry than I had at the time realised.

I began by suggesting that my point of view involved poetry as divination, as a restoration of the culture to itself. In Ireland in this century it has involved for Yeats and many others an attempt to define and interpret the present by bringing it into significant relationship with the past, and I believe that effort in our present circumstances has to be urgently renewed. But here we stray from the realm of technique into the realm of tradition; to forge a poem is one thing, to forge the uncreated conscience of the race, as Stephen Dedalus put it, is quite another and places daunting pressures and responsibilities on anyone who would risk the name of poet.

## POLITICS

The poet is responding somewhat obliquely to political violence and present-day killings. He is using the Bog People material as an analogy, and, by setting up ironic similarities and contrasts, he is able to comment on the present Troubles.

One common motif linking past, present and future is that of a journey: the man's last sacrificial journey 'as he rode the tumbril', the fatal journey of the brothers, 'trailed | For miles along the lines', and the poet's pilgrimage ('driving'). The ironic contrast between the consenting sacrificial death ('his sad freedom') and the brutality of the twentieth-century killing is surely intended. This refers to an incident in the nineteen-twenties in which four brothers were massacred by loyalist paramilitaries. Their bodies had been dragged along the railway lines over the sleepers as a kind of degrading, hate-filled mutilation. The shocking detail of the description ('Tell-tale skin and teeth | Flecking the sleepers') brings home the frenzy and inhumanity of that event; it contrasts poignantly with the quiet dignity of Tollund Man's last journey. We get the impression that he at least had some control over events: he 'rode' the tumbril, he wasn't dragged, and it was for him a kind of 'freedom'.

The stark Anglo-Saxon poeticism of 'old man-killing parishes' links pagan past and Christian present in its hyphenated image. The same linkage is evident in

I could risk blasphemy,
Consecrate the cauldron bog
Our holy ground ...

Iron Age martyrs, modern-day martyrs – both become symbols, icons, sacred territory.

Is Heaney saying that present-day atrocities, albeit more brutal, are just modern versions of an age-old pattern of human activity? That in every society people are sacrificed to a political or religious goddess, are driven by inscrutable forces and desires to accept death for a cause, are mere pawns in the service of a community? And where does the poet stand on this issue? We don't know, because he doesn't comment explicitly. But we do know that he empathises, has a feeling for the situation. On his pilgrimage he will experience something of the feelings of the dispossessed, if only because he will be dispossessed of language.

Watching the pointing hands
Of country people,
Not knowing their tongue.

Cultural dispossession has been an important element in his writings about nationalist community identity in Northern Ireland. He feels that he will share too the estrangement and unhappiness of the victim, a situation oddly familiar to him:

I will feel lost,
Unhappy and at home.

Feelings of estrangement and familiarity together produce this inconclusive, paradoxical ending, where 'home' does not seem very secure or comforting.

The critic Edna Longley complains about the 'ambiguous resolution' of this ending, but feels that this may be as far as he can go and points out that he has reacted to tragic circumstances in a similar way in other poems. What we can say is that Heaney understands the nature of the victim in this poem; and, as the critic Michael Parker says, 'Composing from a sense of reverence for a victim from the distant past came more easily to him than responding to the all-too-immediate horror of the present.'

RELIGIOUS SYMBOLISM: PAGAN AND CHRISTIAN LAYERS OF MEANING

Though this poem deals explicitly with violence and killing, paradoxically it has the shape and tone of a religious poem. The origin of the first killing is the pagan sacrifice to the Earth Mother, goddess of fertility. The fertility theme is introduced early, in the imagery of the first two stanzas: the 'pods' of his eyelids suggest dormant life, an idea reinforced explicitly in the 'gruel of winter seeds'. The earth as female principle is seen in stanza 4:

> She tightened her torc on him
> And opened her fen ...

'Bridegroom to the goddess', he enters the earth naked to guarantee fertility: spring reproduction. Eros and thanatos – sex drive and death wish – are closely intertwined. So it is primarily a religious fertility rite. Even the poet's prayer is expressed in fertility terms, 'to make germinate'. Tollund Man is seen as a religious figure. He has the preserved body of a religious martyr, itself evidence of holiness ('a saint's kept body'). The adjective 'mild' used to describe his eyelids suggests gentleness. The poet risks blasphemy and prays to him to bring germination (new life, religious life?) to the dead of Northern Ireland.

Edna Longley sees Tollund Man as a Christ figure, 'a Christ surrogate whose death and bizarre resurrection might redeem or symbolise redemption for "the scattered, ambushed | Flesh of labourers".' Heaney's Tollund Man assumes a number of religious roles – sacrificial victim, martyr, saint and Christ figure – and so becomes a powerful religious icon, to whom the poet risks praying and for whom he will undertake a pilgrimage.

Edna Longley has drawn attention to the religious shape of the poem and described its three parts as 'evocation', 'invocation', and 'vocation': evocation, or drawing of the scene, in part I; invocation, or the poet's prayer, in part II; and vocation, or the poet's inner compulsion or need to make a pilgrimage, in part III. The poet, as in the age-old way of pilgrimage, vows to make a journey to the sacred site, seeking enlightenment or divine assistance. The pilgrimage here bridges time and space and gives this the universality of religious poetry. With a little humorous twist it links the Iron Age with the age of the motorcar. Heaney is a twentieth-century motorist-pilgrim. Yet this has all the elements of a genuine pilgrimage: the sombre, reverent mood ('Something of his sad freedom ... Should come to me'); the recitation of prayers and litanies ('Saying the names | Tollund, Grauballe, Nebelgard'); the looking for signs ('Watching the pointing hands').

## How Diction, Imagery and Word Sounds Create Mood

### Part I

The mood of the opening stanza is one of gentle reverence. The first line is one of almost monosyllabic simplicity of language – no musical effects, no repeated consonant or vowel sounds: just a plain simplicity of expression, reflecting the purity of the poet's feelings. Lines 2, 3 and 4 have a pattern of s, p, d and i sounds, which carry the softness of the tone. This mood of gentleness is reinforced by the adjective 'mild', with its Christian associations.

The harsher reality of the event begins to intrude in the second stanza, through the diction (filth, dug, gruel, caked), with its raucous and harsh sounds. The image of 'last gruel … Caked in his stomach' is a vivid reminder of the untimeliness of the death.

The prevailing mood of the third stanza is one of sympathy. The imagery of the pathetic dress, 'Naked except for | The cap, noose and girdle,' reminds us of the unequal odds. The only energy of the entire part comes in the fourth stanza, with the frisson of sexuality in the imagery, describing the deadly sexual embrace.

The mood of quietness returns in the fifth stanza, created by the long o and a sounds and the gentle s sounds. The choice of the word 'reposes' befits the tranquillity of a statue or any religious icon.

### Part II

In the first stanza of this section the diction chosen is full of weighty religious terminology (blasphemy, consecrate, holy ground, pray). This contrasts oddly with the violence of the imagery in stanzas 3 and 4. The unexpectedness of this adds to the shock, but the shape and style of the quatrain has something to do with the effect also. The horrific violence is made all the more poignant by being carried in a neutral style and tone, like reportage. The horrifying images are pruned of all excess words and squeezed into the thin, short-line quatrains. Images flick across the eye in a staccato rhythm, like a film shot at some pace.

> The scattered, ambushed
> Flesh of labourers,
> Stockinged corpses
> Laid out in the farmyards,
>
> Tell-tale skin and teeth
> Flecking the sleepers

Then we get the pathos of 'four young brothers', which draws us back to the image of 'stockinged corpses' and suggests youth, innocence and vulnerability.

These images are among the most telling in the poem and create feelings of both revulsion and sympathy.

## Part III

The mood changes again with the sombre rhythms and sounds here. A sad music is achieved with the rhythmic trochees at the end of each of the first three lines (freedom, tumbril, driving), the *s* alliteration, the plaintive *e* sounds (free, he, me), and the long *a* sounds ('Saying the names'). Out of this doleful music emerges the startling image of a tumbril, anachronistic with its associations with the French Revolution and reminders of state killing in every age.

The mood created in the last two stanzas is somewhat confused, as the poet experiences contradictory feelings. He empathises and is alienated at the same time. The alienation is reinforced by the meaningless litany of foreign sounds and disjointed imagery of fragments of people, the synecdoche of 'pointing hands' and 'tongue'. The poet is lost yet strangely at home in the familiarity of violence. The image of 'man-killing parishes', yoking together the pagan and the Christian worlds, offers a final bleak comment on the state of humankind.

## *Publication of 'North', 1975*

### BIOGRAPHICAL BACKGROUND

Heaney spent the academic year 1970/71 as guest lecturer at the University of Berkeley, California, and found it difficult to settle back into life in Northern Ireland when he returned, a transition he described as 'like putting an old dirty glove on again'. He found the daily ritual of road-blocks, arrests, vigilante patrols, explosions and killings deeply disturbing. There were many flash-points and multiple killings at that time, such as Bloody Sunday in January 1972, when British paratroopers opened fire during a Civil Rights Association march, killing thirteen unarmed civilians and wounding others. Soon afterwards the internal Northern Ireland system of government operating from Stormont was abolished and direct rule from London instituted in its place.

Whatever the background reasons, whether political, family or artistic, Heaney decided it was time to leave Belfast and devote himself entirely to his writing. He resigned his post as lecturer in English at Queen's University and moved with his family to a cottage in Glanmore, Co. Wicklow, during the summer of 1972, determined to go it alone as a poet and freelance writer. Inevitably the newspapers gave the move a political dimension. A Southern paper trumpeted 'Ulster poet moves south', while the *Protestant Telegraph* in Belfast referred to Heaney as 'the well-known Papish propagandist'.

*North,* Heaney's fourth volume, appeared in 1975. The publisher's blurb gives an accurate overview: 'Here the Irish experience is refracted through images drawn from different parts of the Northern European experience, and the idea of the north allows the poet to contemplate the violence on his home ground in relation to memories of the Scandinavian and English invasions which have marked Irish history so indelibly.' In part I, he ranges over two or three thousand years of European civilisation, from the myths of classical Greece to nineteenth-century Irish history, examining stories of conquest, cultural conflict and deeds of violence in an effort to understand the present-day Irish conflict, attempting to illuminate the present through focusing on the past.

If part I deals with conflict, in its broadest scope, at the level of history and myth, exploring the conflict of tribes and nations, in part II the focus narrows to the individual human being caught in this vortex. Heaney attempts to understand his own psyche, to chart his personal journey, to understand the pressures on and prejudices of one individual in Northern Ireland. In 'An Unacknowledged Legislator's Dream' and 'Whatever You Say Say Nothing' we get his personal and philosophical reaction to his present-day divided and war-torn society.

> Smoke-signals are loud-mouthed compared with us:
> Manoeuvrings to find out name and school,
> Subtle discrimination by addresses
> With hardly an exception to the rule
>
> That Norman, Ken and Sidney signalled Prod
> And Séamus (call me Seán) was sure-fire Pape.
> O land of password, handgrip, wink and nod,
> Of open minds as open as a trap
> ['Whatever You Say Say Nothing']

The six poems in 'Singing School' mark milestones in his development as a poet and member of his tribe, the Northern Catholic. In 'The Ministry of Fear', 'Fosterage' and 'Exposure' he charts a fascination with words from his first encounter as a schoolboy in St Columb's College and the encouragement of Michael McLaverty to his present status as writer in exile in Co. Wicklow.

> I am neither internee nor informer;
> An inner émigré, grown long-haired
> And thoughtful; a wood-kerne

Escaped from the massacre,
Taking protective colouring
From bole and bark, feeling
Every wind that blows
['Exposure']

In ' A Constable Calls' he recalls, from a child's perspective, his fear of an alien
law. In 'Orange Drums, Tyrone, 1966' his nationalist view of loyalist
triumphalism during the marching season is charted. 'Summer 1969' suggests
the impossibility of his escaping the conflict, historically or geographically. Even
on holiday in Spain he is confronted with violence in Goya's famous painting
*Shootings of the Third of May*.

This then is a book of enormous scope, examining the violence and savagery
of conquest, at its broadest incidence in myth and international history, but also
at the microcosmic level of the individual human psyche.

This collection of conflict poems is prefaced by two poems of a completely
different sort, two peaceful poems outside the stream of history and time,
recalling the security of childhood, the holistic nature of the old ways of life, the
peacefulness of the countryside, and the stability and certainty provided by family
love and values. These are 'Mossbawn: Two Poems in Dedication'. The first of
these is 'Sunlight'.

# *Sunlight*

Text of poem: New Explorations Anthology page 330

BACKGROUND NOTE

Mossbawn is the family home where Séamus Heaney grew up, a place that was
for him, as home is for all children, the centre of the world and the source of all
life and energy. He says of it:

> I would begin with the Greek word *omphalos*, meaning the navel, and hence
> the stone that marked the centre of the world, and repeat it, *omphalos,
> omphalos, omphalos*, until its blunt and falling music becomes the music of
> somebody pumping water at the pump outside our back door. It is County
> Derry in the early 1940s. The American bombers groan towards the
> aerodrome at Toomebridge, the American troops manoeuvre in the fields
> along the road, but all of that great historical action does not disturb the
> rhythms of the yard. There the pump stands, a slender, iron idol, snouted,
> helmeted, dressed down with a sweeping handle, painted a dark green and
> set on a concrete plinth, marking the centre of another world. Five

households drew water from it. Women came and went, came rattling between empty enamel buckets, went evenly away, weighed down by silent water. The horses came home to it in those first lengthening evenings of spring, and in a single draught emptied one bucket and then another as the man pumped and pumped, the plunger slugging up and down, *omphalos, omphalos, omphalos.* [BBC radio interview, 1978, reprinted in *Preoccupations,* 1980.]

Mary Heaney was his aunt, a kind of second mother to him, for whom he had a special affection. She features in a number of his poems: as one of the family women in 'Churning Day', both as a young girl and as a woman taking the young Séamus on a trip to the seaside in 'In Memoriam Francis Ledwidge', and as the planter of a memorial tree in 'Clearances'. She represents the old secure, stable way of life, a sense of community and traditional rural values.

## SIGNIFICANCE OF THE POEM

Given the context of this poem in a volume dealing primarily with violence, past and present, are we justified in viewing the piece as somewhat escapist? The poet has created a timeless zone of slow days, domestic ritual, natural and human warmth, and companionable silence – a safe haven amid the surrounding violence. We are taken back in time to childhood, pictured here as the golden age of innocence and security. (In general, childhood is not sentimentalised by Heaney: see 'Death of a Naturalist', 'Mid-Term Break' and 'The Early Purges'.) Is this nostalgic escapism or a search for alternative human values, values no longer found in present-day society?

## VALUES

The values featured here are domestic: the value of unspectacular routine work ('Now she dusts the board | with a goose's wing'); the practice of simple culinary skills ('her hands scuffled | over the bakeboard'); the routine of a lifestyle pared down to its essentials of bread, water and love. Far from suggesting deprivation, these bare essentials are imbued with a sense of mystery, a sense of the sacramental, suggesting a religious simplicity of life: the water is 'honeyed', 'the scone rising,' and 'here is love'.

Family feeling is important here. Love grows out of simple shared domestic tasks, love flourishes in an ordinary, unspectacular setting, among ordinary, unglamorous people ('broad-lapped, | with whitened nails | and measling shins'), flowering in the silent spaces between people.

And here is love
like a tinsmith's scoop
sunk past its gleam
in the meal-bin.

Love is associated with the simplest of food staple, lurking in the life-giving meal, unspectacular ('a tinsmith's scoop') yet vital.

The values of silence and peace are also stressed ('sunlit absence', 'each long afternoon', 'here is a space | again', 'the tick of two clocks').

All these values are found by reaching back to a pre-modern time. All the props of the scene suggest an earlier age: the pump in the yard, a griddle cooling, the reddening stove, a goose's wing, the meal-bin. They are rural values, born of a simple life. Yet they are made to appear poignantly appealing, offering an ideal way of living.

### ATMOSPHERE

The atmosphere created is one of warmth, serenity and quiet vitality. This is achieved primarily through the imagery and symbolism. Images of sunlight and heat predominate ('a sunlit absence', 'water honeyed', 'the sun stood | like a griddle cooling | against the wall', 'the reddening stove'). The 'helmeted' pump is both actual and symbolic, a soldier on sentry duty protecting the household. But, more importantly, the pump is in immediate contact with the hidden springs of the earth, the source of life. Its water is mysteriously transformed ('honeyed'). As the critic Michael Parker says, it 'serves as an icon or symbol for the subterranean energies of the place and people.' The sun too is captured by the scene, reduced to domestic proportions ('like a griddle cooling'). The bread and water too are life symbols. The alliterative language (helmeted, heated, honeyed) creates a melodic flow that also helps to build this atmosphere of 'mellow fruitfulness'. Heaney himself is reported as saying that it was intended to be a description of the experience of a foetus in the womb.

But the atmosphere is not lazy. There is a quiet energy in this poem, achieved partly through the style of verse. A great deal is packed into these very short lines. The resulting *enjambment* or continuation of ideas – not just from one line to the next but also from one verse to the next – creates a sense of contained energy. The erratic activities and pauses in the aunt's baking ritual contribute also to this sense of restlessness ('now she dusts the board', 'now sits', 'here is a space').

# A Constable Calls

Text of poem: New Explorations Anthology page 332
[*Note: This poem is also prescribed for Ordinary Level 2005 exam*]

This is one of a set of six autobiographical poems entitled 'Singing School', which deals with the development of Heaney's sense of identity as a poet and as a member of the Northern Catholic community. (For further information see pages 218–20.) It records the sense of fear and guilt experienced as a child when he encountered a figure of the law. Perhaps it is meant to be symbolic of the uneasy nationalist relationship with the forces of law and order, but in truth it could be describing 'any child's encounter with a threatening figure of remote authority' (James Simmons).

The bicycle is described in images and sounds that suggest ugliness and crude strength. The *ow* sound in 'cowl' has a crude primitiveness, and the assonance of 'fat black' emphasises the suggestions of ungainly strength in the adjectives. The 'spud' of the dynamo continues to build, both in image and sound, the pervasive atmosphere of crude, even brutal, strength. Perhaps there is also a hint of aggression, possibly life-threatening, in that dynamo metaphor, 'gleaming and cocked back' (as in a gun?). The feeling of oppression is created quite overtly, indeed without a great deal of subtlety, in the image at the end of the second stanza:

> The pedal treads hanging relieved
> Of the boot of the law.

And all of this is created before we meet the policeman.

The policeman never comes across as a person but is defined in terms of his accoutrements and uniform. A series of disjointed references to the 'heavy ledger', the 'polished holster', 'the braid cord | Looped into the revolver butt' and 'the baton-case' establish the figure of military authority, while the only human reference, to the upside-down cap ('The line of its pressure ran like a bevel | In his slightly sweating hair'), does not serve to humanise this figure but rather repels us further. Under this stern figure of authority the agricultural survey returns have assumed the status of a day of reckoning, and the 'heavy ledger' becomes the 'domesday book'. The brisk official tone of the questioning enhances the impersonal nature of this encounter.

> 'Any other root crops?
> Mangolds? Marrowstems? Anything like that?'
> 'No?'

There are quite divergent critical views on the truth of this poem. Some read it as a specific political statement, the policeman the embodiment of the unionist state and the young boy experiencing the fear, the guilt and the alienation of the dispossessed Irish. Others, such as James Simmons ('The trouble with Séamus' in *Séamus Heaney: A Collection of Critical Essays*, edited by Elmer Andrews), are of the opinion that this is a false reading. Simmons feels that this is quite a weak poem, describing ordinary, exaggerated childish fears, and that it doesn't add very much to our understanding of the nationalist identity.

> The father may have been making a few false returns, but the child has heard of the black hole in the barracks and fears that his father may be carried off for his crimes. This is a pleasant little story, vividly told, but there is little about it to justify its place in a short sequence. A Protestant poet might write an exactly similar piece. False returns and a fear of the law are probably universal, but in the context of Heaney's poem, the very vagueness of the story must be generally thought to be one more example of the horrors of being a Catholic in Northern Ireland.

How do you read this poem? The critic Edna Longley, writing about the falseness of the ending, speaks of 'the caller's bike becoming, even from the child's eye view, an implausibly melodramatic time-bomb'. Do you find this poem real or melodramatic?

## Publication of 'Field Work', 1979

BIOGRAPHICAL AND POLITICAL BACKGROUND

The Heaney family lived a fairly insular rural existence in the cottage at Glanmore, Co. Wicklow, from 1972 until 1976. 'I wanted the kids to have that sort of wild animal life that I had. They were like little rodents through the hedges ... I wanted that eye-level life with the backs of ditches, the ferns and the smell of cow dung, and I suppose I didn't want to lose that in myself.'

Isolated, the family was forced back on its own resources, a process that was different and unsettling but not without its rewards. The children's enjoyment of the simple life enabled Heaney to re-imagine his own childhood and rural values. The isolation also forced husband and wife to rediscover each other. These issues surfaced as themes in his lyrics.

Heaney went back to full-time teaching in the English Department of Carysfort Teacher Training College from 1975 to 1981. And, chiefly to facilitate their growing family, in 1976 the Heaneys abandoned their rural retreat for the convenience of a house in Sandymount, Dublin.

The violence in Northern Ireland continued to increase. In 1975 and 1976 alone over five hundred people were killed and more than five thousand were injured. The poet's cousin Colum McCartney was killed in a random sectarian attack. In 1975 three members of the Miami Showband were murdered by the UVF. Retaliation killings were common. In August 1976 the 'Peace People' movement was begun, after three children were killed by a runaway car in Andersonstown when the IRA driver was shot by a British army patrol. For a while ordinary people north and south raised their voices against the killings – killings that feature in a very personal and poignant way in *Field Work*.

## 'FIELD WORK': THE VOLUME

Published in 1979, *Field Work* is the volume that first reflects Heaney's move to Co. Wicklow. The ten Glanmore sonnets that form the centrepiece capture the atmosphere of the place: the mysterious landscape that doesn't always yield up its secrets, populated by deer and rats, cuckoos and corncrakes, and the kind of rural work practices that make casual appearances: ploughs, tractors, silage, etc. He explores the relationship between language and land.

It might be seen as a retreat from the world, as many a literary figure before him had done. Indeed the scope of the poetry has narrowed considerably from that in *North,* which ranged over continents and millennia, to a field and four years in *Field Work*. But Heaney did not see this retreat as a running away, rather as a time for refocusing, for learning. As he put it (in *Poetry Book Society Bulletin,* autumn 1979): 'Those four years were an important growth time when I was asking myself questions about the proper function of poets and poetry and learning a new commitment to the art.' Indeed he refers frequently to the time spent in 'the hedge-school of Glanmore', with all the image's connotations of peasant learning in the eighteenth and early nineteenth centuries.

Heaney begins the volume in 'Oysters' determined to begin afresh, to cast aside history, to live for the day, and to write freely out of his imagination, unshackled by heritage. But, ironically, his imagination takes him right back to politics and to Ulster in the very next poem. 'After a Killing' was written following the murder of the British ambassador to Ireland, Christopher Ewart-Biggs, in July 1976. In the face of the centuries-old conflict the poet struggles to find some crumb of comfort in nature ('small-eyed survivor flowers') or in unexpected human courtesy ('a girl walks in home to us | Carrying a basket full of new potatoes').

The march referred to in 'At the Water's Edge' occurred in March 1972 amid a protest about the Bloody Sunday shootings of January 1972. 'The Strand at Lough Beg' is an elegy for his cousin Colum McCartney, the victim of a sectarian killing. 'A Postcard from North Antrim' commemorates Seán Armstrong, a friend who was similarly gunned down. 'Casualty' celebrates the determined independence of the fisherman Louis O'Neill, an acquaintance of Heaney's, who was blown up.

There is no escape from Ulster for Heaney, no escape from death, even in this rural retreat of Glanmore, where a foraging nocturnal badger might be taken as the spirit of 'the murdered dead' and where such 'visitations are taken for signs'. The difference in the poetry is that these are elegies recording the poet's personal grief at the loss of friends and relations rather than philosophical pieces attempting to understand the ills of the nation (such as we found in *North*). The focus here is more limited, and the tone is what Heaney himself described as 'a more social voice'. It is as if truth is to be found at the level of individual experience and feeling.

But there are few certainties in this book. *Field Work* is strewn with unanswered and unanswerable questions: Who's sorry for our trouble? ... What will become of us? ... What is my apology for poetry? The old certainties are no longer within reach; instead there is a great deal of troubled questioning.

One of Heaney's responses to the uncertainty is to strive for renewal in his personal life. He attempts to find a new understanding of marriage and to forge a new, real and more equal relationship with his wife. In a series of very personal, even idiosyncratic love poems he explores married life and love. He is enthralled by his wife's alluring charm, whether she is diving into a pool in Tuscany ('The Otter') or rummaging around in a bottom drawer ('The Skunk'). She is a nest in 'Home Comings', a reclaimed marsh in 'Polder' and a tree spirit in 'Field Work'.

In 'Harvest Bow' he looks back again to find reassurance in family and cultural continuity. This poem seems to fulfil a similar function to the Mossbawn poems, in its celebration of the way of life and skills of his father, his aunts, etc.

*Field Work* deals with both political and domestic experience and how they are intertwined. The last two poems exemplify this, where Heaney identifies with Francis Ledwidge, the young poet killed in the First World War, and also with the sufferings of a family from Dante's *Inferno*, tortured for political purposes ('In Memoriam Francis Ledwidge' and 'Ugolino').

# The Skunk

Text of poem: New Explorations Anthology page 334
*[Note: This poem is also prescribed for Ordinary Level 2005 exam]*

## ROBERT LOWELL'S 'SKUNK HOUR'

A comparison with Robert Lowell's 'Skunk Hour' might provide an easy way into the Heaney poem. Lowell was read and much admired by Heaney in the 1970s. The Lowell poem is one of intense isolation, loneliness and depression, where the speaker is driven to be a voyeur of lovers in cars.

A car radio bleats,
'Love, O careless Love ...' I hear
my ill-spirit sob in each blood cell,
as if my hand were at its throat ...
I myself am hell,
nobody's here –
only skunks, that search
in the moonlight for a bite to eat.

Heaney's skunk also fills the night loneliness as, temporarily exiled, the poet sits writing in the Californian darkness, separated from his wife. But Heaney's state of mind is not at all like the tormented, desolate Lowell's; instead he is writing love letters, 'broaching the word "wife" | like a stored cask'. The skunk becomes a regular feature of his evenings ('I expected her like a visitor'). Somehow the skunk's visit recalls his wife's presence, perhaps because of the accidental contemporaneity with the poet's love letters. In a very risky zoomorphic comparison, the skunk takes on the qualities of the absent wife.

And there she was, the intent and glamorous,
Ordinary, mysterious skunk,
Mythologized, demythologized,
Snuffing the boards five feet beyond me.

This Californian encounter is recalled for him in the last verse, when he sees his wife rummaging for a nightdress in a bedroom bottom drawer, striking a quite ridiculous skunk-like posture.

## THE ANALOGY

This is one of a series of poems where his wife is sometimes pictured as an otter, a skunk, a sand martin's nest, etc. These *zoomorphic* comparisons (attributing the form or nature of an animal to something) are unusual and unexpected, rather in the style of metaphysical conceits. While they are startling in themselves, the effect is to emphasise the naturalness of the relationship and to communicate something of the primitive erotic animal attraction involved.

The analogy here is particularly risky, in that the associations normally evoked by the skunk are noxious, unpleasant and anything but erotic. The new associations created by the poet are equally startling ('like the chasuble | At a funeral mass'). Perhaps it is this unexpected mixture of connotations, sacred and sexual, repulsive and erotically inviting, that forms the main appeal of this analogy.

A LOVE POEM

This is a very sensuous poem, where all the senses are assailed at once. A gentle romantic light provides the ambient colour for the poem ('My desk light softened beyond the verandah.') Otherwise the predominant colour is black, but a black that comes with diverse associations: that of wild animal, funeral Mass and alluring nightdress. The sense of smell is evoked with exotic effect ('the beautiful, useless | Tang of eucalyptus spelt your absence.') Smell and taste are combined in a synaesthetic image.

> The aftermath of a mouthful of wine
> Was like inhaling you off a cold pillow.

Sounds too are used to emphasise the primitive nature of the feelings ('snuffing the boards') and also to create the erotic allure ('stirred by the sootfall') with the *s* sounds and the soft *o*.

But the poem goes beyond just creating a sensuous atmosphere. It has a direct erotic appeal. Watching the animal, he is 'tense as a voyeur', fascinated by her glamour, her mysteriousness, in a moment of transferred eroticism. This is re-created in the bedroom scene of the last stanza, a moment described by the critic Neil Corcoran (in *A Student's Guide to Séamus Heaney*) as 'charged with affection and intimacy, turning a faintly ridiculous human posture into an unconscious erotic invitation'.

'Sootfall', a word created by Heaney, conjures up both the delicacy of the discarded clothes and their dirtiness. That they have been used by her is alluring. It is faintly ironic that she is searching for a plunge-line nightdress, as he finds her attractive and exciting without it. The animal analogy here emphasises the basic, primitive nature of sex. It is a moment of stark married intimacy, forthrightly and honestly recalled.

The aspect of love dramatised here is not of the superficial, jazzy, romantic variety. If anything, the poet's attitude is anti-romantic, focusing on the physical attraction of older, imperfect bodies. She must feel that she needs the plunge-line nightdress. The shadowy presence of the skunk emphasises the more banal contexts for erotic attraction. This is about ordinary, everyday, unscrubbed, unperfumed intimacy between real people. Neither love nor the human body is idealised here.

IMAGERY

One of the more exciting technical features of this poem is the unusual imagery, the startling comparisons drawn in similes and metaphors. Some are quite shocking, such as the skunk's tail 'damasked like the chasuble | At a funeral mass'. The suggestion of black here is picked up by the 'plunge-line nightdress' at the end of the poem, creating altogether a combination of unusual associations, sacred and sexual. The uncomfortable honesty of the poet's self-image, where he sees himself 'tense as a voyeur', sets the tone of the poem. 'The word "wife" | Like a stored cask' throws up suggestions about the value of the relationship, its maturity, its age, indeed its hidden and private ingredients.

The combining of sensations in the imagery that has already been noticed ('a mouthful of wine ... inhaling you off a cold pillow') portrays the multifaceted richness of the love, as well as its sensuality. But of all the imagery, the final metaphor must be the most startling: the wife's skunk-like posture at a bottom drawer.

## RHYTHM OF LANGUAGE

The rhythm varies and changes to suit the purpose at particular stages of the poem. He uses self-contained, stopped lines of three or four stresses when setting the scene (for example in stanza 2). The effect is of a picture painted with the economy of four brush-strokes. But he also uses enjambment, with each line running into the next – even into the next verse – to create a sense of urgency and excitement and to allow a flow of feelings. (We can see this at work in stanzas 3 and 4, for example.) The language used ranges from the usual heavily descriptive, conversational style we are accustomed to in Heaney to the more analytical and academic at times ('mythologized', 'demythologized', etc.).

# *The Harvest Bow*

Text of poem: New Explorations Anthology page 336

This poem is in the tradition of 'Digging', 'Follower', the 'Mossbawn' poems and others where Heaney returns to his family, in particular to his father and aunt, and to the ethos and values of his childhood community. Here he considers this artefact, the harvest bow, a woven corn ornament produced by his father, to whom this poem is addressed.

## THE BOW AS A WORK OF ART

To the poet the bow is a work of art that enlightens the viewer ('brightens as it tightens twist by twist | Into a knowable corona'). Notice the emphasis on illumination. In a paradoxical image, the poet hints at its natural – therefore transient – nature but also suggests that it has the enduring quality of all good art ('wheat that does not rust'). Like all art, it carries real feelings and emotional truth (it is a 'love-knot'). Yet it is somehow disposable ('a throwaway') and fragile ('of straw'). Perhaps the somewhat paradoxical nature of the qualities of the harvest bow in the first stanza stem from the use of two different viewpoints:

to the poet it is a work of art; to his father, the maker, it is a mere symbolic trifle ('A throwaway love-knot of straw').

## ARTEFACT AS INSPIRATION FOR THE POET

At any rate, the harvest bow has become a source of inspiration for the poet. He regards it almost as a *fetish* (anything irrationally revered), as he touches it to re-establish contact with his sense of community and heritage.

> I tell and finger it like braille,
> Gleaning the unsaid off the palpable.

It embodies and opens up his heritage for the poet. Fashioned by his father's hands, it reveals a sense both of the traditional work practices and of the sports carried out by those hands:

> Hands that aged round ashplants and cane sticks
> And lapped the spurs on a lifetime of game cocks

It carries something of the spirit of his 'tongue-tied' father, their shared past and the relationship between father and son. These are transmitted through images of simple boyhood activities (fishing, whacking the tops off weeds, silent, companionable walks with his father). This artefact embodies in its form the essence of his community, that skill and effort, the patient repetitive agricultural labour that every year produced works of art, of natural creativity in 'that original townland | Still tongue-tied in the straw tied by your hand.'

So the harvest bow has become for the poet a doorway to a lost communal past, perhaps also a symbol of an age of innocence that attracts and inspires him.

## ART AS SYMBOL

Perhaps it might be considered symbolic in a broader sense also. As a product of nature's richest bounty, it could be seen as the embodiment of the life force, preserving the gold of the sun against time ('brightens as it tightens', 'knowable corona', 'its golden loops'). In the final simile, that 'spirit of the corn' has evaded time's trap ('Like a drawn snare | Slipped') and loosed the life force, leaving the bow 'burnished' and 'still warm'. Paradoxically, the bow seems to be both death snare and symbol of life here. It incorporates both time and timelessness, symbolising the permanence of art and the transience of life.

## THE FUNCTION OF ART IN THE COMMUNITY

What is the significance of the motto *The end of art is peace*? We are reminded of Keats's discovered wisdom in 'Ode on a Grecian Urn': 'Beauty is Truth, Truth Beauty.' Whatever about its meaning, the insight gained here from the contemplation of this work of art is much less confidently asserted than that of Keats ('Could be the motto of this frail device'). Here it is more of an aspiration than definite advice for living. Nor does it seem to grow naturally out of the poem.

And what does it mean? Does it signify personal peace, individual tranquillity of mind achieved through the contemplation of, or the practice of, art? Does he mean social or political peace, achieved through understanding of the ethos and values of communities and apprehended through works of art such as this harvest bow? *The end of art is peace* is a slogan that W.B. Yeats borrowed from the nineteenth-century Pre-Raphaelite poet and essayist Coventry Patmore and that Yeats used to embody his own ideas on the purpose of art in life. In Heaney's poem the motto certainly raises the question of the function of art (including literature) in society.

The literary critic Tony Curtis feels that the central message of the poem is a socio-political one.

> The poem has a simplistic but strong central argument: work with 'fine intent' and hark to your gift, others may then learn, 'Gleaning the unsaid off the palpable.' There may be no easy, clear, instructions from the previous generations, but Heaney and Ireland itself may learn from what does survive, the palpable.

So the sense of tradition and continuity, the value of family relationships, of delicate human craft skills, the even tenor of life lived in a rural setting and the other aspects of rural life so important to Heaney can be apprehended to some extent through surviving art and artefacts. This could be to the betterment of peaceful living.

This argument applies not just to the father's artefact but also to Heaney's own art, his poetry. This poem too is meant to be a force for the enlightenment of society, offering a tiny ray of hope by offering models of better living from a previous generation.

Do you find this line of thought convincing, or is it mere nostalgia on the part of the poet?

A PORTRAIT OF HIS FATHER

There are quite a few differences between this and previous representations of his father. In previous poems the father was associated with strenuous physical activities, such as digging and ploughing. Earlier poems have focused on his rump, his shoulders, etc. Here the focus is on his hands. So a new aspect of his father, as delicate craftsman, is examined here.

The father is also a changed man, a man who has mellowed with age.

> As you plaited the harvest bow
> You implicated the mellowed silence in you

But Heaney does not let us forget the kind of man he was, as he contrasts the delicate dexterity of the present with the rough strength of the younger man, wielding ashplants and lapping the spurs on game-cocks.

The father–son relationship is still complex. The artistic relationship is similar to that of earlier poems: the poet is finding a similarity, a continuity, between his father's skill and his own craft. Here his craft is to interpret, to verbalise the father's craftsmanship. In this poem too the father is still portrayed as a strong, silent figure, unemotional, not good at verbal communication.

There is both a closeness and a sense of distance in this relationship. Silence unites father and son but also separates them. Silence can be both companionable and difficult to interpret. We might also notice that father and son are separated symbolically by the stanza division in stanzas 3 and 4, but united by the run-on lines between the verses.

> You with a harvest bow in your lapel,
> Me with the fishing rod, already homesick

These hints of a less than idyllic relationship save the poem from sentimentality and nostalgia. For all that, the poet has a sense of pride in the father's craftsmanship, in the skill of those hands that 'harked to their gift and worked with fine intent'.

## THEMES AND PREOCCUPATIONS
- The lost rural heritage and the need for a sense of continuity
- The function of art and poetry in society
- The importance of family relationships
- Stable memories of childhood as a well of healing waters to be drawn on when necessary.

## TECHNIQUE

### Stanza form
As befits a weighty philosophical theme and a more narrative style of writing, Heaney is using a bigger verse format of six-line stanzas. There is no regular rhythm or metrical pattern, but lines are predominantly four-stress, with some

three-stress and a few pentameters. It has much of the unstructured rhythm of conversation.

## Sounds

The poem has a musical quality. Verses are structured in couplets, some rhyming but most half-rhyming. These off-rhymes do not draw attention away from the argument and create a pleasant unobtrusive music (bow – you; rust – twist; loops – slopes; midges – hedges; wall – lapel). Internal rhyme and assonance are used to create a musical background, or to draw attention to an image or idea. For example, in the first stanza 'plaited – implicated', 'brightens – tightens' and the repeated long *o* sounds in 'knowable', 'corona' and 'throwaway' create a sense of opening out, an expanding perspective, in tune with the idea and meaning. Other sound effects are used similarly throughout the poem.

## Imagery

Images of corn predominate. The harvest bow is pictured as 'wheat that does not rust', 'love-knot of straw' and 'golden loop' and finally metamorphoses into 'a drawn snare'. Most of these images emphasise the golden colour and the positive life force of the corn. Even the snare is 'burnished' and 'still warm'. The bric-a-brac of the rural scene is realised in great and realistic detail ('Blue smoke straight up, old beds and ploughs in hedges'). There are images too with a more philosophical abstract texture: a 'knowable corona', the 'drawn snare' (of time), etc.

## Tone

The tone is reasonably positive. The poet believes his retrospective exploration is valuable and significant and that the discoveries made are of value to the present generation. The memories are relatively pleasant but realistically drawn, so the tone is one of satisfied retrospection rather than sentimental nostalgia. For all the quiet optimism there is a certain tentativeness about the tone, as the poet realises how frail is the fetish and how experimental is the wisdom gleaned.

> *The end of art is peace*
> Could be the motto of this frail device.

# Biographical and historical background

For Séamus Heaney the 1980s were marked by a number of prestigious international teaching positions, while the publication of his prose heralded a growing reputation as a sharply intuitive literary interpreter and critic. In 1980 his collection of essays and lectures *Preoccupations: Selected Prose, 1968–78* was published. In 1982 he began a five-year contract teaching one term a year at Harvard University. With Ted Hughes he edited *The Rattle Bag*, a hugely varied anthology of poetry for young people, and he received an honorary doctorate from Queen's University.

In 1983 *An Open Letter* was published as a Field Day pamphlet. In this verse letter Heaney objects to his work being included in an anthology of British poetry. 1984 saw him elected to the Boylston Chair of Rhetoric and Oratory at Harvard; and in 1988 he became Professor of Poetry at the University of Oxford. *The Government of the Tongue*, another collection of his lectures and critical writing, appeared also in that year.

Meanwhile at home the political situation deteriorated seriously. In August 1979 Lord Mountbatten, his fourteen-year-old grandson and a fourteen-year-old friend were blown up at Mullaghmore, Co. Sligo. Also at this time eighteen British soldiers were blown up by the IRA at Warrenpoint, Co. Down. The period of March to October 1981 saw the hunger strike by Republican prisoners in Long Kesh and the deaths of ten prisoners, among them Bobby Sands, who had just been elected a Westminster MP.

## Publication of 'Station Island', 1984

Published in 1984 by Faber and Faber, *Station Island* is a very complicated and sophisticated work, which uses a great range of myth, legend, and literary and historical allusion. These come from both Irish and European culture, ancient, mediaeval and modern, and Heaney uses them as entry points, or sometimes as parallels, in order to examine his own culture. Heaney has often been accused of not 'tackling' violence directly, of lack of passionate involvement in the Northern question. However, he does deal with the situation; indeed this volume is full of allusions and references to prisons, cells, compounds, policemen, punishments, informers, betrayals, and victims of violence. But Heaney is happier exploring the situation at one remove, using myth, legend, literature and history as an intermediary, a glass through which it is viewed.

## Publication of 'The Haw Lantern', 1987

*The Haw Lantern*, published in 1987, is chiefly a book about loss, emptiness and absence. The most accessible and moving poems in the book are elegies: 'The Summer of Lost Rachel', for a niece who died in an accident; 'The Wishing Tree', for his wife's late mother; a poem for Robert Fitzgerald, a deceased colleague at Harvard; and 'The Stone Verdict', an elegy for his father. But the most powerful of all are 'Clearances', a sequence of eight sonnets, elegies in memory of his mother, who died in 1984. Some deal simply and movingly with very ordinary, everyday experiences, such as peeling potatoes together or folding sheets. Another deals with the scene at the deathbed. Yet another is written from the vantage point of the house of the dead, drawn with mundane realism, which gives it a surreal quality. Altogether they are a very moving series of poems on the relationship between mothers and sons.

## Publication of 'Seeing Things', 1991

*Seeing Things*, published in 1991, in some ways sees a return to the concerns of the early Heaney. It deals with personal vision and personal history, rather than with politics or historical issues. He returns to childhood memories: football, fishing, sailing, skating; memories of an old bicycle, of market days, of rat poison in an outhouse, of first firing a gun; memories of Glanmore, revisited in a sequence of seven sonnets. He is going back, making a 'journey back into the heartland of the ordinary'. But here Heaney is interested in seeing the ordinary in a different way, looking more deeply into things, as in 'Field of Vision'. He is both the observer we met in the early Heaney and now also the visionary, exploring the significance of these observations. This results in a new, fresh 'seeing', a new excitement, as in 'Fosterling'.

> Me waiting until I was nearly fifty
> To credit marvels.

It leads him to a deeper, more philosophical questioning about meaning:

> Where does spirit live? Inside or outside
> Things remembered, made things, things unmade?

The very title suggests this new, complex vision of the poet. 'Seeing things' could refer to sensitive and accurate observation, or to an ability to imagine what is not really there, or even to a visionary and mythical ability to see into the heart of things.

Underlying the volume is a view of the poet as mediator between states, one who facilitates movement between this world and the next, between the marvellous and the actual, the transcendent and the material world (see 'Lightenings VIII'). Many of these poems therefore feature threshold states, crossings between the ordinary and the fabulous. Heaney claims for poetry a visionary power, an ability to transcend the immediate world of the everyday.

The poet came to terms with the relationship with his mother in the 'Clearances' sequence of the previous volume. His father, who died in 1986, is a recurring presence in this volume. But now there is a more equal relationship, less awe, more affection and an effort to understand the timeless significance of fathers and sons in such poems as 'Man and Boy', 'The Ash Plant', 'Squarings XV' and 'Seeing Things'.

Part I consists of thirty or so individual lyric pieces. Part II has forty-eight twelve-line poems, divided into four groups of twelve under the headings 'Lightenings', 'Settings', 'Crossings' and 'Squarings'. 'Lightenings VIII' is from this section.

The volume opens and ends with two dark, bleak poems. The first is a translation from Virgil's *Aeneid* where Aeneas asks to descend into the underworld, and the last is from Dante's *Inferno* and shows the scene at the shoreside as the damned souls wait for Charon's boat to take them across to Hell. The desire to see beyond boundaries, this gift of 'seeing', can be traumatic and dangerous.

## *Field of Vision*

Text of poem: New Explorations Anthology page 339
[*Note: This poem is also prescribed for Ordinary Level 2005 exam*]

THEME

This is a poem about seeing, about understanding beyond surface viewing, about really seeing into the life of things. The poet receives a lesson in seeing from this solitary woman in a wheelchair. He compares her concentrated attention on the everyday world to looking at a field through a barred gate and being able to see 'deeper into the country than you expected'.

DEVELOPMENT

- The poet is interested in seeing not the spectacular but the mundane aspects of country life ('The stunted, agitated hawthorn bush', 'The same acre of ragwort, the same mountain', 'the field behind the hedge'). Notice that we are not startled or distracted by vivid detail or striking metaphor in the usual Heaney style; instead the images here are tediously real, unmediated by the poet's imagination. There is a sort of minimalist approach to his picturing.
- Silence and stillness are necessary for real seeing, and so he identifies with the wheelchair-bound woman. Perhaps vision can come out of suffering?
- Certainly vision will not be enhanced by emotion but comes rather out of a tough, unsentimental approach to life, where all emotional baggage has been jettisoned. We are taken by the picture of this tough, self-contained, uncomplaining invalid.

> She never lamented once and she never
> Carried a spare ounce of emotional weight.

- Paradoxically, as the depth of vision increases, the object viewed (the 'thing') becomes stranger. As the obvious superficial aspects are no longer the focus, 'the field behind the hedge | Grew more distinctly strange'.

- Paradoxically too the vision is deepened and focused by barriers. It is as if the barriers bring a heightening of awareness. It is as if the gate and pillars frame the scene like a picture or photograph ('Focused and drawn in by what barred the way').

## LANGUAGE

Heaney employs a simple, unadorned style of language, in keeping with the theme. He opens in a conversational style ('I remember this woman ...'), which is maintained throughout ('Face to face with her was an education'). This casualness is maintained through the rhythms of ordinary speech in the four-stressed or five-stressed unrhymed lines. Any embellishments in the language come from a few simple repeated patterns, such as 'unleafing and leafing' or 'The same acre ... the same mountain.'

## IMAGERY

As we have noticed already, the imagery is simple to the point of minimalism. Heaney concentrates on realising the ordinary quite faithfully, as in the 'small calves with their backs to wind and rain'. This unadorned economy makes the few images used all the more striking and effective. 'Her brow was clear as the chrome bits of the chair' carries the aseptic nature of woman and vision.

# *Lightenings VIII*

Text of poem: New Explorations Anthology page 341

## A READING OF THE POEM

This is a whimsical adaptation of a story from the 'Annals of Clonmacnoise'. On the surface it is merely a delightful fanciful anecdote, a surreal visionary story that the sceptical might see as the result of sleep deprivation or too much fasting and the devout interpret as the sign of divine favour. For the poet the entire point of the anecdote is contained in the final line and hinges on that changing point of view. To the sailor of the visionary ship the world of the monastery is marvellous and magical, whereas to the monks at their repetitive prayers and mundane tasks it is the sailor and his ship that are extraordinary and marvellous.

Heaney is asking us to contemplate this distinction between the mundane and the marvellous, between the real and the imagined. And he is suggesting that these are not conflicting states. There is fluid access from one to the other: they may even be two sides of the same experience. As the critic Henry Hart said, 'the visionary and the real are symbiotic rather than exclusive.' By blurring any distinction between the imagined and the actual, Heaney is making a strong plea for the visionary, the created, the imaginative. Perhaps the poem even goes as far as to suggest that everything we know is based on visionary experience, that all knowledge is the product of the imagination.

## Publication of 'The Spirit Level', 1996

Much of the poetry in *The Spirit Level,* published in 1996, seems to double back to the beginning, revisiting scenes of the poet's childhood and reworking some of the preoccupations of his early poetry, though with a less innocent eye.

There is a good deal that is quintessentially Heaney here. We notice his keen awareness of the natural, his ability to wonder at the everyday earth – the sights and sounds of rain, the cleansing purity of clay and the gem-like quality of gravel ('The Gravel Walks'). Yet his feeling for the healing, sacramental qualities of nature is no mere romantic escapism and does not blind him to the inherent dangers and pain, such as that suffered by the child who swallowed an awn of rye and whose throat 'was like standing crop probed by a scythe' ('The Butter-Print').

As in his early poetry, he is fascinated by local characters, probing their spirit or quality (such as that of the blind neighbour in 'At the Wellhead') or celebrating their skill, the work of their hands (in 'An Architect', or the bricklayer in 'Damson'). Hands for Heaney are often the focus of creativity.

Once again the strong figure of his father appears in many of the poems, often evoked by the symbol of the ashplant, which was both cattleman's working instrument and sign of tough authority. It says much that the father is frequently imaged in this way ('Two Stick Drawings' and 'The Strand'). But while there is the generic father–son tension, in a poem such as 'The Errand' Heaney displays more unguarded emotion towards his father, but stops sort of expressing it. Unspoken feelings – the Irishman's notion of balance. We see this in 'A Call':

'Hold on,' she said, 'I'll just run out and get him.
The weather here's so good, he took the chance
To do a bit of weeding.'

          So I saw him
Down on his hands and knees beside the leek rig,
Touching, inspecting, separating one
Stalk from the other, gently pulling up
Everything not tapered, frail and leafless,
Pleased to feel each little weed-root break,
But rueful also ...

Then found myself listening to
The amplified grave ticking of hall clocks
Where the phone lay unattended in a calm
Of mirror glass and sunstruck pendulums ...

And found myself then thinking: if it were nowadays,
This is how Death would summon Everyman.

Next thing he spoke and I nearly said I loved him.


Childhood memories provide the spark for many of his reflections. 'A Sofa in the Forties' was the stimulus for his early imaginative play; the mint plant cut for Sunday cooking wafts down the years; he revisits the swing, or blackberry picking. But there is a sharper edge to Heaney's excursions into the past in this volume. The womb-like security of Mossbawn ('Sunlight', for example) gives way to a less idyllic, more primitive picture in 'Keeping Going'.

> Buttermilk and urine,
> The pantry, the housed beasts, the listening bedroom
> ...
> It smelled of hill-fort clay
> and cattle dung. When the thorn tree was cut down
> You broke your arm. I shared the dread
> When a strange bird perched for days on the byre roof.

The past is viewed here from the standpoint of the present; the whitewashed walls of childhood become the bloodstained walls of today. It is as if the innocence has been spoiled irrevocably by present grown-up knowledge. This tension between then and now features in other poems too, such as 'Two Lorries' and 'The Flight Path'. The coal lorry of childhood has metamorphosed into the bomb vehicle of today. Here is an older, less innocent, more resigned voice. Life is now about bearing up, 'Keeping Going'.

> And this is all the good things amount to:
> This principle of bearing, bearing up
> And bearing out, just having to
>
> Balance the intolerable in others
> Against our own, having to abide
> Whatever we settled for and settled into
> Against our better judgment. Passive
> Suffering makes the world go round.

The sheer banality of the language carries the weariness of the tone. An awareness of mortality informs some of the poems, such as 'Mint', 'A Call' and 'A Dog Was Crying Tonight in Wicklow Also'.

But this heaviness is balanced by the spiritual import of other poems, celebrating the human qualities of Cædmon, an English monk of the seventh century said to have received the power of song in a vision ('Whitby-sur-Moyola'), or St Kevin's reverence for creatures ('St Kevin and the Blackbird'). Heaney often associates human goodness and saintliness with nature's gentle creatures.

As the title of the volume implies, this book's central theme is that of balance, idealism balanced by reality, nostalgia set against present pain, then and now, childhood and old age, memory and illusion, truth and lies, the bleakness of life balanced by spiritual uplift.

## St Kevin and the Blackbird

Text of poem: New Explorations Anthology page 342

From this delightful apocryphal story of St Kevin, Heaney develops ideas about the interdependence of all life, the nature of holiness, of prayer, and contemplation, and even about the nature of the creative process.

The casual idiom of the opening line ('And then there was ...') takes us straight into the world of oral culture and storytelling. And this is a fantastic story: exaggerated, incredible, unreal; but somehow it seems to convey a great deal of truth – a clear philosophy of life. The poem is yet another example of Heaney's fascination with seers, people of insight or holiness who may be able to convey deep truths. Typical too is the fact that the poet is not quite sure, at least at first, whether he is encountering genuine wisdom and sanctity or self-deluded foolishness.

This poetic ambivalence is central to the poem. The ridiculousness of the saint's posture in the first four stanzas is counterbalanced by the delicacy with which he is made to sense the bird in his hand, the sensitivity of his apprehension of 'the warm eggs, the small breast, the tucked | Neat head and claws'. So the poet's feeling grows to one of admiration for the saint's generosity of spirit ('To labour and not to seek reward'), for his self-discipline and ability at extraordinary detachment:

A prayer his body makes entirely
For he has forgotten self, forgotten bird
And on the riverbank forgotten the river's name.

The rhythmic repetition of 'forgotten', acting like a mantra or a repeated prayer, conveys perfectly the self-forgetfulness of religious meditation.

## PHILOSOPHY OF LIFE: IMAGES OF SAINTLINESS

Our first image of the saint is from traditional Catholic devotional culture: arms outstretched in cruciform shape. It is a rather extravagant religious gesture but one that was common in the romanticised 'holy picture' culture of popular piety. Yet for all its stereotypical quality, there are hints here of the real rigours and pain of Christian religious life in the allusion to the 'crossbeam' of crucifixion and in the primitive, unsophisticated, disciplined lifestyle of the 'narrow' cell.

Behind the fantastic story of the bird nesting lies a holistic philosophy of life. St Kevin sees God, humanity, creatures and the world as a continuum, all safely linked together, a satisfying unity. And so through contact with the bird he finds himself 'linked | Into the network of eternal life'. It is this concept of linkage and connectedness that Heaney picks up in the second part of the poem. He seems to view Kevin almost as a conduit between the divine and the earthly. Ostensibly we are focusing on whether or not the saint is hurting: 'From the neck on out down ... his knees'. But we are particularly conscious of the extremities: 'the shut-eyed blank of underearth' and the 'distance in his head'. Humanity, and the saint in particular, is the link between the inanimate, unresponsive earth and space, with its suggestion of freedom and possibilities of the spiritual – the 'distance in the head'.

The poem is a celebration of the traditional religious philosophy of life: that through self-discipline, prayer and meditation it is possible to become detached from the physical and emotional demands of the body and the world and to free one's consciousness into the realm of the spiritual. It is a celebration of mysticism – the ability to reach truth beyond understanding and the rational, that forgetfulness that can link one into 'the network of eternal life'.

## A SELF-CONSCIOUS AND HUMOROUS POEM

A very interesting dynamic or relationship between poet and reader is set up here. The poet breaks the conjuror's illusion, steps outside the poem, and overtly involves the reader in the creative act. The reader is invited to be co-creator with the poet:

And since the whole thing's imagined anyhow,
Imagine being Kevin. Which is he? ...

Apart from emphasising the self-consciousness of the poet, which is a trademark of Heaney's work, this interactive process enables the reader to enter the life of the poem and apprehend it more intimately. It also demonstrates Heaney's sure-footed confidence, his ability to wander within and beyond boundaries, as he does in the St Brendan poem, 'Lightenings VIII'. He is pushing at the boundaries of what is real: which is the vision, which is mere illusion? It illustrates also Heaney's sense of playfulness, the comic imagination in his work. It is as if this was a bit of a game and poetry a creative conspiracy between writer and reader. The more obvious elements of comic imagination are found in the zaniness of the events of the first four stanzas.

## Getting an overview of the poet

1. Read through all the poems, slowly and in any order you like. Using any form you like – sentences, phrases or even single words – jot down your general impressions of the poet's work.
2. What are the poet's chief preoccupations in his writing?
3. How do you understand the poet's outlook on life?
   • What does he think important?
   • What makes him angry, afraid, joyful, excited, etc.?
   • Is he hopeful or pessimistic about the world, or is the attitude in the poems more complicated?
4. What is different about the way he writes? –
   • his use of language (diction, imagery, sounds, rhythms of the language, etc.)
   • the form of the poems – one of the traditional forms, sonnet, ballad, elegy, villanelle, lyric or other
   • stanza format
   • traditional metre or free verse
   • rhymed or unrhymed.
5. How does he see his role as a poet in society? What is his speaking voice: detached observer, passionate participant or what?
6. Compare Heaney with other poets on the course, in areas such as
   • view of life
   • issues and preoccupations
   • unique treatment of similar topics
   • use of language.
7. What has encountering this poet meant to you?
8. Can the poems be grouped in any way: according to certain themes; in chronological progression; according to form or style of poem? Arrange the poems in a way that you feel best reflects the importance of what the poet has to say, and explain your arrangement.

## Overview of some themes and issues

Consider the statements following each heading. Re-examine the relevant poems, and make brief notes or headings, together with relevant quotations, on each theme.

### Irishness – history, myths, politics

1. In the early poems, Heaney was preoccupied with local history, with communicating the experience of his own place and the customs, rituals, atmosphere, characters and myths of Mossbawn (see 'Sunlight', 'The Forge').
2. Then he began to think of history as landscape, exploring downwards, finding evidence of history in the bogs and the very contour of the land, exploring what myth and prehistoric evidence revealed about Irishness (see 'Bogland').
3. Exploring back in time, he makes historical connections between the Iron Age and the present. He draws parallels between prehistory's human sacrifices and contemporary violence in Ulster. Is he suggesting that violence is endemic in all societies throughout history, that human sacrifice is necessary for the integrity of territory, that myths, however savage, are an integral part of the creation of the identity of a people (see 'The Tollund Man')?
4. He explores the divisions of present-day Ulster (see 'The Other Side'). Heaney has met with criticism from all sides regarding his treatment of recent Ulster history. Some critics accuse him of having too much politics in his poetry and others of not having enough – accusations such as
   • obscuring the horrors of recent killings
   • endorsing a 'tribal' position
   • suggesting the inevitability of carnage
   • evading the issues and being non-committal.
'For many readers, Heaney's art is fundamentally an art of consciously and carefully cultivated non-engagement' (Elmer Andrews).

What are your views on these reactions? Is Heaney completely uncritical of his own side? (See 'Bogland', 'The Tollund Man', 'A Constable Calls'.)

### Tradition and identity

1. For Heaney, an awareness of one's tradition is fundamental to a sense of identity. He explains his own roots, celebrating the skills that sustained the farming community that nurtured him: the digging, the ploughing, the water-divining, the bread-making, the skills of the farmer – skills seen almost as sacred rituals (see 'Sunlight', 'The Forge').

2. Sometimes he still hankers back to the security of that life of early childhood (see 'Sunlight'). Sometimes he needs to reforge, reinterpret and understand his links with family in order to rediscover his identity (see 'The Harvest Bow': 'I tell and finger it like braille').

3. 'Our sense of the past, our sense of the land and perhaps even our sense of identity are inextricably interwoven,' according to Heaney (*Irish Press*, 1 June 1974). Finding and maintaining a sense of continuity is vital to Heaney: family traditions, customs, and values (see 'Sunlight', 'The Harvest Bow').

   4. He explores his Catholic roots too, as set against the other tradition (see 'The Other Side'). According to Robert Welch, 'Heaney is engaged upon a cultural and tribal exploration; he is testing out his cultural inheritance to see where the significant deposits are located; but he is not engaged upon a mindless submission to the old tradition of the goddess or whatever' (see 'Sunlight', 'The Harvest Bow', 'The Other Side', 'Bogland', 'The Tollund Man').

5. Community identity is defined in terms of the bog (in contrast to the American landscape) (see 'Bogland').

6. Heaney seems to see himself as the spokesperson for this sense of identity, in the volume *Door into the Dark* in particular – an identity that is picked up from the landscape (see 'Bogland': 'We have no prairies', 'our pioneers').

7. His personal identity has overtones of victimhood about it. He certainly seems to identify with victims ('something of his sad freedom ... should come to me') (see 'The Tollund Man', 'A Constable Calls').

IDENTITY AND POETRY

1. Heaney's identity as a poet is inextricably tied in with his historical and cultural identity. The autobiographical voice of *Death of a Naturalist* becomes the spokesperson of his people in *Door into the Dark* (see 'Bogland').

2. The bog becomes a kind of subconscious racial memory for him, providing inspiration for his poetry. 'The poems have more come up like bodies out of the bog of my own imagination' (television interview, November 1973) (see 'Bogland', 'The Tollund Man').

3. 'He is proposing an idea of poetry which combines psychic investigation with historical enquiry' (Elmer Andrews) (see 'Bogland', 'The Tollund Man'). In the essay 'Feeling into Words', Heaney himself spoke of 'poetry as divination, poetry as revelation of the self to the self, as restoration of the culture to itself; poems as elements of continuity, with the aura and authenticity of archaeological finds, where the buried shard has an importance that is not diminished by the importance of the buried city; poetry as a dig, a dig for finds that end up being plants' (*Preoccupations*, 1980).

4. He sees the craft of poetry not just as something mechanical, but rather a combination of imagination and skill. He described a poem as 'a completely successful love act between the craft and the gift' (see 'The Forge', 'Field of Vision').

5. Heaney's own voice in these poems is often indecisive and ambiguous, his position a hesitant observer on the fringes of the scene (outside in 'The Forge'; 'Forgive ... my timid circumspect involvement' in 'Station Island' vii; 'I could risk blasphemy' in 'The Tollund Man').

6. Poetry may be unimportant in politics but it is vital to a sense of identity. 'Faced with the brutality of the historical onslaught, they [the arts] are practically useless. Yet they verify our singularity, they strike and stake out the core of self which lies at the base of every individuated life' (*The Government of the Tongue*, 1986).

## THE POET AND THE IMPORTANCE OF IMAGINATION

1. Heaney sees the function of the poet as being a mediator between the real world and the imaginary. The poet explores the significance behind things (see 'Field of Vision', 'St Kevin and the Blackbird').

2. Imagination is the ability to accept the undemonstrable (see 'St Kevin and the Blackbird').

3. The imagined, the marvellous, is not opposite to everyday reality, just another way of seeing (see 'Lightenings VIII', 'St Kevin and the Blackbird').

4. Perhaps all knowledge is acquired through the imagination. Certainly the marvellous and the imagined are central to our lives ('Lightenings VIII').

## LOVE

1. There are poems of romantic love, dealing with feelings of excitement, of loss, and of great need (see 'Twice Shy', 'Valediction').

2. Feelings of erotic love are sensitively dealt with (see 'The Skunk').

3. Family love is important to Heaney:
   • an idyllic adult–child relationship in the womblike security of Mossbawn (see 'Sunlight')
   • the uncommunicated closeness of father–son relationships (see 'The Harvest Bow').

## OTHER TOPICS DEALT WITH OR ALLUDED TO

# Death

• Death and violence ('The Tollund Man')
• Has death got meaning? ('The Tollund Man')

## Fear and insecurity
- Associated with love ('Valediction')
- Associated with politics, religion, and everyday living ('A Constable Calls').

## Childhood
- Womblike security of childhood ('Sunlight')
- The relationship with parents ('The Harvest Bow')
- Fears of childhood, real or imaginary ('A Constable Calls')
- The need for continuity between generations ('The Harvest Bow).

THE ROLE OF LANDSCAPE IN HEANEY'S POETRY

1. Heaney is a fine descriptive nature poet. He has an 'extraordinary gift in realising the physical world freshly and with vigorous exact economy. Heaney can bring everyday natural events before his readers' eyes with such telling precision that his images are both recognition and revelation' (Terence Browne) (see any of the poems).

2. But landscape for Heaney is more than just a subject to be painted: it is a living presence, an ever-present force, a sort of third party to human activity in the poems. It is there, sharing in the intimacy of the relationship, in 'Twice Shy' ('sky a tense diaphragm: dusk hung like a backcloth'). It has the same immediate personal presence that we find in Kavanagh and in Wordsworth (see 'Twice Shy', 'Bogland', 'The Tollund Man').

3. The landscape can harbour different faces, the life force ('spirit of the corn'), and a threatening, menacing aspect ('the bottomless bog'), just as the farming tradition of his community is associated with decay and also with growth (see 'The Harvest Bow', 'Bogland').

4. People have a human and a religious relationship with the landscape (see 'Bogland', 'The Tollund Man', 'The Harvest Bow').

5. The landscape is seen as essentially female, often with erotic associations in its relationship with man (see 'The Tollund Man').

6. Heaney's landscape is dominated by the earth rather than the sky, with the bog providing a metaphor for Irish consciousness (see 'Bogland', 'The Tollund Man').

7. 'The landscape for me is image and it's almost an element to work with as much as it is an object of admiration or description.' Heaney uses nature metaphors to express his feelings of frustration and loneliness ('need breaks on my strand' in 'Valediction') or the frustrating attempts at communicating between father and son in 'The Harvest Bow' ('your stick | Whacking the tops off weeds and bushes | Beats out of time, and beats, but flushes | Nothing') (see 'Valediction', 'The Harvest Bow', 'The Other Side').

8. The landscape is a source of creativity and insight: 'poems ... come up ...

like bodies out of the bog of my own imagination' (see 'Bogland', 'The Tollund Man', 'Field of Vision').

## IMAGERY AND SYMBOLISM

Consider the following statements, re-examine the poems for evidence confirming or denying them, and add your own references and quotations.

1. Nature and the farming community are the chief sources of his imagery. The flora and fauna of the countryside abound: hawk, goose wing, snipe, skunk, midges. But the overall import of the natural imagery is of a poor, infertile landscape: marsh weeds, sedge, moss, rushes, the agitated hawthorn bush, the acre of ragwort, and of course the ubiquitous bog. The bog is female-spirited, sometimes erotic, a preserver of racial memories and identity but also at times dangerous and menacing. Natural imagery provides most of the metaphorical or poetic language: 'The ground itself is kind, black butter' ('Bogland'); 'The refrigerator whinnied into silence' ('The Skunk'). Even human bodies are described in natural imagery: 'the mild pods of his eyelids' ('The Tollund Man').

2. The realistic detail is particularly noticeable in the portraiture (see 'The Harvest Bow', 'The Forge', 'Sunlight', 'A Constable Calls').

3. The imagery, particularly that involving recollections, has been filtered through the senses. The sensuousness is immediately striking:
   • the visual: 'unpredictable fantail of sparks' ('The Forge')
   • the tactile and aural: 'her hands scuffled over the bakeboard' ('Sunlight'); 'the sootfall of your things at bedtime' (The Skunk').

4. Some of the recurring imagery and locations take on the depth and fixed value of symbol:
   • the bog – symbol of the poet's racial memory and source of his poetic imagination
   • Mossbawn – symbol of security, family love and rural values
   • the harvest bow – somehow symbolises the secret soul and spirit of that community
   • the pump – a conduit to the life-giving force of the earth, symbol of community, source of life, source of inspiration
   • the anvil – both workbench and altar of the art of writing.

5. Use of the odd Old English *kenning* provides a natural strength or muscularity to the versification: 'man-killing parishes' ('The Tollund Man').

## DICTION

1. Often we find a simple but strong monosyllabic vocabulary, a commonplace language.

> All I know is a door into the dark
> To beat real iron out, to work the bellows
>                              ['The Forge']

2.  Variety is provided by abstract terms of Latin or Greek origin ('juvenilia', 'decorum', 'somnambulant', 'palpable', 'mythologised'), also by French borrowing or words of French derivation ('à la', 'voyeur', 'blasphemy', 'mysterious'). There is evidence of technical vocabulary from a variety of disciplines: geography, archaeology, astronomy ('tarn', 'torc', 'corona').
3.  The conversational vocabulary is realistically colloquial ('Easy now ... it's only me').
4.  The syntax of some lines has a conversational directness and simplicity ('We have no prairies,' 'I remember this woman'; or 'Some day I will go to Aarhus,' which contrasts with the more poetic and descriptive 'To see his peat-brown head, | The mild pods of his eye-lids').

VERSIFICATION

1.  In this selection there is only one use of the tightly disciplined sonnet form: 'The Forge'. Examine this poem as a sonnet, considering the divisions, the development of ideas and the rhyming scheme.
2.  Otherwise Heaney uses a variety of verse forms, often favouring the thin four-line stanza with lines of either three stresses (*trimeter*) or only two stresses (*dimeter*). Some of the poems seem to be imitative or shaped to suit the theme – for example 'Bogland', where the seven stanzas of short, mostly trimeter lines give the impression of depth, of descending through the layers of a boghole. Likewise in 'The Tollund Man', similar thin stanzas of dimeter and trimeter lines could suggest excavation or a long journey. Contrast the verse format of 'Bogland' with that of 'The Harvest Bow', a philosophical exploration of social ritual and custom. Do you find the technique of 'The Harvest Bow' appropriate to the poem? Explain. Heaney also uses the *terza rima* structure, adapted from the Italians, Dante in particular (see 'Station Island' vii).
3.  Heaney uses internal rhyme more frequently than end rhyme, with sounds echoing delicately within verses:

> To *see* his p*ea*t-brown head
> The w*i*ld pods of his *eye*-lids

4.  Comment on the use of end rhyme in 'Twice Shy' and 'Valediction'.
5.  He often uses patterns of imitative sound, i.e. onomatopoeic words. For example in 'The Forge':

> He *grunts* and goes in with a *slam*
> and a *flick*

6. Other common musical effects are found in abundance in Heaney's poetry, such as alliteration, assonance, etc.
   - *everywhere* the *eye* concedes to *encroaching*
   - *b*lack *b*utter
   - *cr*ate full of *air*
   - *f*at *bl*ack *h*andlegrips.
7. We sometimes find the Irish pattern of double alliteration:
   *S*till *t*ongue-*t*ied in the *s*traw *t*ied by your hand.

VOICES OF THE POET

A feature of the richness of Heaney's poetry is his ability to write from different perspectives and to use many voices: those of father, son, lover, child, friend, and spokesperson for his people. With this in mind, consider
   - 'The Harvest Bow'
   - 'The Skunk'
   - 'Mossbawn: Sunlight'
   - 'Bogland'.

A LOOK AT GENDER ISSUES IN HEANEY'S POETRY

Patricia Coughlan, in a thought-provoking article, finds two opposing but possibly complementary representations of sex roles in Heaney's poetry:
- a dominant masculine figure who explores, describes, loves and has compassion for a passive feminine figure, and
- a woman who 'dooms, destroys, puzzles and encompasses the man, but also assists him to his self discovery: the mother stereotype, but merged intriguingly with the spouse'.

It is easy enough to identify the first representation as the speaker of the poems. Coughlan traces male activities and attitudes of the speakers in Heaney's first book, *Death of a Naturalist* – ploughing, digging and its equivalent, writing – as well as significant male attitudes, such as the importance of following in the footsteps of ancestors and imitating their prowess, in poems such as 'Digging', 'Follower', and 'Ancestral Photograph'. She traces the development of male identity in such poems as 'Death of a Naturalist' and 'An Advancement of Learning', where the young boy passes a test of male courage in facing up to a rat. The identification of the speaker with the natural maleness of creatures such as the bull and the trout ('Outlaw' and 'The Trout') is noticed in the second volume, *Door into the Dark*.

Of the poems in this selection we might agree that Heaney views the creative process as a particularly male activity in 'The Forge' – the violence of the activity, the archetypal maleness of the protagonist, leading to the suggestion that the truth of art is forged out of violence and brute strength. But the poetic process of 'seeing things' in the later poetry is a more spiritual, even intuitive practice. The image of the poet changes to one of seer, or mediator between states of awareness ('Field of Vision', 'Lightenings VIII', 'St Kevin and the Blackbird').

Something of the prowess of ancestors is present in the speaker's celebration of his father's gift in 'The Harvest Bow'. It is a quintessentially male prowess ('lapped the spurs on a lifetime of game cocks'), yet the skill involved in making the bow exhibits an understanding of the spirit and a delicate craftsmanship. Indeed, plaiting the bow is a female art form, at least in traditional thinking. So perhaps sex roles are not so clear-cut here, as the male ancestor is celebrated for his prowess at a feminine craft.

The representation of woman in the present selection leads to the consideration of a number of issues.

## Woman as lover

Consider 'Twice Shy' and 'Valediction'. In 'Twice Shy' woman is the love object; perhaps there is even a suggestion in the imagery of being victim to the male ('tremulously we held | As hawk and prey apart'). But this is balanced just after this by an equality of rights, by the mutual recognition that each had a past and that each had a right to be cautious, even timorous, in the new relationship ('Our juvenilia | Had taught us both to wait').

In 'Valediction', roles are reversed. Not only is the woman the source of stability in the speaker's life, but she is in complete control of the relationship ('Until you resume command | Self is in mutiny'). Nevertheless the image of woman here is traditional and somewhat stereotyped: an object of beauty, defined by dress and pretty, natural allusions such as the frilled blouse, the smile and the 'flower-tender voice'. So in these poems there seems to be a traditional visual concept of woman, combined with a more varied understanding of role, both as love object and as controlling force.

Woman in 'The Skunk' is very much sex object, alluring, exciting in a primitive, animal way:

> . . . stirred
> By the sootfall of your things at bedtime,
> Your head-down, tail-up hunt in a bottom drawer
> For the black plunge-neck nightdress.

She is an object of desire, observed with controlled voyeurism by the speaker.

## Woman as mother

In 'Mossbawn: 1. Sunlight' the female figure is associated with traditional domestic skills, in this instance baking. The mother figure is one of the central props in Heaney's ideal picture of rural life. The kitchen is a womb of security for the young boy, radiating warmth, nurture and love, as well as being a forger of identity, offering links with tradition and values mediated by the female figures.

A feminist critique would argue that this representation is denying women the freedom to develop fully, by giving them fixed roles within the domestic environment and by associating them with what is maternal rather than with any intellectual activity. As Patricia Coughlan says, 'Woman, the primary inhabiter and constituent of the domestic realm, is admiringly observed, centre stage but silent.'

## The earth as female

Nature – the earth and both the physical territory and the political spirit of Ireland – is viewed as feminine by Heaney. There was a hint of this in the soft, preserving, womblike quality of the earth in 'Bogland'. This feminine aspect becomes explicitly sexual in such poems as 'Rite of Spring' and 'Undine'. But the female principle is destructive to man in such poems as 'The Tollund Man', where the male is sacrificed to the goddess, who is female lover, killer and principle of new life and growth, all at once.

> She tightened her torc on him
> And opened her fen,
> Those dark juices working
> Him to a saint's kept body.

Coughlan feels that the female energy here is represented as 'both inert and devouring' and that if the poem is understood 'as a way of thinking about woman rather than about Irish political murder, it reveals an intense alienation from the female.' But can it be divorced from its political context? And was not Caitlín Ní Uallacháin always the *femme fatale* of political revolutionaries? And hadn't this fatalistic attraction almost a frisson of sexual passion about it, coupled with maternal devotion? The poem reveals the danger of the attraction, but surely it was a willing consummation. The poet envies Tollund Man 'his sad freedom', so perhaps the poem reveals less an intense alienation than a fatalistic attraction to the female.

The feminist critique certainly throws some light on central aspects of Heaney's writing – among them a very traditional view of woman – but there is too much complexity in his vision to allow us to view the encounter of the sexes in his poetry as simply antagonistic.

## Questions

1. 'One of Heaney's greatest skills is that of portraiture: the vivid, realistic drawing of characters, sometimes nostalgic, often unflattering.' Discuss this statement in the light of the poems you have read.
2. What picture of the Irish character and mentality emerges from a reading of Heaney's poetry?
3. 'Heaney takes a pessimistic view of life, reflected in a downward-looking stance and a predominance of bleak imagery.' Discuss, with reference to the poems.
4. 'Heaney's poetry is motivated by a vain search for the lost heritage of childhood and by a sense of tribal identity.' Discuss this view, with reference to the poems you have read.
5. Would you agree that Heaney is an essentially backward-looking poet, finding answers only in the past?
6. 'Heaney, in a fair and balanced way, searches for insight into both cultures of Ulster.' Discuss.
7. 'The importance of tradition and a sense of place are key concepts in the poetry of Heaney.' Discuss this statement in the light of the poems by Heaney you have studied.
8. Would you agree that Heaney's love poetry is filled with insight and honesty?
9. 'Heaney's poetry, whether overtly or hidden, is autobiographical in the main.' In the light of the poems you have studied, would you agree with this statement?
10. 'There is a quality of vivid sensuousness in the poetry of Heaney.' Discuss, with reference to the poems you have read.
11. 'Heaney habitually finds mystery and significance behind ordinary objects and events.' Discuss this statement, referring to the poems for evidence.
12. 'In imagery and in rhythms of language Heaney is essentially a poet of rural Ireland.' Discuss, with reference to the poems you have read.
13. What image of woman emerges from the poems by Heaney you have read?
14. 'Heaney constantly experiments with verse forms in order to find a vehicle suitable to his particular poem.' Would you agree? Examine two or three poems in the light of this statement.

# Main works by Séamus Heaney

POETRY (PRINCIPAL VOLUMES)

*Death of a Naturalist,* London: Faber and Faber 1966.
*Door into the Dark,* London: Faber and Faber 1969.

*Wintering Out,* London: Faber and Faber 1972.

*North,* London: Faber and Faber 1975.

*Field Work,* London: Faber and Faber 1979.

*Selected Poems, 1965–1975,* London: Faber and Faber 1980.

*The Rattle Bag: An Anthology of Poetry* (selected by Séamus Heaney and Ted Hughes), London: Faber and Faber 1982.

*Sweeney Astray,* Derry: Field Day 1983.

*Station Island,* London: Faber and Faber 1984.

*The Haw Lantern,* London: Faber and Faber 1987.

*New Selected Poems, 1966–1987,* London: Faber and Faber 1990.

*Seeing Things,* London: Faber and Faber 1991.

*The Spirit Level,* London: Faber and Faber 1996.

*Opened Ground: Poems, 1966–96,* London: Faber and Faber 1998.

PROSE

*Preoccupations: Selected Prose, 1968–1978,* London: Faber and Faber 1980.

*An Open Letter,* Derry: Field Day 1983.

*The Government of the Tongue,* London: Faber and Faber 1988.

*The Redress of Poetry: Oxford Lectures,* London: Faber and Faber 1995.

*Crediting Poetry: The Nobel Lecture, 1995,* Oldcastle (Co. Meath): Gallery Press 1995.

DRAMA

*The Cure at Troy* [a version of Sophocles' *Philoctetus*], London: Faber and Faber 1990.

# *Bibliography*

Andrews, Elmer, *The Poetry of Séamus Heaney: All the Realms of Whisper,* London: Macmillan 1988.

Andrews, Elmer (editor), *Contemporary Irish Poetry: A Collection of Critical Essays,* London: Macmillan 1992.

Bloom, Harold (editor), *Séamus Heaney: Modern Critical Views,* Edgemont (Penn.): Chelsea House 1986.

Browne, Terence, *Northern Voices: Poets from Ulster,* Dublin: Gill and Macmillan 1975.

Corcoran, Neil, *A Student's Guide to Séamus Heaney,* London: Faber and Faber 1986.

Coughlan, Patricia, 'Bog queens: the representation of women in the poetry of John Montague and Séamus Heaney' in *Gender in Irish Writing,* edited by

Toni O'Brien Johnson and David Cairns, Milton Keynes: Open University Press 1991.

Curtis, Tony (editor), *The Art of Séamus Heaney*, Dublin: Wolfhound 1994.

Fennell, Desmond, *Whatever You Say, Say Nothing: Why Séamus Heaney is No. 1*, Dublin: Elo Publications 1991.

Foster, John Wilson, *The Achievement of Séamus Heaney*, Dublin: Lilliput 1995.

Foster, Thomas, *Séamus Heaney*, Dublin: O'Brien 1989.

Johnson, Dillon, *Irish Poetry After Joyce*, Notre Dame (Ind.): University of Notre Dame Press 1985.

Kenneally, Michael (editor), *Cultural Contexts and Literary Idioms in Contemporary Irish Culture* (Irish Literary Studies, 31), Gerrards Cross (Bucks.): Colin Smythe 1988.

Kenneally, Michael (editor), *Poetry in Contemporary Irish Literature* (Irish Literary Studies, 43), Gerrards Cross (Bucks.): Colin Smythe 1995.

Lloyd, David, 'Pap for the dispossessed: Séamus Heaney and the poetics of identity', *Anomalous States: Irish Writing and the Post-Colonial Moment* (Dublin: Lilliput 1993), 13–40.

Longley, Edna, *Poetry in the Wars*, Newcastle-upon-Tyne: Bloodaxe 1986.

Maguire, Aisling, *York Notes on Selected Poems of Séamus Heaney*, York: Longman York Press 1986.

Matthews, Steven, *Irish Poetry: Politics, History, Negotiation: The Evolving Debate, 1969 to the Present*, Basingstoke: Macmillan 1997.

Morrison, Blake, *Séamus Heaney*, London: Methuen 1982.

Murphy, Andrew, *Séamus Heaney* (Writers and their Work Series), London: Northcote House 1996.

O'Donoghue, Bernard, *Séamus Heaney and the Language of Poetry*, Brighton: Harvester-Wheatsheaf 1994.

Parker, Michael, *Séamus Heaney: The Making of the Poet*, Dublin: Gill and Macmillan 1993.

Simmons, James, 'The trouble with Séamus', *Séamus Heaney: A Collection of Critical Essays*, edited by Elmer Andrews, Basingstoke: Macmillan 1992, 39–66.

Smith, Stan, 'Séamus Heaney: the distance between' in *The Chosen Ground: Essays on the Contemporary Poetry of Northern Ireland*, edited by Neil Corcoran, London: Sren Books 1992.

Tamplin, Ronald, *Séamus Heaney*, Milton Keynes: Open University Press 1989.

Warner, Alan, 'Séamus Heaney' in *A Guide to Anglo-Irish Literature*, Dublin: Gill and Macmillan 1981.

# 7   *Michael* LONGLEY

*John G. Fahy*

## Life and writings

**M**ichael Longley was born in Belfast on 27 July 1939, of English parents. His father, Richard – who features in the poems 'Wounds', 'Wreaths' and 'Last Requests' from this selection – fought in the First World War and was gassed, wounded, decorated, and promoted to the rank of captain. Between the wars the Longleys moved to Belfast, where Richard was a commercial traveller for an English firm of furniture manufacturers. He enlisted again in the Second World War, ending with the rank of major.

In *Tuppenny Stung*, a short collection of autobiographical chapters, you can read of Michael Longley's childhood: of his twin brother, Peter, and older sister, Wendy; of his ingenious and versatile war-veteran father ('that rare thing, an Englishman accepted and trusted by Ulstermen'); of his crippled and temperamental mother ('It has taken me a long time to forgive her that atmosphere of uncertainty, its anxieties, even fears'); of his irrepressible English grandfather, 'Grandpa George'; and the usual menagerie of eccentric relatives we all accumulate. You can read of his primary and secondary education and the forces on his early cultural formation: Protestant schoolboy fears of the dark savageries supposedly practised by Catholics; an English education system dismissive of Irish culture and history; Protestant Belfast's fear and resentment of the Republic. His early education and local socialisation made him aware of conflicting classes and religions and of the duality of Irish identity.

Later he was educated at the Royal Belfast Academical Institution and in 1958 went to Trinity College, Dublin, where the student population at that time consisted in the main of Southern and Northern Protestants, middle- and upper-class English, and a scattering of Southern Catholics who defied the Catholic Church's ban on attendance. Longley studied classics and wrote poetry but felt very under-read in English literature until taken in hand by his friend and young fellow-poet Derek Mahon:

> We inhaled with our untipped Sweet Afton cigarettes MacNeice, Crane, Dylan Thomas, Yeats, Larkin, Lawrence, Graves, Ted Hughes, Stevens, Cummings, Richard Wilbur, Robert Lowell, as well as Rimbaud, Baudelaire, Brecht, Rilke – higgledepiggledy, in any order. We scanned the journals and newspapers for poems written yesterday. When

Larkin's 'The Whitsun Weddings' first appeared in Encounter, Mahon steered me past the documentary details, which as an aspiring lyricist I found irritating, to the poem's resonant, transcendental moments. He introduced me to George Herbert who thrilled me as though he were a brilliant contemporary published that very week by the Dolmen Press. Herbert, thanks to Mahon, is a beneficent influence in my first collection and provides the stanzaic templates for two of its more ambitious poems.

Longley first worked as a teacher in Dublin, London and Belfast. From 1964 he was one of the group of young writers fostered by Philip Hobsbaum at Queen's University, though Longley felt that his poetry didn't fit in particularly well.

From the beginning Hobsbaum made it clear that his stars were Séamus Heaney and Stewart Parker, who was teaching in the States at this time. Hobsbaum's aesthetic demanded gritty particularity and unrhetorical utterance. Heaney's work fitted the bill especially well: at the second or third meeting which I attended a sheet of his poems was discussed – 'Digging' and 'Death of a Naturalist' (it was called 'End of a Naturalist' then).

By this time I was beginning to enjoy what was for me as a lapsed Classicist a new experience – practical criticism. But I didn't much care for the Group aesthetic or, to be honest, the average poem which won approval. I believed that poetry should be polished, metrical and rhymed; oblique rather than head-on; imagistic and symbolic rather than rawly factual, rhetorical rather than documentary. I felt like a Paleface among a tribe of Redskins. Although I have since modified my ideas, I still think that despite the rigours of practical criticism and the kitchen heat of the discussions, many Group poems tended to be underdone.

Longley worked for the Arts Council of Northern Ireland between 1970 and 1991, when he took early retirement. His work for the arts was driven by a number of guiding principles, among which were the nurturing of indigenous talent (he used to ask, 'How much of what we are doing differentiates us from Bolton or Wolverhampton?'), support for the artists, not just the arts, and the need to transcend class barriers and bring the arts, at an affordable price, to the working class.

He was always a champion of cultural pluralism, fostering the artistic expression of both sides of the religious and political divide. In fact the first event Longley organised for the Arts Council was 'The Planter and the Gael', a poetry-reading tour by John Hewitt and John Montague, in which each poet read poems exploring his particular experience of Ulster. So it was not surprising that Longley should be invited to join the Cultural Traditions Group at its launch in 1988. Its aims are, as he has written, 'to encourage in Northern Ireland the acceptance and understanding of cultural diversity; to replace political belligerence with cultural pride'.

His vision of Ulster culture has always sought to include its many different strands and influences and so encourage a unique hybrid rather than separate, antagonistic cultures. As he has said elsewhere, 'Imaginative Ulstermen (and by extension, Irishmen) could be the beneficiaries of a unique cultural confluence which embraces the qualities of the Irish, the Scottish, the English and the Anglo-Irish' (quoted by Michael Parker).

Longley fostered a great range and diversity of artists, from traditional singers and fiddlers to painters, photographers and drama groups. For the last nine years of his career with the Arts Council he was combined arts director, overseeing traditional arts, youth arts and community arts, while concentrating on his chief preoccupation, literature. Here he directed Arts Council money towards publication, attempting to ensure that as many writers as possible got into print.

Michael Longley is a fellow of the Royal Society of Literature and a member of Aosdána. He is married to the critic and academic Edna Longley.

*No Continuity City* (1969), Longley's first volume, is known for its technically accomplished and learned poetry. Among its concerns are poets and poetry and nature, but it is best known for the learned, witty and sophisticated love poetry, almost in the metaphysical tradition. *An Exploded View* (1973) continues to deal with poetry and poetic issues. Nature is also a preoccupation. 'Badger' is from this volume. This book does respond briefly to the upsurge of violence around this time; in 'Wounds' the violence is seen from the broad perspective of international conflict. A great number of the poems focus on an alternative life in the west of Ireland; 'Carrigskeewaun' and 'Poteen' are among these. This attachment of Longley's for County Mayo also forms the focus of his third volume, *Man Lying on a Wall* (1976).

*The Echo Gate* (1979) demonstrates Longley's now established bifocal view: on Belfast and Mayo. He confronts the political violence in its stark, everyday settings in 'Wreaths' and explores the war experiences of his father as a perspective on this violence in 'Last Requests'. He also explores the folklore, ethos and culture of the west of Ireland and finds a bleak, unconscious parallel between its crude violence and that of Belfast in 'Self-Heal'.

*Gorse Fires* (1991) is centred on Longley's adopted second home of Carrig-skeewaun in County Mayo. But it also includes poems on the Holocaust, the Second World War and the Spanish Civil War. Interspersed with these are some free translations from Homer's *Odyssey*, focusing on Odysseus's return to his home and interpreted by some critics as having strong if oblique references to Longley's own home province. 'Laertes' is from this sequence.

In *The Ghost Orchid* (1995) Longley continues to write perceptively and sensitively about the delicacy of nature: the long grasses by the lake like autumn lady's tresses; sandpipers; the sighting of otters and dolphins; birdsong; and of course the flowers that give the volume its title. These are not so much nature studies in the usual sense as intimate encounters that are shared with the reader in the style of a personal diary. And the locations are wide-ranging, from the west of Ireland to the stone gardens of Japan.

This volume not only celebrates the natural beauty of the world but also affirms the sexuality of life, whether manifested in nature's flowers or in artwork, from sheela-na-gigs to Japanese erotic art. A variety of styles of language is employed, ranging from the simplicity and precision of Haiku-style description to the phonic thunder of Ulster dialect.

In this volume also Longley continues with his very creative free translations, from the Roman love poet Ovid, from Virgil, and also from Homer. 'Ceasefire' is one of these, featuring the meeting between King Priam and Achilles at the end of Homer's *Iliad*.

*Tuppenny Stung* (1994) is a collection of autobiographical chapters, previously published in periodicals or delivered as lectures from 1972 to 1992.

POETRY COLLECTIONS

|  | **In this selection** |
| --- | --- |
| *No Continuing City* (1969) | |
| *An Exploded View* (1973) | 'Badger' |
| | 'Wounds' |
| | 'Poteen' |
| | 'Carrigskeewaun' |
| *Man Lying on a Wall* (1976) | |
| *The Echo Gate* (1979) | 'Wreaths' |
| | 'Last Requests' |
| | 'Mayo Monologues 3: Self-Heal' |
| *Gorse Fires* (1991) | 'An Amish Rug' |
| | 'Laertes' |
| *The Ghost Orchid* (1995) | 'Ceasefire' |
| *Broken Dishes* (1998) | |

# *Badger*
Text of poem: New Explorations Anthology page 346

A READING OF THE POEM

This nature poem celebrates that nocturnal woodland creature, the badger, but it also questions humankind's interference in nature.

The badger's legendary strength is evoked both in the descriptions ('the wedge of his body') and by his activities ('He excavates ... into the depths of the hill'), which personify him as a muscular miner. There is a sense of uncompromising directness and dependability about his 'path straight and narrow' that contrasts with the deceptiveness of the fox and the giddiness of the hare. That ruggedness is also evident from his indiscriminate diet: he can cope with the poisonous dog's mercury and the tough brambles as well as the gentler bluebells.

But it is his relationship with the earth that is most interestingly portrayed. Longley sees the badger as a sort of horticulturalist: he 'manages the earth with his paws'; he facilitates the growth of great oak trees ('a heel revolving acorns'). The picture comes across of an animal at one with the earth, the caretaker of the hill, which in turn takes care of him in death. The animal's close association with prehistoric tombs lends him an even greater aura of significance. Somehow he becomes a symbol of the earth's ancientness, its longevity and mythological power. Longley himself has said that he thinks of animals as spirits. He tries to have an animal in each of his books.

The poem also deals with humankind's destructiveness and cruelty, our interference in the natural world. The poet's criticism of this is communicated through the bleak ironies of section III: digging out the digger, the bitter euphemism of this process being described as a forceps birth, the irony of being 'delivered' to his death:

> It is a difficult delivery
> once the tongs take hold.

There is sympathy for the 'vulnerable ... pig's snout' and implicit condemnation of the brutal treatment ('his limbs dragging after them') and also of the environmental disturbance:

> So many stones turned over,
> The trees they tilted.

This treatment is in marked contrast to the badger's careful management of the earth, unaided by machines or 'tongs' of any kind! A clear environmental statement is made here, but it is subtly put across through the contrast rather than by any kind of didactic statement.

This is a tough, unsentimental poem, recording the perennial secret workings of nature. True, it does romanticise the badger somewhat:

> Night's silence around his shoulders,
> His face lit by the moon.

But it also records the violence, the suffering and the destruction of nature and creatures.

Behind that wealth of observed details and naturalist knowledge we can detect a tone of admiration for the animal's strength and its management of the woodland ('His path straight ... not like the fox's zig-zags ...') and we can certainly feel the poet's sympathy for the vulnerable animal in section III.

# *Wounds*

Text of poem: New Explorations Anthology page 348

## BACKGROUND NOTE

In his autobiographical book *Tuppenny Stung,* Longley elaborates on his father's wartime experiences:

> Having lived through so much by the time he was thirty, perhaps my father deserved his early partial retirement. At the age of seventeen he had enlisted in 1914, one of thousands queuing up outside Buckingham Palace. He joined the London-Scottish by mistake and went into battle wearing an unwarranted kilt. A Lady from Hell. Like so many survivors he seldom talked about his experiences, reluctant to relive the nightmare. But not long before he died, we sat up late one night and he reminisced. He had won the Military Cross for knocking out single-handed a German machine-gun post and, later, the Royal Humane Society's medal for gallantry: he had saved two nurses from drowning. By the time he was twenty he had risen to the rank of Captain, in charge of a company known as 'Longley's Babies' because many of them were not yet regular shavers. He recalled the lice, the rats, the mud, the tedium, the terror. Yes, he had bayoneted men and still dreamed about a tubby little German who 'couldn't run fast enough. He turned around to face me and burst into tears.' My father was nicknamed Squib in the trenches. For the rest of his life no-one ever called him Richard.

## A READING OF THE POEM

The figure of his father features prominently in Michael Longley's poetry. The father is graphically and sympathetically realised and the father–son bond asserted in such poems as 'In Memoriam', 'Wounds', 'Last Requests', and 'Laertes'.

The poet's relationship with his father in 'Wounds' is characterised by intimacy and tenderness. There is an intimacy about their style of communication. 'Two pictures from my father's head' suggests a perfect non-verbal understanding, which the poet has kept 'like secrets'. The caress is tender, repetitive and comforting: 'I touched his hand, his thin head I touched.' The father's sense of humour, even if a little grim, indicates the easiness of the relationship: 'I am dying for King and Country, slowly.' (This refers to the link between his final illness and the old war wounds: see 'In Memoriam': 'In my twentieth year your old wounds woke | As cancer.')

In these repeated father–son exchanges Longley is probing his own identity and defining his background. Much has been written about the supposed identity crisis of the Ulster Protestant writer, shakily situated between the conflicting claims of the English and Irish literary traditions and outlooks. As Terence Brown points out in another context, Longley is a lyric poet nurtured in the English and classical traditions 'attempting to come to terms with the fact that he was born in Ireland of an English father and that he now lives in a Belfast shaken almost nightly by the national question, violently actualised.' This family experience of immigration might be seen to mirror the experience of the Ulster Protestant as immigrant. We catch some of this confusion, this incomprehension of the local view in the father's bemused reaction to the Ulster soldiers' sectarian battle cries:

> 'wilder than Gurkhas' were my father's words
> of admiration and bewilderment.

He expresses admiration, presumably for their courage, but complete bewilderment at the sectarian sentiment. Something of the same bewilderment is evident in the poet's own reaction to present-day violence when he describes the murder of the bus conductor:

> . . . shot through the head
> By a shivering boy who wandered in
> Before they could turn the television down

The air of incomprehension, this slight sense of distance from local realities, which may be the inheritance of the immigrant, is shared by father and son.

In summary, the poet is establishing his identity as the son of a courageous English soldier. There is no direct discussion of an identity crisis, either literary or political; but we do register a sense of bewilderment, something of the outsider's air of detachment in the attitudes of both father and son towards Ulstermen at war.

Longley is using his father's First World War experiences as a perspective on present-day atrocities. Patricia Craig says that the violence of the trenches is 'brought up smack against the dingier violences of present-day Belfast'. Whether it is more or less dingy in the poet's eyes is debatable. The grotesqueness of the slaughter and the indignities of violent death are emphasised in both the world war and the present-day killings. The 'landscape of dead buttocks' that haunted his father for fifty years is hardly less bizarre than the recent image of

> Three teenage soldiers, bellies full of
> Bullets and Irish beer, their flies undone.

What is different and shocking about the portrayal of modern violence in the poem is its invasion of the domestic scene:

> Before they could turn the television down
> Or tidy away the supper dishes.

It is casual, perpetrated by a boy who 'wandered in'. The shocking ordinariness of the violence is underlined by the ridiculous apology, 'Sorry, missus.' It is as if he had just bumped into her in the street. Death is delivered to your home with a casual, polite apology.

ISSUES RAISED IN THE POEM

## Longley's sense of identity
- The poet is defining himself by describing his family background.
- The English military background is an important and accepted facet of the poet's identity.
- The sensitive and humorous portrait of his father communicates an easy and tender father–son relationship.
- The importance of that father-figure generally in the poet's life: the long-dead man is still a powerful reality.
- The violent city is part of his identity also.

## Violence
- The 'wounds' of the title refers to old war wounds, lingering psychological wounds (haunting images), and new wounds.
- The universality of killing: the world of the poem is a world of violence, whether legitimised as war or condemned as illegal. Does the poem differentiate between war violence and present-day atrocities?
- The less-than-glorious reality of war

- The indignity of violent death
- The increasing ordinariness of violence: terror at the heart of the domestic scene
- The wanton nature of present-day violence.

## Tone

The opening is conversational, personal. The speaker is sharing a confidence, inviting us in: 'Here are two pictures ... secrets.' There is evidence of a certain wry humour, which successfully deflates any possible attempt at glorifying either his father or the war ('I am dying for King and Country, slowly'; 'A packet of Woodbines I throw in, | A lucifer').

Is there a note of critical irony detectable in the parson's fussiness about dress in the face of death, and a hint of religious cynicism in the apparent indifference of God to human suffering and evil ('the Sacred Heart of Jesus | Paralysed')? The emotional impact is frequently disguised behind the relentless listing of details, but it is there, for example in 'heavy guns put out | The night-light in a nursery for ever'. And the understatement of the last line packs quite an emotional punch.

## Visual impact

This particularly visual style relies heavily on Longley's eye for incongruous details, such as the sectarian battle-cries as the soldiers go over the top; the chaplain with the stylish backhand; the domestic details of the three teenage soldiers, lured to their deaths by the promise of sex; the bus conductor who 'collapsed beside his carpet-slippers,' etc. And they all make the point about how brutally unglorious death is.

# *Poteen*

Text of poem: New Explorations Anthology page 351

A READING OF THE POEM

The description of illicit whiskey-making turns into a statement about national identity. The primitive, superstitious act of 'one noggin-full | Sprinkled on the ground' as a sort of votive offering to the spirits opens up other atavistic echoes and race memories. It conjures up images of other illegal activities, rebel plottings, also carried on in remote bogland and similar inaccessible areas. Poitín-making becomes a symbol of historical Ireland, the Ireland of the dispossessed, of the rebel, with all the paraphernalia of secret societies, stored weapons, and furtive plottings (souterrains, sunk workshops, cudgels, guns, the informer's ear, blood-money).

So it becomes a poem about 'the back of the mind' (suppressed race memory), and the racial consciousness evoked is one of furtive living, blunt violence ('cudgels, guns'), and seamy betrayals ('the informer's ear'). It is not exactly an idealised picture, but rather a bleak and realistic psychological portrait where greed and romantic aspiration go hand in hand ('Blood money, treasure-trove').

# Carrigskeewaun

Text of poem: New Explorations Anthology page 353

## A READING OF THE POEM

We notice that Longley's view of County Mayo is certainly not the romanticised one of the tourist or holiday weekender, but more like the realistic perception of the native who sees the landscape in all its harshness and its beauty. He presents its arid face to us, a landscape of boulders and dry-stone walls, a harsh territory inimical to human and animals alike, the graveyard of many.

> This is ravens' territory, skulls, bones,
> The marrow of these boulders supervised
> From the upper air:

But he also presents the serene beauty of nature, in the image of the lake 'tilted to receive | The sun perfectly'. His interest is primarily in the physical landscape and the flora and fauna rather than in the people; in fact he seems to enjoy his solitary, Crusoe-like existence, dislodging mallards, discovering cattle tracks, etc., in this sparsely populated place.

He has a keen naturalist's eye, as we can see from his perceptive descriptions of the birds in 'The Path'. Kittiwakes 'scrape' the waves; mallards' necks 'strain' over the bog; and the 'gradual disdain' of the swans is captured. He understands both their movements and their psychology. And his treatment of them is gentle, as evidenced by the verbs used to describe his actions: 'dislodge', 'to nudge', etc. There is a sensitive and perceptive naturalist at work here.

For all the harshness of the scene, Longley is at ease with it. In a primitive and slightly crude way he shares a sense of identity with the people's forebears, who also 'squatted here | This lichened side of the dry-stone wall'. He feels that he is part of the life cycle of the place, part of the process of erosion, as when he notices the effect of his footprints in the strand:

> Linking the dunes to the water's edge,
> Reducing to sand the dry shells, the toe –
> And fingernail parings of the sea.

And he enjoys the atmosphere of serenity and acceptance in 'The Lake', as if he too were one of the 'special visitors'.

Family and the human community are but a shadowy presence here. Ghost-like memories of his children are conjured up ('my voice | Filling the district as I recall their names'), or they are registered merely as footprints in the sand. Images of family domesticity he carries in his head, as one might carry a photograph of loved ones:

> Smoke from our turf fire
> Recalls in the cool air above the lake
> Steam from a kettle, a tablecloth and
> A table she might have already set.

So, in some ways, the image of the poet here is the traditional romantic one of the figure alone in the landscape, communing with nature. Yet this poet's home and family are never far away, a constant presence in his mind. Peter McDonald sees Carrigskeewaun as Longley's home from home and says that here Longley is 'bringing one home into contact with another through naming the elements that are missing. Here, it is the family "home" that is named in the stern solitude of a mountain landscape.'

## THEMES

- The poet's appreciation of this western landscape, its elemental harshness and its quiet welcoming beauty, its solitude, its abundance of wildlife, etc.
- An exploration of the relationship between humans and nature: the calm sense of belonging, etc.
- Yet an awareness that humankind is but a tiny part of the process of nature's cycle, helping to dispose of 'the dry shells, the toe | And fingernail parings of the sea.' This generates a sense of philosophical perspective.
- The love of family, children and domesticity that is somehow inspired by this wild place.

## THE SIGNIFICANCE OF THE WEST OF IRELAND IN LONGLEY'S POETRY

Longley's preoccupation with the west of Ireland can be traced throughout his poetry. 'Carrigskeewaun' and 'Poteen' are from his second collection, *An Exploded View*, which contains poems from 1968 to 1972. So even as he was focusing on the erupting violence of the times (in such poems as 'Wounds') he was also contemplating an alternative. His attachment to the west grew as a result of long summers spent in County Mayo, and this is evident from Longley's third volume, *Man Lying on a Wall* (1976). And his fifth volume, *The Gorse Fires* (1991), is centrally focused on Carrigskeewaun, which had become his second home.

Critics have interpreted this fascination with the west in various ways. Terence Brown asks: 'Which is the poet's Ireland – Belfast or Mayo?' He believes this relates to the poet's confused sense of national identity, in attempting to be an Ulsterman and an Anglo-Irishman. Brown believes that the problem of confused identity 'can partially be solved in an identification with the Irish landscape'. And he notes how unusual 'Carrigskeewaun' is in Longley's work for the sense it creates of a person 'at ease with himself and his fellows'.

Peter McDonald takes a slightly different approach, regarding the west as an issue of perspective rather than identity. He feels that the west is in fact a way of undoing the settled nature of the poet's identity and that what it does is provide a new sense of perspective, an angle from which home can be reappraised, 'can be reapproached without the encoding of tribal claims to certain territories'.

Gerald Dawe argues that while Longley accepts his northern roots, the ties of family, home, class and country, he is also searching for an alternative, imagined ideal, 'a compensatory order to transcend these'. He says: 'For Longley, the west of Ireland is seen as an embodiment of some kind of alternative life, a fictional life that compensates for certain values and attitudes missing in the real, given, historical world ... Longley itemises that vision into the simple sights of landscape and nature which, common to the west of Ireland, take on in his work a symbolic potency all of their own.'

What values and attitudes are embodied in 'Carrigskeewaun', and what is symbolised by the landscape? What values are missing from Longley's real, historical world?

# Wreaths

Text of poem: New Explorations Anthology page 357

## A READING OF THE POEM

In 'Wreaths' Longley deals directly with what is euphemistically described as the 'Troubles'. He describes the violent killings, in graphic detail, in their ordinary, everyday settings: a kitchen, a shop, the roadway. In each case his focus of attention is the human consequences of this violence, the loss of life, the deranged grief of relatives, or the psychological effect on the general population as it forces people to relive memories of family deaths.

'The Civil Servant' was written in memory of Martin McBirney QC, a lawyer and friend who was murdered by the IRA. This poem shows violence invading the heart of domestic life: the kitchen. It is the contrast between the ordinariness and intimacy of the setting and the incongruity of the violence that makes the greatest impact in this poem.

He was preparing an Ulster fry for breakfast
When someone walked into the kitchen and shot him ...
He lay in his dressing gown and pyjamas
While they dusted the dresser for fingerprints

The language rhythms too record that incongruity. The prosaic, conversational rhythms of the first line leave us unprepared for the violence of lines 2 and 3. The insignificance of life is recorded. It is regarded as of temporary and symbolic importance only, like the transitory outing of a red carpet, walked on and forgotten:

They rolled him up like a red carpet and left
Only a bullet hole in the cutlery drawer;

The emotional control of the narration adds to the strangeness of this piece. The killing is described in a matter-of-fact tone, in the neutral and precise language of a police witness ('A bullet entered his mouth and pierced his skull'). The loss is recorded in cultural terms only ('The books he had read, the music he could play'). The only indication of feeling comes in the disturbed actions of the widow, who 'took a hammer and chisel | And removed the black keys from his piano.' And even that is narrated in measured, controlled language: 'Later his widow ... and removed ...' It is this control of feeling that is one of the most chilling aspects of this poem.

Matter-of-fact descriptions and conversational rhythms of language also characterise the narration of 'The Greengrocer', written about a local shopkeeper, Jim Gibson. Yet the tone here is laced with a bleak irony:

He ran a good shop, and he died
Serving even the death-dealers
Who found him busy as usual ...

The ironic timing of the violence is emphasised. The Christmas wreaths, celebrating a birth, become his burial wreaths and also provide the general title for the pieces. We register the inappropriateness of this death amid the Christmas fare and the exotic fruit ('Dates and chestnuts and tangerines'). It is ironic too that the killing is overtly linked to the Christmas story ('Astrologers or three wise men'). Is there a bitterness towards the powerlessness of religion here?

'The Linen Workers', based on the Bessbrooke sectarian murders, has a more psychological focus, exploring how public political violence impinges on private thoughts and memories. Strangely, it is also the most personal of the three poems, written in the first person and dealing with the poet's personal memories.

The setting for the massacre of the linen workers is once again an ordinary everyday venue: the roadside. Death is seen as the scattering of the personal bric-a-brac of living:

> . . . spectacles,
> Wallets, small change, and a set of dentures:
> Blood, food particles, the bread, the wine.

While some of these images have symbolic value (for example the bread and wine, symbolic of self-sacrifice, renewal and eternal life), it is the set of dentures that resonates in the poet's mind, triggering bizarre memories of his dead father. The effect is surreal: the Christ figure, like some giant hoarding, 'fastened for ever | By his exposed canines to a wintry sky' in a parody of the Crucifixion. The father, once a victim of world war violence, is disinterred to witness the fruits of violence yet again ('Before I can bury my father once again | I must polish the spectacles ... And into his dead mouth slip the set of teeth'). The images are of victims, religious and familial. Also we see the ubiquitous nature of violence, stretching through history, erupting in the modern community and reaching into the individual psyche, where it shakes up disturbing past and private memories.

THEMES
- The casual 'ordinariness' of violent death in the community
- The ubiquitous nature of violence, in kitchen, shop or street, in the mind
- Human insignificance in the face of violence ('The Civil Servant')
- The bitterness of unseasonal death ('The Greengrocer')
- The psychological effects of violence, reaching right through people's lives, invading the psyche, interlacing public horror and private memory ('The Linen Workers')
- The ineffectiveness of religion in the face of this onslaught ('The Greengrocer'; 'The Linen Workers').

IMAGERY
For the most part the images consist of background details of domestic living, of insignificant private possessions: an 'Ulster fry', dressing-gown, pyjamas, dresser, cutlery drawer, holly wreaths for Christmas, spectacles, etc. They evoke ordinariness, urban banality, and the insignificance of ordinary lives.

Details of the killings are restrained, devoid of horror or gory detail. They are either rendered in stark simplicity ('A bullet entered his mouth and pierced his skull') or conveyed in general terms ('he died,' 'they massacred'). The impact is always in the consequences, conveyed through the telling details, such as the pathetic list of personal bric-a-brac ('spectacles | Wallets, small change, and a set of dentures'). The surreal images of a gap-toothed Christ and a long-dead bespectacled father convey the psychological disturbance of violence.

## TONE

The deadpan, largely unemotional tone of the narration, particularly in 'The Civil Servant' and 'The Greengrocer' (see 'A READING OF THE POEM' above), serves to emphasise the air of unreality and the incongruity of violent death in these everyday settings. 'The Linen Workers' is less controlled. For example, 'massacred' has overtones of horror and revulsion. In this poem there is more evidence of the poetic voice involved in the drama, commenting, not just recording details but interpreting also. 'Blood, food particles' are seen as 'the bread, the wine'.

But Longley does not approach this violence from any sectarian or political point of view, or indeed with any moral attitude. Certainly there is no sympathy for the violence, no attempt to explain or understand the killings. Neither is there outraged condemnation, just a patient recording of the facts. And through these facts, this list of intimate consequences, we see the pointlessness of the violence. Longley's slightly disengaged attitude and neutral tone allow the reader a clear view.

## *Last Requests*

Text of poem: New Explorations Anthology page 360
[*This poem is also prescribed fro Ordinary Level 2005 exam*]

### A READING OF THE POEM

This poem focuses on death and once again on the death of his own father. The two parts are complementary, part I dealing with the father's earlier brush with death in the trenches and part II focusing on his actual death-bed scene. Perhaps the earlier scene is meant to serve as a comfort: he could have died so many years before.

The death-bed scene is treated with a mixture of pathos and humour. The sense of separation, the impenetrable distance of death is physically illustrated: 'I … Couldn't reach you through the oxygen tent.' The onlooker's feeling of helplessness and inadequacy is recorded in the wry comment by the poet: 'I who brought you peppermints and grapes only'. Yet there is humour occasioned by the speaker's misinterpretation of the father's hand movement. The poet needs to interpret it as a last romantic gesture, a kiss, whereas it signifies the dying man's more prosaic need for nicotine, like the need for that last sacramental cigarette before a battle. Perhaps this can be read as yet another sign of the separation wrought by death: a mental as well as a physical distance from loved ones.

Despite the humour, we are in no doubt of the effect of the scene on the poet.

Every detail is etched into his mind: 'the bony fingers that waved to and fro'. The memories carry not only the gesture but the mood of the moment.

> The brand you chose to smoke for forty years
> Thoughtfully, each one like a sacrament.

There is real feeling here behind the façade of wit. The seamier side of war is also adverted to ('Your batman ... Left you for dead and stole your pocket watch'). Once again Longley views military exploits with a jaundiced eye.

# Mayo Monologues – Self-Heal
Text of poem: New Explorations Anthology page 362

## CONTEXT OF THE POEM

This is one of the sequence of four poems – 'Brothers', 'Housekeeper', 'Self-Heal', and 'Arrest' – collectively entitled 'Mayo Monologues' from the volume *The Echo Gate* (1979). They deal with the pathetic and flawed relationships of some isolated and lonely people.

## A READING OF THE POEM

The poem deals with the tragic consequences of an inherently flawed relationship between the young female narrator, a teacher, and a mentally retarded boy. At first the relationship was one of innocent education, centring on the communication of beauty.

> I wanted to teach him the names of flowers,
> Self-heal and centaury; on the long acre
> Where cattle never graze, bog asphodel.

But it is an unequal pairing, incompatible intellectually and physically, the delicacy of the flowers contrasting strangely with the grotesque figure of the boy-man whose 'skull seemed to be hammered like a wedge | Into his shoulders, and his back was hunched, | Which gave him an almost scholarly air.'

The intellectual frustration is described in the natural image of the butterfly:

> Each name would hover above its flower
> like a butterfly unable to alight.

But the only delight he can comprehend and reach for is sexual. A community taboo is broken, and enormous and brutal consequences, out of all proportion to the deed, fall on him with the weight of a Greek tragedy, souring beauty and stunting humanity further. The savage treatment meted out to him unleashes a terrible savagery within himself.

## THEMES

- A view of the dark undercurrents in rural society, involving sullied innocence, thwarted sexuality, ignorance and prejudice, and the crude violence and brutality just beneath the surface
- Insensitive treatment of the mentally retarded
- The almost insignificant origins of tragedy.

### A POEM OF PRIMITIVE ENERGIES

This poem is highly charged with elemental human passions. The female narrator, exhibiting a dangerous innocence, was taking risks. Though innocent of any complicity, she is sensitive enough to question her motivation –

> Could I love someone so gone in the head
> And, as they say, was I leading him on?

– and, discounting what was a reasonable reaction on her part, she does not completely exonerate herself from her role in precipitating the consequences:

> I wasn't frightened; and still I don't know why,
> But I ran from him in tears to tell them.

So there is a traumatic, sexually charged moment, a sense of sullied innocence, and a hint of regret that perhaps things could have been handled differently.

We are confronted with the basic animal nature of humankind, lurking just beneath the surface; the unexpected sexual advance is later represented in animal imagery: 'I might have been the cow … and he the ram'. The primitive animal brutality, coupled with ignorance and lack of any tolerant insight into this condition, is shocking.

> He was flogged with a blackthorn, then tethered
> In the hayfield.

The belief that violence is effective begets a cycle of wanton cruelty: the cow's tail docked with shears and 'The ram tangled in barbed wire | That he stoned to death when they set him free.' And one cannot help but be overawed by the disproportionate nature of the consequences, as if one were viewing a world out of control.

### AS A VIEW OF THE WEST OF IRELAND

The poem paints an unflattering picture of the dark undercurrents, the barely tamed savagery, the pain of ignorance and prejudice just beneath the surface of rural society.

## Tone

Sympathy, revulsion and anger all swirl beneath the surface of this poem. Yet all feelings are controlled by Longley's matter-of-fact descriptions, by the quiet, conversational rhythms of the language and the balanced point of view of the narrator. The narrator herself is the victim of sexual advances, yet in many ways she is a detached and sympathetic observer. She both questions her own motives and understands the actions of the retarded man. So we are drawn in to sympathise with both parties. We understand her sense of regret and her bewilderment at it all: 'and still I don't know why, | But I ran ...' We cannot help but be revolted by the brutality, narrated in matter-of-fact, unadorned language: 'He was flogged ... tethered ... dock with shears ... the ram tangled ... he stoned to death ...'

But overall we register the deep irony of these events. A worthy desire to educate, enlighten and beautify has created instead a dark, brutal monster. And we note the irony of the title: the plant produces no healing properties on this occasion; there are no immortal flowers for his mind, or indeed for hers.

Longley relates these dark deeds not with condemnation and bitterness but with a quiet understanding that this is how things are.

## Relevance to Northern Ireland?

Séamus Heaney's comment on this poem follows a psychological approach in Jungian terms and argues that poetry is the symbolic resolution of lived and felt conflict. He accepts that Longley had no deliberate notion of writing a poem relevant to the 'Troubles'; yet he suggests that the innocent and yet not quite detached female voice in the poem might be the voice of poetry, understanding the victim and the violence and embellishing it with her vision. This is the role of the poet in a violent society; this is how the poet deals with the conflict.

> So she might be an analogue for the action of the poetic imagination as we have been considering it: by comprehending and expressing the violent reactions of the victim in relation to the violent mores of the community, by taking all this into herself and embalming it with flowers and memory, she turns a dirty deed into a vision of reality.

The action of poetry, he says,

> is a self-healing process, neither deliberately provocative nor culpably detached.

# An Amish Rug

Text of poem: New Explorations Anthology page 364

*[Note: This poem is also prescribed for Ordinary Level 2005 exam]*

A READING OF THE POEM

The Amish rug, a gift from the speaker to his lover, carries with it his memories of that culture and community and so enriches the poet's life and love.

The Amish experience of the world is deliberately limited ('a one-room schoolhouse') and calls for simplicity and lack of adornment ('as if ... our clothes were black, our underclothes black'). Mechanisation and industrialisation are avoided ('boy behind the harrow,' etc.) and marriage is signified by its religious element and its simplicity rather than any ostentation ('Marriage a horse and buggy going to church'). Children are a natural, elemental part of the landscape ('silhouettes in a snowy field'). The predominant black-and-white colouring emphasises the simplicity of the culture and the uncompromising nature of the moral values.

The rug, symbol of cultural encounter, and very different from indigenous Amish artefacts, yet transmits the Amish values of naturalness and religious belief. Its colours are described in images from nature, 'cantaloupe and cherry'. Depending on its placing in the room it can be either 'a cathedral window' or 'a flowerbed'. The unspoken wish seems to be that it may bring something of its natural beauty into their lives.

This is a love poem of great charm and elegance. The lover's gift is a simple patchwork quilt. The lovers' desire is for a simple life and uninhibited naturalness in their relationship:

> So that whenever we undress for sleep or love
> We shall step over it as over a flowerbed.

# Laertes

Text of poem: New Explorations Anthology page 366

BACKGROUND NOTE

This poem is based on an episode from Homer's Greek epic poem 'The Odyssey'. Odysseus, king of the island of Ithaca and one of the Greek heroes of the Trojan war, was for ten years prevented from returning home, blown hither and thither by the storms of Poseidon. Many in Ithaca presumed him dead. Suitors seeking to marry his faithful wife, Penelope, gathered at his palace and wasted his estate in continuous feasting.

Odysseus returned, disguised to all at first except to his son, Telemachus, and killed all the suitors in a great and bloody slaughter. As these were the sons of local princes and prominent nobles, there were likely to be repercussions. Before facing these, Odysseus slipped out to the hill country to visit his father, Laertes, who had retired to his vineyards. And this is where the poem is set.

Longley rendered a number of episodes from the *Odyssey* in a fairly free translation, as he explained in the notes with *Gorse Fires*:

> In differing proportions and with varying degrees of high-handedness but always, I hope, with reverence, I have in seven of these poems combined free translation from Homer's 'Odyssey' with original lines.

A READING OF THE POEM

Here Longley returns to his recurring theme of father–son relationships, this time in the classical context of Homer's *Odyssey*. The poem offers interesting psychological insights into the roles people fulfil in a relationship and how these roles alter over time. Odysseus's memories of his childhood centre on a dependent, persistently questioning child–parent relationship, 'traipsing after his father | And asking for everything he saw'. Despite the fact that he now returns as the conquering hero, his first instinct is to revert to his child role and run to the parent for comfort, blurting out his tale. But now the roles have been reversed. The father is now a fragile old man ('So old and pathetic'), and the erstwhile child has become the protector and comforter:

> Who drew the old man fainting to his breast and held him there
> And cradled like driftwood the bones of his dwindling father.

Another interesting aspect of the encounter is the son's need to be recognised. The dramatic delaying tactic practised by Odysseus – the drawing out of the old man to see if he remembered – may seem pointlessly cruel to a modern reader. 'So he waited for images ... Until Laertes recognised his son'. But, psychologically, Odysseus seems to need to be recognised, at least in the outward physical aspect. Perhaps this could be read at a deeper level also and seen to refer to the son's need for a father's recognition of his deeds, his achievements, his independent separate self. In Homer's original version, as we can see from the extract, old Laertes is made to undergo a more formal, rigorous testing, and so the recognition becomes highly significant.

The father–son relationship in this poem, as in the other Longley poems on the same theme, is emotional and tender:

> Odysseus sobbed in the shade of a pear-tree for his father
> So old and pathetic that all he wanted then and there
> Was to kiss him and hug him and blurt out the whole story,

The need for comfort, for emotional closeness, for recognition, for protection and the joy of meeting are at the heart of this father–son relationship.

The poem also makes a statement about home. Home here is a place of familial love, psychological and emotional support and affirmation. But, taking the broader context of the Homeric allusion into account, we cannot evade the awareness that home is also a place of strife and intrigue, civil wars and bloody retribution. And we can hardly avoid drawing parallels between the Homeric world of Ithaca and Northern Ireland. Perhaps this is the greatest value of the allusion. It allows Longley to contemplate the perplexing realities of background, obliquely and from a distance.

## Odyssey

BOOK 24 (EXTRACT)

(Translated by E.V. Rieu)

When they reached the spot, Odysseus said to Telemachus and his men: 'Go into the main building now and make haste to kill the best pig you can find for our midday meal. Meanwhile I shall try an experiment with my father, to find out whether he will remember me and realise who it is when he sees me, or fail to know me after so long an absence.'

As he spoke, he handed his weapons of war to the servants, who then went straight into the house, while Odysseus moved off towards the luxuriant vineyard, intent on his experiment. As he made his way down into the great orchard he fell in neither with Dolius nor with any of the serfs or Dolius' sons, who had all gone with the old man at their head to gather stones for the vineyard wall. Thus he found his father alone on the vineyard terrace digging round a plant. He was wearing a filthy, patched and disreputable tunic, a pair of stitched leather gaiters strapped round his shins to protect them from scratches, and gloves to save his hands from the brambles; while to crown all, and by way of emphasising his misery, he had a hat of goatskin on his head. When the gallant Odysseus saw how old and worn his father looked and realised how miserable he was, he halted under a tall pear-tree and the tears came into his eyes. Nor could he make up his mind at once whether to hug and kiss his father, and tell him the whole story of his own return to Ithaca, or first to question him and find out what he thought. In the end he decided to start assuming a brusque manner in order to draw the old man out, and with this purpose in view he now went straight up to his father.

Laertes was still hoeing round his plant with his head down, as his famous son came up and accosted him.

'Old man,' said Odysseus, 'you have everything so tidy here that I can see there is little about gardening that you do not know. There is nothing, not a green thing in the whole enclosure, not a fig, olive, vine, pear or vegetable bed that does not show signs of your care. On the other hand I cannot help remarking, I hope without offence, that you don't look after yourself very well. In fact, what with your squalor and your wretched clothes, old age has hit you very hard. Yet it can't be on account of any laziness that your master neglects you, nor is there anything in your build and size to suggest the slave. You look more like a man of royal blood, the sort of person who enjoys the privilege of age, and sleeps on a soft bed when he has had his bath and dined. However, tell me whose serf you are. And whose is this garden you look after? The truth, if you please. And there's another point you can clear up for me. Am I really in Ithaca? A fellow I met on my way up here just now assured me that I was. But he was not very intelligent, for he wouldn't deign to answer me properly or listen to what I said, when I mentioned a friend of mine and asked him whether he was still in the land of the living or dead and gone by now. You shall learn about this friend yourself if you pay attention to what I say. Some time ago in my own country I befriended a stranger who turned up at our place and proved the most attractive visitor I have ever entertained from abroad. He said he was an Ithacan, and that Arceisius' son Laertes was his father. I took him in, made him thoroughly welcome and gave him every hospitality that my rich house could afford, including presents worthy of his rank. Seven talents of wrought gold he had from me, a solid silver wine-bowl with a floral design, twelve single-folded cloaks, twelve rugs, twelve splendid mantles and as many tunics too, and besides all this, four women as skilled in fine handicraft as they were good to look at. I let him choose them for himself.'

'Sir,' said his father to Odysseus, with tears on his cheeks, 'I can assure you that you're in the place you asked for but it's in the hands of rogues and criminals. The gifts you lavished on your friend were given in vain, though had you found him alive in Ithaca he would never have let you go before he had made you an ample return in presents and hospitality, as is right when such an example has been set. But pray tell me exactly how long ago it was that you befriended the unfortunate man, for the guest of yours was my unhappy son – if ever I had one – my son, who far from friends and home has been devoured by fishes in the sea or fallen prey, maybe, to the wild beasts and birds on land. Dead people have their dues, but not Odysseus. We had no chance, we two that brought him into the world, to wrap his body up and wail for him, nor had his richly dowered wife, constant Penelope, the chance to close her husband's eyes and give him on his bier the seemly tribute of a dirge.

'But you have made me curious about yourself. Who are you, sir? What is your native town? And where might she be moored, the good ship that brought you here with your gallant crew? Or were you travelling as a passenger on someone else's ship, which landed you and sailed away?'

'I am quite willing,' said the resourceful Odysseus, 'to tell you all you wish to know. I come from Alybas. My home is in the palace there, for my father is King Apheidas, Polypemon's son. My own name is Eperitus. I had no intention of putting in here when I left Sicania but had the misfortune to be driven out of my course, and my ship is riding yonder by the open coast some way from the port. As for Odysseus, it is four years and more since he bade me farewell and left my country – to fall on evil days, it seems. And yet the omens when he left were good: birds on the right, which pleased me as I said goodbye, and cheered him as he started out. We both had every hope that we should meet again as host and guest and give each other splendid gifts.'

When Laertes heard this, he sank into the black depths of despair. Groaning heavily, he picked the black dust up in both his hands and poured it onto the grey hairs of his head. Odysseus' heart was stirred, and suddenly, as he watched his dear father, poignant compassion forced its way through his nostrils. He rushed forward, flung his arms round his neck and kissed him. 'Father,' he cried, 'here I am, the very man you asked about, home in my own land after nineteen years. But this is no time for tears and lamentation. For I have news to tell you, and heaven knows there is need for haste. I have killed the gang of suitors in our palace. I have paid them out for their insulting gibes and all their crimes.'

Laertes answered him: 'If you that have come here are indeed my son Odysseus, give me some definite proof to make me sure.'

Odysseus was ready for this. 'To begin with,' he said, 'cast your eye on this scar, where I was wounded by the white tusk of a boar when I went to Parnassus. You and my mother had sent me to my grandfather Autolycus, to fetch the gifts he solemnly promised me when he came to visit us. Then again, I can tell you all the trees you gave me one day on this garden terrace. I was only a little boy at the time, trotting after you through the orchard, begging for this and that, and as we wound our way through these very trees you told me all their names. You gave me thirteen pear trees, ten apple, forty fig trees, and at the same time you pointed out the fifty rows of vines that were to be mine. Each ripened at a different time, so that the bunches on them were at various stages when the branches felt their weight under the summer skies.'

Laertes realised at once that Odysseus' evidence had proved his claim. With trembling knees and bursting heart he flung his arms round the neck of his beloved son, and stalwart Odysseus caught him fainting to his breast. The first words he uttered as he rallied and his consciousness returned were in reply to the news his son had given him. 'By Father Zeus,' he cried, 'you gods are still in your heaven if those suitors have really paid the price for their iniquitous presumption! But I have horrible fear now that the whole forces of Ithaca will soon be on us here, and that they will send urgent messages for help to every town in Cephallenia.'

'Have no fear,' said his resourceful son, 'and don't trouble your head about that; but come with me to the farmhouse here by the orchard, where I sent on Telemachus with the cowman and swineherd to prepare a meal as quickly as they could.'

# *Ceasefire*
Text of poem: New Explorations Anthology page 367

## BACKGROUND NOTE

This poem was first published in the *Irish Times* on 3 September 1994, two days after an IRA ceasefire was announced. It is another 'free translation' of an episode from Homer's classic poem *The Iliad,* which tells the story of Troy's siege by the Greeks. *The Iliad* begins in the tenth year of the Trojan conflict and ends with the burial of Hector, shortly after this episode.

During the conflict, Achilles sulked in his tent and refused to fight, because of a dispute with Agamemnon over a woman. However, with the Greeks in danger of being routed by Hector, Achilles allowed his close friend Patroclus to borrow his armour and his men to defend the Greek ships. But Patroclus was killed by Hector. In a fit of grief, rage and guilt, Achilles went back to the battle and after great slaughter pushed the Trojans back and killed Hector. In a frenzy of vengeance he dragged Hector's body in the dust behind his chariot, round the walls of Troy, and for eleven days thereafter round the tomb of Patroclus. Finally, old King Priam, prompted by the gods, came to the Greek camp bearing a huge ransom to redeem the body. He clasped the knees and kissed the hands of Achilles, urging him to remember his own father of similar age and also separated from his son.

You can read a translation of the original scene below.

## THEMES

This poem deals with the aftermath of war. It explores the sadness of mourning, the feelings of those left behind to pick up the pieces, the emotions of the victors as well as the bereaved. It faces squarely the compromises people make when necessary, the self-abasement that even proud people will suffer for love and grief. And it signals the building of a reconciliation of a sort. So it relates quite aptly to the needs of a post-conflict Northern Ireland. Indeed, Longley himself has said that he kept Gordon Wilson's face as Priam in front of him while he wrote this poem.

## Visual gestures

This dramatic episode is built around extravagant visual gestures: the kneeling; kissing hands; pushing the old king gently away. The set-piece meal also acts as a visual tableau, performed with eyes and looks, more reminiscent of a romantic scene than of a meal between deadly enemies. Much of the poignancy of this poem is communicated through gestures and looks.

## Imagery

The most exciting thing about the imagery is the unusual nature of the similes. 'Wrapped like a present' is shockingly inappropriate. Yet the very lightheartedness of that image seems to heighten the pathos of the scene, the awfulness of that old man's burden, just as an insensitive comment would increase the sympathy felt in such a situation. The hint of eroticism in 'To stare at each other's beauty as lovers might' is equally inappropriate for the recently mortal enemies. Indeed the reversal of roles in the image of the king's self-abasement – on his knees, kissing the hand of his son's killer – is visually shocking.

All this disturbing imagery punctures the heroic concept of war and conveys something of the true discomfort of the moment, the uncertainty and tension of this scene.

## *The Iliad*

### Book 24 (extract)

(Translated by Robert Eagles.)

Priam found the warrior there inside ...
many captains sitting some way off, but two,
veteran Automedon and the fine fighter Alcimus,
were busy serving him. He had just finished dinner,
eating, drinking, and the table still stood near.
The majestic King of Troy slipped past the rest
and kneeling down beside Achilles, clasped his knees
and kissed his hands, those terrible, man-killing hands
that had slaughtered Priam's many sons in battle.
Awesome – as when the grip of madness seizes one
who murders a man in his own fatherland and flees
abroad to foreign shores, to a wealthy, noble host,
and a sense of marvel runs through all who see him –
so Achilles marvelled, beholding majestic Priam.
His men marvelled too, trading startled glances.

But Priam prayed his heart out to Achilles:
'Remember your own father, great godlike Achilles –
as old as I am, past the threshold of deadly old age!
No doubt the countrymen round about him plague him now,
with no-one there to defend him, beat away disaster.
No-one – but at least he hears you're still alive
and his old heart rejoices, hopes rising, day by day,
to see his beloved son come sailing home from Troy.
But I – dear god, my life so cursed by fate ...
I fathered hero sons in the wide realm of Troy
and now not a single one is left, I tell you.
Fifty sons I had when the sons of Achaea came,
nineteen born to me from a single mother's womb
and the rest by other women in the palace. Many,
most of them violent Ares cut the knees from under,
But one, one was left to me, to guard my walls, my people –
the one you killed the other day, defending his fatherland,
my Hector! It's all for him I've come to the ships now,
to win him back from you – I bring a priceless ransom.
Revere the gods, Achilles! Pity me in my own right,
remember your own father! I deserve more pity ...
I have endured what no-one on earth has ever done before –
I put to my lips the hands of the man who killed my son.'

Those words stirred within Achilles a deep desire
to grieve for his own father. Taking the old man's hand
he gently moved him back. And overpowered by memory
both men gave way to grief. Priam wept freely
for man-killing Hector, throbbing, crouching
before Achilles' feet as Achilles wept himself,
now for his father, now for Patroclus once again,
and their sobbing rose and fell throughout the house.
Then, when brilliant Achilles had his fill of tears
and the longing for it had left his mind and body,
he rose from his seat, raised the old man by the hand
and filled with pity now for his grey head and grey beard,
he spoke out winging words, flying straight to the heart:
'Poor man, how much you've borne – pain to break the spirit!
What daring brought you down to the ships, all alone,
to face the glance of the man who killed your sons,
so many fine brave boys? You have a heart of iron.
Come, please, sit down on this chair here' ...

But the old and noble Priam protested strongly:
'Don't make me sit on a chair, Achilles, Prince,
not while Hector lies uncared for in your camp!
Give him back to me, now, no more delay –
I must see my son with my own eyes.
Accept the ransom I bring you, a king's ransom!
Enjoy it, all of it – return to your own native land,
safe and sound ... since now you've spared my life.'

A dark glance – and the headstrong runner answered,
'No more, old man, don't tempt my wrath, not now!
My own mind's made up to give you back your son.
A messenger brought me word from Zeus – my mother,
Thetis who bore me, the Old Man of the Sea's daughter.
And what's more, I can see through you, Priam –
no hiding the fact from me: one of the gods
has led you down to Achaea's fast ships.
No man alive, not even a rugged young fighter,
would dare to venture into our camp. Never –
how could he slip past the sentries unchallenged?
Or shoot back the bolt of my gates with so much ease?
So don't anger me now. Don't stir my raging heart still more.
Or under my own roof I may not spare your life, old man –
suppliant that you are – may break the laws of Zeus!'

The old man was terrified. He obeyed the order.
But Achilles bounded out of doors like a lion –
not alone but flanked by his two aides-in-arms,
veteran Automedon and Alcimus, steady comrades,
Achilles' favourites next to the dead Patroclus.
They loosed from harness the horses and the mules,
they led the herald in, the old king's crier,
and sat him down on a bench. From the polished wagon
they lifted the priceless ransom brought for Hector's corpse
but they left behind two capes and a finely woven shirt
to shroud the body well when Priam bore him home.
Then Achilles called the serving-women out:
'Bathe and anoint the body –
bear it aside first. Priam must not see his son.'
He feared that, overwhelmed by the sight of Hector,
wild with grief, Priam might let his anger flare
and Achilles might fly into fresh rage himself,

cut the old man down and break the laws of Zeus.
So when the maids had bathed and anointed the body
sleek with olive oil and wrapped it round and round
in a braided battle-shirt and handsome battle-cape,
then Achilles lifted Hector up in his own arms
and laid him down on a bier, and comrades helped him
raise the bier and body onto the sturdy wagon ...
Then with a groan he called his dear friend by name:
'Feel no anger at me, Patroclus, if you learn –
even there in the House of Death – I let his father
have Prince Hector back. He gave me worthy ransom
and you shall have your share from me, as always,
your fitting, lordly share.'
                                        So he vowed
and brilliant Achilles strode back to his shelter,
sat down on the well-carved chair that he had left,
at the far wall of the room, leaned toward Priam
and firmly spoke the words the king had come to hear:
'Your son is now set free, old man, as you requested.
Hector lies in state. With the first light of day
you will see for yourself as you convey him home.
Now, at last, let us turn our thoughts to supper' ...

They reached out for the good things that lay at hand
and when they had put aside desire for food and drink
Priam the son of Dardanus gazed at Achilles, marvelling
now at the man's beauty, his magnificent build –
face-to-face he seemed a deathless god ...
and Achilles gazed and marvelled at Dardan Priam,
beholding his noble looks, listening to his words.
But once they'd had their fill of gazing at each other,
the old majestic Priam broke the silence first:
'Put me to bed quickly, Achilles, Prince.
Time to rest, to enjoy the sweet relief of sleep.
Not once have my eyes closed shut beneath my lids
from the day my son went down beneath your hands ...
day and night I groan, brooding over the countless griefs,
grovelling in the dung that fills my walled-in court.
But now, at long last, I have tasted food again
and let some glistening wine go down my throat.
Before this hour I had tasted nothing' ...

# Some themes and issues in the poetry of Michael Longley

NOTE 1

For the purpose of acquiring an overview, it might be useful to re-read the poems in thematic groupings rather than in chronological order. For example:

(1) 'Wounds', 'Last Request' and 'Laertes' deal with the poet's father and thereby with his sense of his own identity and family background.

(2) 'An Amish Rug' features intimate love and home and family values and contributes to our understanding of the poet and his identity.

(3) 'Wreaths', 'Wounds' and 'Ceasefire' deal with violence, past and present, with violent myths, official war, and the present 'Troubles'.

(4) 'Carrigskeewaun', 'Poteen', 'Badger' and 'Self-Heal' feature the Mayo landscape, Longley's second home and alternative culture.

NOTE 2

Consider each general point made, and return to the relevant poems for supporting evidence and quotation. If you disagree, make your argument with supporting reference also. Either way, build up a knowledge of the poetic detail. Make notes for yourself, perhaps in spider-diagram form.

## EXPLORATION OF IDENTITY: POEMS OF SELF-DEFINITION

We can interpret a number of the poems in this selection as pieces exploring the poet's own background, environment, and values. These areas are not covered in any broad and systematic way, but selected subjects serve as anchor points of his identity.

- Family identity is anchored on the figure of his father in these poems. Acknowledgment of his soldier father helps clarify his own identity. As the critic Edna Longley summarised it, 'The father focuses questions of belonging rather than longing: an Englishman who fought twice for his country.'

- Honouring and remembering the dead is a part of this identity: see 'Last Rites', 'Wounds' and 'Laertes'. (The father–son relationship is examined separately, pages 285–6).

- The violent society also is part of that identity: see 'Wounds' and 'Wreaths'.

- Family values, intimate love and a yearning for simplicity are part of this tapestry of identity: see 'An Amish Rug'.

- An alternative culture, the native Irish identity, is explored in 'Poteen', with its emphasis on the rebel race memory: see the critical commentary of 'Wounds' (pages 260–3) for a discussion of conflicting identities.

# VIOLENCE

- A stark treatment of violence in its ordinary, everyday reality: see 'Wreaths'.
- The pervasive nature of violence in society; death invades the home: see 'The Civil Servant' and 'The Greengrocer'; it even invades the psyche: see 'The Linen Workers'.
- Human insignificance and powerlessness in the face of this violence: see 'Wreaths' and 'Wounds'.
- The 'Troubles' are dealt with against a background of wars and other human conflicts; this gives a sense of perspective to present-day violence: see 'Wounds', 'Wreaths', and 'Last Request'. 'He is able to analogise between different kinds and theatres of human conflict in a personal and historically informed and mediated treatment of the troubles' (Peacock).
- Longley presents the pictures of violence in a neutral, non-partisan way and with a slight air of detachment. He concentrates on presenting detailed pictures rather than conveying emotions: see 'Wounds' and 'Wreaths'.
- Examine what Longley himself has to say (in *Tuppenny Stung*) about the relationship between a poet and the 'Troubles':

> I find offensive the notion that what we inadequately call 'the Troubles' might provide inspiration for artists; and that in some weird *quid pro quo* the arts might provide solace for grief and anguish. Twenty years ago I wrote in Causeway: 'Too many critics seem to expect a harvest of paintings, poems, plays and novels to drop from the twisted branches of civil discord. They fail to realise that the artist needs time in which to allow the raw material of experience to settle to an imaginative depth where he can transform it ... He is not some sort of super-journalist commenting with unflattering spontaneity on events immediately after they have happened. Rather, as Wilfred Owen stated fifty years ago, it is the artist's duty to warn, to be tuned in before anyone else to the implications of a situation.'
>
> Ten years later I wrote for the Poetry Book Society about what I was trying to do in my fourth collection, The Echo Gate: 'As an Ulsterman I realise that this may sound like fiddling while Rome burns. So I would insist that poetry is a normal human activity, its proper concern all of the things that happen to people. Though the poet's first duty must be to his imagination, he has other obligations: and not just as a citizen. He would be inhuman if he did not respond to tragic events in his own community, and a poor artist if he did not seek to endorse that response imaginatively. But if his imagination fails him, the result will be a dangerous impertinence. In the context of political violence the deployment of words at their most precise and most suggestive remains one of the few antidotes to death-dealing dishonesty.'

## OTHER CONFLICTS

- War: he deals with the seamier side of war, the grave-robbing, anti-heroic view in 'Last Request'; see also 'Ceasefire'.
- Violence in society: see 'Self-Heal'.

## THE WEST OF IRELAND

- A different landscape, another ethos, alternative values
- Is he claiming kinship with an alternative national identity, as in 'Poteen'; merely fleeing home; or finding a good place of perspective from which to look north? See the critical commentary on 'Carrigskeewaun'.
- Identifying with the Irish landscape? See 'Carrigskeewaun'. 'The sense of a man at ease with himself and his fellows' (Brown)
- The sheer enjoyment of nature, feeling part of the process: see 'Carrigskeewaun'.
- A genuine naturalist's pleasure, the preoccupation with creatures: see 'Badger'.
- The lonely, isolated nature of his western experience, the absence of community, family, and people: see 'Carrigskeewaun'.
- Not a romantic view of the west; he records the harshness, the pain, the violence and the ignorance as well as the beauty: see 'Badger', 'Carrigskeewaun', and 'Self-heal'.
- Again the precise description, the keen eye for detail: see 'Carrigskeewaun', 'Badger'.
- A view of the west as a place of compensatory values: 'a community of realisable values that are personally authentic and yet generally available, such as there seems to be present in nature: particularly in the redemptive landscapes of the west of Ireland' (Dawe).

## THE FATHER FIGURE

- Honouring and acknowledging the dead is part of the process of self-definition: see 'Wounds' and 'Last Requests'.
- But Longley seems preoccupied with the father's dying, his almost-dying in the trenches and then his actual death: see 'Last Requests' and 'Wounds'. Then his psychological disinterment happens in 'The Linen Workers'. Is this becoming a fixation?
- Images of his father are of a frail old man, such as in 'Laertes' and 'Ceasefire', or focus on his teeth and glasses, images of his imperfection: see 'The Linen Workers'. But they are of a man with endearing human frailties, such as the cigarette addiction. And he has a sense of humour: see 'Wounds'.
- Intimacy of the father–son relationship: see the imagery of 'Wounds': 'I touched his hand, his thin head I touched.'

- Interesting reversal of father–son roles in 'Laertes': the hero slipping back into the child's role, the adult still needing recognition or affirmation from the father.
- A father's love and the lengths to which he will go to reclaim a son are evident in 'Ceasefire'.

## THE ELUSIVE 'HOME' IN LONGLEY'S POETRY

- Very few concrete images of home feature in these poems. A bedroom features in an 'An Amish Rug'.
- The father figure, used by the poet to define his identity, is never pictured at home but only in the trenches, in his grave, in the hospital bed: see 'Wounds' and 'Last Requests'.
- Carrigskeewaun is the poet's home from home, yet it produces no concrete home, merely an imagined image: 'Recalls ... a tablecloth and I A table she might have already set.'
- The passages from Homer that struck a chord with Longley are about a man longing for home, prevented for years from returning and on his return finding it taken over by others.

## THE SENSE OF PERSPECTIVE IN LONGLEY'S POETRY

- Peacock talks of Longley's ability to look beyond the immediate issues of his own society and personal circumstances to other historical times and literary traditions. Notice the range of settings and times: present-day Ulster; the west of Ireland; the trenches in Europe, 1914–18; the classical Greece of Homer. The result is 'a catholicity of culture and political outlook which fosters objectivity, non-partisan human sympathy and historically informed understanding' (Peacock).
- The past and present are placed in juxtaposition to achieve a sense of perspective: violence in the First World War and present-day Belfast; the classical past of Ithaca has parallels with modern Ulster ('Laertes' and 'Ceasefire').
- Is present-day violence dingier? Or is all killing pointless?
- Past and present, life and death are no longer distinct: the dead father is ever present in 'The Linen Workers'.

## A GENERALLY UNROMANTIC VIEW OF LIFE

- Dominated by war and violence: see 'Wounds', 'Last Requests', 'Wreaths', and 'Ceasefire'.
- Country life is rendered in all its realistic harshness ('Carrigskeewaun'), its brutality and pain ('Badger'), its ignorance and prejudice ('Self-Heal').

- The exception in this selection is 'An Amish Rug', with its yearning for simple values and loving intimacy.

YET THERE IS SYMPATHY IN HIS POETRY

- for the human condition: see 'Self-Heal'
- for grieving parents and dead heroes: see 'Ceasefire'
- for nature's creatures: see 'Badger'
- for victims of violence, ancient and modern: see 'Wounds' and 'Ceasefire'.

## Style and technique: some points

FIRST-PERSON NARRATIVE

- The personal voice lends an air of intimacy to many of the poems: see 'Self-Heal', 'Carrigskeewaun', and 'An Amish Rug'.
- He uses a female voice in 'Self-Heal'.
- There is a strong autobiographical element in some of the poems: see 'Last Requests' and 'Wounds'.

DETAILED DESCRIPTIONS

- The use of precise detail creates the realism, whether dealing with violence or the beauties of nature: see 'Wreaths' and 'Carrigskeewaun'.
- Longley has an eye for incongruous detail. Often the point of the poem is made through this visual style rather than through any explicit comment: see 'Wounds' and 'Ceasefire'. For example, he views violence in the context of world wars and other violent contexts, and he views love in the context of the Amish culture.

TONE

- The tone is unemotional for the most part, neutral and slightly detached: see 'Wreaths'.
- The concentration is on precise, matter-of-fact descriptions, objectively rendered: see 'Wreaths' and 'Self-Heal'.
- Yet the tone is not callous; he is full of sympathy for the human condition: see 'Self-Heal'.
- The indications of emotion occur in the poems dealing with his father: see 'Wounds' and 'Last Requests'.
- The balanced tone is achieved through this wide perspective he takes up. For example, he views violence in the context of world wars and other violent contexts, and he views love in the context of the Amish culture: see 'Wounds' and 'An Amish Rug'.

INDIRECT TECHNIQUE

- He approaches subjects obliquely at times: for example, he uses his father's war experience to forge a perspective on Northern violence: see 'Wounds'. Or he uses classical Greek poetry to explore the psychological and emotional relationship with his father: see 'Laertes' and 'Ceasefire'.
- This attempt at contrast and comparison is sometimes reflected in the structuring of the poem in two halves, resonating off each other: see 'Wounds'.

SHAPE

- Shape and form are important in Longley's poems. See, for example, the thin, longish poem 'Poteen', resembling a tube; the rectangular picture-postcard sections of 'Carrigskeewaun'; or the rock-like, unbeautiful oblong of 'Self-Heal', immovable as ignorance. Explore the relationship between shape and meaning in the poems.

## Forging a personal understanding of Longley's poetry

1. Which poems do you remember most sharply?
2. Which images have remained in your mind?
3. Choose any poem of Longley's. Place yourself in the scene; view it with the poet's eye. What do you see, hear, smell, etc.? How are you feeling? Why write that poem?
4. What are the poet's main preoccupations? What does he love, hate, fear, etc.? What interests him?
5. What do you discover about the personality of the poet? What do you think are his attitudes to life?
6. What does he contribute to your understanding of Ireland and of human nature?
7. What would you like to ask him?
8. What do you notice that is distinctive about the way he writes?
9. Compare his work with that of Séamus Heaney. What similarities and differences do you notice with regard to themes and styles of writing?
10. Why read Michael Longley?

## Questions

1. Outline the main issues dealt with in this selection of Longley's poetry.
2. 'Violent events are seen in all the pathos of their everyday settings' (Peacock). Would you agree?
3. 'Longley views all military exploits with a jaundiced eye.' Comment on this statement, with reference to at least two poems from the selection.

4. 'The truth of human relationships is an important issue in the poetry of Michael Longley.' Comment on this aspect of his poetry.
5. 'One of the strengths of Longley's poetry is its descriptive detail.' Examine this element of his style, with particular reference to at least two of the poems.
6. Examine the treatment of death in the poetry of Michael Longley.
7. 'The west of Ireland is seen as the embodiment of some kind of alternative life' (Dawe). What aspects of this alternative life does Longley deal with in the poems you have read?

## Michael Longley: writings

*No Continuing City*, London: Macmillan 1969.
*An Exploded View*, London: Victor Gollancz 1973.
*Man Lying on a Wall*, London: Victor Gollancz 1976.
*The Echo Gate*, London: Secker and Warburg 1979.
*Poems, 1963–1983*, London: Secker and Warburg 1991.
*Gorse Fires*, London: Secker and Warburg 1991.
*Tuppenny Stung: Autobiographical Chapters,* Belfast: Lagan Press 1994.
*The Ghost Orchid*, London: Jonathan Cape 1995.

# Bibliography

Allen, Michael, 'Rhythm and development in Michael Longley's earlier poetry' in *Contemporary Irish Poetry: A Collection of Critical Essays,* edited by Elmer Andrews, London: Macmillan 1992.

Brown, Terence, *Northern Voices: Poets from Ulster,* Dublin: Gill and Macmillan 1975.

Craig, Patricia, 'History and retrieval in contemporary Northern Irish poetry' in *Contemporary Irish Poetry: A Collection of Critical Essays,* edited by Elmer Andrews, London: Macmillan 1992.

Dawe, Gerald, *Against Piety: Essays in Irish Poetry,* Belfast: Lagan Press 1995.

Eagles, Robert (translator), *Homer: The Iliad,* New York: Viking Penguin 1990.

Heaney, Séamus, 'Place and Displacement: Reflections on Some Recent Poetry from Northern Ireland' (first Pete Laver Memorial Lecture, Grasmere, 1984) in *Contemporary Irish Poetry: A Collection of Critical Essays,* edited by Elmer Andrews, London: Macmillan 1992.

McDonald, Peter, 'Michael Longley's homes' in *The Chosen Ground: Essays on the Contemporary Poetry of Northern Ireland,* edited by Neil Corcoran, London: Seren Books 1992.

Parker, Michael, 'Priest of the masses' [a review of Longley's Poems, 1936–83], *Honest Ulsterman,* no. 79, autumn 1985.

Peacock, Alan, 'Michael Longley: poet between worlds' in *Poetry in Contemporary Irish Literature* (Irish Literary Studies, 43), edited by Michael Kenneally, Gerrards Cross (Bucks.): Colin Smythe 1995.

# 8  *Eavan* BOLAND

*John G. Fahy*

## A literary life

Eavan Boland was born in Dublin in 1944. Her mother was the painter Frances Kelly and her father was the diplomat Frederick Boland, whose career moves resulted in her roving childhood and youth. From the age of six to twelve she lived in London, then in New York for a number of years, to return to Dublin when she was fourteen.

She was educated at Holy Child Convent, Killiney, County Dublin, then went on to Trinity College, first as a student and later as a lecturer in the English Department. After a few years she embarked on a career as a literary journalist with the *Irish Times*, and she also presented a regular poetry programme for RTE radio.

## 'New Territory'

*New Territory*, her first book of poetry, published in 1967, contains the early poems, written between the ages of seventeen and twenty-two, which were critically acknowledged at the time as talented, well-crafted work. Among its main concerns, this volume showed some preoccupation with the role of the poet, in pieces such as 'The Poets' and 'New Territory'. It also contained the first of her poems about paintings and so introduced what was to become an important theme of Boland's work: the stereotyped view of women in art and literature. 'From the Painting *Back from Market* by Chardin' shows the peasant woman, defined by love and domestic duties, 'her eyes mixed | Between love and market.'

The poet feels that artists throughout the centuries have ignored the real lives of women:

> I think of what great art removes:
> Hazard and death, the future and the past,
> This woman's secret history and her loves ...

In general this volume is in the mainstream of the Irish political – romantic poetic tradition, with its themes of exile ('The Flight of the Earls') and political martyrdom ('A Cynic at Kilmainham Jail'); poems about Irish poets ('Yeats in Civil War' and 'After the Irish of Aodhagán Ó Rathaille'); and the retelling of legends ('Three Songs for a Legend' and 'The Winning of Etain'). But her outlook was soon to change, under pressure of the unfolding political situation.

Religious and political antagonism in Northern Ireland exploded into violence from 1969 onwards. Few people were unmoved or unaffected by this. The violence spread southwards with the bombing of Dublin and Monaghan in May 1974. Eavan Boland conducted a series of interviews in the *Irish Times* with Northern writers concerning their views on the situation, its effects on the work of the writer, and in general concerning the function of art in a time of violence. In a seminal article on 7 June 1974 entitled 'The Weasel's Tooth', she questioned the whole notion of cultural unity and accused Irish writing, influenced by Yeats, of fostering lethal fantasies for political activists:

> Let us be rid at last of any longing for cultural unity in a country whose most precious contribution may be precisely its insight into the anguish of disunity ... For there is, and at last I recognise it, no unity whatsoever in this culture of ours. And even more important, I recognise that there is no need whatsoever for such a unity. If we search for it we will, at a crucial moment, be mutilating with fantasy once again the very force we should be liberating with reality: our one strength as writers, the individual voice, speaking in tones of outcry, vengeance, bitterness even, against our disunity but speaking, for all that, with a cool tough acceptance of it.

## 'The War Horse'

The second volume of poetry, *The War Horse,* published in 1975, reflects Boland's concerns with violence and conflict in both private and community life. She deals with many types of conflict: the Irish–English struggle, worrying families, and the conflict between lovers. The development of this theme ranges from a recognition of the killer instinct inherent in all nature, however domesticated ('Prisoners'), to a consideration of notorious historical public moments of conflict and death ('The Famine Road', 'The Greek Experience' and 'Child of Our Time', which was written after the Dublin bombings of 1974) and the archetypal deadly conflict of fathers and sons ('The Hanging Judge' and 'A Soldier's Son'). The latter poem, in which a father kills his own son, has been read as 'an image of a society at war with its own inheritance and future'. 'The War Horse', both a private and a political poem, brings a vivid personal awareness of destruction and war to leafy Dublin suburbia.

The feminine vision and view of the world is also a force in this volume. In 'The Famine Road' Boland equates the callous official lack of understanding of the famine victims with the offhand, male medical attitude meted out to a contemporary woman suffering from sterility. Racial suffering is equated with female suffering. In 'Suburban Woman' and 'Ode to Suburbia' she deals with the daily grind of the housewife and the conflict between a woman's traditional role and her identity as a poet and creative artist:

> Her kitchen blind down – a white flag –
> the day's assault over, now she will shrug
>
> a hundred small surrenders off as images
> still born, unwritten metaphors, blank pages;
>
> and on this territory, blindfold, we meet
> at last, veterans of a defeat
>
> no truce will heal, no formula prevent
> breaking out fresh again. Again the print
>
> of twigs stalking her pillow will begin
> a new day and all her victims then –
> hopes unreprieved, hours taken hostage
> will newly wake, while I, on a new page
>
> will watch, like town and country, word, thought
> look for ascendancy, poise, retreat,
>
> leaving each line maimed, my forces used.
> Defeated we survive, we two, housed
>
> together in my compromise, my craft –
> who are of one another the first draft.

Boland had by this time married and moved from her city flat and literary lifestyle to the Dublin suburb of Dundrum, where she was rearing her two daughters. These poems and others such as 'The Other Woman' and 'Child of Our Time' reflect an attempt to find and bring together her identity as wife, Irishwoman, poet and mother with her life in the suburbs.

In this volume also there are some beautiful and honest personal poems on family, love and friendship: 'Sisters', 'The Laws of Love', and 'The Botanic Gardens' – all demonstrating peaceful alternatives to conflict.

## 'In Her Own Image'

In 1976 she began to work simultaneously on her next two volumes of poetry, *In Her Own Image*, published in 1980, and *Night Feed*, published in 1982. *In Her Own Image* deals with individual private female identity, 'woman's secret history'. The poems explore taboo issues: anorexia, infanticide, mastectomy, menstruation, masturbation and domestic violence. Here is a cry to look at the reality of woman, her sexuality, desires, feelings of degradation, and failure to be understood.

'Anorexia' explores female suffering; 'Mastectomy' and 'In His Own Image' explore feelings of degradation and see the female body as the object of man's desire and of his need to control and shape:

> He splits my lip with his fist,
> shadows my eye with a blow,
> knuckles my neck to its proper angle.
> What a perfectionist!
> His are a sculptor's hands:
> they summon
> form from the void,
> they bring
> me to myself again.
> I am a new woman.

'Solitary' suggests that only a woman knows the real sensual rhythms of her own body. 'Tirade for the Mimic Muse' and 'Witching' undermine the accepted conventional image of woman. 'Tirade' in particular deflates the traditional male-created image of the muse as a beautiful girl, choosing instead to deal with the less picturesque reality:

> I've caught you out. You slut. You fat trout.
> So here you are fumed in candle-stink
> Its yellow balm exhumes you for the glass.
> How you arch and pout in it!
> How you poach your face in it!
> Anyone would think you were a whore –
> An ageing out-of-work kind-hearted tart.
> I know you for the ruthless bitch you are:
> Our criminal, our tricoteuse, our Muse –
> Our Muse of Mimic Art.

These are angry poems, featuring degraded states of women, in a sort of anti-lyric verse, yet they goad the reader into considering the reality of woman, not the image.

## 'Night Feed'

If *In Her Own Image* featured the dark side of 'woman's secret history', *Night Feed* features the suburban, domestic and maternal: the ordinary, traditional, everyday aspects of woman's identity. The main sequence of poems, 'Domestic Interior, 1–11', focuses on the close bond between mother and child and explores the intensity of that maternal experience. It includes the now familiar 'Night Feed'.

## Night Feed

This is dawn.
Believe me
This is your season, little daughter.
The moment daisies open,
The hour mercurial rainwater
Makes a mirror for sparrows.
It's time we drowned our sorrows.

I tiptoe in.
I lift you up
Wriggling
In your rosy, zipped sleeper.
Yes, this is the hour
For the early bird and me
When finder is keeper.

I crook the bottle.
How you suckle!
This is the best I can be,
Housewife
To this nursery
Where you hold on,
Dear life.

A silt of milk.
The last suck.
And now your eyes are open,
Birth-coloured and offended.
Earth wakes.
You go back to sleep.
The feed is ended.

Worms turn.
Stars go in.
Even the moon is losing face.

Poplars stilt for dawn
And we begin
The long fall from grace.
I tuck you in.

Also in this volume is a group of poems examining artistic images of women: 'Degas Laundresses', 'Woman Posing', 'On Renoir's *The Grape Pickers*' and 'Domestic Interior'. These women are either defined in relation to their work in field or kitchen or else are putting on a false, decorative pose, fulfilling the stereotyped image man created for them. Woman's perceived need to comply with this idealised image of timeless beauty is satirised in such pieces as 'The Woman Turns Herself into a Bush', 'The Woman Changes Her Skin' and 'A Ballad of Beauty and Time'. In this last poem plastic surgery is under the poet's satirical knife:

A chin he had re-worked,
a face he had re-made.
He slit and tucked and cut.
Then straightened from his blade.

'A tuck, a hem, he said –
'I only seam the line,
I only mend the dress.
It wouldn't do for you:
your quarrel's with the weave.
The best I achieve
is just a stitch in time.'

These fake images of woman, romanticised stereotypes, are set against the real defining moments in a woman's history in the 'Domestic Interiors' sequence. On the one hand Boland is saying that it is these family relationships that are real and important, that identity can be found among the washing-machines and children's toys in suburbia. But she is also protesting that, traditionally, a woman has not had a choice about this. She has been imprisoned at hearth and home and so kept to the margins of society, removed from the centre of history-making and power. Boland seeks a more equitable balance between 'hearth and history'.

## It's a Woman's World

Our way of life
has hardly changed
since a wheel first
whetted a knife.

Maybe flame
burns more greedily,
and wheels are steadier
but we're the same

who milestone
our lives
with oversights –
living by the lights

of the loaf left
by the cash register,
the washing powder
paid for and wrapped,

the wash left wet:
like most historic peoples
we are defined
by what we forget,

by what we never will be –
star-gazers,
fire-eaters,
It's our alibi

for all time:
as far as history goes
we were never
on the scene of the crime.

So when the king's head
gored its basket –
grim harvest –
we were gristing bread

or getting the recipe
for a good soup
to appetise
our gossip …

## 'The Journey'

Boland's fifth collection, *The Journey*, was published in 1982 and republished in *The Journey and Other Poems* in 1986. Prominent among its many and complex themes is the quest for identity: the poet's national identity, suburban identity, feminist identity, and identity as mother and wife. Childhood memories in England and the feeling of being different in such poems as 'I Remember', 'An Irish Childhood in England: 1951' and 'Fond Memory' provoked a consciousness of the poet's own nation and how language defines a person:

> ... the teacher in the London convent who
> when I produced 'I amn't' in the classroom
> turned and said – 'you're not in Ireland now.'
> ['An Irish Childhood in England: 1951']

This consciousness of language as part of one's identity prevails throughout the volume. Yet her relationship with her history and the women of history is not an easy one, and she resists going back to it in 'Mise Éire'. She finds the grim reality of Irish women in history, soldiers' whores or helpless immigrants, difficult to confront:

> No. I won't go back.
> My roots are brutal:
>
> I am the woman –
> a sloven's mix
> of silk at the wrists,
> a sort of dove-strut
> in the precincts of the garrison –
>
> who practises
> the quick frictions,
> the rictus of delight
> and gets cambric for it,
> rice-coloured silks.
>
> I am the woman
> in the gansy-coat
> on board the 'Mary Belle',
> in the huddling cold,
>
> holding her half-dead baby to her
> as the wind shifts East

and North over the dirty
waters of the wharf

mingling the immigrant
guttural with the vowels
of homesickness who neither
knows nor cares that

a new language
is a kind of scar
and heals after a while
into a passable imitation
of what went before.

Yet these are the real women of the past, not those images created by many
previous male poets, who idealised women and moulded them into metaphors
of national sentiment and so created mythic national female figures.

## 'Outside History'

*Outside History* (1990), Boland's sixth volume, is divided into three sections:
'Object Lessons', 'Outside History: A Sequence' and 'Distances'. The object
lessons, in the main, are what woman has learned about life. Some poems, such
as 'The Black Lace Fan My Mother Gave Me' and 'The River', reflect on the
puzzling, almost inexplicable relationship between men and women and on their
different perspectives on the world ('Mountain Time'). Couples growing apart
and breaking up are the focus of 'Object Lessons'. We are made to feel in this
sequence how fragile and transient is all human interaction, particularly in 'We
Were Neutral in the War' and 'Mountain Time'.

> ... darkness will be only what is left of
> a mouth after kissing or a hand laced in a hand ...
> ['Mountain Time']

The female speaker senses that she is not regarded as significant, that she is
marginalised, forced to the sidelines and excluded from the centre of happening
history in 'We Were Neutral in the War'.

> Your husband frowns at dinner, has no time
> for the baby who has learned to crease three
> fingers and wave 'day-day.' This is serious,
> he says. This could be what we all feared.

You pierce a sequin with a needle.
You slide it down single-knotted thread
until it lies with all the others in
a puzzle of brightness. Then another and another one.

The female voices in these poems resemble 'The Shadow Doll', a mere replica of a bride, a protected image, locked in a vacuum. But the speaker is a poet, with her own recognised space, metaphorically represented as a room, and she reaches out to other women writers, trying to imagine 'the rooms of other women poets'. She knows that the literary and creative world has been male-dominated, but the gift has passed into her hands.

## Bright-Cut Irish Silver

I take it down
from time to time, to feel
the smooth path of silver
        meet the cicatrice of skill.

These scars, I tell myself, are learned.

This gift for wounding an artery of rock
was passed on from father to son,
        to the father
of the next son;

is an aptitude
for injuring earth
        while inferring it in curves and surfaces;

is this cold potency which has come,
by time and chance,

into my hands.

Boland's response to being marginalised as a woman poet is to explore alternative history. 'So much that matters, so much that is powerful and frail in human affairs seems to me, increasingly, to happen outside history: away from the texts and symmetries of an accepted expression. And, for that very reason, at a great risk of being edited out of the final account' (*Poetry Book Society Bulletin,* winter 1990).

Boland feels that significance is to be found in the margins of life also, that the unrecorded history of individuals is important too. And it is this alternative history that is the focus of the central section of the volume *Outside History*. In it she explores her own history, but this operates at both a personal and a universal level. Her own history can be read as a metaphor for the unrecorded female history of the nation. She explores her own personal history as a developing writer and poet. She is the young immature poet in 'The Achill Woman' who does not fully comprehend the significance of what she has experienced. She attempts to understand her developing self and to make connections between her present persona as a woman poet and her student past in 'A False Spring'. She is forging an identity as a woman poet in 'The Making of an Irish Goddess', and she is the suburban woman seeking to re-establish contact with her natural and cultural roots in 'White Hawthorn in the West of Ireland'. She finds real significance in moments of human experience, not in symbolic happening, in 'We Are Human History. We Are Not Natural History'. She feels trapped by time, and as a woman she is alienated from the male-dominated version of history in 'An Old Steel Engraving'. She feels powerless and unable to influence history in 'We Are Always Too Late'.

Many of the poems record a sense of incompleteness, such as 'A False Spring', which records the failure to find again her younger, student self and integrate that phase of her life with the embodied now. The lost cultural heritage, passed from mother to daughter but forgotten, is recorded in 'What We Lost'.

There is a keen sense of displacement in the poems. The au pair girls in 'In Exile' signify displaced woman, isolated by the barriers of language and by age and cultural differences. In the sequence we see Boland attempting to recover a sense of belonging and completeness by making connections with her personal history and her cultural history, but also by shedding the myth and the stereotyped image:

> out of myth into history I move to be
> part of that ordeal ...

The third section, 'Distances', focuses mostly on the past, the distant past of her childhood memories and the more recent past of occasional moments of insight. These memories are connected to the present as if the poet is at last achieving a kind of quiet wholeness in her life. She is linked to the past, to family, to moments of love and insight, even to the future, in 'What Love Intended', where she imagines herself coming back like a ghost to a radically altered suburb.

## 'In a Time of Violence'

*In a Time of Violence*, her seventh collection, was published in 1994. It is divided into three sections, the first of which is entitled 'Writing in a Time of Violence'. The poems in this section touch on specific national and historical issues and events, such as the Famine ('That the Science of Cartography is

Limited' and 'March 1, 1847. By the First Post'), agrarian violence and the Peep o' Day Boys ('The Death of Reason'), the Easter Rising ('The Dolls Museum in Dublin'), nineteenth-century women emigrants ('In a Bad Light') and language and nationality ('Beautiful Speech'). But each is examined from an interesting and unusual angle, such as the unsympathetic and insensitive view of the Famine from a woman of the ascendancy class in 'March 1, 1847. By the First Post'.

Many of the meditations are inspired by a visit to a museum or an exhibition. For example, the dress in a museum in St Louis featuring the work of Irish dressmakers sparked off thoughts of women's servitude in exile in the nineteenth century ('In a Bad Light'). But each event is re-created with authentic realism and each tale narrated with sympathy and affection. The poems offer fresh insights into old history as the poet focuses on the human experience behind these historical artefacts.

The poems in the second section, 'Legends', focus on women as mothers for the most part. The fierce protectiveness and the maternal side of women is portrayed in poems such as 'This Moment' and 'The Pomegranate'. Woman as mother is playing an age-old role and has universal significance. The ageing woman features in 'Moths', 'The Water Clock', and 'Legends'. Some of the poems stretch back to the poet's own mother and grandmother through remembrance of a particular skill ('The Parcel') or a link with an heirloom ('Lava Cameo'). Some, such as 'Legends', establish continuity with the next generation:

> Our children are our legends.
> You are mine. You have my name.
> My hair was once like yours.
> And the world
> is less bitter to me
> because you will re-tell the story.

The main work of the third section is the title poem, 'Anna Liffey'. It is, in the words of the author, 'about a river and a woman, about the destiny of water and my sense of growing older'. This section concludes with four poems examining the unsatisfactory portrayal of women in myth, art and literature. The idealised images and the stereotypes are false and suffocating.

She appeals for realism and release in 'A Woman Painted on a Leaf':

> This is not death. It is the terrible
> suspension of life.
>
> I want a poem
> I can grow old in. I want a poem I can die in.

## 'Object Lessons'

Her prose collection, *Object Lessons: The Life of the Woman and the Poet in Our Time*, appeared in 1995. In autobiographical mode, Boland traces her own development as a woman poet, recounts her search as a woman for some kind of arrangement with the male-dominated concept of the nation, and reviews the status of women in poetry and history.

MAIN VOLUMES OF POETRY

|  | Poems in this selection |
| --- | --- |
| *New Territory* (1967) | |
| *The War Horse* (1975) | 'The War Horse' |
| | 'The Famine Road' |
| | 'Child of Our Time' |
| *In Her Own Image* (1980) | |
| *Night Feed* (1982) | |
| *The Journey* (1982) | |
| *The Journey and Other Poems* (1986) | |
| *Selected Poems* (1989) | |
| *Outside History* (1990) | 'The Black Lace Fan My Mother Gave Me' |
| | 'The Shadow Doll' |
| | 'White Hawthorn in the West of Ireland' |
| | 'Outside History' |
| *In a Time of Violence* (1994) | 'This Moment' |
| | 'Love' |
| | 'The Pomegranate' |
| *Collected Poems* (1995) | |

# The War Horse

Text of poem: New Explorations Anthology page 400

THEMES AND ISSUES

The poem stems from an encounter with a roving horse and also the excerpt from *Object Lessons* (page 304), which occurred, coincidentally, during an upsurge of disruption and violence in Northern Ireland. The poet's response is a metaphor poem with political overtones. The horse became the poetic incarnation of all those statistics of violence and death that were pouring nightly from the television screens.

The poem operates on a number of levels of significance. At an immediate level it confronts the issue of violence. We notice the seeming casualness of it, the arbitrary nature of this violence: 'the clip, clop, casual | Iron of his shoes as he stamps death | Like a mint on the innocent coinage of earth.' The treatment of the violence may be metaphorical, yet there is an awareness of the reality of death and wanton injury, which is carried in the imagery. The beheaded crocus is 'one of the screamless dead', the uprooted vegetation 'like corpses, remote, crushed, mutilated', and the eaten leaf merely 'of distant interest like a maimed limb'. The ungainly and often directionless nature of violence is suggested in the motion of the animal as 'he stumbles on like a rumour of war'. The overtones of the language become more overtly political as the poem proceeds: the rose is 'expendable ... a volunteer'; and 'atavism', 'cause' and 'betrayed' are the verbal coinage of revolutionary groups.

Could we read this poem as reflecting a Southern view of the Northern conflict – a middle-class, slightly nationalist Southern view? The speaker feels threatened by the 'casual iron of his hooves', vulnerable with 'only a rose' to form 'a mere | Line of defence against him', and afterwards breathes a sigh of relief that this only partly understood phenomenon is gone:

> But we, we are safe, our unformed fear
> Of fierce commitment gone ...

Lack of interest in this intrusive violence is at first feigned by the speaker. Others pretend he isn't there, 'use the subterfuge | Of curtains.' Yet for all that danger and disruption the speaker faintly admires the beast:

> I lift the window, watch the ambling feather
> Of hock and fetlock ...

She is also slow to blame him: 'No great harm is done. | Only a leaf of our laurel hedge ...' But most significantly of all, at the end of the poem he stirs her race memory ('my blood is still | With atavism') of colonial injustice, English aggression, and the cycle of failed rebellions:

> Of burned countryside, illicit braid:
> A cause ruined before, a world betrayed.

The speaker's attitude to the animal is a complex one and is perhaps contradictory at times, incorporating fear, resentment and relief but also furtive admiration.

Examine what Boland has to say about political poetry in the extract from *Object Lessons* below (page 304).

So, on another level the poem demonstrates how history impinges on the domestic and the artistic, which are frail in comparison. We are made aware, forcefully, of how fragile the domestic is. Boland herself has described the tension in the poem as that of 'force against formality'. The race memory of fighting against imposed order is conjured up by the modern parallel of conflict in a suburban garden, where wild nature reasserts itself over humankind's attempts to tame it. And the speaker can empathise. The rebel is not far beneath the surface of the psyche, despite the suburban veneer.

'The War Horse' is among the first of Boland's poems of the suburbs. The irony is that suburbia was really designed as slumberland, but even in safe, leafy, middle-class dormer territory the 'rumour of war ... stumbles down our short street,' awakening age-old conflicts. Boland is legitimising suburbia as a place of real experience and insight, a fit location and subject matter for poetry.

'The War Horse' is a private 'coming to awareness' of public violence, an intimate 'thoughts inside the head' reflection on the theme. In this aspect it differs from the more public scrutiny of violence in 'The Famine Road' and 'Child of Our Time'.

These notions concerning the influence of history, the relationship between art and society and the search for meaning in suburbia become important and frequently examined issues in Boland's poetry.

FEATURES AND STYLE

## Versification

The poem is composed in open rhyming couplets. Unlike closed couplets, the sense here often runs from one couplet to the next. This gives a flowing rhythm, a fluid energy to the verse, which might be said to reflect the unpredictable energy and purpose of the horse. For example, the sequence of lines from 'I lift the window' to 'his snuffling head | Down', ending two couplets further on, must be read in one breath and might suggest the animal's forward momentum. Following that, the speaker's short gasp of relief ('He is gone') makes an effective contrast and also points up Boland's use of rhythm for effect.

The rhyming is very casual, composed of half-rhymes and off-rhymes for the most part: death – earth, fear – care, limb – climb, huge – subterfuge, street – wait, etc. This offhand casualness accords well with the beast's casual destruction.

## Sound effects

This poet is not deaf to the music of language. Everywhere there are echoes and internal rhymes: 'hock – fetlock', 'Blown from growth', 'fear | Of fierce', etc. The alliteration of 'stumbles down our short street' emphasises the ungainly movement in the confined space. The unobtrusive musical assonance of 'Then to breathe relief lean', with its long *e* sounds, effectively conveys the speaker's sense of release, of escape.

Sound effects are an integral part of the animal portraiture here. The onomatopoeia of 'breath hissing' and 'snuffling head' conveys the threatening unfamiliarity of this beast that has invaded the suburban garden.

## Imagery
The poet employs vivid graphic visual imagery, whether to convey fearsome destructive power ('Iron of his shoes ... stamps death') or beauty ('ambling feather I Of hock and fetlock'). Similes and metaphors are often striking and unusual: the torn leaf is 'Of distant interest like a maimed limb'; the broken crocus is 'one of the screamless dead'. These comparisons are very disturbing and have a nightmarish quality, which brings to consciousness the suppressed terrors that have been unleashed in the speaker by this violent visitation. Altogether the imagery and the language are vigorous and muscular, as befits the scene: 'stamps death I Like a mint'. Notice also the violence of the verbs: stamps, smashed, uprooted, stumble, etc.

## Boland's recollections on the origins and significance of the poem
This extract is taken from her prose collection *Object Lessons* (1995) (chapter 8):

> It was the early seventies, a time of violence in Northern Ireland. Our front room was a rectangle with white walls, hardly any furniture and a small television chanting deaths and statistics at teatime.
>
> It was also our first winter in the suburb. The weather was cold; the road was half finished. Each morning the fields on the Dublin hills appeared as slates of frost. At night the street lamps were too few. And the road itself ran out in a gloom of icy mud and builders' huts.
>
> One evening, at the time of the news, I came into the front room with a cup of coffee in my hand. I heard something at the front door. I set down the coffee, switched on the light and went to open the door.
>
> A large, dappled head – a surreal dismemberment in the dusk – swayed low on the doorstep, then attached itself back to a clumsy horse and clattered away. I went out and stood under the street lamp. I saw its hindquarters retreating, smudged by mist and darkness. I watched it disappear around a corner. The lamp above me hissed and flickered and finally came on fully.
>
> There was an explanation. It was almost certainly a travellers' horse with some memory of our road as a travelling site and our gardens as fields where it had grazed only recently. The memory withstood the surprises of its return, but not for long. It came back four or five times. Each time, as it was startled into retreat, its huge hooves did damage. Crocus bulbs were uprooted. Hedge seedlings were dragged up. Grass seeds were churned out of their place.

Some months later I began to write a poem. I called it 'The War Horse'. Its argument was gathered around the oppositions of force and formality. Of an intrusion of nature – the horse – menacing the decorous reductions of nature which were the gardens. And of the failure of language to describe such violence and resist it.

I wrote the poem slowly, adding each couplet with care. I was twenty-six years of age. At first, when it was finished, I looked at it with pleasure and wonder. It encompassed a real event. It entered a place in my life and moved beyond it. I was young enough to craft and want nothing more.

Gradually I changed my mind, although I never disowned the poem. In fact, my doubts were less about it than about my own first sense of its completeness. The poem had drawn me easily into the charm and strength of an apparently public stance. It had dramatised for me what I already suspected: that one part of the poem in every generation is ready to be communally written. To put it another way, there is a poem in each time that waits to be set down and is therefore instantly recognisable once it has been. It may contain sentiments of outrage or details of an occasion. It may invite a general reaction to some particular circumstance. It may appeal to anger or invite a common purpose.

It hardly matters. The point is that to write in that cursive and approved script can seem, for the unwary poet, a blessed lifting of the solitude and scepticism of the poet's life. Images are easily set down; a music of argument is suddenly revealed. Then a difficult pursuit becomes a swift movement. And finally the poem takes on a glamour of meaning against a background of public interest.

Historically – in the epic, in the elegy – this has been an enrichment. But in a country like Ireland, with a nationalist tradition, there are real dangers. In my poem the horse, the hills behind it – these were private emblems which almost immediately took on a communal reference against a background of communal suffering. In a time of violence it would be all too easy to write another poem, and another. To make a construct where the difficult 'I' of perception became the easier 'we' of subtle claim. Where an unearned power would be allowed by a public engagement.

In such a poem the poet would be the subject. The object might be a horse, a distance, a human suffering. It hardly mattered. The public authorisation would give such sanction to the poet and the object would not just be silent. It would be silenced. The subject would be all-powerful.

At that point I saw [that] in Ireland, with its national traditions, its bardic past, the confusion between the political poem and the public poem was a dangerous and inviting motif. It encouraged the subject of the poem to be a representative and the object to be ornamental. In such a relation, the dangerous and private registers of feeling of the true political poem would be truly lost. At the very moment when they were most needed.

And yet I had come out of the Irish tradition as a poet. I had opened the books, read the poems, believed the rhetoric when I was young. Writing the political poem seemed to me almost a franchise of the Irish poet, an inherited privilege. I would come to see that it was more and less than that, that like other parts of the poet's life, it would involve more of solitary scruple than communal eloquence. And yet one thing remained steady: I continued to believe that a reading of the energy and virtue of any tradition can be made by looking at the political poem in its time. At who writes it and why. At who can speak in the half-light between event and perception without their voices becoming shadows as Aeneas's rivals did in the underworld of the Sixth Book.

In that winter twilight, seeing the large, unruly horse scrape the crocus bulbs up in his hooves, making my own connections between power and order, I had ventured on my first political poem. I had seen my first political image. I had even understood the difficulties of writing it. What I had not realised was that I myself was a politic within the Irish poem: a young woman who had left the assured identity of a city and its poetic customs and who had started on a life which had no place in them. I had seen and weighed and struggled with the meaning of the horse, the dark night, the sounds of death from the television. I had been far less able to evaluate my own hand on a light switch, my own form backlit under a spluttering street light against the raw neighbourhood of a suburb. And yet without one evaluation the other was incomplete.

I would learn that it was far more difficult to make myself the political subject of my own poems than to see the metaphoric possibilities in front of me in a suburban dusk. The difficulty was a disguised blessing. It warned me away from facile definitions. The more I looked at the political poem, the more I saw how easy it was to make the claim and miss the connections. And I wanted to find them.

# The Famine Road

Text of poem: New Explorations Anthology page 402

## A READING OF THE POEM

Boland is drawing parallels between certain aspects of the famine experience and the experience of woman today. The famine road, symbol of purposeless, thwarted lives, is equated with female sterility. The supercilious treatment of the suffering people she sees as akin to the unfeeling arrogance meted out to the childless woman.

> You never will, never you know
> but take it well woman, grow
> your garden, keep house, goodbye.

Boland feels that being a woman gives her a unique perspective on Irish history, as she elaborated in response to the question, 'What does being Irish mean to you?'

> Apart from the fact that it connects me with a past, I find it a perspective on my womanhood as well. Womanhood and Irishness are metaphors for one another. There are resonances of humiliation, oppression and silence in both of them and I think you can understand one better by experiencing the other. [From the interview in *Sleeping with Monsters*]

If we explore the poem's comparison in detail we find that both the Irish in history and women in society are generalised about and so misunderstood: 'Idle as trout in light Colonel Jones | these Irish ...' The woman in the monologue is a mere faceless statistic ('one out of every ten ...'). Neither are treated rationally ('could they not ... suck | April hailstones for water and for food'). The cruel indifference of these people's treatment is linked to the nonchalant lack of medical explanation ('Anything may have caused it, spores ... one sees | day after day these mysteries'). Both groups are different, physically or mentally segregated, condemned to an isolated life or death.

> They know it and walk clear. He has become
> a typhoid pariah, his blood tainted, although
> he shares it with some there ...

> > Barren, never to know the load
> > of his child in you, what is your body
> > now if not a famine road?

Boland links this oppression and humiliation of the sterile woman with that of the famine people. Their blood too is wasted ('could I they not blood their knuckles on rock'). This image is an impotent echo of that authoritative gesture of Trevelyan's ('Trevelyan's I seal blooded the table') as they too put their seal on their work.

The following bleak humorous image conveys their humiliations, shows the primitive state to which they were reduced: 'cunning as housewives, each eyed – I as if at a corner butcher – the other's buttock.' Both woman and famine people are silent sufferers. Disenfranchised, they are allowed to make no contribution. The superior discussion is carried on above their heads and is quite dismissive: 'Might it be safe I Colonel, to give them roads,' and 'grow I your garden, keep house, goodbye.'

The lack of understanding, the unfeeling treatment, the callous oppression, the silent suffering, the feelings of humiliation, of uselessness, the pointlessness of it all, the sense of failure – these are the links between womanhood and Irishness in this poem.

# Child of Our Time

Text of poem: New Explorations Anthology page 406
[*Note: This poem is also prescribed for Ordinary Level 2005 exam*]

BACKGROUND NOTE

The poem was inspired by a press photograph showing a firefighter carrying a dead child out of the wreckage of the Dublin bombings in May 1974.

A READING OF THE POEM

First and foremost this is an elegy for the untimely death of a child. It bemoans the senselessness and irrationality of the child's slaughter in an act of public violence.

> This song, which takes from your final cry
> Its tune, from you unreasoned end its reason;
> Its rhythm from the discord of your murder ...

In the second stanza the keen sense of loss is encouraged by the mournful litany of the literary rituals of childhood, naming again the associations of intimate moments, the rituals around sleeping and waking:

> rhymes for your waking, rhythms for your sleep,
> Names for the animals you took to bed,
> Tales to distract, legends to protect ...

This sense of loss is compounded by guilt, in that it is the adults who should have been the guardians and guides of the child:

> We who should have known how to instruct
> With rhymes for your waking ...

The elegy finishes in a prayer that adult society will learn from this horror, expressed in the paradox 'And living, learn, must learn from you dead,' and so construct a better method of social interaction so that the death will not have been in vain ('find, for your sake whose life our idle | Talk has cost, a new language.') The poem is also a searing condemnation of violence. Society stands accused ('our times have robbed your cradle'), accused also of this barbarous irrationality ('your unreasoned end' ... 'the discord of your murder'). The only hope is that society would awaken to the reality of its actions and that the child might 'Sleep in a world your final sleep has woken.'

The poem could also be read as a comment on the failure of communication. The entire poem is couched in language terminology. It is a 'lullaby', a 'song', inspired by a 'final cry', a 'tune' with 'rhythms'. In the second stanza, loss is expressed in terms of language deprivation and child rearing seen in terms of language fostering: 'rhymes for your waking', etc. The only way forward from this conflict and violence is described as 'a new language'.

So the failure of language is associated with death and destruction. But language is the only bulwark against chaos, and this is the positive message of this bleak poem. Poetry, the most artistic expression of language, can be created out of this pain – this 'tune' from 'your final cry'. It signals a victory of order over chaos, reason 'from your unreasoned end', rhythm from 'discord'. It offers a chance to rebuild broken images and visualise a better society.

## FEELINGS

A delicate balance of emotions is achieved in this poem. The brutal reality of the killing is never denied, and the fact of death is faced squarely, as in 'And living, learn, must learn from you dead,' where the placing of the last word in the line gives it finality and emphasis. But the references to death are sometimes veiled in poetic terms: 'your final cry' and 'your final sleep'. Or they are intellectualised, as in 'the discord of your murder'. Here the aspect of death dwelt on is its discordance, its out-of-tuneness, the disharmony of death. Or the child's broken body is rendered as 'your broken image'. The inversion of the natural order of life and death, in the killing of a child, is expressed in the paradoxes 'from your final cry | Its tune,' 'from your unreasoned end its reason;' and 'Its rhythm from the discord of your murder'. Consideration of this death is poeticised or intellectualised to some degree.

But this is no anodyne reaction. Feelings of grief, loss, guilt and resolution to learn a better way are all conveyed. Yet there is a delicacy and gentleness to the mourning, made all the more poignant by the fact that the poem is a sort of final lullaby. So the slightly euphemistic treatment is appropriate. Death is a kind of sleep. 'Sleep in a world your final sleep has woken.' Altogether the poem seems to be an interesting combination of dirge and lullaby.

# The Black Lace Fan My Mother Gave Me
Text of poem: New Explorations Anthology page 408

A READING OF THE POEM

The poem focuses on courtship and deals with the messy and sometimes enigmatic relationship between the sexes. Just as the blackbird engages in its courtship ritual, human lovers too participate in a sort of courting dance.

> She was always early.
> He was late. That evening he was later.
>
> She ordered more coffee. She stood up.

The staccato rhythms of the verse here, created by the short sentences, draw attention to a choreographed sequence of movements, as a ritual to be played out. There is evidence too of disharmony, never the perfect entry together but rather of fretting and bad timing. If the weather is a barometer of the emotions, then the indications are of a stormy relationship, oppressive and explosive: 'stifling'; 'A starless drought made the nights stormy'; 'the distance smelled of rain and lightning'; 'An airless dusk before thunder.'

The fan is seen as a symbol of courtship, both with humans and in nature. It is a thing of beauty, associated with sensual allure, a romantic symbol. And so it functions here, but it also has darker associations of plunder and violation. The tortoiseshell has been pillaged from its natural habitat, killed off, and 'keeps … an inference of its violation.' As Boland herself saw it, 'as a sign not for triumph and acquisition but for suffering itself' (*Object Lessons*). It becomes a symbol of pain rather than an erotic sign. Still, in nature it retains its sensual overtone, 'the whole, full, flirtatious span of it.' So it carries these contradictory associations, reflecting the real-life complexity of the love relationship, not some stereotyped romantic image.

In other ways too it is an unusual love poem. There is no clear perception of the lovers, no clear recollection of the emotions, no detail of the moment:

> And no way to know what happened then –
> none at all – unless, of course, you improvise.

It is an oblique love poem that focuses on the love token that has lost much of its particular significance, yet is somehow still linked (by means of the blackbird) to their perennial courtship in nature. Its most positive statement is to assert the eternity of courtship, of love gestures. It makes no claims about eternal memories or the triumph of love against time. Rather the opposite, as the particulars of the emotional encounter are lost, eroded by time. Time erodes significance, and even cherished keepsakes lose their importance. There is emphasis also on the darker undertones of love, the tempests and the suffering.

## IMAGERY AND SYMBOLISM

The style of communication in this poem is somewhat oblique. Nothing is actually said: rather, we come gradually to apprehend the nuances and feelings. The core of meaning is communicated through the connotations of the images and symbols. And these images manage to transmit something of the complexity of the emotions and relations.

The fan itself, as the poet has mentioned, is not just an erotic object but also carries some notion of the violations of love, through the pain and plunder of its past. So the symbol deepens the understanding of love in the poem. The parallel image of the blackbird's wing restores some of the sensuality to the love symbol.

The tempestuous nature of the relationship is suggested in the weather imagery, as the atmosphere parallels the emotion: 'An airless dusk before thunder.' It is interesting too that all the references are to dusk or night, not the romantic kind but 'a stormless drought'. The poem explores more the darkness of the emotions than the starry insights of love.

## SOME IDEAS IN THE POEM

- The love relationship is mysterious, inaccessible to outsiders and to history.
- The sensual courtship gestures in a love affair are universal, common to humans and nature.
- But here the symbol of courtship is not just an erotic object, but also a sign of pain.
- What remains are the gestures; the particular emotions are forgotten, eroded by time.
- History and memory fail us in the search for truth: we are forced to invent.
- Yet nature remains flirtatious always.

# The Shadow Doll

Text of poem: New Explorations Anthology page 411

## A READING OF THE POEM

This poem has similarities with 'The Black Lace Fan My Mother Gave Me', in that it too uses a symbol to tease out some truths about the image of woman and the nature of the male–female relationship. We are offered the bride's perspective, a female insight on the wedding, which is portrayed in all its turmoil, an occasion 'to be survived'.

Boland uses the symbol of the doll to point up the discrepancy between the image of woman, particularly nineteenth-century woman, and the less glamorous reality. The manufactured image is elegant, in virginal white ('blooms from the ivory tulle'; 'oyster gleam', etc.), a model of discretion and sensitivity, devoid of sexual appetites ('discreet about | visits, fevers, quickenings and lust'), certainly too polite to talk about these taboo subjects. The reality is that of real-life emotional woman ('feeling satin rise and fall with the vows') and nervous repetition of vows amid the chaotic clutter of wedding preparations.

There may even be a slight envy of the doll's calmness; yet somehow the fevered reality is more appealing than the 'airless glamour' that is 'less than real', like the stephanotis. However, speaker and doll share a sense of confinement: the doll 'Under glass, under wraps,' the speaker restrained by vows and, like the suitcase, pressed down and locked.

## VIEWS OF WOMAN

- The false image versus the reality: the pure, asexual creature of 'airless glamour' is set against the emotional and physical turmoil of the reality.
- Oppressed woman is emphasised: woman confined, repressed, under glass, under vows, locked in.

## IMAGERY

The imagery mediates the theme very effectively. The delicacy of 'blooms from the ivory tulle' and the 'shell-tone spray of seed pearls' helps create the notion of frail beauty, elegant if bloodless. The unreality is reinforced by the flowers ('less than real | stephanotis'). The colours, too, help to create this lifeless perfection: ivory and oyster. And of course the symbolism of the doll, which is a mere replica, underlines the falsity of this image of woman. Both the glass dome and the locked case carry, in their different ways, suggestions of oppression, secrets to be locked away, lack of true freedom.

# White Hawthorn in the West of Ireland

Text of poem: New Explorations Anthology page 414

## A READING OF THE POEM

This is one of a group of poems from the volume *Outside History*, in which the poet is attempting to 'make connections' with her world – to establish continuity in her personal life, family traditions and lore, to find a working relationship with her cultural history and, here, to re-establish the age-old connection with the natural world.

In this poem she is going back to nature, fleeing 'suburban gardens. | Lawnmowers. Small talk.' This toy-house neatness and inconsequential chatter of suburbia is contrasted with the wild, uncultivated beauty, the primitiveness and the naturalness of life in the west:

> Under low skies, past splashes of coltsfoot,
> I assumed
> the hard shyness of Atlantic light
> and the superstitious aura of hawthorn.

She identifies immediately with the naturalness, is at home with the earth. Her enthusiasm is communicated in the energetic rhythms of the language, the flowing, run-on lines:

> All I wanted then was to fill my arms with
> sharp flowers,
> to seem, from a distance, to be part of
> that ivory, downhill rush. But I knew ...

Contrast this enthusiasm with the minimalist staccato phrases of lines 3 and 4: 'I left behind suburban gardens. | Lawnmowers. Small talk.'

The hawthorn is associated with supernatural forces, primitive beliefs, the strange sub-rational powers of the earth. The power underneath the ordinary benign face of nature fascinates the poet here. Like hawthorn, water has a gentle fluency combined with enormous power ('able | to re-define land'), a power that is usually veiled under the river's more usual appearance of a recreational amenity or a landscape bearing for lost travellers. Nature dominates all human exchange – 'the only language spoken in those parts.'

## THEMES

- The poem contrasts two ways of life, the 'cultivated' suburban versus the natural primitiveness of life in the country.
- The superiority of the natural is proclaimed, with its excitement and energy.

- This is an 'earth poem', exploring the power beneath the ordinary face of nature, the hidden sub-rational depths.
- It might also be read as a symbolic journey, of the deracinated poet, the suburban dweller, searching for her real roots – her roots understood in both a geographical and a metaphysical sense. She is searching for a place and also for a philosophy. The undefined time of year, the 'season between seasons', seems to point up the poet's sense of 'out-of-placeness,' her unsettled state of mind.

# Outside History

Text of poem: New Explorations Anthology page 416

A READING OF THE POEM

Boland rebelled against the mythicisation of Irish history: the songs, the ballads, the female icons of the nation, the romantic images. Myth obscures the reality, manipulates history. It is outside real lived history, a remote, unchanging image, a false construct.

Here Boland, as a poet, rejects myth in favour of real history as the proper authority for her poetry and her idea of nation.

The stars are symbolic of outsiders, remote and unreal, 'whose light happened | thousands of years | before our pain did'. Paradoxically, though they appear unchanging and are symbols of eternity, their illumination is thousands of years out of date when it reaches us. Ironically, it is the light that is an illusion: the darkness is real. The stars' unrelenting, cold, hard wintry light is shown in direct contrast to human vulnerability ('our pain'). The alternative to this remote, unchanging mythical framework for viewing life is the vantage point of human history, with its real suffering and mortality:

> Under them remains
> a place where you found
> you were human, and
> a landscape in which you know you are mortal.

It is necessary to choose between the two outlooks. Boland has chosen to move 'out of myth into history', to be part of the real pain and suffering of life. Only now does she begin to experience the real torment of lives endured by countless people throughout the years. In a nightmarish, Armageddon-type image suggestive of famine disaster ('roads clotted as | firmaments with the dead') she invites us in to comfort all the dying in history, real history:

> How slowly they die,
> as we kneel beside them, whisper in their ear.

The critic Jody Allen-Randolph has described it as follows: 'In a moment of power and dignity, the dead are finally allowed to die, however slowly and painfully, as both poet and audience move in to whisper the rite of contrition. Their deaths are not manipulated to serve any cause beyond their suffering which survives in the poem as a moment of collective grief.' It is a final laying to rest of the nationalist dead. But it is too late ('And we are too late. We are always too late'). This melancholic ending echoes an awareness of the suffering caused by this mythical view of history and realises that it cannot be undone fully.

# This Moment

Text of poem: New Explorations Anthology page 418
[Note: This poem is also prescribed for Ordinary Level 2005 exam]

A READING OF THE POEM

At one level this is a simple nature lyric celebrating the moment of dusk in the suburbs. The scene is filled with the usual furniture of a suburban evening: darkening trees, lighted windows, stars, moths, rinds, children, and mothers calling them in. It is a romantic evocation of suburban twilight, creating an atmosphere of calm, of continuing growth, ripeness and natural abundance: 'One window is yellow as butter ... Moths flutter | Apples sweeten in the dark.' Boland is celebrating the ordinary, having discovered that even banal suburban routines can stimulate the poetic in her.

Yet for all its outward ordinariness there is a hint of the mysterious:

> Things are getting ready
> to happen
> out of sight.

This might refer simply to nature's continuing growth in the secrecy of night ('Apples sweeten in the dark') or to some deeper significance of this scene.

Notice that the really significant part of the moment is the reuniting of mother and child. There is a subtle dramatic build-up to this, with intimations that something is being held back slightly: 'Things are getting ready | to happen ... But not yet.' The intervening images serve to heighten the wait for the finally revealed moment:

> A woman leans down to catch a child
> who has run into her arms
> this moment.

This stanza is emphasised by having the only significant activity in the poem: 'leans', 'to catch', 'runs'. With that activity 'this moment' has arrived. So the moment celebrated is maternal, a physical demonstration of the bond between mother and child, with all its connotation of love, security and protection.

The fact that this is happening everywhere, in suburbs all over the world, gives it a universal significance, lends a mythic quality to the gesture. The woman in the poem is connected to all women in history who must have performed a similar action.

So the poem is about dusk, a moment of transition in nature; but it is also about a universal moment in woman's experience: the confirmation of maternal love.

## IDEAS IN THE POEM

- The ordinary beauty and richness of nature at the mysterious hour of dusk
- That the suburbs can be poetic
- That significant moments are moments of human encounter
- A woman sharing in the universal experience of motherhood.

# *Love*

Text of poem: New Explorations Anthology page 420

## BACKGROUND NOTE

'Love' is one of a sequence of poems entitled 'Legends' that explores parallels between ancient myths and modern life. In some of the poems, such as 'Love' and 'The Pomegranate', the exploration of myth is used to deepen an understanding of woman as mother. Other poems explore themes of faithfulness, the creation of images of love, the fragility of all life, etc. In general, the point being made is that legends, myths and such stories point up the similarity of human experience throughout the ages and show a line of continuity from present days to ancient past.

Towards the end of the sequence Boland examines the end of this continuum line, her own family history, when she is prompted by personal memories or significant objects, such as an heirloom brooch or other keepsake.

In classical Greek and Roman mythology a number of the stories feature visits by the living to the underworld, Hades, the kingdom of the dead. So 'the hero' who 'crossed on his way to hell' might be the hero Odysseus, who conjured up the spirits of his dead companions by offering sacrifice on the banks of the river Ocean. But it is even more likely that the speaker refers to the story of Orpheus and Eurydice, a tale of the anguished separation of ardent lovers found in Virgil's fourth 'Georgic'. Orpheus went down into Hades to rescue his beloved Eurydice, who had been killed by a snake bite. His songs to her on his lyre had held all spellbound, and he was allowed to leave with her on condition that he did not look back. But

> He halts. Eurydice, his own is now on the lip of
> Daylight. Alas! he forgot. His purpose broke. He looked back.
> His labour was lost, the pact that he had made with the merciless king
> Annulled. Three times did thunder peal over the pool of Avernus
> 'Who', she cried, 'has doomed me to misery, who has doomed us?'

> Thus she spoke: and at once from his sight, like a wisp of smoke
> Thinned into air, was gone.
> Wildly he grasped at shadows, waiting to say much more,
> But she did not see him; nor would the ferryman of the Inferno
> Let him again cross the fen that lay between them.

The story goes on to chart the months of weeping and mourning suffered by Orpheus, wandering through caves and forests, where his sorrow touched even the wild animals and the trees. Boland uses the myth as a framework for exploring ideas of love and loss and the impossibility of recovering the passionate intensity of first love.

## LAYERS OF MEANING

As with many a Boland poem, this has a number of layers of significance. At one level it is a love poem, in which the speaker reflects on her present loving relationship with her husband but still yearns for the intensity of their early love, when they first lived in this American town with their young family many years before. But the speaker's thoughts are drawn continually to classical myths and legends, in which she finds experiences parallel to her own. She uses these mythical allusions to explore the infant's brush with death, the nature of her relationship with her husband, and her female consciousness and role. She identifies with the female voice in the myth, thereby establishing the continuity and importance of the female experience throughout the ages.

So this is a poem about love, about family, about female experience, and about the centrality of myth to our lives.

The poem has a number of overlapping time frames: present, recent past, and ancient time.

## THEMES AND ISSUES

### Love

Different facets of love are touched on in this poem. The passion and delicacy of first physical love is most keenly registered.

And we discovered there
love had the feather and muscle of wings
and had come to live with us,
a brother of fire and air.

The bird metaphor conveys the elemental nature, the naturalness, the strength and grace of love. Indeed there is an almost nostalgic yearning for the intensity of this early love: 'Will we ever live so intensely again?' etc. With great honesty she admits her need to cast her lover in a heroic mould, to see the beloved as hero. Here she is creating myths, manufacturing an image of love and lover, a classical hero in suburban America: 'I see you as a hero in a text ... with snow on the shoulders of your coat | and a car passing with its headlights on ... the image blazing and the edges gilded ...'   The love she speaks of in the present tense is described in terms of language – love seen as communication:

We love each other still ...
we speak plainly. We hear each other clearly.

Yet a problem is hinted at here. We have less than perfect communication:

But the words are shadows and you cannot hear me.
You walk away and I cannot follow.

The underlying mythical allusions augment this sense of failure, as they all deal with separation and loss and the creation of insufferable barriers between lovers. So the love between speaker and husband here carries connotations of failure, of unheard words.

She also deals with love in a family context, amid kitchen tables and threatened tragedy:

We had two infant children one of whom
was touched by death in this town
and spared;

This is the quiet familial love of the suffering mother who can only watch and wait.

## The significance of myth and legend
Human affairs are seen in the long tradition of history, even prehistory and mythology. Love, death, pain and separation are the universal human experience. The poet uses mythical allusions to create an awareness of the continuity of human experiences and to deepen an understanding of some of them. For example, the threatened loss of her child is explored through a parallel myth. The sense of loss, the separation of death, the awful failure of communication and the waste of life's opportunities are all evoked by reference to myth.

When the hero
was hailed by his comrades in hell
their mouths opened and their voices failed and
there is no knowing what they would have asked
about a life they had shared and lost.

Is the effect of this to distance and lessen the mother's anguish?

The experience of love is seen in the heroic terms of myth and legend, as we have seen: 'I see you as a hero in a text', etc. It is as if the ordinary, everyday reality of love is insufficient and there is a need for the heroic, the superhuman, the extraordinary quality of myth in human lives. She imagines the hero-husband edged with an aura like a god of mythology, though it is merely the effect of car headlights behind him – 'the image blazing and the edges gilded'.

But perhaps the most significant aspect of myth is that it allows the speaker to tap into female experience and the universal female voice.

## THE FEMALE VOICE

The secondary role of woman is much in evidence here, yielding precedence and importance to the male hero, viewing her partner as a 'hero in a text', etc. She is silent, voiceless, but longing 'to cry out the epic question | my dear companion'. She is the unheard voice of woman, throughout myth and history: 'But the words are shadows and you cannot hear me.'

Even her role as mother here is essentially powerless in the face of the threatened death of her infant. She adopts a passive, stoical attitude, as if life and death are completely in the hands of fate. The child 'was touched by death ... and spared ... Our child is healed.' Perhaps this episode could be seen as referring back to an earlier theme of Boland's in 'The Journey': the fears of women with sick children.

Overall, the poet is asserting the universality of female experience, whether it be in Ancient Greece and Rome or modern America, on the banks of the mythical river Styx or a bridge over the Iowa river. By identifying with female voices of myth, and particularly with that of the abandoned Eurydice in the last lines ('You walk away and I cannot follow'), she again registers the powerlessness of women.

## Imagery

The poem opens and closes with images of darkness and shadow. The prevailing darkness and Stygian gloom of the first stanza ('Dark falls ... Dusk has hidden the bridge ... hell') recurs in the final lines ('words are shadows'). So the poem is bracketed by gloom, which qualifies and balances the enthusiasm of the love theme. In contrast to this darkness, the hero is silhouetted in light ('the image blazing and the edges gilded'). So we get a very primal contrast of colours, reflecting love and death, good and evil. Family love and life are mediated in images of ordinary domesticity: an old apartment, a kitchen, an Amish table, a view. References to speech and dumbness abound. Death is pictured as voicelessness, love as plain speaking, and the failure of love as a failure of speech.

Perhaps the most exciting metaphor is that of love as a bird, communicating the natural energy and beauty of the emotion ('love had the feather and muscle of wings').

## Form
The poem is written in loose, non-rhyming stanzas, in which the natural rhythms of speech are employed to carry the reminiscences and the personal narrative. Might it be significant that the stanzas gradually diminish in size? The first three are of five or six lines, then one of five lines, three stanzas of four lines, and finally a two-line stanza to finish. Might this mirror the diminishing scope of love as treated in the poem?

# *The Pomegranate*
Text of poem: New Explorations Anthology page 422

A READING OF THE POEM
This poem deals with the value of myth to life, with the universal truth of legend. The poet explores this theme by recalling the interlinking of life and legend in her own experience.

She first encountered this particular legend when she was a child in exile in London, 'a city of fogs and strange consonants'. The story of separation and confinement in an alien world must have resonated powerfully with her own experience then. Another facet of the legend's theme, the mother's anguish for her lost child, struck a chord with the poet at a later stage in her life, when she 'walked out in a summer twilight | searching for my daughter at bed-time.' She also takes to heart one of the myth's bitter truths: the ravages of time and the seasons on nature and humankind.

> But I was Ceres then and I knew
> winter was in store for every leaf
> on every tree on that road.
> Was inescapable for each one we passed.
> And for me.

The legend assists the poet in understanding her daughter. Insights so gained vary from the startlingly banal fact that 'a child can be | hungry' to the deeper understanding that she must allow her daughter space, the freedom to grow up: 'I will say nothing.' The stories of legend are archetypal and run parallel to human experience in all ages, and it is a worthwhile experience, an enrichment, to move in and out of the different worlds and time zones through 'such beautiful rifts in time'.

The poem also explores the relationship between mother and daughter. It paints a picture of intimate moments, as the mother views the teenage clutter with eyes of love:

> My child asleep beside her teen magazines
> her can of Coke, her plate of uncut fruit.

The poet shares with Ceres that fierce maternal protectiveness. And moving through the beautiful rift in time, the images of Persephone and her own daughter fuse, and the poet's maternal instinct is to warn and protect the child then and the child now:

> I could warn her. There is still a chance
> The rain is cold. The road is flint coloured.
> The suburb has cars and cable television.
> The veiled stars are above ground.
> It is another world.

Yet she realises that the girl must experience the truth of the legend for herself, must be free to experience the temptation ('the papery flushed skin in her hand'), to make mistakes, to suffer pain. If the mother protects her too much the wisdom of the legend (the gift) will mean little: 'If I defer the grief I will diminish the gift.' And what better inheritance can a mother bequeath than the eternal wisdom of myth and legend?

> But what else
> can a mother give her daughter but such
> beautiful rifts in time?

ISSUES RAISED IN THE POEM

- The value of myth to life: how legend embodies universal truth, conveys vital understanding, and illuminates the present.
- The relationship between mother and daughter: the intensity of the bond, the fierce protectiveness, but also an awareness of the independence of the child and her need to experience life, truth, love and passion for herself.

IMAGERY

Some images are used in a symbolic way. The pomegranate, for instance, has mythological significance, a fruit sacred to the underworld, drawing those who eat it down into darkness. Here it fulfils a similar function, with overtones, perhaps, of sexual temptation.

> She will hold
> the papery flushed skin in her hand
> And to her lips.

Has the uncut fruit connotations also of the temptation and loss in the Garden of Eden? Is the mother attempting to protect her daughter from the griefs associated with sexuality?

Much of the imagery is of darkness, twilight, the underworld, etc.: 'hell', 'the cracking dusk of the underworld', 'a city of fogs', 'twilight', 'it is winter | and the stars are hidden', and 'The road is flint-coloured.' This motif of darkness is associated with both the legend and the poet's present experience and creates a somewhat bleak atmosphere. But it is a fitting setting for the poet's anxiety and the pain she suffers in conferring freedom on her daughter. The modern bedroom, if not 'a place of death' as in the legend, is still 'full of unshed tears'.


# Overview of the issues in this selection of Boland's poetry

## Boland's view of Irish history and the idea of nation

- Boland deals with the reality of Irish history, the familiar story of oppression, defeat and death ('The Famine Road'). The sense of national identity that comes across from 'The Famine Road' speaks of victimisation, being downtrodden and living out pointless lives: see also the suffering in 'Outside History'.
- Opposed to that view is the male-created myth, involving heroic struggle, battle and glorious defeat: see the image of the dying patriot immortalised by art in 'An Old Steel Engraving'. The woman poet feels excluded from that cultural tradition – 'One of us who turns away.'
- Boland resists this mythicisation of history, insists on the necessity of confronting the reality, facing the unburied dead of history and laying them to rest ('Outside History').
- She shows concern for the unrecorded history, for the significance of lives lived on the margins of history, away from the centre of power, far from the limelight of action. She mourns the forgotten lives in 'That the Science of Cartography is Limited'.

- In her prose writings Boland explores the idea of nation and the difficulties it produces for her as a woman poet.

> So it was with me. For this very reason, early on as a poet, certainly in my twenties, I realised that the Irish nation as an existing construct in Irish poetry was not available to me. I would not have been able to articulate it at that point, but at some preliminary level I already knew that the anguish and power of that woman's gesture on Achill, with its suggestive hinterland of pain, were not something I could predict or rely on in Irish poetry. There were glimpses here and there; sometimes more than that. But all too often, when I was searching for such an inclusion, what I found was a rhetoric of imagery which alienated me: a fusion of the national and the feminine which seemed to simplify both.
>
> It was not a comfortable realisation. There was nothing clear-cut about my feelings. I had tribal ambivalences and doubts, and even then I had an uneasy sense of the conflict which awaited me. On the one hand, I knew that as a poet I could not easily do without the idea of a nation. Poetry in every time draws on that reserve. On the other, I could not as a woman accept the nation formulated for me by Irish poetry and its traditions. At one point it even looked to me as if the whole thing might be made up of irreconcilable differences. At the very least it seemed to me that I was likely to remain an outsider in my own national literature, cut off from its archive, at a distance from its energy. Unless, that is, I could repossess it. This proposal is about that conflict and that repossession and about the fact that repossession itself is not a static or single act. Indeed, the argument which describes it may itself be no more than a part of it.

## VIOLENCE IN SOCIETY

- 'The War Horse' explores suburban, middle-class attitudes to political violence. It is really a psychological exploration of the theme 'how we respond to violence'.
- Race memory and the old antagonisms to English colonial rule still exist just beneath the surface ('The War Horse').
- The real human consequences of political violence are portrayed in 'Child of Our Time'. The poet acts as conscience of our society here.
- Violence is seen as the result of a failure of language, an inability to communicate ('Child of Our Time').

## THE SIGNIFICANCE OF MYTH

- In one sense myth is seen to play a positive and enabling role, even in modern life. It gives the poet a framework for exploring human truths such as themes of love and death ('Love'). The wisdom of myths enables her to deal sensitively with her growing daughter ('The Pomegranate'). Mythical stories demonstrate the universality of human experience. The poet sometimes feels part of this tradition by doing the ordinary things and so shares in the long history of woman's experience and becomes a part of myth or universal truth ('This Moment').

- But created images can be false, limiting and confining. Idealised or mythicised images of woman are fixed in time, unable to love, breed, sweat or grow old (see 'Time and Violence').
- Boland often challenges the image of woman in mythology (also in art and literature), particularly when it shows woman as marginalised, silenced, subservient to her husband the hero, as in 'Love'.
- History is laced with myths. The unreality, the coldness and the distance of myth from real lives is symbolised in the stars of 'Outside History'.

## THE EXPERIENCE OF BEING A WOMAN

Boland's strong feminine perspective lends an extra dimension of insight to all her themes. But she also considers specific issues relating to the portrayal and the treatment of women.

- The image versus the reality: 'The Shadow Doll' explores that false image of woman, specifically nineteenth-century woman, but it has universal relevance. The image is one of elegance, dignified control of emotions ('an airless glamour'), and suppressed sexuality ('discreet about | visits, fevers, quickenings and lust'). Women are forced to conform to a false image, repressed, metaphorically enclosed in glass, locked away ('The Shadow Doll').
- The image of woman in art, literature and mythology is often idealised or stereotyped. The mythological allusions in 'Love' conjure up an image of woman as powerless and silent, yearning in vain for a heroic love.
- The sufferings of woman are equated with the oppression of the nation ('The Famine Road').
- The traditional role of woman is validated in such poems as 'This Moment', which show woman as mother. That maternal gesture of catching the child in her arms is the key to the poem. The protectiveness of mothers features in 'The Pomegranate'. Also her wisdom is displayed in allowing the daughter freedom to learn for herself.
- Woman as lover features in 'The Black Lace Fan My Mother Gave Me' and 'Love'.
- Suburban woman features in many of the poems: e.g. 'The War Horse' and 'This Moment'.
- The puzzling relationship between men and women features in 'The Black

Lace Fan My Mother Gave Me': the mistimings, the tempests of love, the sensual allure. Love diminishes in time, like the importance of the fan. This makes an interesting alternative view to the blinkered one of idyllic romance.

- Boland challenges the patriarchal tradition of Irish poetry. In *Object Lessons* she elaborated on her objections to the images of woman in literature.

> The majority of Irish male poets depended on women as motifs in their poetry. They moved easily, deftly, as if by right among images of women in which I did not believe and of which I could not approve. The women in their poems were often passive, decorative, raised to emblematic status. This was especially true where the woman and the idea of the nation were mixed: where the nation became a woman and the woman took on a national posture.
>
> The trouble was [that] these images did good service as ornaments. In fact, they had a wide acceptance as ornaments by readers of Irish poetry. Women in such poems were frequently referred to approvingly as mythic, emblematic. But to me these passive and simplified women seemed a corruption. For they were not decorations, they were not ornaments. However distorted these images, they had their roots in a suffered truth.
>
> What had happened? How had the women of our past – the women of a long struggle and a terrible survival – undergone such a transformation? How had they suffered Irish history and rooted themselves in the speech and memory of the Achill woman, only to re-emerge in Irish poetry as fictive queens and national sibyls?
>
> The more I thought about it, the more uneasy I became. The wrath and grief of Irish history seemed to me, as it did to many, one of our true possessions. Women were part of that wrath, had endured that grief. It seemed to me a species of human insult that at the end of all, in certain Irish poems, they should become elements of style rather than aspects of truth.

## AGEING

- In the later poems, such as 'The Pomegranate', Boland is conscious, in a personal sense, of the ageing process.

## REPRESENTATION IN ART

- In other poems Boland is particularly concerned with the representation of women in painting.

- In all these areas explored – history, art and love – Boland is striving for truth and searching out the reality rather than the glittering image.

POETRY IN THE SUBURBS

- A good deal of her poetry is set in the suburbs, a setting not associated traditionally with poetic aspiration.
- The fragile nature of the beauty and order created in the suburbs is brought out in 'The War Horse'.
- The toy-house neatness of suburbia is no match for the wild, elemental attractions of nature in 'White Hawthorn in the West of Ireland'.
- In the later poems we encounter a romantic evocation of a suburban twilight ('This Moment'). Nature has colonised the suburbs ('Stars rise. | Moths flutter.' and 'One window is yellow as butter').
- But the real bleakness of the suburban street is not hidden: 'The rain is cold. The road is flint-coloured' ('The Pomegranate').

## Forging a personal understanding of Boland's poetry

Think about the following points and make notes for yourself or discuss them in groups.
1. On reading Boland, which poems do you particularly like?
2. On reading Boland, what were the main issues the poems raised for you?
3. What settings, colours and moods do you associate with Boland's poetry?
4. What general understanding of the poet did you form?
   - What is important in her life?
   - How does she see herself?
   - Is she a happy or a sad person? etc.
5. Did reading her poetry add anything to your understanding of Irish history? What, and in which poems?
6. Consider her thoughts on the treatment of women in society and in history. Do you consider that she makes an important contribution to feminist thinking?
7. What insights did she give you into suburban life?
8. Would you consider her a radical poet? Explain your views.
9. Why do you think we should read her poetry?
10. What aspects of Boland's poetry strike a chord with you: particular themes; settings; point of view on the world; the images she creates; the feeling and tones in the poems? What appeals to you?

## Questions

1. Outline three significant issues dealt with in the poetry of Eavan Boland. Explore, in detail, the poet's treatment of any one of these issues.
2. Do you find the poet's view of Irish history particularly bleak? Comment.
3. 'The attempt to shed the constricting husk of myth and enter the nightmare of history is an important theme in Boland's poetry' (R. Smith). Discuss.
4. 'Boland's poetry shows a consciousness of the sustaining power of cultural heritage, whether through primitive Irish superstition or classical mythology.' Discuss this statement in the light of the poems you have read.
5. 'Boland's poetry shows how idealised images of women need to be set beside the reality.' Discuss.
6. 'While she takes a feminist line, maternity and suburbia feature prominently in Boland's poetry.' Consider this statement in the light of at least two poems you have read.
7. 'The relationship between mother and daughter is an important preoccupation in Boland's' poetry.' Discuss, with reference to at least two of the poems you have read.
8. 'Boland is always conscious of the natural context in which human events occur.' Consider Boland as a nature poet.
9. 'Boland's imagination thrives in the shadows.' Would you agree?
10. 'Finding significant moments of human experience is the goal of much of Boland's poetry.' Discuss this statement, with reference to at least three poems.

# Bibliography

Allen-Randolph, Jody, 'Écriture féminine and the authorship of self in Eavan Boland's In Her Own Image', Colby Quarterly, vol. 27 (1991), 48–59.

Allen-Randolph, Jody, 'Private worlds, public realities: Eavan Boland's poetry, 1967–1990', Irish University Review, vol. 23 (1993), no. 1, 5–22.

Boyle Haberstroh, Patricia, Women Creating Women: Contemporary Irish Women Poets, Syracuse (NY): Syracuse University Press 1996, 59–92.

Dawe, Gerald, 'The suburban night: Eavan Boland, Paul Durcan and Thomas McCarthy' in Against Piety: Essays in Irish Poetry, Belfast: Lagan Press 1995, 169–93.

Denman, Peter, 'Ways of saying: Boland, Carson, McGuckian' in Poetry in Contemporary Irish Literature (Irish Literary Studies, 43), edited by Michael Kenneally, Gerrards Cross (Bucks): Colin Smythe 1995, 158–173.

Kiberd, Declan, Inventing Ireland, London: Jonathan Cape 1995.

Longley, Edna, 'From Cathleen to anorexia: the breakdown of Irelands' in A Dozen Lips, Dublin: Attic Press 1994, 162, 187.

McGuinness, Arthur, 'Hearth and history: poetry by contemporary Irish women poets' in *Cultural Contexts and Literary Idioms in Contemporary Irish Literature* (Irish Literary Studies, 31), edited by Michael Kenneally, Gerrards Cross (Bucks): Colin Smythe 1988, 197–220.

Mahoney, Rosemary, *Whoredom in Kimmage: Irish Women Coming of Age,* New York: Houghton Mifflin 1993.

Matthews, Steven, *Irish Poetry: Politics, History, Negotiation: The Evolving Debate, 1969 to the Present,* Basingstoke: Macmillan 1997.

Meaney, Geraldine, 'Sex and nation: women in Irish culture and politics' in *A Dozen Lips,* Dublin: Attic Press 1994, 188–204.

Ní Chuilleanáin, Eiléan (editor), *Irish Women: Image and Achievement,* Dublin: Arlen House 1985.

Roche, Anthony, and Allen-Randolph, Jody (editors), *Irish University Review Special Issue: Eavan Boland,* vol. 23, no. 1 (spring–summer 1993).

Ward, Margaret, 'The missing sex: putting women into Irish history' in *A Dozen Lips,* Dublin: Attic Press 1994, 205–24.

# *Ordinary Level,* 2005 EXAMINATION

## *Explanatory note*

Candidates taking the Ordinary (Pass) level exam in 2005 have a choice of questions when dealing with the prescribed poems. They can answer either (*a*) a question on one of the poems by a poet prescribed for Higher Level for the 2005 exam, or (*b*) a question from a list of other prescribed poems (i.e. the alternative poems discussed on pages 330–352).

(*a*) The poems by Higher level poets that may also be answered by Ordinary level candidates in the 2005 exam are as follows:

| | | | |
|---|---|---|---|
| **Wordsworth** | She dwelt among the untrodden ways (p.6)<br>It is a beauteous evening, calm and free (p.9)<br>Skating (extract from *The Prelude*) (p.11) | **Eliot** | Preludes (p.135)<br>Rannoch, by Glencoe (extract from *Landscapes IV*) (p.156) |
| | | **Kavanagh** | Shancoduff (p.180)<br>A Christmas Childhood (p.185) |
| **Dickinson** | 'Hope' is the thing with Feathers (p.45)<br>A narrow Fellow in the Grass (p.60) | **Heaney** | A Constable Calls (p.221)<br>The Skunk (p.224)<br>Field of Vision (p.234) |
| **Yeats** | The Lake Isle of Innisfree (p.86)<br>The Wild Swans at Coole (p.91)<br>Swift's Epitaph (p.114) | **Longley** | Last Requests (p.267)<br>An Amish Rug (p.271) |
| | | **Boland** | Child of Our Time (p.308)<br>This Moment (p.315) |

(*b*) The alternative poems that Ordinary level candidates sitting the exam in 2005 may choose to study instead are discussed on pages 330–352

CONTRIBUTORS

Carole Scully        John McCarthy
John G. Fahy        David Keogh
Bernard Connolly

## Robert Herrick
### *Whenas in silks my Julia goes*
Text of poem: New Explorations Anthology page 431

A READING OF THE POEM

The opening line of this poem immediately sets the scene for the reader. Herrick watches Julia, who is dressed in silken clothing, move about in front of him. However, despite her name being mentioned in the first line of the poem, we learn nothing more about her.

The following five lines are concerned with Herrick's reaction to what he sees, particularly the silk fabric. His thoughts are 'sweetly' filled with the 'liquifaction of her clothes'. His eyes are captivated by the 'brave vibration'. He is spellbound by the 'glittering'.

For Herrick, the image of Julia 'in silks' is a sensual and erotic one. However, the sensuality and eroticism do not come from Julia or the silken fabric, but rather from Herrick's perception of the fabric. In this way, they originate from within Herrick himself. It is Herrick's response to the silk that makes it sensual and erotic. He finds it erotically suggestive, arousing and full of sensual promise, while another may simply see it as a piece of cloth. So, in the first three lines, he is engulfed by the sensuality of the silk, likening it to liquid flowing smoothly and 'sweetly'. His own excitement increases in the second three lines, where the 'brave vibration' of the moving fabric sweeps over his internal being.

It is evident from such words and phrases as 'methinks', 'I cast mine eyes' and 'taketh me' that the emphasis of the poem is firmly placed on Herrick himself and his reactions. In this respect, Julia becomes little more than a shadowy object in the background, a mechanism to produce movement in the silken fabric.

THEME

Although at first this poem appears to be about Julia, in reality it focuses on Herrick's personal responses. He is attracted and aroused, not by any of Julia's unique features or qualities, nor by the fineness of the silken fabric; they are simply objects that trigger a series of reactions within him. Herrick finds the intensity of these reactions both enjoyable and disturbing.

## LANGUAGE

Herrick chooses his words carefully, so that the actual sounds of the words help to reinforce the images he creates. So, lines 2-3 are filled with the letters 'l' and 's' to suggest a sense of liquid. The very sounds of these letters help the reader to 'feel' something of the sensory quality of liquid. Similarly, the letters 't', 'i' and 'e' in the final line create brittle words that convey the sparkling, reflected light of the moving silk, encouraging the reader to 'see' the fabric.

Herrick uses rhyme in a similar way. The first three lines end in 'goes', 'flows' and 'clothes', all 'liquid' in their sounds, while the second three lines end with the shorter 'see', 'free' and 'me', echoing an increase in excitement and the 'brave vibration'.

By using these techniques, Herrick creates vivid images that help the reader to understand the sensual nature of his response.

## TONE

The tone of this poem is filled with a sense of tension. On the one hand, Herrick is attracted by, and clearly enjoys, the movement of the silk, using phrases such as 'how sweetly flows'. On the other, he seems to feel overwhelmed by the intensity and depth of his reaction. The final line: 'O how that glittering taketh me!' expresses his awareness that this is an irresistible and disturbingly uncontrollable response that consumes him.

# John Milton
# *When I Consider*

Text of poem: New Explorations Anthology page 436

## A READING OF THE POEM

In the octet of this sonnet Milton reflects on his blindness, and how his disability affects his performance of what God expects of him. Milton opens by describing his blindness in terms of light and money: 'When I consider how my light is spent'. He uses 'Talent' in the dual sense of a unit of money (referring to the 'Parable of the Talents') and as a faculty or sense. In essence the octet asks, 'Doth God exact day-labour, light deny'd'; does God expect the same productivity from him as would be expected from a fully sighted person?

In the sextet 'patience' answers 'that murmur' of complaint. 'God doth not need | Either man's work or his own gifts'. Acceptance of God's will is seen as the path to salvation: 'who best | Bear his milde yoak, they serve him best'. The majestic creator – 'his State | Is Kingly' – has a multitude of servants who are constantly in motion to do his bidding: 'Thousands at his bidding speed ...

without rest'. Milton's consolation is stated in the final line: 'They also serve who only stand and waite.' Christian resignation in the face of the will of God helps Milton to deal with his scrupulous conscience.

## IMAGERY

'Light' is used in the poem to represent the faculty of sight, 'day-labour' means the work potential of a sighted person, and 'light deny'd' refers to the condition of blindness.

Financial terminology is used to illustrate the 'Parable of the Talents'. Milton speaks of his light being 'spent' and a 'Talent ... Lodg'd with me ... and present I My true account'. The power and majesty of God is suggested by 'his State I Is Kingly'. This omnipotent figure does not require 'man's work'; acceptance of his will is described as 'his milde yoak'.

# Samuel Taylor Coleridge
# *The Rime of the Ancient Mariner (part IV)*
Text of the poem: New Explorations Anthology page 443

## A READING OF THE POEM

Part IV of the 'Rime of the Ancient Mariner' opens with the wedding guest in fear of the old sailor's appearance: 'I fear thee ... I fear thy skinny hand ... thy glittering eye'. The mariner assures him that he is not a ghost: 'This body dropt not down.' He describes, in the third stanza, his terrible loneliness and suffering: 'Alone, alone, all, all alone ... My soul in agony.' In the following stanza he describes 'That many men so beautiful!' who are all dead. The mariner feels guilt at his own survival: 'a thousand thousand slimy things I Lived on; and so did I.' His spiritual despair is suggested by his inability to pray: 'and made I My heart as dry as dust.' He closes his eyes so as not to see the disapproving looks of his shipmates: 'The look with which they looked on me I Had never passed away.' The mariner wishes he was dead, 'And yet I could not die.' It is the appearance of the water-snakes that marks a turning point for the mariner: 'I watched their rich attire: I Blue, glossy green, and velvet black'. The dormant heart of the sailor is touched: 'A spring of love gushed from my heart, I And I blessed them unaware'. In the final stanza there is a highly symbolic action – 'The Albatross fell off, and sank I Like lead into the sea.' By blessing the water-snakes the mariner has begun his spiritual regeneration.

## THE ROLE OF THE SUPERNATURAL

Supernatural events are at the centre of the poem's narrative; the killing of the albatross – 'a bird of good omen' – unleashes the sequence of events leading up to part IV of the poem. In the extract the mariner is surrounded by the bodies of his dead shipmates: 'Nor rot nor reek did they'. They still stare contemptuously at the mariner: 'The look with which they looked on me I Had never passed away.' The becalmed ship casts a ghastly supernatural shadow: 'The charmed water burnt alway I A still and awful red.' Overcome with the joy of watching living creatures, the mariner blesses them 'unaware'. He attributes this action to the work of 'my kind saint' and repeats, 'I blessed them unaware.' The final supernatural event in part IV is 'And from my neck so free I The Albatross fell off'. In the marginal gloss Coleridge wrote, *The spell begins to break.*

## THE BALLAD FORM

Coleridge uses the conventions of the ballad form and its idiom to create an architecture of poetic sound. The *ballad rhythm* gives the narrative drive and entices the reader into the poem – see lines 255–258, with the description of the moon. *Direct speech* is used dramatically: 'I fear thee, ancient Mariner! I I fear thy skinny hand!'. Coleridge varies the length of the lines to achieve particular effects. Look at the penultimate stanza, where six lines, instead of the usual four or five, describe the climactic moment of blessing the water-snakes. *Repetition* occurs for functional purposes as well as being part of the ballad format: 'And I blessed them unaware' (lines 277 and 279). *Assonance* combines with repetition to remarkable effect in 'Alone, alone, all, all alone, I Alone on a wide wide sea!' There is a primal *simplicity in the language* that reflects the elemental simplicity of the subject matter: 'The Albatross fell off, and sank I Like lead into the sea.' 'The Rime of the Ancient Mariner' retains the direct *storytelling*, characteristic of all ballads, but does so at greater length. Development of *character* and motivation is as *underdeveloped* and *superficial* as in the traditional form. Coleridge adds a depth of spirituality and symbolism that is more characteristic of the Romantic movement than the traditional ballad.

# William Carlos Williams
# *The Red Wheelbarrow*
Text of poem: New Explorations Anthology page 452

## A READING OF THE POEM

Williams opens his poem with four words describing his emotional reaction to the image that is at the centre of this piece: 'so much depends I upon'. He deliberately tries to convey to the reader a sense that this is an object of importance and significance in the world.

It comes as something of a surprise, then, that the image turns out to be that of a red wheelbarrow. There does not seem to be anything particularly important or significant about such an ordinary object.

However, it is this very surprise that Williams wants his readers to feel. The contrast between the expectations he created with the first four words and the reality of the image in the subsequent twelve words encourages us to go back and reassess our view of the red wheelbarrow. Williams expresses his appreciation of it in almost loving terms. He is grateful that the wheelbarrow exists as an object.

## THEME

Williams deliberately challenges the idea that everyday objects are unimportant. He believed that the reality of an object gave it importance, an importance that could touch the human heart. He wanted to capture this reality in his work: 'I was interested in discovering about life, I put down daily impressions. Certain poems are very real because I was touched by real things.' For Williams, familiarity should never breed contempt!

## STRUCTURE

Williams was determined to develop a style of poetry that was uniquely American. He sometimes called it 'a United Stateser way' of writing. Rather than use a poetic type of language, he decided to use the everyday speech of the American people to provide the rhythm in his poetry: 'The rhythmic pace was the pace of speech, an excited pace because I was excited when I wrote ...' In order to strengthen this sense of excitement Williams wrote in short lines.

He rejected other poetic devices such as rhyme and the use of capital letters at the beginning of each line of poetry, deciding that they were part of 'the old order which, to me, amounted to restriction.'

## IMAGERY

Above all, Williams wanted to achieve simplicity in his poetry: 'I try to say it straight, whatever is to be said.' For this reason, he avoided complicated imagery. In this poem the image of the wheelbarrow is conveyed vividly by his use of the words 'red' and 'glazed'. These two words make it easy for us to imagine the brightness of the wheelbarrow, a brightness that suggests the special importance of this everyday object. The vividness is further heightened by the contrast between the shining red wheelbarrow and the feathery whiteness of the chickens. Although he uses only twelve simple words to describe two uncomplicated images, Williams achieves an overall effect of depth and detail. It is as if we are there with him, looking out at the scene and suddenly appreciating the unique and special importance of that familiar red wheelbarrow.

# D.H. Lawrence
## *Piano*
Text of poem: New Explorations Anthology page 455

### A READING OF THE POEM

The poem opens quietly, 'Softly in the dusk', as a singer is performing. Childhood memories are called to mind as the poet sees a picture of himself as a child, sitting at his mother's feet as she plays the piano. Line four uses significant detail to suggest the mother's character: 'And pressing the small, poised feet of a mother who smiles as she sings.' She is presented as accomplished, 'poised' and warm – 'who smiles'. In stanza two the poet describes how he is overcome with nostalgia 'till the heart of me weeps to belong | To the old Sunday evenings at home'. Lawrence finds the memory so painful that it is 'In spite' of himself that the singing 'Betrays me back'. A cosy idyllic picture is painted: 'And hymns in the cosy parlour' with 'winter outside'. In the third stanza the poet describes that no matter how loudly the singer sings or the accompanist plays, the music of the present will always be lost as he is taken back to the past. He says, 'The glamour | Of childish days is upon me'. His control of his emotions is loosened: 'my manhood is cast | Down in the flood of remembrance'; there is a terrible intensity in his feelings of loss and grief: 'I weep like a child for the past.'

### SOUND EFFECTS

In this poem Lawrence achieves a verbal music, as the singing and accompaniment is reflected in the language. Assonance – 'Softly, in the dusk, a woman (echoing the u in dusk) is singing to me' – combines with a sibilant 's' to create a musical pattern. Rhyme enhances the musical effect: 'me – see, string – sings'. Sound echoes sense (onomatopeia) in the description of the piano sounds from the child's perspective: 'in the boom of the tingling strings'. The harshness of the contemporary singer's voice, when compared to the memory of the Sunday evening hymns as his mother played, is suggested by the choice of the word 'clamour'.

### A NOVELIST'S EYE IN CREATING SCENES AND SUGGESTING CHARACTER

Lawrence has the capacity to describe scenes vividly with an economy of detail. The opening line paints a highly atmospheric picture with the minimum of information: 'Softly, in the dusk, a woman is singing to me'. In the same stanza a family scene of great warmth and charm is described, as the deep love between mother and child is apparent: 'A child sitting under a piano . . . And pressing the small, poised feet of a mother who smiles and sings.' In these two lines Lawrence has portrayed his mother as a confident, accomplished woman who gave joy and love to her children. The second stanza has a strongly atmospheric description of Sunday evenings, singing hymns in 'the cosy parlour'. Physical cold on the outside – 'with winter outside' – serves to highlight the emotional warmth inside, with a loving family and a sense of religious certainty.

# Edwin Muir
## *The Horses*

Text of poem: New Explorations Anthology page 459

### A READING OF THE POEM

Muir quickly establishes the background to his poem in the opening three lines. There had been a 'seven days war' that, despite its brief duration, produced such a terrible effect on the world that it was put 'to sleep'.

Muir develops this concept of a sleeping world by describing the changes that occurred in the emotional lives of the ordinary people. They were catapulted into a state of shock, unable to communicate and haunted by a sense of terror: 'We listened to our breathing and were afraid.' Muir uses the vivid image of nations 'Curled blindly' in the foetal position, a recognized response for a traumatized person, to convey the extent of this terror. It is clear that the enormity of the war was such that those who survived it were forced, for their own sanity, to close down their emotional and psychological responses, to put these parts of their beings asleep. Even though time has passed, the people are still unable to cope with this worldwide emotional and psychological devastation, it 'confounds' them 'with its strangeness'.

In the aftermath of the 'seven days war' the world, as a whole, retreats away from the technology on which it had once depended. Muir unfolds a series of images that show the prewar machinery gradually becoming less relevant. The radios no longer work; the warships are useful only for transporting dead bodies; a plane crashes into the ocean; the tractors 'lie about our fields' unused. The world that was once filled with the humming of engines is now a silent one. This silence indicates that the world, too, has had to close down a part of its existence, to put it 'to sleep'.

The people come to regard machinery and technology as representing the 'old bad world' that had given birth to the war, the war that 'swallowed' their children. Radios had been used to circulate news of the war so, Muir tells us, even if they were once more 'to speak', they would be ignored because they would speak of a world the people 'would not have ... again.'

Into this sleeping world come 'the strange horses'. They signal their arrival with a cacophony of sound that shatters the world's silence. The 'distant tapping' grows into a 'deepening drumming' and then into a 'hollow thunder'.

They move with a noisy energy that frightens the people who have become used to listening to their own breathing. Nevertheless, the horses stir up old memories, leading the people to recall the way in which the technology of the prewar world had totally changed the lives of the horses. The horses had been willingly sacrificed to 'buy new tractors', just as the human children had been sacrificed in 'one great gulp'. Muir makes a clear contrast between the vibrancy and strength of the horses and the lifeless tractors that lie like 'dank sea-monsters', to emphasize how this movement towards technology had been a grave error.

Gradually, the horses reawaken the sleeping people. Images of 'fabulous steeds' and 'knights' fill the minds that had been shocked into closing down. The horses offer a 'long-lost archaic companionship' that warms emotions for so long repressed. They bring with them a way of connecting with the life that the people once had, before technology and machinery took over. The horses carry something of the purity of 'Eden', the perfect world that God created for Adam and Eve. They remind the people that there is a life-force that will persist even in the 'wilderness of the broken world'. In this way, the arrival of the horses changes everything and signals a 'beginning'.

## IMAGERY

Muir uses a series of vivid images to convey the world that has been brought about by the 'seven days war', and to help the reader to share in the emotions felt by the people who experience it. There is real horror in the image of the children being 'swallowed' in 'one great gulp', and a terrible sadness in the 'nations' huddled like terrified babies.

He conveys the energy and the healing power of the horses with a series of extremely effective images. They engulf the people like 'a wild wave', washing away the effects of the war. They enable the people to break away from a world of inescapable drudgery, suggested by the 'oxen' with the 'rusty ploughs'. The image of the 'half-a-dozen colts' being born in 'some wilderness of the broken world' captures the unyielding urge of the horses to survive, and it is this that inspires wonder and hope in the people.

## TONE

Muir controls the tone of this poem with great skill. His conversational tone creates a great sense of immediacy, as if we are actually talking to a survivor of a terrible war.

The emotions of the speaker are raw and real, as with the resignation in the line 'By then we had made our covenant with silence', and the desperate determination filling 'We would not listen' and 'We would not have it again.'

After the arrival of the horses the tone changes to one of hope: 'Our life is changed; their coming our beginning.'

# Louis MacNeice
## *Autobiography*
Text of poem: New Explorations Anthology page 473

For this poem to have any real effect it must be read aloud. Louis MacNeice has written some of the most multifaceted poems written in the twentieth century. 'Autumn Journal' is a sprawling yet controlled masterpiece that chronicles life in 1930s Europe like no other. Its language and rhythm are complex and masterful. The poem, however, seems very simple;  but its simplicity can be underestimated. One must ask why he chooses such a simple, understated style.

The answer comes in the first line. This poem, this story of his life is set in his childhood. So he has decided to give voice to the child that he was. There is no room for complex voices and rhythms in the minds of children, and it is that state of mind that he wishes to convey. From the evidence in the poem, this mind seems to be frustrated, confused and afraid.

The first two lines give some of the few positive images in the poem. The simple rhyme between 'green' and 'seen' adds to the childlike atmosphere in the poem. The openness suggested by nature and the idea of variety might give an early impression that this place is one that is worth remembering. We soon see that it may not be.

When the chorus comes in, it is in italics; it feels as though it should be whispered, but with menace. There is an ultimatum in the threat that was made. The word 'never' seems particularly harsh.

When the poet brings in the father, he too seems harsh. The manner of his approach is very definitive. It is clear to the child that there is something wrong with the father, and in particular the way in which:

> He wore his collar the wrong way round.

The mother is different. She is remembered in terms of brightness, with a reassuring 'yellow dress', and because of  the contrast between his father – who 'made the walls resound' – and her attitude of 'Gently, gently, gentleness.'

The four stanzas that follow are all negative. Their colours are bleak with 'the dark ... talking to the dead' and the 'lamp was dark' and 'the black dreams'; again these are in contrast to his mother's 'yellow dress'. There is a vacuum instead of hope. Nobody listens to this child except to issue the repeated ultimatum. The child seems to be haunted by 'silent terror' and then neglected.

When the child becomes old enough we see that he has had enough:

I got up; the chilly sun
Saw me walk away alone.

The sun that is looking over him with a fresh start, like at the beginning of a new day, represents the yellow of his mother's dress. This time when the chorus is thrown at him he is more defiant; he seems to take it as an opportunity not to return.

# Dylan Thomas
## *Do Not Go Gentle Into That Good Night*
Text of poem: New Explorations Anthology page 478

### A READING OF THE POEM

Dylan Thomas wrote this poem about his father's impending death. The poem uses a fusion of imagery and sound to suggest how the poet feels.

In line one Thomas uses the imperative, as he appeals to his father not to embrace death too readily. Death is represented as 'that good night'. He asserts that 'Old age should ... rage against the dying of the light' – another symbol of the extinction of life. It may also be significant that Thomas's father went blind as his health failed. The second stanza reflects on the fact that sensible men know that death is inevitable and that it must be accepted: 'know dark is right', but still cannot practise what they preach. Thomas uses the dramatic enigmatic image of 'forked no lightning' to represent how this accepted wisdom does not inspire real resignation. The image of not going 'gentle into that good night' is repeated as a refrain reiterating the poet's appeal to his father. Stanza three refers to how good men at the end, 'the last wave by', conscious of the good they might do – 'how bright | Their frail deeds might have danced in a green bay' – would not willingly embrace death, which is once again symbolised as 'the dying of the light'. In stanza four Thomas describes how 'Wild men', who lived life with great intensity – 'who caught and sang the sun in flight' – and become aware 'too late' of their reckless ways, also do not go easily into the 'good night' of death. In stanza five Thomas puns on 'Grave men' who paradoxically see with 'blinding sight', and whose 'Blind eyes could blaze like meteors'. These men too 'rage against the dying of the light.' In the final stanza Thomas reaches a pitch of even greater emotional intensity, as he prays for his father: 'And you, my father,' to 'Curse, bless, me now with your fierce tears'. The stanza is extended to accommodate both refrains in a remarkably passionate conclusion.

## Use of Sound Effects

Dylan Thomas uses the sound of the language to suggest the dramatic intensity of his emotions.

*Alliteration:* The repetition of 'g' and 't' sounds adds to intricate patterns of sound in line one, 'Do not go gentle into that good night.'

Alliteration is used for emphasis throughout the poem: 'deeds ... danced' and 'blind ... blaze'.

*Assonance:* Verbal music is created with the patterns of repeated vowel sound in the poem; 'age | rave | day', 'dying | light' and 'Blind eyes ... like ... blaze ... gay'.

*Rhyme:* The first and final line in each stanza rhyme. In an unusual rhyme pattern the second lines of each stanza rhyme: 'day | they | bay | way | gay | pray'.

*Repetition:* Lines and phrases are repeated to achieve a chant-like effect (lines 1, 6, 12 and 18 are identical, as are lines 3, 9, 15 and 19).

*Colloquialisms:* The choice of 'gentle' rather than the more grammatical adverb 'gently' reflects a colloquial quality that is often present in the work of Dylan Thomas.

*Antithesis:* 'Curse, bless' is an example of opposite ideas being placed side by side to express the intensity and conflicting nature of the poet's overwrought emotions.

*Puns:* 'Grave men' has a black humour that is unexpected, given the poem's theme.

*Paradox:* 'See with blinding sight' is an apparent contradiction that highlights the clarity of thought of those who are near death.

## Imagery

Many of the images Dylan Thomas uses cannot easily be paraphrased, but have immense powers of suggestion. The central images of 'that good night' and 'the dying of the light' are immediately comprehensible, but 'have forked no lightning' and 'how bright | Their frail deeds might have danced in a green bay' are more problematic. These two metaphors are drawn from the natural world and testify to the poet's imaginative vision and sensibility.

It is the interplay of symbolism and language that give the poetry of Dylan Thomas its unique appeal.

# Denise Levertov
## *What Were They Like?*
Text of poem from New Explorations Anthology page 486

This is a direct, angry, political poem about the Vietnam War. The poet sets up a question-and-answer session. Six questions are asked, and then later they are answered. The tension is felt all through the poem. There is a boiling anger, yet the speaker in the poem is trying her best to be reserved and cautious.

The questions come first, and seem to be coming from an anthropologist who is trying to find information about a lost society. They seem to be harmless, but when they are balanced by the answers their significance becomes obvious. The questions refer to innocuous items like 'lanterns of stone', 'opening of buds', 'laughter', 'ornament', 'poetry' and 'speech and singing'. But when we hear the tenor of the responses, we know these things to be very important indeed.

In the first answer, the speaker turns the metaphor of stone from referring to their lanterns to referring to their hearts. In fact the thought of even asking about lanterns seems anathema to the speaker. She implies that it cannot matter about light when you have no heart.

Next she explains that without life or the beginnings of life there was no place for flowering beauty, never mind celebrations of that. The third answer is perhaps the most terrifying and bleak: yet also the plainest.

> Sir, laughter is bitter to the burned mouth.

It is obvious from the fourth answer that ornament is only an afterthought, when you consider that the people barely had bodies to put the ornament on.

In the fifth answer she explains that the victors often write history. There is nothing in these people's immediate history that they would want to celebrate. Even Nature was destroyed for them. They could not look in pools of water and see themselves any longer. Their language had been reduced to the language of the panicked:

> When bombs smashed those mirrors
> there was time only to scream.

Again, the speaker tells us that singing can no longer be heard from these people, who have been frightened into silence. She gives us the most beautiful image in the poem when she tells us that when they did sing 'their singing resembled | the flight of moths in moonlight.' This encapsulates the great, unified beauty that they were once capable of. She reminds us then of the fact that all that beauty is now irrelevant, for there is nothing left to see or hear.

This is a hauntingly powerful poem that tells the story of a forgotten people.

# Elizabeth Jennings
## *One Flesh*
Text of poem: New Explorations Anthology p.491

This poem is a meditation by the poet on her parents and their relationship. She examines her parents in old age and ponders on whether or not they were always like this. To do so, she ponders on them in bed.

The poet goes straight into the poem; immediately the parents are presented as being in two beds in the same room, the father reading to himself and the mother tossing and turning. They are both trying to get to sleep. They have come to a pragmatic arrangement to facilitate this. Their sleeping apart should mean that they will sleep more easily, but it doesn't work. Instead they both lie in silence and 'it is as if they wait | Some new event:'.

The poet does not comprehend how her parents can have drifted so far apart, 'like flotsam from a former passion'. She is fascinated by the way 'They hardly ever touch' and finds that if they do, it is done with hesitancy and fear. The parents' lives seem to have come full circle. They have returned to the chaste lives that they may have had before they were married.

In the last verse the poet points out the contradiction in the parents' relationship, and sees that they are:

> Strangely apart, yet strangely close together,

She sees that the silence is their way of communicating now that they are ageing slowly but surely, like 'a feather touching them gently'. Finally the poet comes to the conclusion that they may not even be conscious of the differences that are coming into their relationship; they may not be fully aware that:

> These two who are my father and my mother
> Whose fire from which I came, has now grown cold?

This may seem at first like a rhetorical question, but perhaps it is not. The poet may genuinely not know how her parents, who were once in love, can seemingly have fallen out of love – especially since they are still together.


# Thomas Kinsella
## *Mirror in February*
Text of poem: New Explorations Anthology page 496

### A READING OF THE POEM

The poem opens abruptly with the dull alliteration of 'The day dawns ...'; there is staleness apparent: 'scent of must and rain'. In the bedroom where the poet is standing the air is dry, and 'Under the fading lamp' suggests a generally lethargic atmosphere. The details the poet gives regarding his appearance are unflattering: 'a dark exhausted eye, | A dry downturning mouth'. The second stanza moves from description to reflection: 'Now plainly in the mirror of my soul'. Kinsella considers the processes of growth and decay 'In this untiring, crumbling place of growth', and sees 'that I have looked my last on youth'. He is aware of the inevitable decline he is now facing and compares himself to Christ: '... they are not made whole | That reach the age of Christ.' In the final stanza the poet uses the trees in the garden as a metaphor to represent the ravages of time. He reflects in highly dramatic language on how the trees have been trimmed and pruned: 'hacked clean', suffering 'brute necessities'. He asks rhetorically, 'And how should the flesh not quail that span for span | Is mutilated more?' He recoils from this physical decay, this mutilation 'in slow distaste'. The mood changes as Kinsella displays his resignation by the gesture of folding the towel 'with what grace I can'. He faces up to the difficult realities of life with an assertion of basic human dignity: 'Not young and not renewable, but man'.

## A DRAMATIC POEM

Kinsella dramatises a moment of psychological insight in this poem. The act of physically looking in the mirror represents the poet's assessment of his life, as he has looked his last on youth. Kinsella's use of the present tense throughout the poem adds a sense of immediacy: 'The day dawns ...', 'my brain ...', 'idling ...', I read ...', 'I fold'. He uses the scene in his garden to reflect on the process of ageing and uses language dramatically, with alliteration: 'Hacked clean for better bearing', and chooses words like 'brute ... defaced' and most striking of all, 'mutilated'. The poem concludes with a gesture expressing the poet's acceptance of his mortality and his resolve to move on: 'I fold the towel with what grace I can, | Not young and not renewable, but man.'

## IMAGERY

Kinsella suggests his state of mind using the description of the morning bedroom scene with its 'scent of must and rain', 'dry bedroom air', 'fading lamp'. Details of the poet's appearance suggest a generalised exhaustion and depressed mood: 'a dark exhausted eye, | A dry downturning mouth'. It is only in the second stanza that Kinsella states how he feels and what he is thinking about. The natural processes of growth and decay are referred to in the paradoxical metaphor of 'this untiring crumbling place of growth'. His moment of self-realisation is encapsulated in the central image of the poem, 'Now plainly in the mirror of my soul'. Kinsella's reference to his age, that of Christ, has associations with crucifixion and suffering: 'for they are not made whole | That reach the age of Christ.' The trees in the final stanza represent the suffering associated with ageing and the pain of life's events. Mankind's suffering is worse as the 'flesh ... span for span I Is mutilated more'. There may well be a spiritual significance in the 'grace' with which the towel is folded in the final two lines. This physical action completes the morning's routines in the bathroom, and is a symbol of resignation and the poet's getting on with life.

# U. A. Fanthorpe
# *Growing Up*
Text of poem: New Explorations Anthology page 501

## A READING OF THE POEM
Growing up was a difficult process for U. A. Fanthorpe, and in this poem she traces her feelings of alienation at the various stages in her life. Babyhood is described in the first stanza: 'I wasn't good I At being a baby.' She learned to conceal her feelings and perspective on the world at an early age: 'Masking by instinct how much I knew I Of the senior world'. Her refusal to conform to the stereotypical norms of infant behaviour is demonstrated humorously in 'Shoplifting daintily into my pram'.

As a child she realised that she did not fit in with children: 'Children, I Being childish, were beneath me'; nor with adults: 'Adults I despised or distrusted.' Grown-ups considered her *'Precocious, naïve'*; her defence was 'to be surly'.

Adolescence made her feel even more 'out of step'. Her physical development 'nudging me ... To join the party', she found puberty especially traumatic, 'With hairy, fleshy growths and monthly outbursts'. Her feelings are powerfully summed up in 'Was caught bloody-thighed, a criminal I Guilty of puberty.' Emily Dickinson was her role model; she admired her for being 'intransigent' and because she 'Never told anyone anything'.

In the fourth stanza she relates how difficult she found social interaction: 'Never learned I The natives' art of life.' She developed a strategy for social survival by staying 'mute', except for 'the hard-learned arcane litany I Of cliché'. She concludes that she was 'Not a nice person'.

There is a change of mood in the final stanza, even though the art of social life is still mysterious: 'Masonic', she has found 'A vocation even for wallflowers.' She observes 'the effortless bravura I Of other people's lives'. Fanthorpe cannot take for granted what she describes in the simile 'like well-oiled bolts, I Swiftly and sweet, they slot into the grooves I Their ancestors smoothed out along the grain.' Her feelings of alienation are lifelong, but she has found a niche as an observer of other people's lives.

Fanthorpe's style is conversational – 'I wasn't good | At growing up' – and direct. She manipulates sound cleverly, as her use of alliteration for emphasis testifies: 'Called to be connoisseur, I collect'. The smoothness of other people's lives is suggested by the 's' sounds in 'Swiftly and sweet, they slot into the grooves'. Fanthorpe has a mischievous sense of humour: 'Biting my rattle, my brother (in private), | Shoplifting daintily into my pram.' Her images are drawn from the familiar world: 'cliché, my company passport', and the 'well-oiled bolt'. Her allusion to 'Emily' tells much about her own character and the qualities she aspires to: 'intransigent ... Struggled to die on her feet ... Never told anyone anything.'

# Brendan Kennelly
# *Night Drive*

Text of poem: New Explorations Anthology page 514

This poem describes a journey. The journey is obviously a painful one. The poet and Alan, possibly his brother, are going to see their father, who is on his deathbed. The poem is in three parts. The first deals with the journey to the father. The second, shortest piece is spent with the father. The final part is the journey home. The poem is a mixture of narrative and dialogue. Kennelly deals with the drama of the situation expertly. While the poem deals with his father's imminent death, it spends little time with the father physically present, yet the father is a spectral presence all the way through. He is the reason for the journey.

The first section describes the frustration felt by the brothers as they make their journey 'Along the road to Limerick'. The conditions are obviously awful and while Alan tries to make conversation, the poet is rendered speechless by the thoughts of what is to face him when he reaches his destination. Kennelly animates the horrendous weather conditions. The rain 'hammered' and it is 'Lashing the glass'. The wind's swirling motion is detailed by showing it to have a fist that 'seemed to lift the car | And pitch it hard against the ditch.'

The sense of doom is continued with the description of the violence of the river that is 'A boiling madhouse roaring for its life'. It is ripping the countryside to shreds and is described as 'insane' and 'murderous'.

'Nature gone mad' as a theme repeats in this poem. It is seen at its most vivid in the scene with the frogs. The frogs have left their haven in the swamps and fields that have become too wild and flooded for them to cope with. They are forced onto the road, where they are being squashed beneath the tyres of cars. Like the poet and his brother they have become 'Bewildered refugees, gorged with terror.' The people have no choice but to go on their journey, which means that they have to contribute to the slaughter of the frogs. They are forced to focus on the task of going to see their dying father and do not have time to comment on the 'Carnage of broken frogs.' Their focus is made obvious by the line where Alan asks himself: '"How is he now?"'

Where there was a fierce unflappable energy in the first section, there is calm in the second. The serenity is heightened by the image of the pillow and the 'white hospital bed'. The contrast is striking. In both cases there is a determination not to let the ravages of nature get in the way. Where the brothers in the car were not going to let nature get in their way and fought against it and succeeded, their father also tries to fight back the inevitable and succeeds temporarily. However, it seems clear that whatever small battle he may win, the war is beyond him. This is seen when it has reduced his ability to 'rail against the weather'.

The third section allows time for reflection. Darkness returns in the last section. The brothers have been made sombre by their experience and death is the first thing to greet them as they make their journey home. Alan is distracted by having to focus on his driving and does not have as much room to contemplate as his brother does. Alan shows optimism when he suggests; '"I think he might pull through now."'

On the other hand, Nature has left the poet in more pessimistic mode as he is haunted: 'In the suffocating darkness | I heard the heavy breathing | Of my father's pain.'

Nature has become too much for him.


# Roger McGough
## *Let Me Die a Young Man's Death*
Text of poem: New Explorations Anthology page 518

This is a witty look at mortality, and more specifically how the poet wants to live rather than die. Immediately he dismisses the traditional poetic way of dying, where somebody goes silently and makes their last prophetic pronouncement before 'popping their clogs'. He uses clever rhyme in the last line to stretch the line, so that the reader is just out of breath when they get to say the phrase 'peaceful out of breath death'.

He then gives comic instances of the way he'd like to go. He uses a clever pun on the rhyme between tumour and humour. So at 73 he wants to die quickly from a bit of flash exuberance. He even insists on being on his 'way home | from an allnight party.'

At 91 he imagines himself in a Mafia film like *The Godfather* or *Goodfellas*, when all of a sudden he is shot down. Again he uses a spectacular moment to describe the way he'd like to go. He also puns on the idea that he would be having a haircut, with the manner of his death being to 'give me a short back and insides'.

At 104, if he survives the 'tommyguns' and the 'bright red sports car', he plans to be murdered by his mistress. Not only does he plan to be lively enough to have a mistress, he plans to be caught 'in bed with her daughter'. After he is cut 'up into little pieces', he thinks that his mistress will want one part of him. He doesn't tell us which part this may be but he leaves us to guess ...

In the first verse he tells us how he doesn't want to go. In the next three he tells us how he wants to die. In the final verse he again reminds us of his original message. He insists that there should be nothing sacred about his demise. Above all, he doesn't want people to say, 'What a nice way to go'; it is clear from the previous verses that he is more interested in making a big splash on his way out.

# Eamonn Grennan
## *Daughter and Dying Fish*
Text of poem: New Explorations Anthology page 520

In this poem Grennan describes the death of dogfish and his daughter's innocent non-reaction to it. The poem is a good example of how a poet can use sound to convey what he wants almost as much as he can use the words themselves. This is never more obvious than when the poet dominates the poem with alliterative 's' sounds. They almost smother the poem, resonating with the sliding along of the fish as they contort their way towards death.

Take the third stanza as an example:

> sliding the slow length of one another
> as spines stiffen, scales shimmer, glaucous
> sea-eyes pop with shock and resignation.

The reader can feel the water slurp around as the fish splashes against the rock pools. It is a worthwhile exercise to trace the 's' sounds all the way through this poem and to notice how dominant they are in each stanza.

The first three stanzas just show the fish as they lie, about to die. The poet describes all elements of them from their mouths to their tails. In the fourth his daughter enters. As she walks across the pier she bends to pet the fish, and then continues on her way as if this were an everyday thing. The poet is surprised at this, especially as he is fascinated by the final death dance of the dogfish.

He returns to what they were like when they were alive, and how their movement then was so smooth compared to their graceless state now: 'How they would glide, barely brushing | one another, bodies all curve and urgency'.

Now they are reduced to 'a hapless | heap of undulant muscle'. When life finally leaves them, the poet feels that he can compare them to the stone of the pier and they are as dead as that.

His daughter, meanwhile, goes on about her business, undisturbed by the death that has surrounded her that day. He revels in her innocence and in her 'cheerful small voice | still singing.'

## Sharon Olds
## *The Present Moment*
Text of poem: New Explorations Anthology page 525

This thoughtful meditation concerns issues of ageing and of how we perceive the ageing process. A daughter sees her father in hospital, where he is terminally ill, and she tries to reconcile the image she once had of her father as somebody who was strong physically and mentally with the frail figure who lies before her. Through the poem she gives a powerful description of what illness does to people, of how it can ravage the body and the mind at the same time in a ruthless manner.

She combines the body and the mind at the start of the poem. She shows how the father has gone in such a short time from being someone who was active to being just a passive entity on the edge of existence. The first instance comes when she sees him just lying on his hospital bed. He is now motionless, facing towards the wall. This is becoming her dominant image of him now, instead of the image that she had of him before he entered the hospital and he 'sat up and put on his reading glasses'. At that stage he was actively reading, taking things in, his eyes alive as the 'lights in the room multiplied in the lenses.'

She uses the image of food to show the changes he has gone through. He now is dependent on food that will pass through him for energy, not for taste. He eats 'dense, earthen food, like liver', which is pure tasteless fuel – not something more unusual and aesthetic, like pineapple with its exotic connotations.

She follows this by noticing the changes to his body over the years. He is none of the more appealing figures that he used to be. She goes in reverse chronological order through his phases of life. She describes him as a portly man with a 'torso packed with extra matter'. As a young man he was a 'smooth-skinned, dark-haired boy'.

She admits to not knowing him obviously when he was a baby, but she notes his dependence back then, when he would 'drink from a woman's | body'. Once again he is being fed. And his 'steady | gaze' now is again like when he was just born: where sleep brings only relief to him now, just as it did then.

She finishes with a metaphor of a swimmer, only her father is swimming towards death: and want as she might to help him, she is helpless. She can only look on while he continues in his struggle.

# Carol Rumens
## *Passing a Statue of Our Lady in Derry*
Text of poem: New Explorations Anthology page 527

**Note: This poem was written before the beginning of the peace process.**

This hushed, subtle lyric is a poem that is based on simple observation and allowing that observation to flow. As the title suggests, the poet sees a statue of the Virgin Mary near a bus stop in Derry. This sets off a series of associations in the poet's mind; she has recollections and she has musings on the peculiarities of the significance of the Virgin Mary in the town of Derry.

She begins by describing the statue as she sees it. The statue is animated by her and she feels sympathy for it straight away. The statue 'appears tired'. In fact throughout the poem the statue appears world-weary. We see it bowing 'pleadingly' and the image of a 'frail', 'stranded' creature; an exasperation is apparent.

This is contrasted with innocence and a sense of hope; her 'fresh, white stone' and 'her narrow, girlish hands'. This contradiction seems to be what drives her fascination with the statue.

In her childhood the poet obviously had tremendous reverence for the Virgin Mary. This comes through in her recollection of the humming repetition and 'lyric boredom of the rosary'. Back then, time was taken to reveal 'small contritions' and 'miracles seemed at our fingertips'. This was a different time from now, when rushing for a bus is more likely.

In the final verse the poet brings to mind what the statue symbolises; hope. In her eyes, this 'frail, human idea' is what the people of Derry were hanging on to. The innocent-looking statue represents hope to them: a chance for a new beginning and to give them what they want, to move on, like the progression from childhood to being an adult.

# Ciaran Carson
## *Soot*
Text of poem: New Explorations Anthology page 530

The narrator in 'Soot' describes a scene where a woman is preparing a room for the chimney sweep to call and clean out her chimney. We are told that 'It was autumn,' a time when the first fire is ready to be lit after not being used at all over the summertime.

As she is preparing for the visit, she goes through a well-rehearsed ritual of sorting out the furniture and moving 'the ornaments from the mantelpiece'; the narrator gives us an idea of the type of place that it is when he describes the emotion of the woman who was:

> Afraid his roughness might disturb
> Their staid fragility.

'His roughness' is the only impression that we get of the sweep in the first verse. In the second verse, however, he doesn't seem at all rough. Indeed, he is described as entering 'shyly' and being 'ill-at-ease'. The woman stays dominant for a while, talking to him and watching him. When he starts his work, he takes over. He is confident when he is dealing with a topic in which he is an expert. When the circumstances of the transaction change, then so does he:

> He asked her to go outside and look, and there,
> Above the roof, she saw the frayed sunflower
> Bloom triumphantly.

There is reluctance on both their parts to become involved in this relationship. He is 'Too busy with his work for speech'; whereas when she needs to pay him she does it hesitantly: 'grimacing | As she put the money in his soiled hand.'

Towards the end of the poem we see the effect that the man had was anything but 'soiled'. Indeed, the opposite was true: 'Everything was spotless.'

In the final verse we see how even a dead material like soot has regenerative properties. It is considered useless and dirty, but here we see that with time it can have an effect that is beautiful and wondrous. Despite its appearance it can be used to bring beauty to the world – just like the chimney sweep.

# Moya Cannon
## Crow's Nest

Text of poem: New Explorations Anthology page 544

This poem uses a specific instance encountered by the poet to examine the nature of being and existing.

The poet begins with great specifics. She gives us the date, the 26th of December. She gives an almost exact location, 'Near the cliffs on Horn Head' in County Donegal. This poem depends on building from a definite real event. Its descriptions are beautifully and poignantly portrayed, drawing the reader into the scene immediately.

The idea of chance and fate are brought up almost immediately as the poet tells us that she 'came upon a house'. A picture of neglect and decay is presented, as we are allowed to picture the state of the house with its 'roof beams long since rotted into grass'. Then she sees what becomes the focus of the poem: 'a crow's nest in a dwarf tree.'

This disturbs the poet initially. A nest like this is not usually expected to be so close to the ground. The poet examines the artistry of the builders of the nest. The poet is under no illusions that the builders were artists rather than craftsmen. They have worked with passion to create their home, to build their 'great tangled heart'. They have used nature to create a place of nurture:

> heather sinew, long blades of grass, wool and a feather,
> wound and wrought
> with all the energy and art
> that's in a crow.

Her thoughts then focus on 'why?' in the final verse as she ponders:

> Did crows ever build so low before?
> Were they deranged . . . ?

## Simon Armitage
### *It Ain't What You Do, It's What It Does To You*
Text of poem: New Explorations Anthology page 546

This is a beautifully simple poem about the difference people can make and about how people can be important, even if they are not living exotic lives. The poet sets up four exotic scenarios and contrasts them with four seemingly banal instances, giving each equal credence. This poem could easily be compared with Patrick Kavanagh's poem 'Epic' in the way that it contrasts the local with the universal.

The first contrast is between a Bohemian travelling across the USA, living 'with only a dollar to spare, one pair | of busted Levis and a Bowie knife', and simply living with 'thieves in Manchester'. The banality of the place Manchester, which is local and drab, compared to the living-on-the-edge lifestyle in the States, is also emphasised by the simplicity of the line.

Next, he tells us that he doesn't get his spiritual wholeness from one of the wonders of the world, but from the energy used in skimming stones across an old lake in northern England. He finds himself at one with the energy of the Black Moss, instead of with the glamorous Taj Mahal. He points out here that what is important is the feeling it gives him, rather than the location.

Finally he refers to two different actions. The first is daring and brave – getting ready to take a parachute jump where life and limb are seemingly risked.

The second is simply caring for a mentally handicapped boy in a help centre. He obviously feels that the latter is more important. He goes on to assess what this does to him, and finds that it gives him a 'tightness in the throat' and a 'tiny cascading sensation'. He thinks that these feelings give him a purpose in life. They give him a 'sense of something else.'